ARCHAEOLOGICAL T
THE POLITICS OF CULTURAL
HERITAGE

Archaeology is meant to be an impartial science, concerned with seeking the truth about the past for the benefit of all humankind. But as the practices and values of archaeology have been enshrined in cultural resource management, they have also gradually become entwined with the apparatus of state power and control, and bound up in bitter political conflicts with Indigenous communities.

Laurajane Smith's controversial new book dissects the nature and consequences of this clash of cultures. Her lucid appraisals of key debates such as NAGPRA, Kennewick and the repatriation of Tasmanian artefacts show how Indigenous communities in the US and Australia have confronted the pre-eminence of archaeological theory and discourse, and how this has challenged traditional archaeological thought and practice.

This is a much-needed survey of how relationships between Indigenous peoples and the archaeological establishment have got into difficulties, and a pointer towards how things could move forward. It will be essential reading for those concerned with developing a just and equal dialogue with Indigenous peoples about the role of archaeology in the research and management of their heritage.

Laurajane Smith is Lecturer in Cultural Heritage Studies and Archaeology at the University of York, UK. She previously taught Indigenous Studies at the University of New South Wales, Sydney and worked as a cultural heritage consultant for many years.

ARCHAEOLOGICAL THEORY AND THE POLITICS OF CULTURAL HERITAGE

Laurajane Smith

Routledge
Taylor & Francis Group

LONDON AND NEW YORK

First published 2004
by Routledge
2 Park Square, Milton Park, Abingdon, Oxfordshire OX14 4RN

Simultaneously published in the USA and Canada
by Routledge
29 West 35th Street, New York, NY 10001

Reprinted 2006

Routledge is an imprint of the Taylor & Francis Group

© 2004 Laurajane Smith

Typeset in Garamond by
HWA Text and Data Management, Tunbridge Wells
Printed and bound in Great Britain by
The Cromwell Press, Trowbridge, Wiltshire

British Library Cataloguing in Publication Data
A catalogue record for this book is available from the British Library

Library of Congress Cataloging in Publication Data
Smith, Laurajane.
Archaeological theory and the politics of cultural heritage / Laurajane Smith.
p.   cm.
Includes bibliographical references and index.
1. Archaeology and state. 2. Archaeology–Political aspects. 3. Aboriginal
Australians–Antiquities. 4. Indians of North America–Antiquities.
5. Australia–Cultural policy. 6. United States–Cultural policy. I. Title.
CC135.S58 2004
930.1–dc22   2004002064

ISBN 0–415–31832–7 (hbk)
ISBN 0–415–31833–5 (pbk)

For Gary, Hamish and Mahalia
Also in memory of Bampot (Ansavon Royal Duchess, CD)

CONTENTS

ACKNOWLEDGEMENTS

This volume is based on several years of research, and along the way I have spoken to many people about their experiences in cultural heritage management, and about the content of this book. In particular I have benefited from conversations with the following who kindly gave up their time to give me background information: David Andrews, Emogene Bevitt, Anne Bickford, Karen Brown, John Cain, Gavin Clarke, Robert Clegg, David Collett, Miki Crespi, Bill Ellwood, Ronald Emery, Josephine Flood, Jill Gallaghar, Carol Gartside, Mick Harding, Dick Henry, Jeannette Hope, Ray Kelly, Jim Kennan, Greg Lehman, Anne McConnell, Angie McGowan, Francis McManamon, Paula Malloy, Marilyn Nickels, Patricia Parker, Don Ranson, Denis Rose, Stewart Simmons, Stephen Stanton, Sharon Sullivan, Peter Ucko – all opinions and errors are my own, however. Rodney Ross, Centre for Legislative Archives, US National Archives and Records Administration provided me with invaluable help whilst researching aspects of this work.

The following people read and commented on drafts of this work and I am grateful for their patience, time, and insights: John Carman, Martin Carver, Mathew Collins, Jon Finch, Jane Grenville, Richard Howitt, Patricia Reynolds, Sven Schroeder, Emma Waterton, Kate Wescombe, and Larry Zimmerman. I extend a special thanks to Larry, who was extremely generous with his time and insights, and Emma and Sven for all their time. Support from colleagues at the Department of Archaeology, University of York was important for allowing me to finally finish this work. In particular, I wish to thank Jane Grenville, Martin Carver, Tania Dickinson and Kevin Walsh for their support and encouragement.

I owe a very great debt to Gary Campbell. Throughout the lengthy germination of the book, and the research on which it is based, he has been a constant source of encouragement, support and, most importantly, inspiration. He has discussed and debated with me every aspect of the work, and has read, reread, edited and commented on all drafts. He, along with Hamish and Mahalia Campbell-Smith, has suffered with me during the writing stage, and I thank all three for their tolerance and sense of humour. Cindy has had to deal with a long separation caused, in part, by this book and I thank her for her forbearance.

ACKNOWLEDGEMENTS

The book comprises substantially unpublished material. However, the Australian section of Chapter 7 draws on, but substantially expands, Smith (2000) and the later sections of Chapter 9 draw on, but again substantially expand on and contextualize, discussions of the 1995 events between TALC and La Trobe discussed in Smith (1999, 2001).

ABBREVIATIONS

AAA	Australian Archaeological Association
AACA	Australian Association of Consulting Archaeologists
AAPA	American Association of Physical Anthropologists
AAV	Aboriginal Affairs Victoria (Victoria, Australia)
ABC	Australian Broadcasting Commission
ACHP	Advisory Council on Historic Preservation (USA)
AFA	Asatru Folk Assembly
AHC	Australian Heritage Commission
AHPA	*Archaeological and Historic Preservation Act*, 1974 (USA)
AIAS	Australian Institute of Aboriginal Studies (later became, Australian Institute of Aboriginal and Torres Strait Islander Studies)
AIATSIS	Australian Institute of Aboriginal and Torres Strait Islander Studies
AIM	American Indian Movement
ALB	*Aboriginal Law Bulletin*
ANZAAS	Australian and New Zealand Association for the Advancement of Science
AP	Associated Press
ARPA	*Archaeological Resources Protection Act*, 1979 (USA)
BIA	Bureau of Indian Affairs
CRAR	Committee for the Recovery of Archaeological Remains (USA)
CRM	Cultural Resource Management
Cwlth	Commonwealth of Australia
DOI	US Department of the Interior
EES	Environmental Effects Statement
EIA	Environmental Impact Assessment
FOAP	Friends of America's Past
ICOMOS	International Council on Monuments and Sites
IRA	*Indian Reorganization Act*, 1934
IUPPS	International Union of Prehistoric and Protohistoric Sciences

KIC	Koori Information Centre (Victoria, Australia)
NAGPRA	*Native American Graves Protection and Repatriation Act*, 1990
NCAI	National Congress of American Indians
NHPA	*National Historic Preservation Act*, 1966 (USA)
NPS	US National Park Service
NPWS	NSW National Parks and Wildlife Service (NSW, Australia)
NSW	New South Wales, Australian State
PWS	Parks and Wildlife Service (Tasmania, Australia)
SAA	Society for American Archaeology
SHPO	State Historic Preservation Officer (USA)
SMH	*Sydney Morning Herald*
SOPA	Society of Professional Archaeologists (USA)
TAC	Tasmanian Aboriginal Centre (Australia)
TALC	Tasmanian Aboriginal Land Council (Australia)
Tas	Tasmania, Australian State
THPO	Tribal Historic Preservation Officer (USA)
TWS	Tasmanian Wilderness Society
UNESCO	United Nations Educational, Scientific and Cultural Organisation
VAS	Victoria Archaeological Survey (Victoria, Australia)
Vic	Victoria, Australian State
WAC	World Archaeological Congress
WWW	World Wide Web

1

INTRODUCTION

In the mid-1990s two extremely public conflicts occurred between archaeologists and Indigenous peoples over the repatriation of items of cultural heritage significance. Although separate conflicts – one occurred in Australia, the other in the USA – and focused on very different material heritage, there were significant similarities in the ways in which these conflicts were conducted, regulated and expressed. In Australia, what has been called the 'La Trobe Affair' developed over the control over secular material culture and was popularly believed to have precipitated the 'death of archaeology' (Maslen 1995a). What became known as the 'Kennewick Man' case in America centred on the repatriation of human remains, and has been defined as the case that 'will determine the course of American archaeology' (Preston 1997: 72). The aim of this book is to provide a theoretical framework for understanding the social consequences of archaeological theory and practice. My intention is to illustrate how conflicts over the disposition of cultural heritage, like those above, are framed by archaeological discourse and how, in turn, the politics of cultural heritage and archaeological theory are inextricably intertwined.

Since the 1980s there has been a growing acknowledgement in the Western discipline of archaeology that what we do as archaeologists is 'political', and has significance beyond the accumulation of abstract knowledge about the past. However, what is actually meant by 'politics' – how is archaeology political, and what is the relationship of politics and archaeological knowledge and discourse? What does archaeological knowledge and discourse *do* outside of the academy that makes it political?

One of the principal things that archaeologists do outside of academia is cultural resource management (CRM). Although defined in more detail below, CRM refers to the process and procedures, often underpinned by public policy and legislation, used to protect, preserve and/or conserve cultural heritage items, sites, places and monuments. Although often perceived as a process that is in some way separate from the 'real' business of archaeological research, or at least as an adjunct area of archaeological practice, it is nonetheless integral to the discipline. Not only does CRM employ a significant number of archaeologists, it is the process through which the archaeological database is preserved and maintained, but also ultimately defined for future research. It is explicitly through the day-to-day processes of CRM that archaeologists encounter other groups and interests who perceive the 'cultural resource' not as data but as 'heritage'. If we accept that practice and theory inform each other then the practices of CRM cannot be dismissed as insignificant.

Subsequently, my aim is to critically explore and theorize the nature of CRM, and the interrelationship it has with the development and maintenance of archaeological discourse, theory and practice, and in so doing identify its 'political' nature. The politics of archaeology is examined through a comparative exploration of the way in which archaeological theory, especially the 'New Archaeology', played a constitutive role in the creation of CRM policy, practice and legislation in the USA and Australia. I argue that through CRM archaeology becomes actively engaged in the politics of cultural identity, which has profound consequences not only for the discipline itself, but also for those who define the 'things' that are 'managed' by archaeologists as part of their cultural heritage. The book examines the conflicts between archaeologists and Indigenous peoples in America and Australia, and demonstrates the political nature of archaeological knowledge and discourse. The analysis draws on and brings together detailed examinations of archival documents, newspaper and other media publications, as well as analyses of academic archaeological discourse and theory, and archaeological practice.

This book contends that through CRM archaeological knowledge and expertise is mobilized by public policy makers to help them 'govern' or regulate the expression of social and cultural identity. Material culture, as cultural heritage, is often used to give tangible and physical representation to intangible concepts and notions of cultural, social or historical identity, such as a sense of place, community or belonging. The way in which any heritage item, site or place is managed, interpreted and understood has a direct impact on how those people associated with, or who associate themselves with, that heritage are themselves understood and perceived. The past, and the material culture that symbolizes that past, plays an important part in creating, recreating and underpinning a sense of identity in the present. The past is used both to legitimate and to understand the present. Various groups or organizations and interests may use the past to give historical and cultural legitimacy to a range of claims about themselves and their experiences in the present. These claims may, from time to time, stand in opposition to archaeological knowledge or understandings of the past. However, archaeology as a form of expertise and as an intellectual discipline occupies a privileged position in Western societies, and in debates about the past. The scientific discourse of much archaeological theory tends to underwrite and help maintain the sense of expertise, and therefore the disciplinary authority, that ensures archaeology a privileged position in these debates. However, the consequence of this is that archaeological knowledge, as one area of expertise about the past, becomes what Rose and Miller (1992) refer to as a 'technology of government'. This is defined as the process whereby the knowledge, techniques, procedures and so on of a particular discipline become mobilized in the regulation of populations (Rose and Miller 1992: 175, see Chapter 4 for details). Archaeology becomes mobilized as a 'technology of government' in the regulation or governance of social problems that intersect with claims about the meaning of the past and its heritage. Archaeological knowledge is particularly useful in this context because it is used to judge the significance of physical objects or places. As a technology of government, archaeological discourse and knowledge may be utilized by governments, bureaucracies and policy makers, and ultimately, through the practices of CRM, may help them clarify and arbitrate over competing demands and claims made about the past by various interests. Moreover, it may be used to help define the interests and populations that are linked with, or define, a particular social problem that may itself intersect with an understanding of the past.

The use of archaeological knowledge in the legitimization or de-legitimization of interests may occur without the consent or knowledge of archaeological practitioners, but its use nonetheless places archaeology at odds with others who have an interest in the cultural and social uses of the past. This is particularly the case for Indigenous people in colonial, and so called post-colonial, contexts who may seek to establish the legitimacy of their cultural claims to land, sovereignty and nationhood through discrete links to the past and its material cultural heritage.

In effect, archaeology is a form of expertise that must, and does, become embroiled in social and cultural debates about the past and its meaning for the present. This is not a purely intellectual or academic exercise. Rather the consequence of this process is that archaeology, as a privileged form of expertise, occupies a role in the governance and regulation of identity. This means that archaeological knowledge, and the discourse that frames this knowledge, can and does have a direct impact on people's sense of cultural identity, and thus becomes a legitimate target and point of contention for a range of interests. Conflicts over the meaning of the past become more than just conflicts over interpretation or differing values, they become embroiled in negotiations over the legitimacy of political and cultural claims made on the basis of links to the past. This conflict and the degree to which various interests, most notably Indigenous interests, contest archaeological knowledge and practices has serious consequences for the discipline of archaeology, which has been extensively criticized, and made the focus of politicized action by Indigenous peoples throughout the world (Watkins 2001a). Certainly, the archaeological literature that discusses this conflict expresses a sense that the discipline feels besieged (McGuire 1989: 180; Zimmerman 1998a). In response, archaeology has tended to maintain a discourse that stresses its position as an expert, neutral and value free practice, despite a number of post-modern incursions into the discipline. This response ensures that the power/knowledge strategy that underpins archaeological expertise is maintained in the face of the critiques and challenges offered by Indigenous peoples. The archaeological discipline must continue a discourse informed by 'processual science' if its position as a technology of government, and its role in governing cultural identity, is to be maintained. Ultimately archaeological discourse and archaeological theory become governed by involvement in the governance of cultural identity. Archaeological discourse must maintain its scientific, if not scientistic, values to maintain its position in CRM and thus ensure access to the discipline's data.

During the 1990s, international and national archaeological organizations and individuals have moved to incorporate Indigenous criticisms into archaeological theory and practice (for instance WAC 1990; AAA 1991; and chapters in Davidson *et al.* 1995; Nicholas and Andrews 1997; Swidler *et al.* 1997; Dongoske *et al.* 2000). These initiatives will be limited and partial, for both Indigenous peoples and archaeologists, unless two things are recognized. First, the discipline has to gain a clearer understanding of the way its discourse uses power and ideology, and is in turn contested on those grounds. Second, the consequences of the discipline's involvement in the governance of certain social problems must be recognized. By understanding these issues, negotiations over access to sites and heritage items, with both Indigenous peoples and other interests, may commence from a deeper understanding of the 'politics' involved, and of the power/knowledge relations that must themselves be negotiated if equitable resolutions are to occur for both parties.

Although this analysis is developed in the context of American and Australian Indigenous heritage management, the model developed here is applicable in other contexts. My examination draws on Indigenous issues and cultural politics in these countries because of the stark political nature of these debates and archaeological involvement in them. The nature of these debates makes them easier to illustrate and define than other debates in heritage management and archaeology, where the protagonists are less clearly culturally or politically defined by post-colonial political and cultural conflicts. However, as conflicts over the management of sites such as Seahenge and Stonehenge in Britain, and Ayodhya in India, and debates over the interpretation of labour history, women's history, African-American history and many more suggest, the analysis developed here has relevance and applicability for understanding the role of archaeology in other conflicts and social and cultural debates.

The social problem

Archaeology is drawn on to help explain, regulate and govern social problems that intersect with issues of identity and the past. In the 1960s and 1970s a number of coincidental developments and events coincided to create a set of social problems and opportunities that facilitated archaeology's use as a technology of government. These events created an opportunity to develop not only a formalized role for archaeological engagement with the governance of identity issues, but also an explicit role that became institutionalized through state bureaucracies and heritage agencies.

The first development was an increase in competing demands about the meaning and nature of material culture as either someone's heritage or as an archaeological resource. In America and Australia this was intimately connected with the development of nationwide assertive Indigenous political movements.

By the late 1960s and early 1970s, national and organized Indigenous political and cultural movements had gained media and public attention in both American and Australia. The development of these movements, and subsequent increasing public awareness about Indigenous cultural politics meant that both the American and Australian states were confronted with new social problems. The problems posed by these movements for the state were particularly acute given the tensions over the development of national identities experienced in all post-colonial countries.

The second development was the increasing concern in many Western countries about the fate of cultural heritage, and public debates increased exponentially through the 1960s and 1970s about the need to conserve and preserve 'the past' (Lowenthal 1990). A range of reasons has been suggested for this marked increase in interest. Some have identified it as part of wider debates about concern for the environment and the rate of post-war development (Lowenthal 1979: 554; Rains *et al.* 1983; Glass 1990). Others that it was a result of increased leisure time (Hunter 1981) or even the growth of cultural tourism (Urry 1990), or an obsession with nostalgia as Western public life grew more abstract and impersonal (Chase and Shaw 1989; Lowenthal 1989). Still others considered that it was associated with nascent, but explicit, conservative political tendencies and 'it was better back then' ideologies (Wright 1985; Hewison 1987; Shanks and Tilley 1987b; Bower 1995). Some see it as part of modern attempts to reassert and explore perceptions of social, cultural or national identities (Bickford 1981; Lowenthal 1995). Whatever the cause there was increasing social debate about heritage and its significance to Western societies.

The third development was that archaeologists became active players in this debate, lobbying governments in America and Australia for legislation to protect archaeological resources (see Chapter 7). At this time the discipline also increased its 'professional' and institutional profile, with archaeological organizations such as the Society for American Archaeology (SAA) producing codes of conduct, while actively defining and developing its lobbying role during the 1970s (SAA 1961; Adams 1984; Knudson 1984; McGimsey 2000). In 1964, the Australian Institute of Aboriginal Studies (AIAS) was formally established (now the Australian Institute of Aboriginal and Torres Strait Islander Studies), followed by the Australian Archaeological Association in 1973. Both commenced sustained lobbying and provided codes of conduct for researchers (see Chapter 5).

This lobbying was largely successful, and in both America and Australia legislation was developed in the 1960s and 1970s to protect Indigenous 'archaeological resources' or 'relics' as they were often called (Chapter 7). This legislation and associated policy underwrote the development of CRM as a formal management process. Although the development of CRM in America can be traced to the *Antiquities Act* of 1906, and the impetus given by the 1940s and 1950s reservoir salvage programmes, it was not until the 1960s that CRM was extended and given greater legal and policy formality and nationwide substance (see Chapters 5–7). The CRM model developed in the USA was imported into

Australia in the late 1960s and early 1970s (Sullivan 1973, 1975a; Chapter 7). Part of the success of the lobbying by archaeologists rests with the development of professional organizations that gave the discipline greater authority and legitimacy in the process. The advent of the 'New Archaeology' in the 1960s, which strenuously professed a rational discourse emphasizing a new identity for the discipline as a 'science', was highly significant here. The scientific discourse of processual theory was made very public as many of those advocating a new and rational archaeology were also engaged in attempts to make the subject more 'relevant' to the public. This was done from the 1960s onwards through increased archaeological participation in outreach and educational programmes as part of CRM, and through the continued lobbying by archaeologists for the protection of archaeological resources from development and looting.

What was significant about this new archaeological discourse was that it was easily understood by the modern liberalism of Western governments. The discourse of rationality and objectivity, and the scientific values that informed it, found synergy with and 'made sense' in the context of the 1960s and 1970s liberal forms of governance in both America and Australia (Chapter 6).

These were all coincidental developments that facilitated the uptake of archaeological knowledge, through CRM, as a technology of government by providing, in the first instance, a social problem complete with a truculent population that needed identifying and defining by governments, in this case Indigenous Australians and North Americans. Then, in the second instance, archaeology as a discipline was increasing its public profile through its professional-ization and lobbying activities, and moreover was presenting a newly minted *discourse* that rendered the new social problem understandable to the rationalities of liberal governance.

What is cultural resource management?

Cultural resource management is the term currently used in the USA, although replaced in Australia since the early 1990s with the term 'cultural heritage management'. The phrase was changed in Australia following Indigenous criticism that the term 'resource' implied that their heritage could be accessed and was of equal significance to allcomers, while the term 'heritage' recognized that certain groups could and do have a special relationship with some places, sites or artefacts. The term CRM is used here not only because it is still current in the US but because of its historical significance in both countries. The idea of 'resource' also encapsulates much of the discourse surrounding the development of management policy and practices, and was part of a discourse that influenced the relations between archaeologists, Indigenous interests, public policy and legislation.

The standard definition of CRM, constructed within the established discourses of power/knowledge of the discipline of archaeology, argues that it is simply the technical processes concerned with the management and use of material culture perceived by sectors of the community as significant (e.g. McGimsey 1972; Cleere

6

1984c, 1989; Hunter and Ralston 1993; Pearson and Sullivan 1995; Hall and McArthur 1996; King 1998). These processes of management are regulated by codes of professional ethics, legislation and government policy (King 2000). Discussion has also focused on describing the legislative and government policy base of CRM (e.g. McGimsey and Davis 1977; Fowler 1982; Darvill 1987; Cleere 1984a, 1984b, 1993a; Flood 1987; Hunter and Ralston 1993; Hall and McArthur 1996; King 2000). Other debates or definitions of CRM have been focused on particular issues, such as 'who owns the past', or issues raised by community proposals to rebury human remains, repatriation, and tourism issues, to name but a few (e.g. McKinlay and Jones 1979; Green 1984; McBryde 1985; Cleere 1989; Shanks and Tilley 1987a, 1987b; Davison and McConville 1991; McManamon and Hatton 2000; Skeates 2000; Layton *et al.* 2001).

However, as some have begun to argue, CRM is (or at least can be) more than this (Byrne 1991, 1993; Carman 1991, 1993, 2002; Smith 1994; Graham et al 2000; Meskell 2002a). CRM's association with archaeology is a significant one, as it both influences and is influenced by the ideologies and politics of archaeology (Byrne 1991, 1993; Carman 1993). Heritage is also used to symbolize perceptions of social, cultural and historical identity at individual, community and national levels as a growing literature on this phenomenon testifies (e.g. Lowenthal and Binney 1981; Lowenthal 1990; Friedman 1992; Johnston 1992; Dicks 2000; Graham *et al.* 2000; Emerick 2001). The management and use of heritage must impact upon the meanings individuals and communities give to the past. Heritage, for instance, is used by Indigenous peoples and other community groups to challenge received and normative perceptions of their pasts and identities (see for example Wylie 1992a; Tunbridge and Ashworth 1996; Graham *et al.* 2000; Watkins 2001a). Heritage can also be used, as Hewison (1987) notes, to support conservative versions of social development, in which class exploitation is rendered invisible by the preservation of sanitized industrial sites without the retention of associated cramped housing and squalid urban areas. In addition, the traditional subaltern roles and positions of women, working-class communities and migrant and ethnic communities in the present can be reinforced or challenged by providing uncritical or radical interpretations of the historical continuity of these roles (for instance, Bickford 1981, 1985, 1993; S. Watson 1992; Reekie 1992; Johnston 1993; Leone *et al.* 1995; Tunbridge and Ashworth 1996; Ruppel *et al.* 2003). These and other uses of heritage mean that archaeologists employed in CRM become involved, whether they wish to or not, with debates over the meanings given to the past and heritage, and with notions and perceptions of cultural, historical, social and national identities. In the process of doing CRM they also engage with these issues in the context of government policy and legislation.

Definitions and analyses of CRM or archaeology which consider the *interaction* of 'heritage' as the physical and symbolic embodiment of 'identity', archaeological ideology, discourse and practice, and government policy, agencies and legislation, are rare in the literature. Current definitions of CRM, which stress the technical aspects of CRM practice, have two important effects on debate. First, the defining of issues that engage archaeologists (e.g. issues surrounding the definitions of cultural and other identities, access to sites, reburial and repatriation) as being primarily 'heritage' issues causes them to cease to be *archaeological* issues. They become issues that archaeological theoreticians can comment on and discuss in abstract terms, but they are not then issues with which the whole of archaeology must engage, or actively address. CRM is often used or conceptualized as an intellectual 'buffer' or barrier between political and cultural issues, and archaeology conceptualized as an intellectual and/or 'scientific' discipline removed and insulated from such issues by its position within the academy. By associating CRM with political issues, archaeology as a discipline is one step removed from cultural and heritage politics.

Second, CRM, as an arena in which particular issues are dealt with, is very neatly divorced from the rest of archaeology. CRM *simply* becomes an area of practice that intersects with other interests in heritage. This conceptualization of CRM has meant that little intellectual space has been made for conceiving of CRM as a process which is influenced by, and which in turn influences, archaeological theory and practice.

Descriptions that concentrate on outlining CRM practice, the relevant legislation and policies and the issues CRM deals with, have helped to create a perception that CRM is separate from archaeology and that it has no real influence on the discipline. This has often lead to the marginalization of CRM within archaeological discourses, and CRM is often devalued as an area that contributes little to archaeological research (Renfrew 1983; Carman 1991). Indeed many archaeologists working in CRM report that they are often criticized for not 'doing *real* archaeology' (Clarke 1993). CRM, however, 'protects' and manages the archaeological database – the dismissal of CRM as either irrelevant to archaeology, or completely outside archaeological control (as Jennings 1986; Shanks and Tilley 1987b, 1989a, amongst others, have implied), cannot be supported without directly threatening the database upon which the discipline depends for its credibility. The way in which archaeological sites are managed, and what is chosen to be conserved or destroyed, has obvious and sometimes irreversible influences on archaeological research. As an embodiment of archaeological practice that is influenced by archaeological theory and discourse, the separation of CRM from archaeology in general has confused attempts to define, discuss and theorize CRM.

Archaeological practices, discourses and knowledge are the underpinning elements in the development and enactment of CRM processes – archaeology cannot credibly be seen as an innocent bystander. One of the consequences of CRM for archaeology is to construct and formalize relations between intersecting interests in the past and material culture. These relations constituted by public policy and legislation set the parameters and aims for the practices involved in the management of material culture. One of the broad aims of CRM is to mitigate conflict over heritage when and where this occurs (Pearson and Sullivan 1995; Kerr 1996; King 1998). Consequently, the procedures of CRM define the interrelations between all interests. Interests may also intersect with, for example, the concerns of developers, tourist operators, antiquities traders and others who may wish to utilize Indigenous material culture. When such interests intersect, new relations are developed and formulated. However, the core relations that will be represented in any conflict over Indigenous heritage will be those between Indigenous people, archaeologists and government agencies. Relations established with developers, tourist operators and so forth are more ephemeral.

Thus, CRM is defined as the processes, informed by public policy and heritage legislation, that manage and protect Indigenous cultural heritage, and in doing so, construct and define relations between archaeologists, Indigenous interests and governments. These relations are defined, maintained and negotiated within CRM ostensibly for the purpose of resolving and mitigating conflict over the disposition and interpretation of Indigenous material culture.

The theoretical context of the argument

The argument to be developed throughout the following chapters contends that the conflict between Indigenous people and archaeologists needs to be considered in a context that exposes not only the privileged position of archaeological discourse, but also *how* this discourse has come to be privileged. It is knowledge of what archaeology *does* outside of the discipline, and what is *done* with archaeological knowledge, that is important for comprehending the extent of Indigenous criticism and reaction to archaeological knowledge. CRM represents an area of archaeological practice that has a significant impact upon what is *done* with archaeological knowledge. In effect, it is the relations between archaeology, government and their bureaucracies and Indigenous communities in post-colonial contexts that determines and defines the political nature of archaeology.

To elucidate this relationship and its consequences for both archaeology and Indigenous people the later work of Foucault, and his idea of 'governmentality', is drawn on. Foucault's governmentality thesis argues in short that certain mentalities, hence govern*mentality*, become important tools in the processes of liberal government and administration (Dean 1999: 2). That is, the mentalities and calculations that regulate the 'conduct of conduct' are derived from disciplined intellectual knowledge and thought (Foucault 1991b). The literature on govern-mentality argues that intellectual knowledge is incorporated into the act of governing populations and social problems by subjecting them to analysis (Rose and Miller 1992: 182). This process is based on the authority of liberal modernity, which stresses rational universal 'truths' (Pavlich 1995). The claims of intellectuals to meta-professional authority, superior knowledge, and their search for the attainment of 'truth', underwrites the often privileged position of the intellectual in Western societies (Bauman 1987) and thus the role of intellectual knowledge in governing social problems.

Archaeological expertise, emphasized by the logical positivism of processualism, became useful in defining populations through both their 'archaeological' past and the heritage objects and places that were defined as representing that past.

9

Claims to the past, or to an authorized version of the past, are often important to a range of groups for defining their identity, a sense of community and belonging, and a sense of place. Community identity, whether of Indigenous North Americans or Australians, or communities bound by certain class, social or ethnic alliances, often come into conflict with each other and/or national projects and perceptions of a wider collective identity. This conflict often centres on how the past is understood and thus how it may legitimize the construction of certain identities. These claims are rendered tractable when scientific 'value free' archaeological knowledge and expertise is called upon through CRM to arbitrate over these claims.

Expert knowledge thus becomes included in the 'political' arena. Yet at the same time, expertise is de-politicized as it is seen to rest on technical rationalist calculation, which must operate above competing interests. Within archaeology, the discursive power of logical positivism stresses objectivity and ensures technical rigour. This apparent depolarization of archaeological knowledge allows it to be covertly re-politicized in its use in the governance of social problems and to reinforce its usefulness. Moreover, by rendering social problems as subject to the intervention of 'rational' knowledge, the problems that are governed in this process are themselves rendered non-'political'. Material culture, or heritage, renders archaeological knowledge tangible, 'evidential' and thus 'real'. This physicality further renders the social problems that interact with heritage open to intervention and regulation.

However, two problems with the 'governmentality' literature need to be identified and stressed. First, it tends to over-privilege the authority of knowledge, to overly abstract resources of power, and second, it has yet to deal with the consequences of contestation of expert knowledge and discourse. The point to be made here is that although archaeological knowledge and discourse gains significant power in its mobilization as a technology of government, this does not mean that it cannot at times be successfully challenged. Because of this, power may be reshuffled and the authority of the intellectual, at least temporarily, renegotiated. Many groups and communities do passionately target archaeologists and their knowledge. The governmentality thesis certainly reveals why this criticism is often so passionate and sustained. However, it is unable to chart the consequences of this resistance to archaeological governance.

To remedy the overly abstract nature of Foucauldian theorization of power/knowledge these relations and negotiations are firmly situated within the apparatus of the state. The governmentality literature has, quite rightly, been accused of obscuring the concrete realities of the state and its bureaucracies in the deployment of intellectual knowledge. However, this analysis is also informed by the work of Bob Jessop who corrects Foucault's overemphasis on the discursive construction of 'the state', neglect of the strategic and structural aspects of state power, and, importantly, the bases for resistance to that power. Indeed Foucauldian analyses tend to ignore institutional and organizational factors (Jessop 1990), and the extent to which the state may play a privileged role even in diffuse and de-centred networks of power (Hunt 1993). The state is a set of institutions that mediate power and by situating the analysis within the state, the bureaucracies that administer the process of CRM are identified as giving concrete expression to the governance of material culture and the social problems connected with it. Moreover, it also allows for recognition that archaeological knowledge can be and is contested and challenged, and the state itself provides a focus for Indigenous resistance.

Through the heritage management process archaeological knowledge becomes mobilized within the state. Since the early 1970s, archaeological knowledge and values have become inextricably tied into the heritage management process to help govern a range of social problems, particularly those posed by Indigenous peoples in post-colonial contexts. The whole process of CRM, which emphasizes the technical application of knowledge and expertise, works effectively to render wider political debates about the legitimacy of cultural and social claims on the past as non-political. It does this in two ways. First, by redefining these issues as issues of access, or even 'ownership', of certain discrete heritage sites and objects, so that wider social problems become narrowed down and redefined as conflicts over single heritage sites. Second, claims are further de-politicized by redefining them as technical issues of site management. In this process archaeology, in constituting 'heritage' as part of its database and as part of the 'resource' it seeks to protect and objectively interpret, de-politicizes 'subjective' claims to 'heritage'. This then renders 'heritage', and the claims made about it, more readily 'governable'. The governance of heritage facilitates the de-politicization of Indigenous claims about cultural identity. This has significant consequences for Indigenous people where cultural identity has become an important resource used by both Indigenous communities and governments in negotiations over the legitimacy of Indigenous political interests.

CRM provides the institutions, policies and legislative frameworks that effectively mobilize archaeology as a technology of government. Archaeological knowledge and discourse, particularly that informed by processual theory, has been incorporated and embedded within CRM practice, policy and heritage legislation. Thus, it is through CRM that archaeology has established a role for itself in the 'governance' of material culture, and consequently influences claims about the nature of Indigenous cultural identity. In relations established by CRM processes between archaeologists, Indigenous people and state institutions and policy makers, archaeological knowledge may be utilized in public policy and legislation to interpret and arbitrate on, or 'govern', the use and disposition of material culture. This has consequences for Indigenous claims about cultural identity based on material culture.

The relations established by CRM are not static, and CRM practitioners around the world, Indigenous peoples and other stakeholder groups have questioned the dominant discourse. There are a range of examples wherein CRM practitioners, and archaeologists more generally, have attempted to subvert the dominant assumptions and values embedded in CRM, and to be less technical, scientific and bureaucratic (for instance Zimmerman 1989a, 1998b; McGuire 1992; Pardoe

1992; Clarke 2002; Dongoske *et al.* 2000; Emerick 2003; Derry and Mallory 2003 amongst others). Policy developments in some countries, such as Britain and Australia, have moved actively toward social inclusion and community involvement (Newman and McLean 1998; ICOMOS 1999). A number of writers and theorists have also made more explicitly theoretical interventions (for instance Byrne 1991, 1993; Walsh 1992; Shanks and Tilley 1987a, 1987b; Hodder 1999; Meskell 2002a), questioning the empiricism and cultural politics of the discipline.

However, and this argument is developed in more detail throughout the book, the dominant discourse in archaeology is still just that – dominant. Too much loosening of claims to scientific expertise runs the risk of making the discipline just another interest group, which lessens the discipline's utility as a technology of government. As innovative and refreshing as many of these interventions have been, they are still in a sense more the exception that proves the rule than the wave of the future.

The privileged position of archaeology over the management of material culture assures access to the database but this position is also resisted and contested by Indigenous people through criticism of archaeological practices and research. This criticism is often crystallized in debates about the repatriation and reburial of human remains, the return of artefacts collected and held by archaeologists, or disagreements over the interpretation of the past. Indigenous contestation of archaeological practice and knowledge has led to shifts between, and renegotiations of, the relations established under CRM. The continual renegotiation of power within these relationships is exemplified by the case studies discussed in Chapters 8 and 9. The history of archaeological, Indigenous and governmental interactions over the sites and remains at Kennewick, USA, and in southwest Tasmania, Australia not only reveal the changes in relationships that occur over time as power is negotiated, but they also illustrate the consequences this has for both Indigenous interests and, ultimately, the expression and development of archaeological theory and practice.

The consequence of archaeological knowledge and practice and its mobilization and institutionalization within CRM is that archaeological knowledge enters into state strategies concerned with the governance of Indigenous cultural identity. For Indigenous people the presence of archaeology in this process means that what the discipline does *not* do is develop neutral and passive interpretations of the past. Rather the discipline and individual archaeologists generate knowledge that is explicitly used by or against Indigenous people in negotiations with state agencies. Therefore, in political negotiations archaeology becomes one of a number of factors that has to be controlled or managed. For archaeology, the consequences are that it becomes directly and intimately engaged in the politics of Indigenous cultural identity. This in turn has consequences for, and influences the expression of, archaeological theory and practice. This is a point that needs to be stressed, as it is central to this work. For archaeologists to maintain access to their database they must continually invoke the discourse of processual rationality or risk undermining the authority of intellectuals and their usefulness as a technology of government. Subsequently archaeological knowledge and discourse becomes *itself* regulated and governed by its position as a technology of government. Processual discourse must continue to set the archaeological agenda or the position of archaeological expertise becomes jeopardized within CRM.

Scope and methodology

As stated above, American and Australian Indigenous CRM and the archaeological practices and theories that inform CRM are the foci of this book. As noted, this is in part due to the stark and well discussed nature of the politics of Indigenous CRM in these countries. Both countries are examined to illustrate the extent to which the engagement of archaeological knowledge in programmes of governance produces very similar sets of relations and consequences for archaeologists in both countries. That is, the consequences for archaeology and Indigenous interests identified in this analysis are not necessarily confined by or shaped by particular cultural or national circumstance, but are rather defined by the relations established within CRM between Western forms of liberal governance, Indigenous cultural politics and archaeological knowledge and discourse. Although the processes identified in this analysis have produced similar constraints and influences on archaeological discourse and theory, Australia provides a useful counterpoint to the USA. This is because Australia, to a certain extent, has been able to advance the debates between archaeologists and Indigenous peoples beyond the point reached in the USA so far. The Australian situation, which is still to escape the impasse created by the need to maintain archaeological authority on the one hand and the desire to be more inclusive of Indigenous concerns and aspirations on the other, does offer some practical ways forward nonetheless.

In the USA this study examines CRM at a Federal level only and does not explore the multitude of State practices and conservation laws. Although individual State laws, policies and practice influence CRM processes, it is Federal legislation and policy that regulates, defines and sets the overall agendas in American CRM (see King 1998). The opposite is, in fact, the case in Australia. In Australia, State heritage laws and policies set the agenda, although many Federal laws and policies have developed from similar principles and guidelines. While Australian Federal legislation and policy exists, it can only be acted upon in very specific circumstances within each State (see Chapter 7). A network of State specific legislation largely governs the work of Australian archaeologists and cultural resource managers. An examination of the practices of CRM across Australia becomes, therefore, a massive project – well outside the scope of this work.

Since one of the central issues of this book is to explore the interplay between archaeological practice and theory and Aboriginal politics of identity, the examination of CRM practices will be confined to the three southeastern States (New South Wales (NSW), Victoria and Tasmania).

In these States the politics of cultural and historical identity are particularly volatile and represent a political resource that is constantly contested in public debates about the nature of Aboriginal culture and society in this region of Australia. In southeastern Australia, Aboriginal cultural identity has been constantly questioned by powerful white settler discourses that have maintained that Aborigines in this region 'died out' or vanished shortly after 'settlement' (Ryan 1981; Creamer 1988; Broome 1995; Goodall 1995). When, or if, Aboriginal people are recognized as still existing in these States it is often assumed that Aboriginal culture has been completely or largely 'lost' (Creamer 1988). This works to deny the cultural associations of contemporary Aboriginal people to past and present material culture. Thus, the book will analyze the development of CRM policy and legislation and archaeological practice in the context of these dominant perceptions that persist in government policy in these States. This, in turn, provides some insight into the consequences of archaeology and CRM for the politics of Aboriginal cultural identity.

The case studies chosen for this analysis are those that have very publicly challenged and contested the position of archaeological knowledge and discourse established by CRM and the legislation that underpins it. The Kennewick case study examines the debates and court challenges over the identity and custodianship of human remains estimated to be 9,200 years old. This case, which hinges on the interpretation of the *Native American Graves Protection and Repatriation Act* (NAGPRA), allows for a charting of the continual negotiation and renegotiation of power, privilege and position within the relations established by CRM and the consequent impact that this has had and continues to have on archaeological practice and theory.

The southwest Tasmanian case study, as with Kennewick, has been a focus of public and governmental attention. Archaeological evidence used in the 1978 film *The Last Tasmanian* (Haydon 1978) sparked debate about whether or not Tasmanian Aboriginal people were extinct. Knowledge about archaeological sites in the southwest played an important role in the Franklin Dam dispute and the subsequent important environmental court case and victory in 1983. The southwest sites have also been the focus of public debate in the so-called 'La Trobe Affair' about the nature of archaeological research and its relationship with Aboriginal people and organizations (e.g. Murray and Allen 1995; TALC 1996). These very public debates provide a useful focus for an investigation into the consequences for both archaeology and Aboriginal communities of archaeological practice and interpretation.

The arguments developed in this study are based on analyses of a) archaeological academic literature and archaeological popular literature, film, internet publications and sites, and newspaper and magazine accounts of archaeological and Indigenous debates; b) the Indigenous academic and non-academic literature; c) policy and other documents held in the libraries and archives of State and Federal heritage authorities and agencies; d) in Australia Hansard and other government documents and publications, and in the USA Congressional Records, House

Reports, and other government documents. This material has been supported by interviews with archaeologists directly concerned with the development of CRM and/or employed within State and Federal heritage agencies, Indigenous people working within CRM or areas related to CRM practice, and government Senators/ Ministers who were concerned with the development of legislation.

All the above material is constituted as *data* insofar as it forms the basis of arguments and evidence for propositions advanced in this analysis. This material has been critically examined and used to reveal attitudes and ideologies within the discipline and CRM. Analysis centres on the discourses (see Chapter 4) employed in the above materials. These are used to help identify underlying philosophical and ideological positions current in the archaeological literature.

Position of the researcher

While the primary sources of data have been archival research, relevant literature, and interviews, my reading of this material and the development of my arguments have been in part informed by my own experiences working in CRM and archaeology in Australia. Certainly, my working experience with Indigenous Australians has influenced the position I take in this book, and throughout my career I have endeavoured to pay attention to and facilitate the critical inclusion of Indigenous concerns in my work as both a cultural resource manager and later as an academic. My political position is clear on many issues to do with Indigenous heritage – what is done with Indigenous heritage must be done with the full, frank and informed consent of Indigenous people. It is important to negotiate and perhaps work out compromise where this is possible, but in such negotiations archaeologists will often, as this book reveals, be starting from a position of privilege and power. Until the relations of power are equalized and until Indigenous people are in control of *their* heritage, any negotiations that archaeologists enter into must be informed by a clear understanding of the potential political and cultural consequences of those negotiations.

2

THE CULTURAL POLITICS
OF IDENTITY
Defining the social problem

Indigenous peoples throughout the world recognise that, at the core
of the violation of our rights as peoples, lies the desecration of our
sovereign right to control our lives, to live according to our own laws
and determine our futures. And at the heart of the violation has been
the denial of our control over our identity, and the symbols through
which we make and remake our culture and ourselves ... Recognition
of a people's fundamental right to self-determination must include
... the right to inherit the collective identity of one's people, and to
transform that identity creatively according to the self-defined aspirations of one's people and one's own generation. It must include the
freedom to live outside the cage created by other peoples' images and
projections.

(Michael Dodson – Aboriginal and Torres Strait Islander Social
Justice Commissioner – 1994: 5)

Since the late 1960s and early 1970s, the Western discipline of archaeology has
come under continuous and explicit criticism by Indigenous peoples from around
the world. This criticism has been particularly pointed and public in countries
such as the USA and Australia. As many archaeological commentators on this
conflict have noted, this criticism developed both within, and was integral to,
the new and public political movements for civil rights, sovereignty and land
(for instance, McGuire 1992, 1998; Zimmerman 1997, 1998a). The demands
by Indigenous peoples that they control how, or if, their heritage will be studied
and understood by archaeologists are more than assertions or expressions of
religious or cultural relativity. These assertions were, and continue to be, part of
wider negotiations with governments and their policy makers about the political
and cultural legitimacy of Indigenous claims to specific rights, not least of which
are rights to land.

Many of the demands and claims made by Indigenous people to land and
other rights rested on Indigenous knowledge and experiences, which were simply
not compatible with Western knowledge, experience and post-colonial expediency.
Indigenous demands and negotiations with Western governments rested not only

on a particular understanding of colonial history, legalities, and moralities, but also on Indigenous understandings of cultural identity, as well as Indigenous law and knowledge about the nature of land and other resources. Here 'knowledge' refers not only to religious knowledge and understanding, but also to other forms of Indigenous cultural understandings about the world and their experiences within it. To make sense of Indigenous demands governments and their policy makers turned to various forms of expertise to help them translate and understand Indigenous knowledge and claims. However, to both underpin the legitimacy of Indigenous demands, and to ensure that responses to them were culturally meaningful to Indigenous peoples, it became important for those demands to be accepted on their own terms – that is on the basis of Indigenous knowledge, law and sovereignty. The consequence of this was that archaeology, as one of the various forms of expertise that governments mobilized to help them understand the problem before them, became a target of Indigenous criticism designed to undermine the utility of archaeology in this process.

The central argument of this book is that archaeological discourse and knowledge may become mobilized as a technology of government to govern particular social problems and issues. In this process, archaeological knowledge and discourse may be utilized by governments and their bureaucracies to help them to define, understand and regulate truculent populations and the social problems and the issues that they present for the state. This chapter identifies and examines the social problem within which so-called 'prehistoric' archaeology became entangled. It is this problem together with the coincidental development of discourses on archaeological 'science' and 'professionalism', together with the emergence of CRM, that led to the implementation of archaeology as a technology of government in the governance of material culture and cultural identity.

Indigenous cultural identity as a political resource

Material culture, the artefacts, sites and places, which are perceived by archaeologists to represent or have meaning in a particular culture, is the focus of archaeological analysis. Indigenous people perceive the very things that archaeologists identify and define as 'data' as heritage. Heritage, with its ability to provide physical and tangible links with the past, plays an important role in the development, maintenance and contestation of a wide range of 'identities' (Zimmerman 1998b; Graham *et al.* 2000). To understand the consequences of archaeological practice and interpretation, and archaeology's intersection with Indigenous interests, identification and discussion of the political importance of Indigenous cultural identity is required. The development of an American Indian political Movement and the Australian Land Rights Movement in the late 1960s and early 1970s in association with what may be defined as a 'cultural revival' or resurgence (Creamer 1988, 1990; Gulliford 2000; Hill 2001) have been important in the re-assertion of Indigenous cultural identity. Material culture has played an important role in supporting and symbolizing this highly political re-assertion.

An important element in Indigenous resistance to colonization has been the contestation of received notions of Indigenous identity and white settler perceptions of the history of American and Australian colonization. Normative constructions of history in both countries tend to characterize Indigenous and white settler relations as a simple relation of domination and subordination, where either defiant 'savage' populations needed to be actively subdued, or where they simply and peacefully vanished as the colonial frontiers expanded (Reynolds 1986; Markus 1990, 1994; Zimmerman 1996; Churchill 1998; P. Deloria 1998). The idea that Indigenous people faded away was a perception facilitated by nineteenth-century Social Darwinism. Interlinked ideas of cultural and physical evolution underwrote much of the mythologies that were used to both classify and understand Indigenous peoples, while at the same time justified the colonial process.

Ideas propagated by early scholars, such as John Lubbock and Lewis Henry Morgan, suggested that American Indians and Australian Aborigines were, in an evolutionary sense, physically and culturally arrested in their development (Dippie 1982; Trigger 1989). Indigenous people were defined as the primitive 'other', and as McGuire (1992: 817) notes in the case of American Indians, whether characterized as noble savages or savage savages Indigenous people were defined nonetheless as primitives (see also Attwood 1989; Markus 1994 for Australia). The identification of Indigenous peoples as primitives justified colonization and the 'special treatment' they received, in particular the removal of people from land and the various attempts made by colonial governments at cultural assimilation. Linked to the idea of primitiveness was the idea of wilderness. The perception that North America and Australia were wilderness to be tamed by settlement is a pervasive mythology in the colonial history of both countries and non-Indigenous contemporary understandings of that history (Deloria 1992b; Durham 1992; Langton 1995; Head 2000). The characterization of these continents as wilderness reinforced the idea that they were vacant, or virtually vacant, and that Europeans had a natural right to occupy them (Reynolds 1982; Stiffarm and Lane 1992).

The mythologies of vanishing primitive peoples drifting through a wilderness, facilitated the persistent underestimation of Indigenous populations in both countries (Reynolds 1982; Stiffarm and Lane 1992). In addition, they reinforced dominant perceptions that Indigenous peoples had either vanished or that they were no longer 'real' Indians or Aborigines because cultural practices had changed following the depredations of colonization (Reynolds 1982; Dippie 1982; Durham 1992; McGregor 1997). In the southeastern states of Australia, these mythologies were particularly persistent and Aboriginal people in these regions were held to have either died out completely or 'lost' their culture entirely (Ryan 1981; Broome 1995; Goodall 1996). A related and significant mythology based on ideas of primitiveness in America was the Moundbuilder myth. This denied that earthworks in the Ohio and Mississippi regions were part of the heritage of local Indian communities (McGuire 1998: 69). Instead, these were seen as evidence of earlier 'civilized', probably 'white', groups that had been displaced by barbarians and thus colonists were morally right to seize land in this region by continuing not only a tradition, but by revenging lost civilizations (Hinsely 2000).

Within the first decades of the twentieth century the idea of vanishing peoples became increasingly harder to sustain in both countries, and government actions towards Indigenous peoples became increasingly driven by policies of cultural assimilation (Dippie 1982; Lippman 1992; Bordewich 1996). Significant in the processes of assimilation was bureaucratic surveillance, which was achieved through both legislative control and state classifications of Indigenous peoples (Nelson and Sheley 1985; Robbins 1992; Goodall 1995: 60; McGrath 1995b: 34f; Deloria and Lytle 2002). By the early twentieth century in Australia, each State government had enacted legislation to control the movement of Aboriginal people and to 'encourage' or force their segregation onto reserves and missions. Under these acts Aboriginal lives were highly regulated, their movements, living conditions, social lives, employment and pay were controlled and overseen by Protection and Welfare Boards and welfare inspectors (see chapters in McGrath 1995a). Children were routinely removed from families to be 'brought up white' or were sent to orphanages to be trained as rural and domestic labourers (Read 1982; Edwards and Read 1989; McGrath et al. 1995; Wilson 1997). State legislation, as Goodall (1995) argues, facilitated assimilation not only by the activities it legalized, such as child removal, but also through the establishment of mechanisms of surveillance (see also Bennett 1989; Lippmann 1992; McGrath 1995b).

These processes were also similarly at play in America and underpinned by legislation and bureaucratic surveillance. The Bureau of Indian Affairs (BIA), established in 1824, was charged with Indian welfare and included such responsibilities as administration of reservations and reservation land, and the operation and subsidization of schools and other educational programmes (Officer 1984; Iverson 1998). Underwriting all BIA activities were policies of assimilation (Bolt 1987; Iverson 1998). These policies became more pronounced in 1849 with the removal of the BIA from the Department of War and its inclusion in the Department of Interior, and then again in 1910 with the passage of the *Omnibus Act* which strengthened BIA authority over Indian lives and land (Deloria and Lytle 1998: 34). As in Australia, children's education became a significant focus of attempts at assimilation and boarding schools were established in the 1880s to facilitate assimilation (Deloria and Lytle 2002: 241). Through its education programmes the BIA attempted to break down Indian languages and religions, and attempted to teach Indians to be farmers, tradespeople or domestics (Iverson 1998). In 1887, the *General Allotment Act* saw the subdivision of reservations into 160-acre allotments, which were distributed to tribal members while all surplus land was sold to the Federal government and opened up to homesteaders. This Act attempted to attack the notion of community-held land while fostering Western notions of individual land ownership (Coulter and Tullberg 1984: 200–1; Deloria and Lytle 1998: 25).

The *Indian Reorganization Act* of 1934 (IRA) saw the establishment of a level of self-government through the development of tribal governments. This Act arose from public support for changes to Indian policy following 1920s reform movements and public recognition of poverty levels on reservations (Cornell 1988: 90-1). With the establishment of decentralized tribal governments, the 'bureaucratic stranglehold and paternalistic orientation of the BIA' was modified (Deloria and Lytle 2002: 101). Further, it put an end to the allotment process and helped to maintain and expand the tribal land base while aiding the recognition of the existence of tribal communities (Cornell 1988: 93). Although significant in facilitating tribal self-government, the IRA has received criticism from some Indigenous commentators. Often the forms of tribal administration that emerged under the Act were based on European forms of government and the BIA drafted a model constitution for use by tribes (Deloria and Lytle 2002: 101). These factors have led some to argue that despite the gains made under the IRA, the act may also be seen as a continuation of assimilation policies (see Hauptman 1984; Lacy 1985; Churchill and Morris 1992; Robbins 1992).

The post-World War Two American policies of termination and relocation, and the acts that enforced these policies, attempted to further undermine tribal communities. 'Termination' aimed to terminate Federal responsibility over certain Indian nations and tribes, and consequently saw local tribal and reservation economies suffer (McGuire 1992; Thomas 2000; Deloria and Lytle 2002). An important consequence of termination was the relocation of Indigenous peoples into urban centres, facilitated by the establishment of urban job training centres for American Indians under the *Relocation Act* of 1956 (Robbins 1992; Churchill and Morris 1992: 16).

Bureaucratic and government definitions of identity are important in the surveillance of Indigenous people (Goodall 1995). As Dodson observes 'supposedly objective definitions are ideological tools, designed to assist the state in applying its policies of control, domination and assimilation' (1994: 4), an observation echoed by numerous other Indigenous authors (V. Deloria 1969, 1998; Langford 1983; Fourmile 1989c; Jaimes 1992; Langton 1993; Churchill 1998). Initial bureaucratic definitions were based on early anthropological concerns about racial origins, where blood quantum was used to define a person's identity as Aboriginal or Indian (Sykes 1989; Maykutenner 1995; Stiffarm and Lane 1992; Fogelson 1998). The percentage of Aboriginal or Indian 'blood' was used as the basis for determining access to certain Federal or State provided resources (Lippman 1992; Jaimes 1992; McGrath 1995b). In America access to land under the *General Allotment Act* of 1887 was determined by degree of Indian blood, so that under this Act only those with half or more 'Indian blood' could receive land while those with less than 'half blood' were disenfranchised (Jaimes 1992: 126). In Australia, the classification of a person as Aboriginal effectively rendered that individual exempt from recognition by the Federal government, which meant that they came under the auspices of their local State law that regulated their movements and employment. Before the 1967 referendum that brought alterations to clauses in the Federal constitution, Aboriginal people had to sever relations with Aboriginal kin and friends, and effectively renounce their identity as an

Aboriginal person to gain Federal citizenship and thus 'exemption certificates' from control by State Welfare boards (Bennett 1985; Goodall 1995). A similar process of conferring citizenship occurred in the US before the *Indian Citizenship Act* of 1924, prior to which granting of citizenship symbolized 'the determination of the individual to cast aside traditions and customs and assume the dress, values, and beliefs of the larger society' (Deloria and Lytle 2002: 221).

In Tasmania Aboriginal people were denied their identity altogether because of the racial classification of Indigenous people. The normative perception in this State held that Truganini who died in 1876 was the 'Last Tasmanian' Aboriginal (Ryan 1972, 1981; Maykutenner 1995). She was the last so-called 'full-blooded' Tasmanian, and following her death Tasmanian Aboriginal people were redefined as 'descendants' only and their legitimacy as Aboriginal people was denied (Ryan 1981). Ideas of 'race' have also played a significant role in underpinning polices of 'assimilation' (Cowlishaw 1987; Markus 1994). Assumptions that cultural identity is biologically determined drove the emphasis on blood quantum (Tatz 1992: 80). The removal of children to be brought up or educated off reservations or reserves was often driven by blood quantum issues as those with 'white blood' were seen as more easily assimilated into 'white' society and culture (Read 1982; Wilson 1997). The policies and practices of assimilation were an attempt to reduce Indigenous resistance to colonization through both surveillance and instilling European cultural values into Indigenous peoples (Morris 1989). Further, in Australia at least, these policies were part of a process of colonization that reconstructed Aboriginal people as domestic and rural workers (Williams and Thorpe 1992: 97). This was a significant process in the colonization of Australia and the development of its rural industries, as Aboriginal people were, and continue to be, a significant and vital source of cheap labour in many economically important rural industries (McGrath 1987; May 1994; Brock 1995).

Sykes (1989: 10) has argued that the emphasis on blood quantum arose from the influences of anthropologists on government policy, as it was to the advantage of anthropologists to have a group set aside as 'full bloods' that they could access for the purpose of study. Indigenous people have, since first contact with Europeans, been subjected to close scrutiny by a range of academic disciplines and intellectuals. The study of Indigenous culture, social practices and material culture has produced continuous academic and public debate about the identity of Indigenous people (Langton 1993; V. Deloria 1998; Hill 2001). Anthropology has played an important role in colonial history by providing governments and their bureaucracies with ways for understanding, classifying and surveying Indigenous populations (Cowlishaw 1992; Biolsi 1998). Certainly, incorporation of academic and technical discourses into the control and management of Indigenous peoples' lives was well established by the time governments sought to extend their interests into the management of heritage. Certainly, in America, anthropological and archaeological expert witnesses gave evidence in treaty-based land claim and compensation hearings under the *Indians Claims Commission Act* of 1946 (Churchill 1992; McGuire 1992; Downer 1997). Although many of these witnesses may have attempted to support land claims, the issue here is that expertise was being utilized to translate and understand Indigenous land claims.

A significant part of the whole process of colonization has been the active denial of the history of oppression and Indigenous resistance to it. Although this resistance commenced with the onset of colonization, it is only since the late 1960s that the nature of American and Australian history and race relations has been actively debated in public arenas. The development of nationwide movements, that marked a new way of 'doing' politics in the 1960s (Matthews 1990), was significant in moving Indigenous resistance into the arena of public consciousness and debate. Central to the development of these movements was the process of questioning and debating normative accounts of American and Australian post-contact history. In Australia, a significant event in this process of contestation was the formation of the Australian Aborigines' League in Melbourne in 1934. One of the actions of this League was to proclaim Australia Day in 1938, which marked the 150th anniversary of Australia's 'settlement', as a Day of Mourning (Broome 1995: 147). This was a significant action, which questioned perceptions of the Australian nation and nationhood, and inspired similar demonstrations during the 1988 bicentennial (Broome 1995: 148). Throughout the twentieth century, Aboriginal people and communities, with the support of unionists and the Communist Party of Australia, undertook strike action to protest their treatment, pay and conditions of employment, and their citizenship status (see McLeod 1987; McGrath 1987; May 1994; Watson 1995).

In 1966, the Gurindji walked off Wave Hill Station in protest over wages and conditions (Hardy 1968). The walk-off was spectacularly successful in that it not only denied pastoralists a vital source of labour (Read 1995: 291), but also inspired other communities and helped lead to the development of the Land Rights movement (Maddock 1983). As part of the strike the Gurindji occupied Wattie Creek, land traditionally owned by the Gurindji, thus a strike for better conditions became a land rights claim on Wattie Creek (Hardy 1968; Maddock 1983). Subsequently the late 1960s saw the development of the Land Rights Movement, which as Miller (1986: 194) states gave direction to Aboriginal political activism. The American Civil Rights Movement initially influenced the aims and form of the Australian movement. Although Miller (1986: 194) noted that he and other activists quickly recognized that, unlike in the Civil Rights Movement, basic issues of sovereignty and rights to cultural expression had to underlie the Australian movement. Two significant events in the early 1970s cemented the issue of sovereignty and cultural identity and expression as central to this movement. In 1972, the Aboriginal Tent Embassy was erected on the lawns of Parliament House in Canberra, and signified both the alienation of Aboriginal people from wider Australian society and the assertion of Aboriginal sovereignty. This and subsequent arguments that Australia was 'invaded' rather than 'settled' challenged normative perceptions of Australian nationhood. In 1971 the Aboriginal flag was developed and adopted and symbolized the development of a 'pan-Aboriginality' that, while acknowledging the diversity of Aboriginal cultural expression and experiences, also unites Aboriginal people in opposition to non-Aboriginal discrimination and oppression (Keefe 1988; Attwood 1989). As Archer (1991) argues, these events encouraged a re-modelling of Aboriginal identity during the 1960s and 1970s that saw the rise of 'pan-Aboriginality' as a sub-state nationalism. This is a modern development with no pre-colonial history; it was a development of an Aboriginal consciousness, which occurred in terms of reciprocal contact with colonizers and state institutions (Archer 1991; Attwood 1989, 1995).

In America, collective protest has also had a long history, however, Cornell (1988) suggests that with the IRA and the formal recognition of tribal governments Indian protest took on an added dimension. He argues that tribalization facilitated cooperative relations between diverse and distant Indian communities and provided a focus for political and community organizations (1988: 101–4). Organizations such as the National Congress of American Indians (NCAI), the Council of Energy Resource Tribes and National Tribal Chairmen's Association and other organizations began to form from the 1940s onwards (Cornell 1988; Nagel 1997; Iverson 1998). The oldest of these, the NCAI, was founded in 1944 and agitated on a range of issues, combating in particular the policies and practices of Termination and Relocation (Iverson 1998: 113–15). The American Civil Rights Movement added a further dimension to Indian activism, and 'fish-ins', protests over fishing rights in the northwest, began to occur in the early 1960s (Nagel 1997: 161). However, as in Australia, Indigenous Americans perceived that issues such as treaty rights, sovereignty and land rights could become subsumed within the wider civil rights movements and a distinct Indian political movement developed in the late 1960s (see Nagel 1997; Deloria and Lytle 1998). In 1969, the San Francisco Bay Area's Indians of All Tribes occupied Alcatraz Island and a land claim was made (Smith and Warrior 1996). Nagel (1997) argues that this occupation represented the beginning of the Red Power movement and of accelerating American Indian activism. The American Indian Movement (AIM), founded in Minneapolis in 1968, went on to develop chapters in a number of other cities and States, and established itself at the forefront of much of the activism of the early 1970s (Means with Wolf 1995; Smith and Warrior 1996). Central to AIM and the wider Indian political movement were issues of sovereignty, self-government and land. The Indigenous movement was initially developed within the urban diaspora created by the removal of Indians from their land (Churchill 2003: 264). The urban origins ensured that not only were land access issues central to the movement, but also the need to challenge normative views about Indian identity and wider American nationhood. AIM, in particular, was highly effective in ensuring the development of public debate about Indigenous issues and land claims. From 1971, under the influence of several Indian activists, such as Russell Means, AIM initiated a sequence of public protests and events that specifically targeted normative ideas about American history, nationhood and the legitimacy of colonization (Smith and Warrior 1996; Churchill 2003). Some of these demonstrations were directed specifically at archaeologists; for instance, in 1971 members of AIM disrupted an excavation in Minnesota by backfilling trenches and burning field notes (Deloria 1973). These protests were underwritten by Deloria's (1969) highly influential manifesto *Custer Died for Your Sins,* which challenged not only the colonial nature of the American state, but also identified the role of anthropologists in the colonial process and offered a scathing, if humorous, attack on the validity of the discipline.

Interlinked with these protests were attempts to regain Indian control of cultural identity, and to challenge a range of American mythologies and stereotypes. For instance, in 1968, the NCAI commenced a campaign to challenge the use of Indian stereotypes in popular media and in the use of mascots and other images (Thomas 2000: 203). In response to the 1992 Columbian quincentennial American Indians celebrated their survival and argued that America must recognize its invasion, rather than settlement, of Indian lands (Wylie 1992a; Gulliford 2000).

In 1973, AIM occupied the Wounded Knee battle site on the Oglala Lakota Pine Ridge Reservation, an occupation that lasted for 71 days and resulted in a major and unsuccessful standoff against Federal marshals (Means with Wolf 1995; Smith and Warrior 1996; Nagel 1997). Although the events at Wounded Knee saw active and successful attempts by the American government to repress AIM, this organization had, as Robbins (1992: 268) points out, significantly raised public awareness of Indian issues. AIM, and other similar organizations, not only gave direction to continued Indian political activism, it also provided a sense of solidity and purpose to that activism (Smith and Warrior 1996; Rawls 2001). Moreover, as Russell Means argues, AIM reasserted a sense of American Indian cultural pride that underwrote the cultural revival movement (1988, quoted in Churchill 2003: 285–6).

Miller (1986) also identifies a sense of cultural revival that both underpinned and developed out of the Australian Land Rights Movement. These revivals were both an act of resistance and of survival in the face of the history of assimilation and contemporary racial stereotyping and discrimination (Keefe 1988; Gulliford 2000; Hill 2001). As a further act of resistance and assertion of the control of cultural identity, names such as 'Koori' from southern Australia and 'Pallawah' from Tasmania were used to challenge the racist cultural baggage that underwrites the name 'Aborigine'. In America debate has also arisen over the use of the term 'Native' in recognition of the colonial baggage and mythologies of primitiveness embedded in that term (Zimmerman 1996).

A sense of cultural revival also underwrote the development of the Red Road or 'Indian Way', an approach applied to various social problems, such as unemployment and alcoholism, to find culturally meaningful solutions (Zimmerman 1996: 156). This process reaffirmed Indian identity and offers an important counter to assimilation and the encroachment of dominant Euroamerican values on Indian communities (Zimmerman 1996: 156; Gulliford 2000). In Australia, a sense of pan-Aboriginality drew not only on cultural similarities between Aboriginal peoples, but more importantly on the commonality of experiences under colonization and dispossession (Dodson 1994: 9). Its development was important in publicly asserting, amongst other things, claims for land, compensation and the end of discriminatory practices. As a political tool, Australian Aboriginal cultural identity has taken on further weight and force with the 1992 judgment in the *Mabo and Others* v. *State of Queensland* land claim case. In this judgment it was determined that the native title over the Murray Islands by the Meriam people had not been extinguished by European settlement (Bartlett 1993; Butt and Eagleson 1993). This has challenged the legal assertion that Australia was *terra nullius* (that is legally unoccupied) at the time of Cook's 'discovery' of Australia and its subsequent colonization by Britain. Under the *Native Title Act 1993* (Cwlth), which arose from the 'Mabo Judgment', Aboriginal people may claim ownership of land provided they can demonstrate cultural ties to it (McIntyre 1994: 122). Again, the negotiation and definition of cultural identity becomes a significant focal point in the negotiation of land claims or access to compensation for land.

As a tactic, the development of both unifying cultural and political movements provided a coherence and force to Indian and Aboriginal political activism that could be more easily understood and listened to by governments. Why this is so is discussed in more detail in Chapter 4; however, in terms of representational politics these developments were crucial. The development of a coherent and integrated movement, with organizations and symbols of representation, gained political legitimacy with governments and policy makers in ways that individual community action and activism could not.

The revival of cultural pride and identity helped to give coherence and unity to the political movements, and cultural identity itself became a resource of political power. Claims to cultural identity and survival reinforced arguments for land (Harris 1979; Miller 1986; Churchill 2003). Further, the expression by Aboriginal and Indian peoples to self-conscious, confident and assertive claims to cultural identity challenged wider societal preconceptions. Not only were perceptions about the nature of history challenged, but the security of Australian and American cultural and national identity was also destabilized. The existence of coherent unified political movements, in which its members asserted their sovereignty and identity while challenging the idea of a single American or Australian nation, works, as Purvis (1996: 55) states, to 'call into question the stability of dominant conceptions of how and where politics is done in the contemporary world'.

Indigenous challenges to the idea of the 'nation', threaten the traditional processes involved in the government of Indigenous people. Indigenous cultural identity has been a focal point around which the treatment of Indigenous people has been determined, and through which Indigenous people have asserted not only their rights, but also the fact of their existence and experiences. As Dodson states:

> Those Aboriginalities have been, and continue to be, a private source of spiritual sustenance in the face of others' attempts to control us. They

are also a political project designed to challenge and subvert the authorised version on who and what we are.

(Dodson 1994: 10)

Indigenous cultural identity is an important resource of power that has been used both by and against Indigenous people. The control of cultural identity is significant in the development and assertion of Indigenous politics. Indigenous material culture as a physical symbol of cultural identity also becomes an important political resource in this context. As Langford (1983) pointed out to an Australian archaeological audience, the control of Aboriginal heritage is not only important in the negotiation of land claims, but also important in the control and maintenance of community cohesion and identity, and in asserting a sense of self-sufficiency and self-worth. She noted that if control of heritage was not returned to Aboriginal people then the perception of Aboriginal people as powerless victims would be propagated: 'if we Aborigines cannot control our own heritage, *what the hell can we control?*' (1983: 4, emphasis in original). Control of heritage, and thus cultural identity, is not only a vital resource in political negotiations, but it is also a vital resource for Indigenous cultural expression and community continuity and cohesion.

Indigenous criticism of archaeology

Criticisms levelled at the discipline of archaeology were integral to measures to take control of cultural identity, and its use in the wider negotiations of political legitimization. Archaeological excavations were not only disrupted by AIM, but Indigenous people also began to question publicly and forcefully the very legitimacy of the discipline (Deloria 1973; Langford 1983). From the 1970s, Indigenous people began attending archaeological conferences, not only to present papers challenging archaeological practices and concepts, but also to initiate and engage in arguments and debates from the floor (see for instance, Barunga 1975; Marika 1975; Langford 1983; Hammil and Cruz 1989; Antone *et al.* 1992; Reid 1992; and Grimes 2000 who comments).

Indigenous criticism of archaeology questions the 'relevance' of archaeology to Indigenous people (Williams 1975; Eaglehawk and Crow quoted in Mulvaney 1979: 215; Langford 1983; Cambra 1989; Turner 1989; Mihesuah 2000). The cultural legitimacy of archaeological interpretations has also been challenged and Indigenous people have argued that their past and history is known by them and thus that archaeological interpretations have little if anything to offer that understanding (Langford 1983; Anawak 1989; Hammil and Cruz 1989; TALC 1996). While some communities acknowledge the ability of archaeology to augment Indigenous knowledge about the past (for instance, chapters in Davidson *et al.* 1995; chapters in Swidler *et al.* 1997; Field *et al.* 2000), others have questioned the universalizing tendency of archaeology and warn against the archaeological appropriation of the past (Cambra 1989; Fourmile 1989c).

Archaeology assumes that the past is inherently open to study, and that as experts archaeologists have an inherent right to access that past (Klesert and Powell 1993). Indigenous people on the other hand question this 'right', and argue that this archaeological belief will only result in an appropriation of a community's past (Langford 1983; Vizenor 1986; Fourmile 1989c; Mihesuah 2000). This is because archaeological study redefines the Indigenous past as understandable only in terms of dominant Western understandings of human history. As such, it alienates that past and the meanings and significances it has to local community identity.

Others have identified the inherent racism in archaeological discourse and practice, identifying that terms like 'prehistory' denies the legitimacy of Indigenous knowledge about that past and undermines a sense of Indigenous history (Deloria 1973, 1997). Further, it is a term that is also underlined by a colonial discourse that classified peoples as 'primitives' or 'civilized', and that saw the period of prehistory as inherently primitive. Indeed the discourse of much contemporary archaeology is embedded with terms that carry unpleasant colonial baggage. For instance, the use of terms such as 'civilization' to describe cultures with extensive material assemblages, or the use of 'evolution' in describing cultural or technological development, or the adherence to the three age system of dating (stone, bronze and iron), amongst others, are all implicated in and embedded with colonial cultural chauvinism. Both the history of anthropology and archaeology have been scrutinized by Indigenous people who point out that these and other disciplines were integral in the colonial process and underpinned the process of assimilation and other attempts at cultural or physical genocide. As Vine Deloria (1998: 220) observes 'the politics of political institutions and the attitudes of American society toward tribal peoples have been shaped largely by the descriptions forged by the social sciences' and he and other Indigenous people have challenged archaeology to accept the political and moral responsibilities of this history (see also Langford 1983; Fourmile 1989c).

The issue of consultation has also been a significant theme within Indigenous criticism. Heritage agencies and archaeological organizations have been heavily lobbied by Indigenous people to ensure that they be consulted and informed about archaeological research activities that are likely to impact on their communities. Indigenous people have argued for the ability to veto archaeological research, given the ability of that research to materially affect the way that non-Indigenous Americans and Australians understand and regard Indigenous peoples.

Much of this debate and criticism has been centred on and tied up with debates over the reburial and repatriation of Indigenous human remains. The indiscriminate collection of human remains has a long and unpleasant history in both Australia and America (see Griffiths 1996; Thomas 2000). For many Indigenous communities it was culturally and religiously vitally important that their ancestors were afforded respect through obtaining appropriate cultural treatment and disposition for their remains (Wettenhall 1988; Hammil and Cruz 1989; Turner 1989; Pullar 1994; Thornton 1998; Riding In 2000). The excavation and storage of Indigenous remains by archaeologists and physical anthropologists is simply culturally unacceptable to most Indigenous communities (Fourmile 1987; Richardson 1989; Pullar 1994). Moreover, how Indigenous ancestral remains are treated speaks forcefully about the attitudes archaeologists hold about not only the people in the past, but also the people in the present who are descendent from and culturally linked to those remains. Reoccurring in this debate is the lament that Indigenous people are often treated as fossils or specimens with no ability to assert a sense of their own sense of self and place in history. Significant here is the event that is often cited as one of the touchstones in the American Indian movement for reburial and repatriation. In 1971 during reconstruction of Highway 34 in Iowa, a cemetery containing a number of graves of European settlers and the grave of an Indian woman and infant was uncovered. The remains of the Europeans were reburied in a local cemetery, while those of the Indian woman and child were removed for study. Protest by the Indigenous community, led by Maria Pearson, emphasized the inherent discrimination of this act (Horizon 1995). The differential treatment of Indigenous and non-Indigenous remains underscores not only the history of discrimination, but also the continuation of discrimination and social and political disenfranchisement (McGuire 1989; Rivera 1989).

The range of criticisms identified above were by no means confined to reburial debates, however, it was this debate that gained particular archaeological and popular media attention. This was in large part because it is a fundamentally significant religious and cultural issue for many Indigenous communities, and is often at the forefront of Indigenous criticism. For many communities the disturbance of burials is simply anathema to religious and cultural beliefs and values. However, this criticism also focused archaeological attention because archaeological access to data was directly threatened by demands for repatriation. The initial archaeological response to this challenge was to debate whether Indigenous people had the 'right' to claim control over skeletal material and artefacts and asserted the rights of archaeological science to access its data (for instance, Buikstra 1981; Meighan 1984; and Sprague 1974; Winter 1980 who comments on this). This debate became quickly characterized as a debate between science and religion. Archaeologists questioned the legitimacy of religious belief to censor and control academic research and many archaeologists were staunch in their stance against reburial (for instance, Cheek and Keel 1984; Mulvaney 1991; Knusel and Roberts 1992; Meighan 1992; and Zimmerman 1998a who analyses this). While there were indeed fundamental differences in understanding and perspectives on the value and significance of human remains and the worth of archaeological research, the characterization of this debate as one between religion and science missed the point. The need for many Indigenous people to control their heritage is not only about defending belief systems, but is embedded in wider struggles to control identity and the cultural and political legitimacy that Indigenous people are afforded by governments and society.

The forcefulness of Indigenous criticism of archaeological research has helped to spark internal archaeological debates that have challenged the epistemological and ontological security of the discipline. Many archaeologists have critically engaged with Indigenous criticisms and have explored the implications of it for the development of archaeological research practices and theory (notable among these include Zimmerman 1989a, 2001; Pardoe 1990, 1992; McGuire 1992, 1998; Bray 1996, 2001; Ferguson 1996; Greer *et al.* 2002; Clarke and Paterson 2003; McNiven and Russell in press). Some organizations have now established codes of ethics that recognize the need for community consultations and negotiations (for instance WAC 1990; AAA 1991; Davidson 1991a, 1991b; Lynott and Wylie 2000). Certainly, the move to establish consultation processes was part of a genuine attempt by many archaeologists and government heritage or cultural resource agencies to address Indigenous criticisms, or at least to further understand them. Many individual archaeologists and heritage agencies have also now instigated a range of practices to work with Indigenous and other communities (see chapters in Davidson *et al.* 1995; Swidler *et al.* 1997; Dongoske *et al.* 2000; Marshall 2002; Fforde *et al.* 2002; Derry and Malloy 2003), while some Indigenous communities have themselves either employed or chosen to work alongside archaeologists on Indigenous-led projects (see for instance, Adams 1984; Ferguson 1984; Anyon and Ferguson 1995; Anyon *et al.* 1997, 2000; Ross 1996; Dongoske and Anyon 1997; Greer *et al.* 2002; Stapp and Burney 2002; Smith *et al.* 2003).

Some Indigenous responses to archaeological consultation and other practices have tended to be positive (Kelly 1979, 1980; Tjamiwa 1992; Xiberras and du Cros 1992; chapters in Dongoske *et al.* 2000). However, there have been criticisms that early attempts by archaeologists at consultation were only 'tokenistic', and pragmatic, and that Indigenous people learned or gained little concrete from it (for instance, Barunga 1975; Marika 1975; Fesl 1983; Cook and Morris 1984; Fourmile 1989a, 1989c; Moore 1989). Despite the development in the 1990s of codes of ethics and the implementation of consultation policies by many government heritage or cultural resource agencies to standardize consultation practices, criticism has continued (e.g. Fourmile 1992; Geering and Roberts 1992; Organ 1994; Ah Kit 1995; Forsman 1997; Lippert 1997; Ravesloot 1997; Watkins 2003). Recent criticism of archaeological consultation practices has stressed that many archaeologists do not 'listen' to, or negotiate, with Indigenous people, and have characterized consultation processes as 'just telling'.

While archaeological attempts at consultation and community inclusion have often been prompted by genuine desires for Indigenous participation, the perception by some Indigenous critics that negotiation is not part of the consultation process results from three issues. First, there can be a lack of explicit recognition or understanding of the resources of power that archaeologists bring to any consultation process. This then impedes the possibility of, or the nature of, negotiations (Watkins 2001b). Impeding the success of the consultation processes and other initiatives is the issue of archaeological expertise. Some commentators have identified that in joint projects it is archaeological expertise, rather than Indigenous knowledge, that is listened to by governments and other audiences (Greer and Henry 1996; Lippert 1997; Cash Cash 2001). As argued in the following chapter archaeological knowledge is underpinned by the discourse of logical positivism that stresses objectivity and rationality. This discourse, alongside archaeological claims to professionalism, underwrites the authority of archaeological pronouncements while, at the same time, devaluing the authority of Indigenous knowledge.

Second, consultation and community inclusion can falter because there is limited archaeological understanding of the consequences of archaeological practice and knowledge outside of disciplinary confines. There is little sense or understanding of what Indigenous people might stand to lose or gain in the consultation process, and the discipline has yet to come to terms with the consequences it has for the politics of cultural identity.

Third, the processual underpinning of much American and Australian archaeology does not provide the intellectual tools to incorporate non-positivist Indigenous knowledge into either the practice of archaeology or the development of research agendas. This is not to say that archaeologists *must* incorporate Indigenous knowledge into their research, however, the current theoretical framework of the discipline allows little space for this to actually occur, and this impedes meaningful community inclusion when attempts are made. This tension is witnessed in recent debates about the value of what the American literature refers to as 'oral traditions'. The research utility for both archaeologists and Indigenous communities of incorporating oral history or knowledge into archaeological research has been argued by Echo-Hawk (1997, 2000). However, Mason (2000) retorts that the use of oral tradition will only compromise the integrity of archaeological research and its ability to seek 'truth', as tradition cannot be verified. He notes, that 'like religion, you believe oral tradition or you don't' (2000: 263). As Whiteley (2002: 408) points out, the issue here is power/knowledge; both positions have political consequences for the legitimacy of the knowledge claims made by both parties. For each to incorporate the other's knowledge system, one or both must compromise and this has wider consequences. For archaeology, it is to risk losing access or control over data and knowledge of the past; for Indigenous peoples it risks further alienation from their cultural knowledge and traditions.

In Australia, this situation is exacerbated by the contradictory situation created by the Australian Archaeological Association code of ethics on the one hand, and adherence to processual theoretical concerns on the other. The Australian Archaeological Association code of ethics recognizes the priority of Indigenous access to the data of archaeology and encourages Indigenous participation in the generation of research questions and practices (AAA 1991). Yet, this stance is contradicted by the Australian discipline's adherence to positivist notions of science and its hesitation in debating postprocessual or other theoretical positions that abandon the essentialism and reductionism of processual theory (Burke *et al.* 1994; Smith 1995a; Lahn 1996). Any inclusion of non-positivist knowledge about the past into archaeological practice requires a surrendering of disciplinary authority. By inference, any move to support Indigenous claims calls into question the authority of archaeology established through the discipline's assertion of scientific objectivity. This is because any recognition of Indigenous claims to 'the past' must implicitly acknowledge the plurality of interpretations of the past. In effect, any desire to acknowledge the Indigenous politics of archaeology places in jeopardy the very values that have been used to justify archaeological involvement in Indigenous history and material culture in the first place.

Conclusion

In both theoretical and practical terms, archaeology has achieved the status of a conundrum. At one level, it seeks to accommodate Indigenous knowledge claims and answer the moral charges made against it. At another level the discipline seeks to maintain unfettered access to its data, and cannot jeopardize the authority of expertise and professionalism that ensures that access. This impasse sends contradictory messages to Indigenous peoples and helps, as argued in the next chapter, to undermine the theoretical attempts made by postprocessualism and other critical theories to find a concrete and politically sensitive way out of the situation. This impasse is facilitated by the wider discipline's failure to understand the extra-disciplinary consequences of what the discipline *does*. In effect, it lacks the theoretical acuity to understand the role that archaeological knowledge plays outside of the discipline and the way that role is perceived both by governments and a range of other stakeholder groups, in particular Indigenous peoples.

An understanding of these consequences is central to the development of archaeological practice and theory that aims to deal equitably with Indigenous demands and claims. Any negotiation that aims to be honest and equitable is better served when the resources of power/knowledge used by negotiators are identified and understood, and when the consequences of negotiation to both parties can be identified. It is the aim of this book to begin to offer a theoretical insight and understanding of the consequences of archaeological knowledge and practice outside the academy. To begin to do this, this chapter has placed the criticism levelled at archaeology into the wider context of the history of Indigenous cultural politics. The development of a new way of doing politics in the 1960s and 1970s is important for understanding the consequences of the collision of archaeological and Indigenous interests. The development of Indigenous political 'movements' and the use of the past in defining the political identity and legitimacy of these movements are significant.

Although the history of Indigenous political protest in both America and Australia began with, and is as long as European occupation, the 1960s marks an era of increasing public awareness of Indigenous politics. Not only were public debates sparked about land and sovereignty rights, but the point was also publicly driven home of the simple fact that Australian Aboriginal and American Indian peoples had survived despite colonial denial of their cultural and physical presence. Individual community concerns were given added political voice and legitimacy through representation by a movement united on basic common issues. Community interests could be more forcefully represented and lobbied for as the movements could claim representational political legitimacy (Matthews 1990; Abbott 1996).

The agenda of Indigenous politics is concerned with a wide range of issues, notably housing, health, education, employment and so forth, however, an important underpinning aspect of the movement is land rights (Charlesworth 1984; Coulter and Tullberg 1984; Churchill 2003). Claims to land were based on historical, economic and cultural ties, and in particular an ability to demonstrate long-term cultural and physical ties (Hiatt 1989; Brody 2001). Indigenous material culture/heritage are important resources in helping communities to put their case, and in helping governments determine the 'legitimacy' of claims. Indigenous culture and its representation in material culture plays an important part in maintaining, but also proclaiming, Indigenous cultural identity. The physicality of material culture is not only important in providing tangible links to the past, it is also a powerful symbol or statement to others of what constitutes a population's past and present cultural affiliation and identity. The importance of controlling the meanings given to material culture has underpinned Indigenous criticism of archaeological interpretations, possession of ancestral remains, as well as lack of negotiation in consultation and the hesitation in returning information about the past back to communities.

By the 1970s it had became important for governments to regulate the newly articulated demands and claims of Indigenous political and cultural movements, and to make sense of emerging Indigenous identities that utilized the past and Indigenous heritage in negotiating political legitimacy. This coincided with more effective archaeological lobbying of governments about their concerns for the preservation of cultural resources that were increasingly threatened by development and commercial looting. As is documented in the following chapters, the development of CRM and the legislation that underpins it ignored Indigenous input and explicitly incorporated archaeological concerns and concepts in an attempt to de-politicize claims to Indigenous cultural identity. The past, on which this identity hinged, became the construct of objective archaeological science, which in turn was regulated through cultural resource legislation and the CRM process.

3

ARCHAEOLOGICAL THEORY AND THE 'POLITICS' OF THE PAST

In Chapter 1, Indigenous CRM was defined as the process of interlinked and contested relations between archaeologists, Indigenous people, governments and their bureaucracies. The central problem addressed by this chapter is how to make sense of and explain these interrelations and, more specifically, to consider whether current archaeological theory offers a suitable framework for understanding the nature and practice of archaeology within CRM. Can contemporary archaeological theory make sense of what archaeology 'does' within the context of CRM?

Theoretical discussion within Anglophone[1] archaeology has been ostensibly polarized since the mid-1980s between 'processual' and 'postprocessual' theories. They differ significantly in how they believe the discipline should theorize its data, and how or whether the discipline should construct, reconstruct, think about and critique itself, its practices and its knowledge construction. This chapter reviews processual and postprocessual theories, the main theoretical positions within Anglophone archaeology, and examines their ability to ask meaningful and useful questions about archaeological discourse, practice and knowledge.

The focus of this review is on processual and postprocessual theoretical developments for a number of reasons. First, processual theory significantly influenced and still underpins the development of American and Australian archaeology and Western CRM in particular (Redman 1991; Hodder 1993; Carman 2002; see Chapter 5). Second, postprocessual theory, although not widely debated within US and Australian archaeology, explicitly attempts to analyse and explain the political context of archaeology. Various proponents of postprocessual theory have made the claim that it can offer critical analyses and perspectives on the interaction of archaeology with Indigenous politics and/or heritage interests (e.g. Shanks and Tilley 1987a, 1987b; Leone *et al.* 1987; Hodder 1989c, 1992, 1999; Tilley 1989b, 1989d; Meskell 2000b; Olivier 2001). These claims make postprocessual theory an obvious departure point for any analysis of CRM and the interaction of archaeology, Indigenous politics and heritage bureaucracies. This chapter reviews both processual and postprocessual writings as theories of knowledge and practice, and concentrates on the ability of each position to pose self-reflexive questions about the practice of archaeology in CRM.

The principal conclusion from this review is that archaeological theory explains only itself. Current theoretical debate offers some insight into the construction and development of knowledge and discourse used within the discipline, but it is fundamentally self-referential. It offers little insight into the practices of archaeology, and the uses of archaeological knowledge, outside the academy. It thus offers little explanation or insight into the consequences of archaeological practice within CRM, and the interaction of archaeological theory and practice with governmental and Indigenous political concerns.

This conclusion has two significant implications that are explored in the following chapters. The first is that we must turn to the wider social sciences for theoretical frameworks that might make sense of the interaction of archaeology, Indigenous politics and heritage bureaucracies (Chapter 4). The second is that archaeological theory must itself become subject to analysis within this work (Chapter 5). The ideological underpinnings of both postprocessual and processual theory must themselves be examined for the contributions they make to archaeology's role within CRM. What may then be identified is the influences this role, in turn, has had on the development of archaeological theory and discourse (Chapter 6).

Processual theory

What is processual theory?

Processual theory, or the 'New Archaeology',[2] represented the avant-garde of archaeological theory during the 1960s and early 1970s (Patterson 1986a, 1986b). Processual theory, or 'processual archaeology' (Renfrew and Bahn 1991: 14), developed in the USA in the early 1960s as a reaction to the perceived inadequacies of the 'culture history' approach (Watson 1973a; Trigger 1984b, 1989). By 1980, advocates of processual archaeology could successfully claim that, during the 1970s, processual theory had become 'mainstream' (Patterson 1986a: 44). Certainly, today processual theory is claimed as the dominant theoretical position in American, British and Australian archaeology despite challenges by postprocessual theories and residual 'culture history' adherents (Murray 1987; Daniel and Renfrew 1988: 173–4; Johnson 1999).

The New Archaeology brought about important and fundamental changes to the discipline. It embraced logical positivism during the 1960s, and worked to make this epistemological framework basic to the discipline during the 1970s (Gibbon 1989). It repositioned archaeology away from its early twentieth-century associations with history, and aligned it with the natural sciences (Binford 1968a, 1972; Flannery 1973). As well, the need to implement a rigorous and systematic research methodology within the context of a research design was stressed (Binford 1964). Significantly, it also argued the need to *explain* the archaeological record rather than simply describe and catalogue site and regional assemblages, as the preceding culture history approach was claimed to have done (Binford 1962;

Watson *et al.* 1971; Renfrew 1973). Explanation was to be achieved through the explicit implementation of theory, which would be developed using hypothetico-deductive methodologies (Watson *et al.* 1971). The archaeological record was to be understood in terms of human behaviour. It was argued that the culture history approach, concerned as it was with identifying individual 'cultures' through the archaeological record, and then documenting and recording changes over time, had failed to add any overall understanding about the nature of human cultural development and behaviour (Binford 1964; Watson 1973a).

Processualists conceived human behaviour, although manifested in a variety of cultural expressions, as being influenced by common or inherent attributes or 'processes' which were to be identified (Binford 1962, 1964, 1968a). This would allow the development of 'law like propositions' that would inform and explain the archaeological record (e.g. Fritz and Plog 1970; Watson *et al.* 1971; Watson 1973b; Binford 1978; Read and LeBlanc 1978). In addition, the natural (as opposed to cultural) processes which influenced the deposition and conservation of the archaeological record, together with the limitations and influences on interpretation caused by archaeological method and concepts, were to be identified and understood (Binford 1962, 1988; Schiffer 1976). Subsequently, the New Archaeology highlighted the importance of rigorous scientific methodology and engendered explicit and self-conscious debate on the nature of theory and method within the discipline.

It also triggered considerable polemical debate within the US and British literature (Flannery 1973; Salmon 1982; Daniel and Renfrew 1988). The polemic of the processual reaction to the 'sterile' description of the then dominant culture history approach (Caldwell 1959; Binford 1962) promised a New Archaeology which was to be more 'relevant', dynamic and theoretically sophisticated. The need to establish the unambiguous 'relevance' of archaeology was stressed in much of the processual material of the 1960s and 1970s (e.g. Binford 1962; Flannery 1967; Ford 1973; Fritz 1973; King 1977). Although what it was to be relevant to was never clearly defined, there emerges a sense that with the advent of processual theory archaeology had 'lost' its 'innocence' (Clarke 1973). Its 'innocence' was certainly discarded in a more self-conscious approach to theory and method. A push to make the discipline and its knowledge more 'socially responsible' (Binford 1962; Clarke 1973), more clearly definable and testable (Binford 1968b; Clarke 1968; Watson *et al.* 1971; Gumerman 1977; Watson 1991), and ultimately more socially and scientifically 'relevant' was expressed through rhetorical claims to 'maturity' (Binford 1962, 1986, 1988; Flannery 1967; Fritz 1973; Watson 1973a; Renfrew 1982). For instance:

> We suspect that unless archaeologists find ways to make their research increasingly relevant to the modern world, the modern world will find itself increasingly capable of getting along without archaeologists.
>
> (Fritz and Plog 1970: 412)

During the 1960s and 1970s, archaeology embraced what Chalmers refers to as the 'common sense view of science' (1979: 1). The perception of 'science' incorporated into archaeology was one easily identifiable by most lay people. Science was deemed by the science to have established archaeology as a 'mature', relevant and authoritative science (Renfrew 1982) that, moreover, was publicly seen as such. As Gibbon (1989: 89) notes, processual archaeology attempted broadly to deal with the issue of the 'purpose of archaeological research'. It dealt with this issue in a very explicit and public way, specifically via debates about why the past should be conserved and preserved (e.g. McGimsey 1972; McGimsey and Davis 1977; Deetz 1977; Fowler 1977; Mulvaney 1970, 1979, 1981b; Megaw 1980). Processual theory had consequences for public debate and conflict over material culture. For instance, archaeology as an expert science assumed an authoritative position in these debates, and, through the processual scientific discourse, heritage objects became (and were publicly seen to become) archaeological data. This aspect of processual archaeology and its consequences is discussed in Chapter 5.

Archaeology's new 'relevance' was to be measured against its publicly proclaimed scientific maturity. Linked to this was its (asserted) ability to comment on the present as well as the past. It was argued that by identifying the basic processes underlying human behaviour it was possible to predict or comment upon present and future 'problems', including such things as population growth, environmental degradation and so forth (e.g. Fritz 1973; Fletcher 1981; see also Dark 1995: 34 who comments on this). Trigger (1989) argues that the discourse of 'relevance' in the US literature was also linked to the failure of the culture history approach to help American archaeologists make the American Indian past 'meaningful' to American society generally. By defining universal processes, American archaeology, and Indigenous research generally, became more 'relevant'. Further, the so-called 'maturity' archaeology gained from its identification with 'science' (Clarke 1973; Hodder 1981) provided archaeology with a certain relevance for state agencies. Graham Clark foreshadowed this in 1934, when he noted that archaeology should only be incorporated into state agencies concerned with the management of antiquities and relics when it had 'reached a degree of accuracy' (1934: 414).

In the search for 'relevance', Binford and others called for a rejection of the historical particularism of culture history, with its aims of simply reconstructing and describing the histories of past societies. To achieve this, archaeology was to reject its links with history, which the discipline had made during the first half of the twentieth century, and realign itself with anthropology (Binford 1962; Longacre 1970; Fritz 1973; Watson 1973a). Anthropology itself was seen as having scientific goals, a view that anthropologists in the 1960s regarded as theoretically dated (Leone 1971). However, anthropology with its assumed (by archaeologists) aim to '*explicate* and *explain* the total range of physical and cultural similarities and differences characteristic of the entire spatial-temporal span of man's [*sic*] existence' (Binford 1962: 217, emphasis in original) was seen to offer a more useful, 'relevant' and theoretically informed insight into human behaviour than the cataloguing of assemblages characterized as the culture history approach. Binford (1988: 30) stressed the need to define and ask what he referred to as the 'Big Questions' about human cultural evolution and processes. During the 1960s and 1970s there was a quantum change in what it was that archaeology did – it became a more standardized form of expertise – and thus could be applied to particular problems surrounding the 'governing' of material culture. It was able to apply technical procedures and science to conflicts over material culture, and de-politicize issues through the employment of its expertise.

Processual archaeology as a theory of knowledge

The explicit goal of the New Archaeology was to make archaeology more 'scientific' and to bring archaeology closer to the natural sciences (Binford 1988: 22). To this end processual theory employed the framework of logical positivism, taking the view that empirical verification was the only source of true knowledge (Gibbon 1989: 8).

Processualists, in challenging the usefulness of particularistic and descriptive studies of cultural change, stressed the need to establish generalizing law-like evolutionary propositions that would explain human behaviour (e.g. Renfrew 1983; Binford 1968b; Watson et al. 1971; Watson 1973a). Subsequently, processual theory held that archaeology needed to identify and explain universal cultural 'processes', and reject particularistic studies of cultural change (Binford 1962). The main aim of archaeology was thus the establishment of generalized laws about cultural development (Flannery 1967; Fritz and Plog 1970; Watson et al. 1971; Watson 1973a). Material culture was defined as reflecting social behaviours, or reflecting the natural processes of deposition and taphonomy, all of which could be scientifically described and explained (Binford 1962; Schiffer 1976, 1988). Processual theory was successful in its incorporation of the natural sciences insofar as rigorous scientific method came to underpin disciplinary practice, and knowledge and methodology from the natural sciences were incorporated into the discipline through interdisciplinary projects (in particular from areas such as biology, earth sciences, palaeontology etc.).

However, processual archaeology has failed to identify convincing cultural processes and produce law-like generalizations. Although, as Trigger (1989) notes, the view that human social behaviour was a process of adaptation to the natural environment focused research on environmental adaptations, such as subsistence strategies, technological development and trade. Concern with the natural environment is reflective of processual archaeology's incorporation of the methodology of the natural sciences. The identification of more discrete 'cultural' processes was not facilitated by 'borrowing' from the natural sciences, and the lack of engagement with social science concepts rendered any understanding of 'culture' problematic in the context of these borrowings (Shanks and Tilley 1987a).

The emphasis on ecological models and environmental adaptations and interactions dominated much of the US processual research during the 1970s and 1980s and was readily incorporated into British research (Daniel and Renfrew 1988). This followed on from the influential functionalist work of Graham Clarke, whose important excavation into the ecological and subsistence aspects of Star Carr in northeast England laid the groundwork for this aspect of processual concerns (Johnson 1999). Clarke's functionalism also found synergy with the processualist aim of identifying underlying and interacting processes.

The positivistic assumptions underlying processual research include the perception that science is an objective and rational practice, producing neutral and value free knowledge (Watson 1973a; Watson 1991; Bell 1994). A further assumption inherent in processual theory is the idea of the universality of knowledge – archaeological interpretations, because of their empirical, law-like and objective nature, are of universal applicability and 'relevance' (Binford 1988, 1990; Bell 1994). These assumptions have led to a view of material culture as holding intrinsic value and information, which can be obtained through systematic and rigorous research. Although this is not necessarily articulated in an overt manner, the idea that material culture has inherent value is one that nonetheless emerges in the processual literature (Tainter and Lucas 1983).

Importantly, processual archaeology also reoriented the relationship between practice and theory in archaeology. The idea that theory could and should be clearly defined in 'research designs' was emphasized in processual debate (Gumerman 1977; Schiffer 1988; Bell 1994). Three different 'levels' of theory were applied to the study of the archaeological record. Binford, in acknowledging that archaeologists interpret the past from their expectations in the present, identifies 'constructs' as the first level of theory (Binford 1962). On the second level, processualists define 'middle range theory' which represents the groups of principles concerned with deriving archaeological data from the past and transforming them into statements about cultural systems (Binford 1977). On the third level processual archaeologists defined higher-level theories or general or system theories (Schiffer 1988; Watson 1991; Redman 1991). At this level, theories are developed to identify and explain the cultural processes and systems that are the concern of processual archaeologists. In addition processualists also advocate the development of 'experimental laws' to complement theory building (Schiffer 1988: 464).

Despite the recognition of different levels of theorizing, 'constructs' and ideological assumptions and perceptions often become obscured in processual theory building and implementation (Shanks and Tilley 1987a; Hodder 1989a; Wylie 1992b). Although the aim was to identify and control, where possible, ideological assumptions by identifying 'constructs' and implementing self-conscious research procedures, the privileging of empiricism, 'objectivity', and hypothesis testing has worked to reinforce top-down theorizing. Thus, despite its aim to do so, the ontological assumptions about the 'naturalness' of the archaeological record have not been challenged by processual theory.

The underlying principles of the so-called 'high' theory offered by Binford and others have become so much part of archaeological discourse and knowledge that they are no longer challenged – they are seen as part of the 'common sense' (or 'normalization') of archaeology. As Richard Watson argues 'archaeology is based on all the ... sciences and on common sense', and it does not need to 'challenge' common sense (1991: 278).

Later processual theoretical debate has centred on defending itself from the postprocessual critique (e.g. Renfrew 1989; Binford 1987, 1990; Watson 1990, 1991; Redman 1991; Bintliff 1993). Binford has dismissed postprocessual and critical theories generally as 'religion' (1990: 62), while others maintain the rationality of science (Bintliff 1991, 1993; Watson 1991, 1992; Bell 1994; Pardoe 1994), accusing postprocessualists of making 'a mockery of science, reason and archaeology' (Watson 1990: 687). However, adherents and others sympathetic to processual theory acknowledge that a certain sterility has entered into processual research, which Bradley calls a 'loss of nerve' or self-confidence (1993: 131), and that research has lost itself in the particulars of data, and become science for science's sake (Redman 1991; Trigger 1991a).

Processual theory established itself as the dominant position in American prehistoric archaeology during the late 1960s and 1970s. However, in Australia, its establishment was more difficult, but was effectively tied into the emergence of the discipline itself in that country. Prehistoric[3] archaeology as a recognizable and university-based discipline began in Australia in the late 1950s and early 1960s (Golson 1986; Mulvaney 1989, 1993a; Bowdler 1993). Australian archaeology as a professional discipline is therefore relatively recent, and although fieldwork before the 1950s and 1960s was undertaken by museum staff and interested individuals, it was not until the 1950s that researchers specifically trained in archaeology (most notably at Cambridge in the UK) began to conduct fieldwork (see Moser 1995b). The late development of the discipline has had several important implications for the importation of processual theory into the study of Australian prehistory.

As numerous commentators have noted, there has been little explicit debate in Australia about theory and the underlying principles and concepts of archaeology (Murray and White 1981; Huchet 1991; Murray 1992a; Bowdler 1993; Burke et al. 1994; Smith 1995a, 1998). While Bowdler (1993) contends that many Australian archaeologists do not overtly identify with processual theory, the key themes of positivistic science and processual theory are nonetheless evident (Murray 1992a; Moser 1995b).

Authoritative calls were made in the late 1960s and early 1970s by Megaw (1966), Jones (1968a), and Mulvaney (1971a, 1971b), all influential academic archaeologists, for Australian archaeology to adopt the methodology and philosophies of the emerging American literature. The adoption of processual theory, and subsequently scientific rigour, was seen as ensuring disciplinary maturity and offered a way for the developing discipline to avoid parochialism. As Megaw states:

We have still far to go in what has been regarded as the last state in the evolution of our archaeology: systematic search and theorizing with the aid of processual analysis.

(Megaw 1966: 308)

Megaw advocated a more scientific archaeology, and the adoption of the latest theoretical trends from the USA, to ensure archaeological maturity in the eyes of the international community – even at the expense of making his and others' Cambridge training 'old fashioned' (1966: 308). Mulvaney (1971b: 243) also called for 'more sophisticated techniques and sounder logic', saying that Australian archaeologists would 'do well to consult American literature, particularly ... *American Antiquity*' (see also 1971a). In 1961, Mulvaney also warned against parochialism: 'our isolation is such ... there is a danger that [Australian archaeology] could become parochial' (quoted in Megaw 1966: 301). In 1963, at an Australian Institute of Aboriginal Studies (AIAS) conference Jack Golson, another eminent Australian archaeologist, is also reported to have advocated that Australian archaeology adopt the theoretical and methodological techniques being developed in the USA (Mulvaney 1971a: 373; see also Golson 1986). Jones, too, in 1968 warned against the simple collection of data and artefacts by professional archaeologists, and argued that archaeology needed a cohesive theoretical framework, especially because:

In terms of the 'mainstream of history', Australia is a peripheral eddy. If we are content merely to document this local sequence, we consign our work to a footnote of world prehistory.

(Jones 1968a: 535)

Processual theory was thus a vehicle for the newly emergent Australian archaeology to gain international recognition and acceptance. As Mulvaney (1981a: 63–4) reports, the concept of Aboriginal people as 'relic savages' also engendered intellectual contempt that saw Australian archaeology ignored internationally. The need to prove the 'relevance' and usefulness of Australian research helped facilitate attempts within the discipline to draw on the authority of 'science'. Subsequently, processual method and theory were *explicitly* adopted into the Australian discipline, as Moser (1995b: 181–2) documents, when they were incorporated into the teaching of prehistoric archaeology at Sydney University. During the 1960s and 1970s this was one of the main teaching departments of archaeology in the country, and many of those who taught in the department, or went through as students during these decades, have held, or continue to hold, influential positions within the discipline (Moser 1995b; see also Allen and Jones 1983).

However, as in America, Australian archaeology did not entirely abandon the preceding culture history approach (McBryde 1986). Australian archaeology pursued the development of its scientific and theoretical credentials on top of the old 'culture history approach', a process which Allen and Jones (1983: 166) refer to as Australia's 'hybridization'. Nonetheless, the influences of 'culture history' were satirized as a theoretically bankrupt 'dig and see' mentality (Murray and White 1981). Certainly, the *discourse* of processual science came to dominate in Australia, and became significant in framing research questions, even if the archaeology that was actually done did not entirely abandon prior practices and methods. The 1960s and 1970s have been characterized in Australia as both a 'scientific revolution' and the arrival of 'modern' archaeology (Jones 1993: 106, 115).

Processual theory and CRM

Despite the rapid emergence of CRM as an important area of archaeological practice in the 1960s and 1970s, many archaeologists did not, and in terms of their philosophies of science could not, treat CRM as 'real' science or 'real' archaeology (see Renfrew 1983, who identifies this phenomenon). For them, CRM is a consequence of the science, not an influence on it. It provides a technical area of employment for archaeologists, but it does not alter the way in which knowledge is produced or interpreted.

Because of this, most archaeological literature that addresses CRM tends to discuss technical issues of management and practice, offering no real examination of the philosophical or ideological underpinnings of CRM. Once CRM's association with archaeology is acknowledged, it is seen as simply an area of technical practice. However, processual theory did become important in the development of CRM as it provided its rigorous methodological underpinnings (Redman 1991: 298; Hodder 1993; Murray 1993a). The CRM approach took positivism as its starting point (Bintliff 1988; Byrne 1991, 1993; Carman 1993; Smith 1993a), and accordingly processual theory provided CRM with the scientific principles and values to assess which aspects of the database to conserve and preserve and which to allow to be destroyed. Finally, it also provided CRM with intellectual authority through its association with archaeological 'science'. These issues are further discussed and illustrated in Chapters 5 and 6. However, for the purposes of this review, the processual literature on CRM may be characterized as concerned with establishing and maintaining archaeological scientific practice within CRM. Apart from a concern to maintain archaeological scientific standards within CRM, there is no critical or analytical discussion of the role of archaeology within CRM.

The naturalization of processual theory as processual archaeology

Processual theory does more than underpin archaeology. It has become the 'natural' theoretical position in Anglophone archaeology. 'Naturalization' has meant that processual theory cannot problematize the 'taken-for-granteds' in archaeology. The paradigm constructs these in a way that renders them 'natural' and, therefore, virtually invisible. Processual theory not only dominates how archaeological practice and research is perceived, it also constructs and explains the very identity of archaeologists. A powerful position that follows on from this is that archaeologists are scientific, rigorous, systematic, and, above all, they excavate and record. The 'doing' of archaeology, epitomized by the scientism of excavation,[4] has established disciplinary identity.

Embedding processual assumptions within the discipline has a highly emotive consequence, because the discipline as a whole, and many individual archaeologists, are enmeshed within a reinforcing circle of what it *is* to be an archaeologist. Archaeological identity, the identity of the discipline and of individual archaeologists, becomes linked with how archaeologists theorize and think about research and practice. Processual theory is not just an abstract intellectual framework used to inform research – it has a tangible, emotional reality as part of the identity of many archaeologists.

The identity of archaeology as an objective science is also tied to archaeologists' access to the archaeological record. One of the unproblematized assumptions in archaeology, which derives from its positivist philosophy, is that the archaeological record exists 'naturally'. This paradigm constructs material evidence as part of 'nature' and thus as objective reality. Bhaskar (1986, 1989a) argues that all disciplines assume a naturalism about what they study, that the object of their study is simply there to be studied. This is then linked to an unproblematic acceptance of what a discipline is. In the case of archaeology the unproblematized assumption is that archaeology is a science, which in turn gives authority to the discipline and ensures privileged access to what the discipline calls the 'archaeological record', or more precisely its data.

Processual theory has a threefold value for archaeology. First, as a theoretical tool it provides a methodological and explanatory framework, and underpins the philosophy and ideology of Anglophone archaeology. Even where aspects of the culture history approach remain, scientific methodology and philosophy are theoretically dominant.

Second, and more importantly, processual theory provides an identity, a sense of coherence, a consciousness, an explanation of what it is to be an archaeologist. In effect, the naturalization of processual theory and scientific practices provides a sense of cohesion within the discipline. The discipline socializes its members, and processual theory ensures that this socialization pivots around the development of the 'archaeological scientist'.

Third, processual theory ensures disciplinary authority. Western culture invests considerable intellectual authority in 'objective' science. The rhetoric of social 'relevance', which was to be gained through scientific rigour and empirical work, was important in providing an authoritative assertion of the discipline's identity.

This review is largely concerned with the successful establishment of the theoretical project attempted by the processualists in the 1960s and 1970s. This took place during the 1970s despite the growth of politicized Indigenous and other interests in material culture and heritage issues. Moreover, the success and institutional power base of processual theory has not yet been successfully challenged by later critiques and oppositional theoretical positions. Certainly, most oppositional theories, such as feminist archaeology and postprocessual theory, have yet to offer alternative methodologies to those informed by processual theory. Processualism has been successful in that it dominated theory and practice within the discipline. It has, in effect, become the hegemonic position.

Processual theory and the problematizing of archaeology

Does processual theory offer a useful framework with which to analyse the role archaeological practice and knowledge plays within CRM? The answer to this question is unequivocally no. First, processual theory makes no pretensions to provide a self-reflexive analysis of the consequences of archaeological knowledge and practice. Processual theory provides the intellectual tools required to interpret the archaeological record and other data, but it does not aim to turn analysis back onto itself.

Second, processual theory in assuming a certain form of rationality, 'objectivity' and 'scientific rigour' cannot incorporate a self-reflexive practice even if it wanted to. Privileging empirical knowledge leaves little room for analysing the *experiences* of archaeological and non-archaeological participants in debates over material culture. Nor does it consider the consequences of archaeological knowledge and practice relevant to the construction of archaeological knowledge. Any consideration of consequence must deal with competing knowledge systems, such as Indigenous perceptions of the past, which may contradict archaeological knowledge. Further, it must also consider that this knowledge has some measure of *legitimacy* (at least to someone, if not archaeologists). Within processual theory, the legitimacy of knowledge rests on its rationality, logical plausibility, and on its testability. A consideration of the consequences of archaeological knowledge makes little archaeological sense within processualism given the assumed universal applicability of rational and tested knowledge.

Third, the assumption about the universal applicability of rational knowledge has lead, as argued above, to the naturalization of archaeological practice and philosophy. This naturalization makes certain underpinning perceptions and constructs invisible, and thus difficult to scrutinize.

Postprocessual theory

Postprocessual theory rejects the positivism of processual theory and offers itself up as a 'new' way of theorizing archaeological data. More significantly, however, it claims to offer the theoretical tools that allow the discipline itself to become the focus of analysis. It also aims to incorporate non-archaeological knowledge claims into its interpretations of the past and into the construction of archaeological knowledge (Leone 1981; Leone *et al.* 1987; Shanks 1992; Shanks and Tilley 1989a; Wylie 1992a; Leone *et al.* 1995; Shanks and Hodder 1995; Hodder 1999).

Given these claims, postprocessual theory would appear to offer a useful position from which to analyse archaeological practice, politics and the consequences of archaeological knowledge in CRM. Postprocessual theory thus appears to be a most useful and appropriate departure point for my argument, and as such warrants critical attention.

However, this section concludes that, like processual theory, postprocessual theory is too self-referential to be of use in the real politics of CRM. Further, it does not abandon, and indeed helps to recreate, the intellectual authority obtained for the discipline by processual theory. This means that postprocessual theory's ability to engage with the nature and consequences of archaeological interactions with Indigenous and other forms of knowledge and practice is limited.

What is postprocessual theory?

Postprocessual theories developed in the mid-1980s as a reaction to the scientistic positivism of processual theory, and its failures to contextualize and understand the construction of knowledge (Patterson 1989). It takes as its starting point a rejection of the 'myth of objectivity' (Shanks and Hodder 1995), and self-consciously draws upon debates in the wider social sciences (Shanks and Tilley 1987a). In particular, it incorporates a great deal of postmodern literature, although it is selective in drawing on it.[5] In its broadest application, the label of postprocessualism may be defined as all critical theories that in some sense come 'after' processualism. This approach would include feminist and Marxist theories within the postprocessual stable (Hodder 1986a, 1991a, 1992; Preucel 1995). As with the advent of processualism, the emergence of postprocessual theory was marked by polemical debate, in which the proponents of postprocessual theory aimed to impress, and to stake out as much theoretical ground as possible (Wylie 1992b, 1993). The rhetoric and polemic of both postprocessual theory and post-modernist writings (from which many key features of postprocessualism have been partly derived) have been criticized for using dense language as a 'jobs for the boys strategy' (see Smith and du Cros 1994: 118; also Gilman 1987; Mascia-Lees *et al.* 1990) – a strategy not unknown in the 1960s processual debate. As part of the staking out of theoretical space, feminism and Marxism, which have long histories in archaeology, have tended to be subsumed within postprocessualism (Engelstad 1991; Smith 1995c). In a sense, both feminism and Marxism may be claimed as *post*-processual archaeologies, in that they are critical of positivistic positions. However, they need to be separated from the 'postprocessualism' that has dominated theoretical debate in the last two decades.

The principal forms of postprocessual theory have focused on responding to debates with processualism, and have failed to incorporate or address issues raised by feminist and Marxist archaeology. The bibliographies of most self-proclaimed postprocessual writers are marked by an almost complete absence of reference to feminist and Marxist work. Although postprocessualism has, as Shanks and Tilley (1989a) acknowledge, presented a fluid definition of itself, this apparent fluidity is misleading. What emerges in the theoretical debates is a core body of literature (with an intense presence in bibliographies and citations, and several commercial texts) that takes as its starting point an explicit rejection of processual theory. Thus, in the following discussion 'postprocessualism' refers to this body of theory, and does not incorporate other 'post' processual critical theories.

Postprocessual theory is an attempt to offer a critical understanding of and engagement with material culture and the archaeological past that is integrated with self-reflexive practice. A range of approaches to the interpretation of the past may be identified, for instance the earlier contextual approaches of Hodder (1984, 1986a), and post-structuralist work of Shanks and Tilley (1987a, 1987b, 1989a) and later 'interpretive' approaches (Hodder *et al.* 1995; Thomas 1996; Shanks 1999), the use of phenomenology (Tilley 1994; Bender 2002), and structuration and agency (Dobres and Robb 2000; Dornan 2002), amongst many others. Within this, however, a significant analytical focus is placed on discourse, texts and metaphor. Shanks (1992; with Tilley 1987a, 1989a; with Pearson 2001), Tilley (1989c, 1991, 1993a, 1993b, 1999), Thomas (1993b, 1996), and Hodder (1988, 1989b, 1992, 1999), for example, have emphasized notions of discourse and text, drawing on the work of Lacan, Foucault, Ricoeur and Derrida. All interpretation of the past is informed by self-critical reflexive analysis, and thus, postprocessual theory offers a framework for the critical examination of the discipline itself through an explicit attempt to illuminate the interrelation between theory and practice. Postprocessualism also claims to include Indigenous and other 'marginalized voices' through a 'democratizing' of dialogues (for instance, Leone 1986; Leone and Preucel 1992; Hodder 1999; Bender 1999, 2001; Buchli and Lucas 2001b). These claims have immediate relevance to any attempt to understand the consequences of CRM practice, and it is these aspects that are examined here. While postprocessualism has had a significant presence in theoretical debates, its impact outside this arena is difficult to measure. However, at some level postprocessualism, particularly the work of Hodder, Shanks, Tilley and Leone has begun to influence attempts at archaeological research and CRM that is inclusive of community interests. For instance, Goldstein (2000) calls on the work of Leone and Preucel, and chapters in Derry and Malloy (2003) reflect on the ability of Hodder's work to provide frameworks for critical community based archaeological practice. Postprocessual debates continue, at some level, to influence the work of archaeologists in exploring contested fields of archaeological research (for instance, Meskell 1998; Buchli and Lucas 2001a; Bender and Winer 2001; Biehl *et al.* 2002).

The development of postprocessual theory

Though postprocessual theory arose to criticize 'the notion of an impartial, value free observer and scientist' (Shanks and Tilley 1989a: 2), a number of specific 'politicizing' issues were the impetus for their rejection of processual positivism.

Hodder notes that the expansion of postprocessual theories occurred in association with 'a heritage boom in which there were wider interests in interpretive issues' (1991c: 7). Proponents of postprocessual archaeology often state that it was concern about increasing conflict over the meanings attributed to heritage that sparked a consideration of archaeological 'politics' (Leone 1981; Leone *et al.* 1987; Rowlett 1987; Leone and Potter 1992; Leone and Preucel 1992; Champion 1991; Wylie 1993). Indeed postprocessualists were concerned that the heritage industry in the UK was offering 'a rose-tinted vision of the past' (Champion 1991: 141), or observed that archaeology was 'serving political aims' via heritage management (Leone *et al.* 1987: 284; see also Shanks and Tilley 1987b, 1989a). In America, archaeologists involved in negotiating conflicts over the interpretation of colonial Williamsburg and eighteenth- and nineteenth-century Annapolis cited the need to challenge normative perceptions. They also argued that the negotiation of interpretations with marginalized 'voices' is a useful springboard to help archaeologists identify ideology and subjectivity in the discipline (Leone 1981, 1984, 1986; Leone *et al.* 1987; Leone *et al.* 1995). The existence of a plurality of meaning led to the claim that a key role for critical archaeology was to see 'the interrelationship between archaeology and politics [in order to] ... allow archaeologists to achieve less contingent knowledge' (Leone *et al.* 1987: 284).

In the UK, heritage was viewed less as offering a problem of negotiation and conflict, than as appropriating archaeological knowledge to serve Thatcherite reinterpretations of the 'nation' and its past (Shanks and Tilley 1989a: 5). Archaeological knowledge was seen as being 'commodified' by its involvement in the heritage industry (Shanks and Tilley 1987b; Champion 1991; Hodder 1991c). However, the role of archaeology in challenging normative assumptions through heritage interpretation was a point grasped not only in the US, but also in the UK. For example, Shennan suggests that material culture has 'an active and creative role in social change', and in a statement reminiscent of the processual discourse on 'relevance', asserts that this 'has an interesting positive effect on archaeology: it makes it more important' (1986: 333).

Politicization of archaeology, and increasing emphasis on its role in challenging normative perceptions about the past and present has been stressed as an important aim by many postprocessualists (e.g. Miller and Tilley 1984b; Olsen 1986; Shanks and Tilley 1987a, 1987b; Leone *et al.* 1987; Hodder 1992). Archaeology's role in challenging perceptions about the past and present is, of course, one that is recognized by many traditional processualists (e.g. Binford 1988; Connah 1988). The significant difference between processualist and postprocessualist approaches, however, is the latter's determination to renegotiate the archaeological position to create a 'democratic pluralism' (Shanks and Tilley 1989a: 10; see also Leone *et al.* 1987; Leone *et al.* 1995; Hodder 1999). For some proponents of postprocessualism, this 'democratic pluralism' was also seen as an attempt to deal with the criticisms levelled at archaeology by Indigenous peoples[6] and feminist archaeologists (Hodder 1992: 163; see also Miller 1980; Leone 1981; Shanks and Tilley 1987a). Wylie (1993) argues, however, that postprocessual theory fails to rise to the challenges it faces from Indigenous peoples and feminists. She argues that it has obscured the critiques and effectively created new mechanisms of marginalization of Indigenous and feminist voices in the construction and interpretations of archaeological knowledge (see also Engelstad 1991).

Despite its rhetorical commitment to 'democratic pluralism', postprocessualist discourse possesses characteristics which work against both democratic participation in the discourse, and plural knowledge. The use of dense rhetoric and jargon makes much of postprocessual material difficult for the uninitiated. Postprocessualists on the one hand claim that they do not want to confine themselves to writing for other archaeologists (Shanks and Tilley 1989a: 11). On the other hand, they employ dense polemic as a strategic devise to gain critical attention within academic circles – a ploy that is openly acknowledged (see Shanks and Tilley 1989b: 50; Olsen 1989). This contradiction, and the language employed in debate, works to obscure and abstract issues, and fails to 'democratize' debate or encourage Habermas' 'ideal speech situation' as advocated by US postprocessualists in particular (Leone and Potter 1992: 140; also Leone *et al.* 1987; Earl and Preucel 1987; Leone *et al.* 1995; see also Bapty 1989; Baker 1990 for the UK). Further problems over the conceptualization of CRM, the role of archaeology in this area, and its dealing with power and knowledge have also thrown up problems and contradictions in postprocessual theory.

Postprocessual theory as a form of knowledge

Leone (1981: 5) has argued that archaeologists impose meaning on data from the past, and that the present feeds this meaning back onto itself through an understanding of the past. Thus, postprocessualists challenged one of the basic, although often unacknowledged, underlying assumptions of archaeological discourse – that data (material culture) has inherent meaning and value. It was recognized that 'knowledge does not reside in the surfaces of things' (Tilley 1990b: 78).

Subsequently the central aims of interpreting the past was the recognition of plural 'readings' of the past (Leone *et al.* 1987; Shanks and Tilley 1989a; Shanks 1995), the inclusion of the archaeologists' 'experiences' and emotional responses to archaeological data (Tilley 1991, 1994, 1999; Shanks 1992, 1995; Hodder 1992: 155f; Thomas and Tilley 1993), and an emphasis on the development of archaeological 'narratives' rather than more authoritative 'models' or 'hypotheses' (Shanks and Tilley 1987b: 19; Tilley 1989a, 1991; Thomas 1990a; Shanks 1999).

Alongside this aim was the goal of rendering archaeological interpretations or pronouncements about the past less authoritative, and thus privileging 'marginalized voices' (Leone *et al.* 1995; Hodder 1998, 1999; Bender 1999). To facilitate this, postprocessualists have called for a 'politicization' of the discipline, and have argued the need for archaeologists to establish and acknowledge their political agendas (Miller and Tilley 1984a; Rowlands 1986; Leone *et al.* 1987; Shanks and Tilley 1987b, 1989a; Tilley 1989b, 1991; Bapty and Yates 1990).

The establishment of explicit political agendas, and negotiated and democratized debate over the meaning and interpretation of the past will, they argue, facilitate pluralist approaches to archaeological work and the management of heritage.

These arguments have led to criticism that postprocessualism is flawed by a relativism that devalues the work of archaeologists (Renfrew 1989; Binford 1990; Watson 1990, 1991; Berglund 2000; amongst others). Others have argued that postprocessualists have not yet provided a solution to the problem of how to acknowledge pluralism on the one hand, and prevent the associated slide into relativism on the other (Trigger 1989, 1991a, 1991b; Bintliff 1991; Kohl 1993; Wylie 2000a). Still others (e.g. Lahn 1996; Zimmerman 1998a) have noted that the advocacy of a politicized archaeology is necessary for theoretical development and engagement with Indigenous criticisms. However, as they point out, the details of what the political agenda should be, or how it is to be implemented, have never been made explicit (see also Bradley 1987).

The postprocessual response to the charge of relativism has been varied. Hodder in attempting to develop a 'method' for interpreting the past turned to hermeneutics (1991b: 10–12, 1999). Hermeneutics is concerned with how we understand and identify the conditions that make understanding of 'otherness' possible (Johnsen and Olsen 1992: 420). Moreover, the subject of analysis becomes a text, as its existence can only be understood through signs that must be deciphered or 'interpreted' (Moore 1990: 88). Specifically, it is Gadamer's use of hermeneutics that Hodder and others advocate:

> Time is no longer a gulf to be bridged, because it separates, but it is actually the supportive ground of process in which the present is rooted. Hence temporal distance is not something that must be overcome ... In fact the important thing is to recognize the distance in time as a positive and productive possibility of understanding. It is not a yawning abyss, but is filled with the continuity of custom and tradition, in the light of which all that is handed down presents itself to us.
> (Gadamer 1975, cited by Johnsen and Olsen 1992: 429)

History is not just something we interpret, but is also active in shaping this understanding (Johnsen and Olsen 1992: 430). This is similar to Giddens' idea of the 'double hermeneutic' employed in Hodder's work (1999), in that our interpretive processes are both contingent upon our experiences in the social world and on our understanding of these interpretive processes (Outhwaite 1991: 76; also Trigg 1985). Hodder argues that the use of hermeneutics provides a form of methodological rigour, if not a 'guarded objectivity of the past' (1991b: 10), and provides a response to the charge of relativism. The idea of hermeneutics as a form of 'method' is criticized by Johnsen and Olsen (1992: 432), who argue that hermeneutics is an attempt to understand the social sciences. However, Shanks and Hodder (1995) and Tilley (1993a) have used hermeneutics to attempt to recreate postprocessual theory as 'interpretive archaeology' to advance the theoretical debate past the relativism charge. 'Objectivity', while still acknowledged as constructed, is redefined by Shanks and Hodder as 'strong statements' (1995: 18), and something that 'holds together when interrogated' (1995: 19). This repositioning then attempts to answer both criticisms, the lack of postprocessual method and relativism, by reasserting the 'importance' and 'strength' (or authority) of archaeological interpretation.

This repositioning of the debate is a response to more than the issue of relativism, but derives from a failure of postprocessualism to deal with issues of power and authority. Indeed, in dealing with the plurality of meanings given to material culture, postprocessualism has been confronted by a significant theoretical impasse. This impasse is caused by the threat to archaeological authority that must follow if the discipline were to abandon both the practical and theoretical tools that allow it to make binding statements about the past. 'Interpretive archaeology', and its particular use of hermeneutics, only recreates this theoretical and political impasse.

To understand this problem further it is useful to examine the postprocessual handling of issues of discourse, ideology and power. The other postprocessual response to accusations of relativism has been one that advocates political action, and the identification of ideology in archaeological knowledge construction for defining politically acceptable meaning:

> There is no way of choosing between alternative pasts except on essentially political grounds, in terms of a definitive value system, a morality.
> (Shanks and Tilley 1987a: 195)

As such, postprocessual theory is also a critical theory of archaeology. It offers a dialectical approach that ensures that the theoretical structures become embedded in the practice of archaeology and the collection of archaeological data. It claims to link practice with theory to become a 'theory *of* and *in* practice' (Shanks and Tilley 1989a: 2, emphasis in original). Critical self-reflection becomes part of the agenda so that postprocessual theory can engage in social critique and negotiation over meanings of the past (Leone *et al.* 1987; Earl and Preucel 1987; Yates 1988; Shanks and Tilley 1989a). In short, 'archaeology is nothing if it is not critique' (Shanks and Tilley 1987a: 213).

Discourse and ideology

The initial call for a self-reflexive archaeology, which positioned the discipline as the object of critical analysis, focused on identifying and examining discourse and ideology (e.g. Miller and Tilley 1984b; Rowlands 1986; Leone *et al.* 1987; Shanks and Tilley 1987b; Nordbladh 1990). Discourse, as a social production of particular meanings, is embedded in language (Laclau 1982), and is constructed by the speaker's association with particular institutions and their socio-political position (Macdonell 1986; Fairclough 1993). Shanks and Tilley (1987a: 64f) argue that these institutions may be identified and 'mapped out', with the underpinning ideology of the speaker or writer being identified through analysis of their discourse. Postprocessualists argue that discourse is inseparable from hegemonic structures and critique the discourses of processual archaeologists (Leone *et al.* 1987; Shanks and Tilley 1987a, 1987b; Thomas 1990b; Last 1995). Shanks and Tilley note that the identity of the person who may make a particular pronouncement is less important than the institution with which the speaker is associated (Shanks and Tilley 1989b: 51). The political power associated with the institutional position of a speaker is what ensures the dominance of a particular discourse (archaeological interpretation, pronouncement, etc.), rather than any internal logic or persuasiveness of the discourse. This position contradicts the position of processual archaeologists who claim that the persuasiveness of an argument is the main factor that ensures the credence of archaeological inter-pretations (Watson 1991; see also Binford 1988; Redman 1991). Shanks and Tilley's concern with the institutional position of a speaker is an attempt to deal with the power/knowledge nexus, but as argued below, they tend to emphasize the discourse at the expense of practice.

The postprocessual approach that requires that the discursive field within which archaeology operates be identified is an important one. 'Discursive field' refers to the range of meanings or different positions taken in a social, cultural and cognitive context (Fairclough 1993). This is then analysed with reference to how those meanings are structured in relation to each other and to broader societal factors. Questions may then be asked concerning how the professional discourse (or meanings) fit into the practice of archaeology and archaeological interpretations (Leone 1984; Miller and Tilley 1984a; Davis 1992).

As noted, the relationship between language and politics is an important concern in postprocessual theory, and Shanks and Tilley in particular expand on it in their work. They, and others, have used discourse analysis to illustrate how particular archaeologists, archaeological interpretations, theories, and archaeological departments are given credence in archaeology (e.g. Tilley 1989c, 1993b; Shanks 1992; also Hodder 1989c; Rowlands 1989; Thomas 1993b). Ironically, postprocessual archaeologists, as they acknowledge, have used the institutions in archaeology that convey power and prestige to put forward postprocessual theory (Shanks and Tilley 1989a; Hodder 1991b, 1999). Although postprocessualists have acknowledged this authority they fail to take the analysis further and examine how archaeological expertise is utilized outside the academy, and the wider consequence this has. Although Hodder's (1998, 1999) recent work at Çatalhöyük attempts to include the local community, the absence of any analysis of relations of power and privilege between archaeologists and local communities is marked. Important work by Leone and colleagues in America has also attempted to challenge normative assumptions about the past by identifying archaeological ideology and placing it within a social context (Leone 1986, 1999; Leone *et al.* 1987; Leone *et al.* 1995). However, as Carman observes (2002), this work has also yet to problematize the political and power relations between archaeological and non-archaeological discourse on the past and material culture.

Shanks and Tilley come close to dealing with issues of power in their consideration of the relativist critique. Although they argue that 'a plurality of discursive forms needs to be recognized' (Shanks and Tilley 1989a: 8), they also argue that no one discourse is essentially, or entitled to be, dominant. They are not saying that everything is relative or that 'anything goes'. Rather they are saying that meaning is constructed through discourse and that truth is not a category in relation to the real world, but a statement in relation to a particular discourse. For example, Renfrew's (1989) criticism of Shanks and Tilley – that ley liners' interpretations of the past are given as much validity as archaeological interpretations misses the point. The discourse of ley liners is not given validity – not because what they say is not true, but because they operate outside the dominant discourse. Despite the recognition of this, postprocessual writings have divorced the concept of discourse from notions of ideological dominance. They have done so as their analyses tend to stress narrative and interpretation as the key features of a critical approach to archaeology. Indeed these elements are stressed to such an extent that texts become more important than practice to them, and intellectual history's proper object of study remains primarily textual.

This separation, and/or a tendency to abstract the relation between discourse and ideology, is one that has also been noted by critiques of the post-modern literature (Purvis and Hunt 1993). The abstraction of ideology is explicitly done as postprocessual writings only address academic archaeological audiences, and never actually mention who the other interested parties in the meanings of material culture actually are. Studies seldom actually identify the social, cultural and political contexts that influence the use and interpretation of material culture, either by postprocessualists themselves, or other groups. The insights they make about the authority of archaeological knowledge have relevance only within the power struggles in the academy. Although more recent critical archaeology attempts to redress this and to engage more directly with the political contexts of archaeology (for instance, Meskell 1998; Bender and Winer 2001) an explicit and developed debate about the extra-disciplinary consequences of archaeological practice and theory is still to be had.

Postprocessual theory and CRM

In terms of practice CRM is seen as being not only a major employment area for archaeologists, it also incorporates archaeological method and codes of practice (Renfrew 1983; Murray 1993a). The archaeological literature on CRM generally defines it as a technical process, which emphasizes archaeological survey, site recording, assessment and, where necessary, excavation or salvage of sites and places (e.g. Hunter and Ralston 1993; Pearson and Sullivan 1995; King 1998). Thus, it is often defined as archaeological practice guided by legislative and government policy guidelines. As an area of practice that must also, by definition, intersect a range of competing non-archaeological discourses and ideologies, it appears to offer a fertile ground for postprocessual analysis.

Hodder (1991c) has noted that it was the increasingly conservative gaze into the past being manifested by the British 'heritage industry' that accelerated the importation of post-modernism into archaeology. Moreover, it was the perception that 'the past' and archaeological knowledge was being 'commodified', and that 'heritage [was] innately conservative' (Baker 1988: 143) that rang alarm bells for many postprocessualists. Archaeological knowledge was perceived to have been relegated to the periphery, or worse, repackaged for its marketability and value for tourism (e.g. Shanks and Tilley 1987b, 1989a; Merriman 1988; Wickham-Jones 1988; Bender 1992; Hodder 1993). Much of this concern was based on the writings of Wright (1985) and Hewison (1987) who linked cultural tourism, and an upsurge in public interest with heritage, to Thatcherite and New Right attempts to sell conservative values with 'it was better back then' rhetoric (see also Corner and Harvey 1991).

In this view of heritage and CRM, archaeological knowledge and privilege is seen as under threat. This situation obviously throws up some concerns for the advocacy of plural pasts. Shanks and Tilley, in advocating political action in defining 'appropriate' discourses, clearly consider politicized action in the CRM context to include the re-privileging of archaeological knowledge.

CRM is used here to refer to all the process of heritage management, and this includes the British definition of the 'heritage industry'. This industry, although often not clearly defined, clearly refers to the commercial marketing of heritage for tourist/public consumption. However, even in England, the use of sites for cultural tourism and other commercial purposes must follow on from government policies, legislation and CRM practice (although admittedly theme parks and private museums fall outside this) (Branigan 1990). Witness the debates over Stonehenge, a site that is the flagship of the 'heritage industry'. It is, however, managed following CRM procedure and policy, and *uncontrolled* touristic and commercial use of this site does not occur.[7] The evident distress that surfaces in the UK postprocessual debates about heritage, and the general UK archaeological literature about heritage conflicts (e.g. Cleere 1988; P. Fowler 1987, 1992; Skeates 2000) clearly warn that 'it is vitally important to ensure that [the heritage industry] remains securely rooted in archaeological information' (Wickham-Jones 1988: 193).[8]

This concern is echoed, although less overtly, in the US postprocessual literature on heritage and CRM. In this literature, the solving of conflicts is advocated by democratic discussion between participants and/or changes to interpretive material. 'Language' is emphasized as a solution, and there is no clear sense of practice or engagement with how power/knowledge may structure conflict over heritage, nor is there any consideration of how governmental agencies may influence conflicts.

The postprocessual response to conflict over heritage is one that emphasizes 'discussion' with no clear sense of power relations or the structuring of those relations between conflicting interests. This occurs even when archaeology is itself threatened by tourism and other economic interests. For example, Shanks and Hodder, in offering Rhys Jones a solution to conflicts between accounts of human origins presented by academic scientists and Australian Aboriginal people, suggest:

> Talk to people, understand them, persuade if necessary; instead of patronising them by playing the expert. Maintain an open and reasoned dialogue.
>
> (Shanks and Hodder 1995: 20)

This is laudable, as far as it goes, but archaeologists *are* experts and are seen as such by wider society. Postprocessualists themselves advocate ensuring the primacy of archaeological knowledge in the use of heritage, and point to the authority of archaeological science (e.g. Tilley 1990c). Why then do postprocessualists advocate 'dialogue' in a political vacuum?

The answer to this question lies in the authority and prestige given to archaeology through its involvement in CRM. Some archaeologists, postprocessualists among them, argue that the interpretation of heritage provides an important role, if not a justification for, archaeology (Baker 1988; Tilley 1989d; Leone and Preucel 1992; Leone *et al.* 1995). Shennan (1986: 333) notes that due to the role of material culture in social and cultural contexts the 'study of material culture, and with it the archaeologists, becomes central rather than peripheral'. This authority, in part, relies on what Buchli (1995: 191) argues is the physicality of material culture. Physicality is both an important attribute in the role of material culture in symbolizing social and cultural meaning, and its ability to move freely from one context to another. Archaeologists, as experts on material culture, play more than the innocent role Shanks and Tilley define for them in CRM.

A failure to engage with how it is that archaeology and CRM interact, or the use of archaeological knowledge in the management of heritage, has produced some curious and theoretically inconsistent responses in the postprocessual literature about heritage conflict:

> this is crucial, responsibility is owed to the past. To ignore what the past is and use it to justify any desired invention is an injustice against the past and an offence against reason.
>
> (Shanks 1992: 117)

We would be excused for assuming this statement derives from a processualist with its appeal to 'reason' and an absolute identifiable past, but this is Shanks' response to the use of 'the past' to reconstruct cultural identity. Shanks' appeal parallels many of the concerns of the processual archaeologists in the 1960s and 1970s, employing concepts they used in establishing the role of archaeology in CRM (see Chapter 5).

Further, in arguing that archaeology through salvage excavation 'rather than conform[ing] to the heritage industry, *ought to be challenging it*' (Tilley 1989d: 279, emphasis in original), we find postprocessualists restating processual debates. Tilley's (1989b) calls for scientific rigour and for regional archaeological studies are identical to those of the 1970s processual archaeologists in the US and Australia. Processualists argued the need for these 'innovations' to make archaeology more 'relevant' to society.

Postprocessualists have more lately argued that archaeology should readopt some of the methodological rigour of processual archaeology that they had previously rejected (e.g. Preucel 1991; Hodder 1999). This argument, along with the adoption of hermeneutics as a methodological approach, is an attempt to ensure the primacy of the discipline in discourses about material culture, the nature and meaning of the past, and the management of heritage.

In accepting the legitimacy of Indigenous and other marginalized pasts, postprocessualists relinquish established claims to academic authority based on the absolute rationality of archaeological science. They have created an impasse. To support the idea of plural meanings and of 'democratic negotiation' of conflicts over heritage, postprocessualists must employ the rhetoric of rationality or risk losing intellectual authority – a risk they do not seem to want to take. To help maintain archaeological authority and its rationality, methodological rigour was 'rediscovered' by postprocessualists as an important issue.

To ensure their intellectual authority, archaeologists also need to position themselves as important in heritage *interpretation* and, moreover, as the key *negotiators* in heritage conflicts. This is also important so that archaeological access to the archaeological database is not jeopardized in heritage conflicts. The label 'Interpretive Archaeology' has helped to reassert archaeological authority. Its political advantage is that it helps to identify the 'relevance' of archaeology in CRM in much the same way as the 'New Archaeology' did when it established archaeology's scientific credentials for its technical application in CRM (see Chapter 5).

Postprocessual theory and the problematizing of archaeology

Chippindale (1993: 35) characterizes postprocessual archaeology as an intellectual game that ignores the social consequences of archaeology. Its textual orientation, its emphasis on 'language', and overall, its failure to deal with concrete political situations and analyses, certainly obscures and abstracts concrete issues of politics and social consequences of archaeological knowledge. Its discussion of politics does not transcend the discipline's own professional idiom (Durrans 1989: 67). This ensures a self-referential positioning of politicized discussion, as well as risking simply restating many of the ideologies of processual theory, as typified by Shanks (1992).

The criticism levelled at post-modernism, that it can become simply an exercise in illustrating the social construction of knowledge without engaging in concrete issues as an exercise to *avoid* politics (Baber 1992: 108; also Jessop 1990; Mascia-Lees *et al.* 1990; Woodiwiss 1990, 1993; Best and Kellner 1991), can certainly be applied to postprocessualism. The timing of postprocessual theory is important in understanding its aims and its failures (Wylie 1993; Berglund 2000). It arose, in part, to address the criticisms of Indigenous peoples and feminists and to address the marginalization of those groups in society whose interpretation of the past occurs outside the dominant archaeological discourse. However, rather than addressing these criticisms and issues, postprocessual theory has reinforced the authority of archaeological knowledge and discourse. Rather than including 'other voices', its ostensibly democratic, pluralist discourse has only worked to reinforce their exclusion from the power constructed by archaeological knowledge. Further, the challenges to archaeological authority posed by a postprocessual 'dialogue' with non-archaeological interests has resulted in the development of debate that is strongly reminiscent of 1970s processual debates over access to data.

Postprocessual theory has not escaped from a self-referential bind that reduces CRM and conflicts over heritage to conflicts over access to data. In short, postprocessual theory does not advance us much further with our understanding of the consequences of archaeology than its predecessor.

Conclusions: Archaeological Theory and CRM

Several issues arise from the state of archaeological theory and its inability to deal with CRM. If, as argued in Chapter 1, CRM has more than a simple technical relation to archaeology, it becomes useful to problematize that relationship. In doing so a mapping of the extent to which CRM constrains and influences archaeological practice and theory and vice versa may be possible, and should result in identifying the influences external to the academy on knowledge construction.

To examine and explain the interrelationships between government, Indigenous and archaeological interests established by CRM, a theoretical understanding of the discipline is required that offers the space to examine archaeological knowledge and practice outside the discipline. In Chapter 1, CRM concerned with Indigenous sites and places was defined as a process of interactions between archaeological knowledge and discourse, Indigenous cultural politics, and government and bureaucracies. Neither processual nor postprocessual approaches have the acuity to successfully identify the consequences of knowledge and discourse outside the academy. In the case of processual theory, it makes no claim to do so, although in the case of postprocessual theory explicit claims are made about its ability to examine power/knowledge relations, archaeological politics and heritage issues. However, postprocessual theory obscures the power/knowledge nexus, and reduces discourse to *only* language issues, while re-privileging archaeological knowledge in the process. It cannot deal adequately with external concerns due to the risk of jeopardizing archaeological authority and the privileged role of archaeological knowledge in the arbitration of heritage issues.

Consequently, archaeological theory, whether it is processual or postprocessual, tends to explain the construction of archaeological knowledge and discourse with little or no reference to influences external to the academy. In short, they refer only to themselves, yet remain incapable of examining their own power/knowledge constructions. Processual theory's use of notions of rationality and objectivity constantly recreate the legitimacy of archaeological knowledge and ensure access to material culture using the discipline's claims to scientific authority. To consider the consequences of archaeology within such a context must de-emphasize the socio-politics of archaeology. Within postprocessual theory, archaeology – its texts, discourse, epistemology, ideology – is re-privileged as the most important focus of analysis, and little sense of 'politics' or consequences outside academic confines is entertained. Postprocessual theory offers few clues to the interplay of archaeology and wider social and cultural issues, although Buchli's (1995) account of material culture moves us a little closer in understanding how archaeological knowledge may move between contexts.

Despite the above reservations postprocessual theory at least offers a *departure* point for examining CRM, in that discourse is a useful focus for analysing and identifying some of the main concepts underlying the discipline. However, the abstraction of discourse and ideology from analyses of politics amounts to a serious flaw. McGuire's point that archaeological theory should be judged on how well it allows archaeologists to engage with a 'real world', which, amongst other things, considers 'how our interpretations of the past serve the interests of the present' (2002: 14), is important in dealing with CRM. The following chapter suggests areas where archaeological theory can be augmented by drawing more explicitly on literature that deals with issues of power, politics and their inter-relation with expertise and intellectuals.

Postprocessual theory can be augmented in three areas. First, epistemological and ontological issues need to be addressed. The archaeological understanding of discourse needs to be re-thought, and links with materiality and the 'real world' of practice and structures need to be made. A satisfactory epistemological solution to the 'dialogue of the deaf' between 'relativists' and positivists in the discipline is also needed – a solution to this will be found in the 'critical realism' literature.

Second, a critical understanding of the role of intellectuals and the consequences of expertise is required. Bauman's work on intellectuals and the literature on Foucault's 'governmentality' provide, as shown in Chapter 4, some useful links between theory and practice. Though Foucault's position is anti-realist, and his emphasis on epistemology needs to be reconciled with the critical realism literature, his insights into the role of intellectuals, and the 'governmental' effects of expertise, markedly improve on Tilley's (1990c) attempts to theorize an 'archaeology of archaeology'. An understanding of the role of intellectuals and expertise should inform the positions archaeologists and Indigenous interests occupy in American and Australian CRM negotiations and the interaction of these interests in the context of governmental mediation.

Third, the critical literature on 'the state', law, policy and politics is considered, particularly in the context of the position of heritage bureaucracies within CRM. How interests are defined and given legitimacy through policy, and regulated through state institutions and bureaucracy is useful in defining the consequences of archaeology and its interaction with Indigenous concerns.

Though falling well short of a fully developed theory, my use of this literature can provide a framework for analysing how state institutions regulate and govern competing interests, and utilize expert knowledge and intellectuals, thus demonstrating a clearer understanding of how and why archaeology is mobilized via bureaucratic structures as CRM. The role of intellectuals and expertise in wider cultural and social debates should help to clarify the use and role of archaeological knowledge in 'heritage issues'. Theories of critical realism should provide links to the 'real world'; yet consider the concrete consequences of archaeological discourse and ideology.

4

ARCHAEOLOGY AND THE CONTEXT OF GOVERNANCE
Expertise and the state

The debate between processual and postprocessual archaeologies has, as in other disciplines, highlighted a polarization 'between objectivism and relativism' (Bernstein quoted in Purvis and Hunt 1993: 476; see also Wylie 2000a). This chapter provides a way between the two, by weaving together some postprocessual insights into subjectivity and discourse with a clearer understanding of the relationships of such issues to 'politics'. The previous chapters brought the argument to a point where a conception of politics is needed that considers the concrete effects of discursive practice, and consequences of the power/knowledge dyad. Although this dyad informs much of the literature on which postprocessual theorists have drawn, it remains significantly under-theorized in postprocessual writing.

In the previous chapter three areas of debate were identified as needing further clarification and development: the need for a position on epistemological and ontological issues that deals with political consequences of archaeological knowledge; a clearer theorization of expertise and the social role of intellectuals; combined with a more comprehensive understanding of the state, law and policy. This chapter, will draw on the wider social science literature, and consider each area in turn to develop a theoretical framework that both engages with and informs an analysis of the social consequences of archaeology.

The first excursion is into critical realism, which aims to do away with the false dichotomy between relativism and positivism posed by the current state of archaeological theory. Critical realism also offers a strong critical social project with which to ground the consequences of archaeological discourse and knowledge within CRM. Chapter 3 identified a problem with the use of theories of discourse in the postprocessual literature, wherein the concrete consequences of discourse within archaeological practice had become obscured. This chapter discusses the Foucauldian approach to discourse, and other traditions of discourse analysis that ground themselves in critical realism (which can loosely be associated with the school of Critical Discourse Analysis) (Wetherell 2001a; Fairclough *et al.* 2003). Though both these traditions treat discourse as a form of social action there is an epistemological distinction between them, in that Foucault is an anti-realist. The argument developed here suggests that, despite the utility of Foucault's work, a stronger sense of the concrete consequences of archaeological discourse can be developed from a critical realist perspective.

A consideration of theories of discourse and the political consequences of archaeological discourses also demands a consideration of the role of the producers of expert texts. If discourse has concrete consequences, what then is the role of the intellectual producers of discourse? In other words, if archaeological discourse has a consequence within CRM, what role do archaeologists play, and what consequences are wrought both by and for archaeologists by the use of archaeological discourse within CRM? A consideration of these questions requires a theorizing of intellectuals and expertise and their role in state agencies. The literature on 'governmentality', which takes Foucault's later work as a starting point, is reviewed. This literature, unlike Tilley's (1990c) or other postprocessual uses of Foucault, goes beyond interpreting texts and considers the role and consequences of expertise outside the academy. However, it is concluded that the governmentality literature over-privileges intellectuals and the power of knowledge, and in doing so makes little room for the contestation of knowledge from outside the academy.

Subsequently, state theory is considered as a remedy for this over-privileging of knowledge. State theory offers alternative insights into the way states operate, and one of the things that is stressed is the need to understand law and public policy to adequately explain the role and consequences of intellectual expertise. By augmenting the governmentality literature with a theory of the state grounded in critical realism, the consequences of archaeological discourse, knowledge and practice may be understood in a wider context than that offered by current archaeological theory.

Ontology and epistemology

The polarization of theoretical debate within archaeology is expressed in its epistemological (questions about knowledge) and ontological (questions about what things exist) problematics. The epistemological position of processual theory is logical positivism, with its ontological foundations in naturalism. Processual theory assumes a naturalistic approach to what it studies – the archaeological record exists both as a 'natural' and unproblematized entity. In contrast, post-processual theory's epistemology is post-positivist and generally eclectic. Its ontology is relativist in so far as nothing is seen to exist in the world as such, but rather, 'things' are created within discourse (Wylie 2000a). The postprocessualists frame their questions in ways that turn upside down the 'sense' that logical positivism makes of the world. For example, they ask questions, such as, 'does the archaeological record exist in reality?', and answer no because the archaeological record can only be understood through discourse, and is itself created by discourse. Conversely, postprocessualists have also proclaimed that the discipline has a 'responsibility' to the archaeological record (e.g. Shanks 1992: 117; Tilley 1989d). These postprocessual posturings are contradictory, and add to the ontological confusion underlying postprocessual theory and its role within the discipline.

Similarly, polarized theoretical debates have also occurred in the wider social sciences, where post-modern relativism is placed in opposition to issues of objectivity. Indeed much of the debate within archaeology has already been played out in sociology and other social sciences during the last two decades. Sayer (1992: 2) notes that social sciences, unable to discover the 'law-like regularities' required by positivistic epistemologies, have focused debate between ontological idealism and empiricism. Post-modern critiques of the social sciences have themselves also been criticized for extreme relativism (Frow 1991; Best and Kellner 1991), adopting an overtly 'textualist stance', playing 'language games' (Norris 1992, 1995; Fairclough 1993), and abstracting and evading concrete political issues (Rouse 1987; Woodiwiss 1990: 30, 1993; Smart 1992).

Solutions to the polarization 'between objectivism and relativism' have been extensively debated in the social sciences literature. The debates considered here are, first, 'critical realism'; and second, the debates surrounding definitions of 'discourse'.

Critical realism

To deal with the impasse created between the different archaeological theoretical camps a clearing of the theoretical and epistemological ground is required. Critical realism fills the space left by this impasse by offering an epistemological position that grounds postprocessual relativism in the 'real world' of consequence.

Critiques of post-modern relativism have been concerned with the reduction of 'truth-claims' to rhetoric (Norris 1995: 111), or simply to issues of discourse (Purvis and Hunt 1993: 476; Van Dijk 1998). This position has been widely criticized as confusing ontological and epistemological issues, if not reducing ontology to epistemology (Norris 1995: 111–12; Woodiwiss 1990: 25; Outhwaite 1991: 32). Both Bhaskar (1986) and Norris (1995: 111) argue that relativists conflate 'intransitive' (or extra-discursive) objects that occur independently of human conceptualization, and the 'transitive' realm of knowledge that is open to socio-political assessment (see also Wetherell 2001a). This relativizes truth-claims and power/knowledge relations, and undermines the analysis of the consequences of truth-claims and research programmes (Norris 1992, 1995). It also undermines any acknowledgement of the effects that discourse and knowledge truth-claims may have, and how they impact on practice and wider social and political debates (e.g. Bhaskar 1986; Purvis and Hunt 1993; Fairclough 1993). Reducing ontological questions to issues of epistemology can also undermine concrete political agendas, actions and consequences in the social sciences (Woodiwiss 1990; Norris 1992). For instance, by conceiving debates over the meaning and control of the archaeological/heritage objects as being constructed only within discourses, the concrete effect that the ability to interpret, control or possess objects from the past may have on those with a stake in the fate of those objects is denied.

Some social scientists believe the work of Bhaskar (1978, 1986, 1989b) can help remedy this problem, seeing his approach as a non-reductionist way to avoid idealism and relativism (e.g. Keat and Urry 1982; Jessop 1990; Outhwaite 1991; Sayer 1992; Fairclough *et al.* 2003; and Gibbon 1989 for archaeology). Bhaskar argues for a 'critical realism' that readily allows for the importance of language and discourse, but stresses the concrete social relations and generative and causal structures that underlie discourse.

Realism, to Outhwaite (1991: 19), is a 'common-sense' ontology in that 'it takes seriously the existence of things, structures and mechanisms revealed by the sciences at different levels of reality'. Realists, while acknowledging that knowledge claims can never be verified or falsified, consider that knowledge of the extra-discursive is possible (Woodiwiss 1990: 6). For Bhaskar:

> Things exist and act independently of our descriptions, but we can only know them under particular descriptions. Descriptions belong to the world of society and of men [*sic*]; objects belong to the world of nature ... Science, then, is the systematic attempt to express in thought the structures and ways of acting of things that exist and act independently of thought.
>
> (Bhaskar 1978: 250)

Critical realism, according to Sayer (1992: 4–5), is a philosophy and not a substantive social theory. For Bhaskar it is a philosophy that acts as an 'under-labourer and occasional midwife' to the sciences and social sciences (1989b: 24). It acknowledges that the world exists independently of our knowledge of it, and that knowledge is fallible and theory-laden, and its production is a social practice. Social phenomena, such as institutions and texts, are seen as concept dependent, and knowledge should be accompanied by skepticism and critique (Bhaskar 1989b: 23–4; Woodiwiss 1990: 25; Sayer 1992: 5–6).

Critical realism, moreover, holds that 'we will only be able to understand – and so change – the social world if we identify the structures at work that generate those events or discourses' (Bhaskar 1989b: 2). The postprocessual turn in archaeology, in seeing language and discourse as the most relevant forms of power in the 'post-modern' world, has chosen to stress subjectivity, yet says little about actual social relations, and the structures and institutions that typify and affect them. As a result, postprocessualists have attracted criticism for failing to deal with concrete political consequences and agendas (Engelstad 1991; Smith 1994; Berglund 2000).

The materiality of 'things' identified by Bhaskar also extends to social structures and relations. Bhaskar (1989a: 4) argues that society exists and is transformed through relational interactions. Social structures depend upon and presuppose social relations, but these social relations may be opaque to social agents who participate in them. Thus, for Bhaskar, society is conceived as an ensemble of social practices, in which social agents, while not creating social practices, presuppose them and thus both reproduce and transform them. The social sciences, in seeking to identify and describe social practices, must be dependent on the understandings and perceptions that agents have about these practices. However, social practices are not reducible to this understanding or consciousness. Contrary to the hermeneutic position adopted by some postprocessualists, social practices are not simply reducible to their conceptual aspect – they 'always have a material dimension' (Bhaskar 1989a: 4). In addition, our understanding about social practices – the knowledge programmes we enter into to describe, classify and analyse these practices – has an effect in reproducing and transforming social relations and practices. In short, the discourses we develop about 'things', 'events' and practices, while not having a reality in a positivistic sense, are nonetheless 'real' in that they have a material consequence.

In arguing that descriptions of the real world are theory laden, Bhaskar (1978, 1989a) is not arguing that 'anything goes' or advocating a naïve epistemological relativism. Rather he wishes to examine how discourses and truth are pursued, legitimated, ignored and so on, in science and society at large (Outhwaite 1991: 34). Critical realism provides an ontological platform, a basis from which to ask questions about the construction and use of knowledge and truth-claims. In maintaining a critical realist ontology the consequences of discourse and knowledge must be considered to have some material interrelation with social practices, institutions and relations.

Critical realism thus anchors discourse in the realm of the real. As Woodiwiss (1990: 28) argues, this does not signify the dissolution of epistemology or the abandonment of a consideration of extra-discursive reality. Rather it provides discourse with a materiality, a substance or an 'identity' for the subjects of discourse. Knowledge, and analyses of the growth of knowledge, must have a material basis otherwise the study of knowledge becomes simply a language game (Norris 1995: 123).

The anchoring of discourse in the realm of the real is important, as it provides a philosophical space to consider the material consequence of archaeological knowledge and discourse within CRM. This is particularly important for understanding Indigenous contestation of archaeological knowledge and discourse. American Indian and Aboriginal reaction and response to archaeological inter-pretations of the past, and archaeological claims about the nature and significance of heritage objects, are not just disagreements over the meaning and nature of the past and heritage objects. It is also a response to the material effects archaeological knowledge has on the meanings given to the Indigenous past, and the management of heritage by government instrumentalities.

Discourse

The term 'discourse' has a variety of interpretations. Wetherell (2001b) notes that the most basic way of looking at discourse is as language in use. In social theory and analysis 'discourse' is used to refer to the different ways of structuring knowledge and social practice (Fairclough 1993: 3). Social meanings and power relations are embedded in language, and represented and reproduced through discourse (Macdonell 1986; Van Dijk 1998). For Foucault (1991a), whose work is needless to say very influential in studies of discourse, they are knowledges that are collected into different disciplines, and deal with the construction and representation of knowledge. There is therefore a strong emphasis on epistemological issues, so that in archaeology, for example, the dominant discourse is one of 'archaeological science' derived from the epistemological position of processual theory, while a competing discourse is that derived from the relativist epistemologies of postprocessual theory.

Discourses do not simply reflect social meanings, entities or relations; they simultaneously 'constitute' them (Fairclough 1993: 3; Wetherell 2001c). The discourse not only represents the object and idea, but also interacts with knowledge to constitute it, reinforce it and alter it (Cousins and Hussain 1984: 29). A discourse is also influenced and constructed by a speaker's position within a discipline, that is, their socio-political values and their association with particular theoretical stances within their discipline (Macdonell 1986). Thus a speaker's discourse, or discursive statements, can be used to map out a speaker's institutional position (Fairclough 1993; Tilley 1990a: 299), and it will also reinforce and 'construct' the speaker's own institutional position (Macdonell 1986). Further, discourses can be mobilized by actors to question other discursive or ideological positions. This can be seen as a strategic or tactical device to maintain the legitimacy of disciplinary positions which link intellectual discourse to political, social and ideological power (Macdonell 1986; Foucault 1991a). As Tilley (1990a) argues this definition of discourse is a useful analytical tool for examining the historical development of knowledge within the archaeological discipline.

Foucault (1972, 1973) examines the growth of knowledge in certain disciplines in the social sciences, and develops the metaphor of 'archaeology' in tracing the development of knowledge (see also Cousins and Hussain 1984; Flynn 1994). This metaphor was not used so much to trace the origins of knowledge, or to capture 'the spirit of the age', but to describe what he termed the 'archive' and its association with discourse. The 'archive' refers to a discipline's set of rules at a given period, and these rules define, limit and form the things that are 'sayable' (Foucault 1991a: 59–60). In short, 'archaeology' provided an epistemological history of knowledge (Foucault 1972). An archaeology of archaeology would thus require a digging down through the layers of knowledge and meaning within the discourse of the discipline to determine the underlying 'archive' – those elements of the discipline that determine and influence discourse and practice.

In his 'genealogical' studies, which developed out of 'archaeology', Foucault's definition of discourse took on a more material basis and he considered power relations in more detail (Flynn 1994; Hall 2001). 'Genealogy' aimed to describe events as transformations of other events, which seem, from our position in the present, to have a 'family resemblance' (Bove 1992: 13). In tracing 'events', Foucault aimed to show transformed domains of knowledge production, and to illustrate the association of discourses with power and materialities (Bove 1992:

13; Pavlich 1995). Foucault was interested in techniques, or technologies, of power rather than general political struggles and processes (Rouse 1987; Fairclough 1993), so via the 'power/knowledge' couplet, knowledge enables a certain control or surveillance of what people do, and thus becomes a technique of power (Rouse 1994: 96). Discourse, representations and constructions of knowledge, reveal forms of power that have effects upon the actions of others (Bove 1992: 3). The idea of power/knowledge was crucial for Foucault's theorization of expertise and intellectual practice.

The material effects of discourse are captured in the term 'discursive practice'. The concept of 'discursive practice' describes the point of linkage between 'what one says and what one does, of the rules one prescribes to oneself and the reasons one ascribes, of projects and of evidences' (Foucault (*L'Impossible Prison*) quoted in Flynn 1994: 30). Clegg neatly restates this as 'knowledge reproduced through practices made possible by the framing assumptions of that knowledge' (1992: 153). For example, within the discipline of archaeology the discourse of 'archaeological science' privileges methodological rigour, and in turn, privileges certain practices, like excavation and other technical practices. The privileged position of practices like excavation are then reflected and reconstructed in the discourse and practice of the discipline.

Fairclough (1993), has criticized Foucault's ideas about discourse for not providing a clear approach or method for investigating social change, as well as for failing to provide a more clear and material link between disciplinary knowledge and wider social issues and practices (see also Sayer 1992). While Foucault stressed the significance of the development of disciplinary, or professional discourses, Purvis and Hunt (1993: 486) argue that his approach neglects 'popular discourses' (see also Van Dijk 1998). This has two implications. First, issues and questions about how 'popular discourses' interact with professional discourses have not been considered. As Purvis and Hunt (1993: 486) note, popular discourses may be influenced by professional knowledge and discourse, but they are not reducible to them. The second implication is the under-theorization of *how* professional discourses affect popular discourse, and *how* professional discourses are contested by non-professionals – for instance, Indigenous peoples' challenges to archaeological accounts of 'prehistory'.

Purvis and Hunt (1993) suggest that 'ideology' may provide a point of analysis for examining shifting deployment of discourses and their material effects. They argue that in the ontological and epistemological confusion produced by attempts to apply Foucault's work, notions of discourse and ideology have also become confused (1993: 487–9; also Norris 1995; Van Dijk 1998). The concept of ideology has been reduced simply to matters of 'interest' and intellectual construction, and has lost a sense of material effect so that questions of the 'consequences' of discourse have become abstracted (Purvis and Hunt 1993: 491; also Eagleton 1991). Issues of consequence, Purvis and Hunt argue, can be asked within the framework offered by Foucault's theory of discourse, provided consideration is given to what they term the 'ideological effect' of discourse. By this they mean that some discourses should be seen as ideological when they are taken up within, or connected to, systems of domination. The effect of these discourses is ideological because they have a material relation to systems of domination and subordination; that is, they are incorporated into lived experience.

The linking of critical realism with discourse analysis has political implications beyond those of intellectual history and disciplinary disputes over knowledge. Contested discourses and the power/knowledge dyads constructed within and between them have material, causal power in shaping real-world experiences. For example, the discourse of archaeological science gains material form in legislation and social practices. At the same time, critical realism acknowledges that there is a dialectical relationship between discourse and the material world as the discursive spaces themselves are simultaneously constructed and constrained by such real-world phenomena.

The implications of discourse theory and critical realism for the discipline of archaeology are that divergent epistemological questions, favoured by practitioners such as Tilley (1990a), Hodder (1999), Binford (1988, 1990), and others, can also be grounded in ontological arguments about the effects of power/knowledge relations raised elsewhere in the social sciences. By considering the ontological and political effects of knowledge and discourse construction and use, questions about the history and development of knowledge can be extended beyond disciplinary boundaries to consider their institutional effects in lived experiences and social practices outside the academy. This is a crucial point – discourse analysis grounded in critical realism contextualizes the specific power/knowledge constructions of archaeology into the wider 'real-world' settings it shapes and is shaped by. For the purposes of my argument, critical realism has provided a more adequate philosophical position from which to trace the institutional position, ideologies and values of the archaeological discipline and its involvement in CRM, and the effects and interrelations that these may have on social practices.

Intellectuals and expertise

In considering the interplay of power and knowledge the social sciences have attempted to describe and account for intellectuals who, traditionally, are associated with developing and wielding knowledge. This section introduces some of the literature on the role of intellectuals that will be useful for offering insight into the position and consequence of archaeological knowledge within CRM.

Despite the discipline's confidence in its own particular expertise, and its effective rendering in legislation, the authority and expertise of archaeology has also been called into question by Indigenous peoples' criticism in post-colonial nations. Indigenous criticisms, and the pragmatic consultative response favoured by archaeologists, places the discipline in a 'de facto relativist' position. Consultation with Indigenous people, at least philosophically (if not in actuality) requires recognition of the existence (if not the legitimacy) of non-archaeological ways of knowing. Clearly recognition in pragmatic terms by the discipline, and a theoretical recognition by the postprocessualists, of different knowledge systems produces the disciplinary impasse discussed in Chapter 3. To surrender the authority of an objective and absolute past, which this recognition implies, jeopardizes archaeological authority. Thus, an understanding of the role and nature of this authority outside the academy will clearly be useful in negotiating a way 'between objectivism and relativism'.

Intellectuals and theories of power

Bauman (1987, 1992) identifies two roles that intellectuals occupy in Western societies, that of legislator and interpreter. The authority of the 'Legislator' is based on the traditional Enlightenment view of intellectuals and knowledge. That is, the legislator makes authoritative statements, the authority for which derives both from the legislator's superior knowledge and their search for the attainment of 'truth'. The 'interpreter', meanwhile, seeks to translate discourses constructed in one knowledge system into other knowledge systems. This latter role represents intellectual practice in a post-modern sense, and aims to facilitate communication between autonomous (sovereign) participants in the social order, rather than choosing 'rational' paths towards an 'improved' social order.

Bauman observes that the two forms of intellectual practice co-exist and that the interpreter role, despite its post-modernist claims, is not necessarily socially or politically progressive, nor an 'improvement' on the legislator role. This is because the interpreter does not abandon the claims of intellectuals to meta-professional authority, which underwrites the privileged position of the intellectual.

Frow (1995), in criticizing Bauman's work, suggests that the traditional definition of intellectuals used by Bauman, that of the high intelligentsia, a small elite group of men and women who act as the spokespersons for disciplines of knowledge, is too limited to capture the diverse array of interactive functions of intellectuals and their knowledge. Rather, Frow (1995: 90) advocates a definition developed by Gramsci as those whose work is socially defined as being based on the possession or use of knowledge, be that knowledge prestigious or routine, technical or speculative.

Gramsci (1971) argued that intellectuals are the group most responsible for social stability and change, as it is they who control or alter the behaviour of the masses. Intellectuals are the purveyors of 'consciousness', they influence notions of national identity (Bocock 1986: 36) and class consciousness (Larrain 1984: 84). However, rather than being a distinct social class, Gramsci (1971) defines 'organic' and 'traditional' intellectuals. Organic intellectuals are perceived as occurring in every social class, and as acting as agents for defining class consciousness:

> Every social group ... creates together within itself ... one or more strata
> of intellectuals which give it homogeneity and an awareness of its own

function not only in the economic, but also in the social and political
fields.

(Gramsci quoted in Femia 1988: 130)

Thus, for Gramsci and his followers, at least some intellectuals are defined
through their immediate social function and are distinguished from other workers
on the basis of their use and possession of knowledge. Classes are also held to
become conscious of their role and work to extend their hegemony 'on the terrain
of ideology' through the mediation of organic intellectuals (Larrain 1984: 84). In
contrast to these 'organic' intellectuals, traditional intellectuals are defined as the
elite group, which includes scholars, artists and clergy (Femia 1988: 131). These
intellectuals play a role in developing and maintaining hegemonic leadership by
providing the state with a world-view or a philosophy and moral outlook, which,
if successful, is reinforced by organic intellectuals (Bocock 1986: 46). This
reinforcement becomes embodied in notions of 'common sense' (Femia 1988:
132). Femia notes, however, that traditional intellectuals may not necessarily
share the world-view of the ruling group, but that compromise is often achieved
through institutional pressure and inducement (1988: 132). For example, intellectual expression in universities or the public service may be influenced by
appointment and promotion procedures, the allocation of research funding and
so forth.

Larrain (1984) argues that intellectual practice is located within the state as
ideology is produced, contested and regulated through the creation of intellectuals
in state funded institutions and state mediated processes of accreditation and
authorization. The extension and negotiation of hegemony is also a process of
construction and reconstruction of a conception of the world, which in turn
entails a process of formation and reconstruction of intellectuals (Larrain 1984:
84–85; also Davidson 1977: 258). Although Bauman's definition of intellectuals
does not consider 'organic' intellectuals, his model provides a useful examination
of how knowledge and expertise is taken up and used by the state and its
institutions. The addition of Gramscian ideas about organic intellectuals widens
the analysis to consider how discourse and its ideological effect, are translated
and contested in hegemonic processes. This is important for understanding what
archaeology does within CRM as it extends intellectual expertise beyond the
academy. It also allows an analysis of archaeological expertise, and importantly
its contestation, in the context of hegemonic processes and their arbitration by
state institutions.

Both processual and postprocessual writings have maintained the traditional
elitist idea of intellectuals in their examination of various 'readings' of the archaeological record. This emphasis has contributed to the intellectual and political
impasse the discipline has reached. Because debate over the past is conducted
within a framework of intellectuals' and 'other' views of the past, the proffered
solutions to Indigenous and other criticism are necessarily self-referential. A lack
of insight into the use of knowledge outside the traditional intellectual arenas

hinders attempts at 'informed consultation' with Indigenous peoples and others concerned with heritage and the past. This intellectual limitation also obstructs the postprocessual appeal for 'democratic dialogue'.

Governmentality and technologies of government

Taking up the Gramscian definition of intellectuals as 'possessing and using knowledge' in Bauman's 'legislative' or 'interpretive' manner, it is useful to consider how knowledge is taken up within social institutions, and to consider the mechanics of the legislative and interpretive roles assigned to intellectuals. One of the most powerful critiques of intellectuals is Foucault's work on 'governmentality'. This was developed in his later work, and followed on from his analyses of the development of expert knowledges in his histories of the social sciences (Foucault 1991b).

The governmentality thesis was developed in analysing changes in techniques of power Foucault perceived as occurring in 'modern' times via 'liberal' government. He argued that the deployment and techniques of power changed in the eighteenth and nineteenth centuries, with the rise of modern liberalism, or 'modernity', as capitalist societies became more complex and populations more diverse (Foucault 1991b: 101; Gordon 1991). Foucault's historical analysis then focused on the role of the emerging modern disciplines in state power, and argued that 'governability' replaced 'sovereignty' as a form of governing populations (Bove 1992: 14).

The links between 'governance' (or 'governability') with modernity (i.e. rationality) and liberalism allows examinations of how governmental needs to 'govern' emerging social problems are entangled with the development of intellectual discourse and knowledge. It shows how the rise of heritage as a social issue and problem may have influenced, and been influenced by, the development of archaeological discourse and knowledge construction. Governmentality allows insight into the relationships between liberalism, science, colonization, and stewardship of the past. The relationship between science, colonialism and stewardship provides a useful historical background to the development of CRM in the context of 'post-colonial' America and Australia. Further, as social problems become more complex and governance becomes an important technique of power, archaeology is translated into institutions concerned with governing the meaning of the past.

As Gordon notes, 'Governmentality is about how to govern' (1991: 7). For Foucault 'governmentality' is the 'ensemble formed by the institutions, procedures, analyses and reflections, the calculations and tactics, that allow the exercise of this very specific albeit complex form of power' (1991b: 102). A certain 'mentality' became the common ground of modern forms of political thought and practice (Miller and Rose 1993: 76; Dean 1999). Western societies can therefore be characterized by the way they address the kinds of problems that should be addressed by various authorities (Miller and Rose 1993: 76; Johnson 1993: 140).

The sovereignty of the state is seen in the governmentality literature as over-emphasized in analyses within the social sciences (Foucault 1991b: 103; Rose and Miller 1992: 176; Marlow 2002). Foucault rejects the idea of a unified state with rigid and absolute functions. Rather, what is important for modernity 'is not so much the *etatisation* of society, as the "governmentalization" of the state' (1991b: 103, emphasis in original). The state becomes a particular form that government has taken (Miller and Rose 1993: 77), and, in Rose's terms, the governmentalization of the state represents 'a transformation of the rationalities and technologies for the exercises of political rule' (1991: 5).

Thus, the process of governing populations rests on the representations of populations and the way that the 'truth' of that representation can be documented so that it can enter into political calculations (Rose 1991; Salskov-Iversen *et al.* 2000). The theories of the social sciences provide for Rose and Miller (1992: 182) a kind of 'intellectual machinery' for government. Intellectuals and their truth-claims provide procedures for 'rendering the world thinkable, taming its intractable reality by subjecting it to the disciplined analyses of thought' (Rose and Miller 1992: 182). This thought is based on liberal modernity and its emphasis on rational universal 'truths' (Pavlich 1995). Thus, the archaeological rationality, provided by processualism, can be rendered useful in defining populations (be they Indigenous peoples or other groups) through both their 'archaeological' past and the material culture (or heritage objects) which are defined as representing their past.

Foucault's examination of the history of power/knowledge places expertise and intellectuals into a network of power relations that developed, in part, out of his examination of the Christian notion of 'pastoral care' (Cousins and Hussain 1984: 249; Marlow 2002). Knowledge and the truth-claims of intellectuals became part of the practices and politics of modern liberal rule. In a sense knowledge and expertise take on a 'stewarding' and pastoral role. This is a role that archaeology takes on with respect to the 'archaeological record' and material culture generally.

The governmentality literature approaches 'politics' as a problematic of rule. In doing so it raises the question of 'what should be ruled, by whom and through what procedures' (Rose 1993: 285). Liberal governance is inextricably linked to forms of expert knowledge of society and expertise in 'scientific' knowledge of the conduct of conduct (Rose 1993: 284). Liberalism, rather than being a philosophy about rule, is a rationality of rule, a form of practice or mode of government (Dean 1994: 198; Marlow 2002). Expert knowledge becomes bound to the maintenance of order in increasingly complex social systems, which have, over time, adopted strategies of 'the state of welfare' for dealing with populations, and that have, in turn, been moulded by the new ways in which advanced liberalism deals with expertise. Government depends on the production, circulation and authorization of truths that construct what is to be governed and how it is to be governed (Rose 1991: 6; Salskov-Iversen *et al.* 2000).

Rose (1993: 290–2) proposes several key features of liberal government:

- a new relation between government and knowledge – government becomes connected to diverse theories, techniques and experts;
- subjects become active in their own government – i.e. individuals are created who participate in their own government;
- expertise is mobilized to manage 'at a distance' newly identified social problems;
- the activity of rule itself is constantly questioned.

Expert knowledge is included, especially in 'welfare' aspects of the state, in the 'political' arena. Yet at the same time, expertise is de-politicized as it is seen to rest on technical rationalist calculation, which must operate above competing interests. Within archaeology the hegemony of processualism stresses objectivity and ensures technical rigour. This de-politicizes archaeological knowledge, as postprocessualists have argued; however, it has more significant consequences than have been identified. Postprocessualists have argued that this de-politicization hinders 'democratic' negotiations with Indigenous peoples and others interested in the meaning of the past. However, more significantly it means that archaeology in providing 'rational' and 'objective' knowledge can be taken up within liberal governance to arbitrate or 'govern' relevant social problems. Further, the application of 'rational' knowledge explicitly renders the social problems it governs as non-'political'.

The above processes have been related to what Rose and Miller have called 'technologies of government':

> The complex of mundane programmes, calculations, techniques, apparatuses, documents and procedures through which authorities seek to embody and give effect to governmental ambitions.
>
> (Rose and Miller 1992: 175)

Notions of intellectual expertise become explicitly entwined with the mechanics or 'technologies' of government. Technologies of government are bodies of knowledge, expertise, disciplines, social theories and so forth, which government mobilizes to get things done (Dean 1994, 1999). The nineteenth-century establishment of 'professions' working alongside formal bureaucracies:

> became incorporated into the processes of governing, but [they] did so in the institutionalized form of independent, neutral colleague associations, controlling recruiting and training, providing codes of conduct and procedures of discipline.
>
> (Johnson 1993: 144)

Political rationalities, which include 'public' ideas of government, moral justifications for exercising and limiting power, and perceptions about its proper distribution, are then deployed and reinforced through technologies of government

(Rose and Miller 1992: 183). Thus political rationality is enforced, negotiated and reconstituted within technologies of government (Dean 1994: 188; Salskov-Iversen *et al.* 2000: 19). This process is not an abstract one. Rather technologies of government seek to translate 'thought' into 'the world of persons and things' (Miller and Rose 1993: 82). This translation is achieved though the mundane techniques of knowledge production (such as experimentation, surveys, question-naires, etc.) and its construction and dissemination in discourse (Miller and Rose 1993: 82; Dean 1994: 188; Hannah 2000). Language is perceived by Miller and Rose (1993: 81) as an 'intellectual technology', in that it renders certain types of actions amenable, and the phenomena to be governed susceptible, to 'evaluation, calculation and intervention'.

This process is, however, not faultless. Technologies of government can, and often do, produce unexpected problems, especially through the intersection of competing technologies, or may be employed in a way not initially intended (Miller and Rose 1993: 86). For example, 1960s archaeological knowledge about the nature of Aboriginal sites in NSW held that few sites would be expected to occur in that State – an assumption that underpinned the development of NSW heritage legislation. This erroneous expectation led to the development of stronger (in the terms of site protection) legislation than originally intended (see Chapter 7). Conversely, James Chatters' statements about the morphology of the Kennewick remains were taken up and used by the media in ways it appears that he did not intend, in particular in questioning the legitimacy of American Indian indigeneity (see Chapter 8). In a similar situation, Rhys Jones' arguments concerning the effects of isolation on pre-contact Tasmanian Aboriginal culture were, as he argues (1992a: 59–60), taken up into wider debates about the identity of Aboriginal people in a way he did not intend (see Chapter 9). Foucault (1991b), because of these possibilities, tends to rest his analyses on examinations of how certain knowledge claims are seen as 'truth', and in identifying the preconditions for certain discourses and claims to expertise (see also Gordon 1991).

While Rose, Miller and Dean emphasize the role of liberalism in replacing sovereign rule, Johnson (1993) argues that governmentality also has an historical association with colonialism. One consequence of the mobilization of expertise in defining the things and phenomena to be governed by liberal rule is the isolation of a subject population through the documentation of its attributes and characteristics (Rose 1991). Discursive practices reproduce and transform the identities of groups within society through the classification and interpretation of the behaviour of populations (Clegg 1992; Finch 1993). Burchell (1991: 119) argues that political power is most keenly felt and articulated when those that are governed are required to alter how they see themselves as governed subjects. Clearly ideologies and discourses within the academy have an impact on real-world experiences. For instance, social Darwinism generally, and the idea in particular that Indigenous people both in North America and Australia were a 'vanishing race', were central in recreating Indigenous peoples as governable subjects. Liberal rule was also a part of 'the early formation of the great territorial, administrative states and colonial empires' (Johnson 1993: 141). The new human sciences were as crucial in establishing colonial rule as force of arms and trade, rendering Indigenous populations understandable, tractable and governable. Technologies of government were utilized in liberal colonial rule in redefining the colonial identity of populations.

In the concept of governmentality, expertise and 'professional' discourses get taken up as technologies of government. Intellectuals, in arbitrating upon and interpreting different and contested knowledge systems, become involved in governing populations, and in constituting and rationalizing social and power relations and alliances. Various studies have examined how individual social science disciplines and theories have been mobilized as technologies of government (e.g. Burchell 1991; Rose 1991, 1999; Robson 1993; Cawley and Chaloupka 1997; Dean and Hindess 1998; Dean 1999). What is suggested here is that by applying this approach to analyses of the hegemonic discourse of archaeology and its various contested alternatives in academic, political and public domains, establishes practices such as CRM and public archaeology more generally as important technologies of governance. In the particular setting of post-colonial America and Australia this is significant because specific elements of archaeological discourse have become so central in creating, not just Indigenous American and Australian identities, but a more complex, robust and multifaceted national identity which is upsetting previous hegemonic forms of governance (e.g. debates over constitutional monarchy, Mabo and *terra nullius*[1] in Australia and post-2001 reflections on America's place in the 'global society').

The governmentality thesis offers an intellectual tool for tracing the historical construction and deployment of knowledge about material culture and its effects on the perceptions of 'identity' held by, and applied to, specific populations. It allows an examination of the effects of archaeological discourse and ideology on political struggles through its effects on notions of identity. Importantly, in viewing archaeology as a technology of government, the postprocessual concern for theorizing the 'politics' of archaeology may be reconstituted outside a concern for intra-disciplinary politics as a concern for extra-disciplinary effects and consequences. Moreover, the governmentality thesis provides an historical and political context for analysing the development of archaeological theory and knowledge in terms of the rise of modernity, and liberal and colonial problematics of rule. The mobilization of archaeological knowledge within institutions of the state through CRM may be understood as not simply technical responses to the physical needs of conservation of material culture, but as part of the processes of identifying, classifying and 'governing' populations who are, in part, identified by their links to material culture – a process which is facilitated by the processual claims of the discipline of archaeology. This is not to say that this process is not resisted or contested, as the critical response by Indigenous and other groups to archaeology shows – but it partly explains why that criticism is often so intense and sustained. Further, it helps explain why Indigenous criticism of the management of sites and places transcends, if it does not completely ignore, the boundaries that archaeologists often attempt to deploy between 'research archaeology' and 'CRM'. However, the observation that archaeological expertise and knowledge is often contested directs us to some of the limitations of the governmentality thesis.

Despite Foucault's interest in the interplay of different and opposing discourses and truth-claims, governmentality fails to make space for contested and competing claims to knowledge (Pearce and Tombs 1998; Smith and Campbell 1998; O'Malley 2000). It offers, for example, little analytical attention to Gramsci's insights into organic intellectuals – how does knowledge and discourse *not* developed in sites mobilized as technologies of government compete and contest acknowledged technologies? This issue is of particular relevance in the history of the colonial and, subsequently, post-colonial forms of government and resistance, areas hardly touched on by the governmentality literature. Further, in privileging knowledge and expertise as the most useful technique and technology of government, opposing or non-technical expertise becomes obscured in this model. This issue is of particular relevance when considering the contestation of archaeological interpretations of the past by Indigenous people.

Foucault also dismisses the law and judicial systems as insignificant in liberal rule, and later governmentality work has not challenged this (Pearce and Tombs 1998). This characterization of law derives from Foucault's (1991b) and Rose's (1993) dismissal of the idea of a unitary state for a notion of 'the state' as a form of authoritarian discourse. In rightly rejecting monolithic notions of the state, the governmentality literature has unfortunately failed to address the mechanics of how expertise is actually mobilized on a day-to-day and material basis (Bove 1992). Further, in taking a critical realist perspective, the state must be seen to have a material form, as well as a discursive precondition (Jessop 2001a).

Although Rose and Valverde examine how instruments of law become integrated into technologies of government, law is reduced to 'a fiction' (1998: 545) and its material consequences become obscured (Pearce and Tombs 1998). By dismissing law the governmentality thesis dismisses a material link between expertise and its deployment in governing target populations. Legislation has become a significant site of archaeological expertise, as heritage legislation often embodies archaeological knowledge (see Byrne 1993; Carman 1993; Smith 1993b; Ellis 1994) and is, itself, in part interpreted by archaeologists employed in state institutions concerned with the management of heritage (Parrott 1990; King 1998). Thus, an understanding of how law is used in the governing of material culture is important for grounding the idea of archaeology as a technology of government in the day-to-day management of material culture.

The anti-realist position on the state advocated in the governmentality literature (Foucault 1991b; Rose and Miller 1992; Rose 1993; Dean 1999) fails to problematize issues of consequence, as there is no material basis for measuring what it is that expertise does in concrete terms. The emphasis on knowledge and discourse tends, as Norris (1995: 118–19) argues, to reduce all to issues of language. Watts (1994) makes a similar point – that a reliance on discourse as language loses track of the materiality of language. A grounded alternative will require:

> producing historically specific accounts of the social practices that involve the activities of states in the production of jurisdictions and interventions, and their employment of intellectually trained personnel and their techniques of communication (such as writing, printing, calculation, the production of statistics and the development of research and constitutive categories).
>
> (Watts 1994: 125)

Expertise has played a crucial role in state formation (Johnson 1993). This role extends beyond the employment of experts, as the state maintains 'a symbiotic yet ambiguous relationship with the intellectually trained not directly employed within the state' (Watts 1994: 145). For instance, within the realms of CRM archaeological experts may be employed directly within state institutions, but may also work as contracted experts in advisory roles, and/or archaeological knowledge may be deployed by non-archaeological bureaucrats or government Ministers/Secretaries in dealing with management issues as they arise. The state both utilizes and is constituted by governmentality, but also provides an identifiable, a *real*, structure for mobilizing directly and indirectly political rationalities and the governance of populations. A notion of the materiality of the state provides the idea of governmentality with a means through which to measure the effects of technologies of government in the world of lived experiences. What that notion of the state might be is discussed below.

State and policy issues

State theory

While Foucault's work acts as a corrective to more functional analyses of the state, the state cannot be dismissed as a fiction. Jessop's (1990) 'strategic relational' theory of the state provides a non-deterministic, non-reductionist analysis of the state, and corrects Foucault's (and many Foucauldians') overemphasis on the discursive construction of 'the state'. It does so by emphasizing the strategic and structural aspects of state power, and the bases for resistance to that power. By grounding analyses of the ways expertise is used to 'govern' in Jessop's work on the state it will be possible to situate the role of CRM as a technology of government more concretely in its institutional setting, and still remain sensitive to issues of ideology and power.

Jessop's theory of the state is useful for four main reasons. First, Jessop (1990) offers a non-reductionist view of the state. He offers a 'relational' perspective which conceives the state as an ensemble of interacting institutions, whose relations, actions and strategies are both contingent and subject to multiple causations. Second, as his work is firmly grounded within critical realist philosophy, he engages with discourse theory without getting subsumed by discourse, or reducing politics to simply language games. Third, Jessop's theorization of the state allows for the existence of multiple sites of power, networks of institutions, discourses and ideologies. Fourth, he integrates work on discourse, ideology, and hegemony in a sophisticated way that allows a perspective on how the state includes and excludes, legitimates and de-legitimates competing interests. In short, his theorization of the state provides tools for an analysis that supplements, in a theoretically satisfying way, the Foucauldian insights of the governmentality thesis with a more explicit analysis of institutions including bureaucracy and law.

Jessop's 'strategic relational' theory of the state commences with the argument that the state is not a thing, rather it is shifting and fluid and undergoing constant reorganization of its institutions and boundaries (1983: 222, 1990: 267, 2001a; see also Cammack 1989; Mitchell 1991; Brown 1992; Hay 1996). He views the state as characterized by the relations between its ensemble of institutions, which are linked through political strategies to re-form the state, or what he terms 'state projects' (1990, 2001b). Politics forms the state, but the structures of the state also influence the conditions of political processes in a complex dialectic between structure and strategy (1990: 149). Thus, the form of the state is a 'crystallisation of past strategies, as well as a privileging of some over other current strategies' (1990: 269).

As opposed to Foucault's account of the state, this approach draws attention to the various interests engaged in political struggles within and outside the institutions of the state. It also draws attention to the structures and conjunctural factors that de/legitimize certain interests and changing modalities of governance. Thus Jessop does not view the state as simply concerned with class struggles, as some more traditional accounts maintain (see for example Hindess' critique 1987), but argues that its functional unity cannot be taken for granted due to the shifting and contested nature of state projects and political interests. The implication of this is that institutions and structures of the state affect the calculation and expression of political interests and strategies, and that as a 'variable institutional ensemble the state system can never be considered as neutral' (Jessop 1990: 268). Moreover, any substantive unity, however transitory, that the state might possess derives from political struggles to impose that unity (1990: 268).

Jessop uses the term 'strategy' in two ways. First, it is used to refer to conscious political strategies to reform policy and state procedure and institutions. Second, the term is also used in the context of the complex social and political relations of the state that result in 'unconscious' changes in strategies (1990: 264). By this he means that policy, practice, and state projects can change without conscious intent through the complex interactions of ideology, bureaucracy, law and institutions. He also argues (1990: 266) that strategies are irreducible to goals, ideas and ideologies, and that they must be understood in terms of their materialization in specific institutions.

Further interests are often represented by the state in relation to specific strategies, and thus the legitimating of interests are not undertaken in absolute terms, but are given legitimizing weight relative to specific political strategies (1990: 268–9). By identifying interests, Jessop also identifies the existence of alternative interests and opens the conceptual ground for competition between them. In addition, he acknowledges that the state itself engenders political interests, these interests are not only those of state mangers ('officialdom'), but are also the interests which have a stake in the forms the state may take, and in the development of policy in the real legal, economic and political structures and settings they create; the real-world landscapes of power, privilege and resistance (1990: 269).

With respect to power, Jessop (1990) argues that the state has, as an institutional ensemble, no power as such. Rather it is a set of institutions that mediate power. He characterizes the power of the state as the power of the forces acting in and through the state, as well as those reacting against or resisting state intervention. He identifies 'forces' as such things as, for example, class forces, gender groups, regional interests, to which could be added Indigenous groups and so forth (1990: 270).

The law

In considering issues of 'state power', it is necessary to consider the role of law as a mediator of power within the state. Hunt (1993), in reviewing the way law has been theorized and studied, has noted that studies of law have recently begun to focus on the concept of 'governance', while rejecting the 'model of rules' to explain the nature of law. The idea of governance leads to a conception of government as a process rather than as an institution, and allows a consideration of the dimensions of the experiences and consequences of being governed (Hunt 1993: 305). Hunt is sympathetic to the idea of governmentality, although cautions against the tendency to expel the state, and to overlook 'the law'.

Hunt (1993: 313) examines the connection between state, law and power by conceiving the process of governance as revolving around the idea of 'regulation'. Regulation is defined as a type of social process, of which law may, or may not be, an aspect (Hunt 1993: 314–15). The idea of regulation rejects the opposition between coercion and consent notions of power. However, regulation builds on the power/knowledge dyad and its embodiment of the role of information, expertise, policies and strategies, by its deployment of specific knowledges encapsulated in legal interventions. Hunt offers a schematic definition of regulation as: 'power/law/knowledge' (1993: 314).

A closer look at Hunt's use of regulation is useful in grounding governmentality in material processes, as it provides an understanding of the role of law within late liberal rule and modernity, and thus is useful in exploring the relation between Indigenous 'heritage' legislation and archaeology. First, Hunt (1993: 315) makes the distinction between 'regulation' and 'control', and argues that control is not necessarily the outcome of regulation. Rather he sees the results of regulation as more open, that regulation is often avoided, circumvented, challenged and so forth. In this conceptualization room is thus made for Indigenous resistance to the use of archaeological expertise in heritage legislation and policy.

Second, Hunt argues that regulation is intentional, and an object of regulation must be constituted (an object can also, as Hunt notes, be similarly dismantled and abandoned). Regulatory interventions are often responses to the apparent 'discovery' of a social problem. The discovery and articulation of a problem is closely connected to the collection of information about the phenomenon (1993: 316). The selection and deselection of objects of regulation very often constitute significant sites of political contestation. For example, Hunt notes that struggles over abortion are struggles over the creation of a particular object of regulation. Further, the desire to regulate is often most strong when a new regulatory project is the subject of controversy and contention (1993: 318). Thus struggles over Indigenous heritage become struggles over objects of regulation. Heritage objects in symbolizing Indigenous cultural identity play an important role in governing or regulating Indigenous cultural expression.

Third, regulation also involves the creation or designation of 'regulatory agents' whose functions may include the collection and recording of information, surveillance, reporting, initiating enforcement actions and so forth. Fourth, 'regulatory knowledge' is produced within the regulatory process, so that the 'identification, acquisition, and deployment of knowledge are central features ... of the construction of objects for regulation' (1993: 317). Hunt sees the collection of knowledge as playing a central role in the formation of regulatory policies and strategies, and he notes that one of the features of modernity is the quest for objective knowledge. The development of processual archaeology, and its discourse, which stresses the 'objective' nature of archaeology, becomes a trigger for the deployment of archaeological regulatory knowledge and agents. Hunt suggests that a key feature of the modern emphasis on objectivity was the emergence of organized social sciences, and a transition from 'amateur' to 'professional' social sciences that occurred in the nineteenth and early twentieth centuries. He argues that there is a connection between the 'professionalism of regulatory knowledge and the growth of systematic regulatory activity' (1993: 317). However, he acknowledges that regulatory knowledge can take on a 'life of its own', that it can go beyond that translated into government action, and that it can come into conflict with political pragmatic considerations of governments.

Regulatory knowledge works to constitute objects of regulation and helps the formation of 'regulatory strategies'. By this Hunt refers to the process whereby knowledge is expressed as a regulatory policy or strategy, which is then incorporated into legislative form (i.e. knowledge is transformed into procedures, rules, statutes etc.) (Hunt 1993: 319). For example, archaeological knowledge was one of the bodies of expertise that has been explicitly used to formulate heritage legislation in both America and Australia (see Chapter 7). It also continues to be used to interpret and administer the legislation, and to inform the practices of CRM that follow from heritage legislation and policy.

The regulatory approach attempts to break away from the idea of law as simply a system of rules, and presents law as part of a network of social relations that can have legal dimensions. The approach is concerned with notions of causality, and with the effects and consequences of the legal dimensions of social relations; it engages with 'lived experience' (Hunt 1993: 326–8). This conception of expert knowledge has an obvious synergy with the governmentality idea of technologies of government. However, Hunt, in focusing on law and legislation, provides a material link between disciplines as technologies of government and governance. Further, a regulatory conception of the law provides a grounding of the govern-mentality thesis in an analysis of the interplay of expertise and state institutions.

Interests and interest groups

In conceptualizing power relations Jessop and Hunt note that the state and law mediate political struggles between various 'interests'. If we conceive the state as a sum of social practices (Jessop 1990; Mitchell 1991), we need to further define how these relations are organized and mediated. If politics is not governed by a sovereign centre of power, but dispersed among multiple centres of power (Abbott 1996), how does executive government identify and organize conflicts over power? In analysing this interplay political scientists identify discrete groups and interests who interact with and lobby government and state institutions in attempts to influence state projects and government policy. Abbott (1996), in his review of the literature on these issues, notes that a variety of terms, including pressure groups, interest groups, organized interests, and so forth, have been developed to designate groups whose aim is to lobby government and influence policy. Following on from Jessop and Hunt, the term 'interest group' favoured by Matthews (1990) is employed here.

'Interest groups' may be broadly defined as cohesive or semi-cohesive groups whose cohesion revolves around shared interests (Matthews 1990). These may be shared political, social, cultural and/or ideological concerns (Abbott 1996). Interest groups lobby to ensure that their interests, their concerns, desires and aspirations, are listened to by government, in the hope of influencing government policy (Matthews 1990; Abbott 1996). As well as 'interest groups', Bennett (1989) defines 'interests'. Groups may possess shared 'interests', but not be necessarily represented by a single static 'interest group'. In particular he identified Indigenous interests as a recognized 'interest', which are not necessarily represented by a single group that can claim to speak for all Indigenous interests or people.

These interests and interest groups will often come into conflict with other interests, and each must compete to gain recognition by government and its agencies (Matthews 1990; Abbott 1996). In complex societies governments respond by 'regulating' conflict through the implementation of policy and legislation, a process that is legitimated through the ideology of democratic representation.

As Jessop (1990) argues, the state mediates interests in relation to specific shifting strategies. In this process various interests and interest groups may be privileged or singled out at specific times by government or the differing arms of the state. Various political resources that are used by interests and by government in identifying privileged or non-privileged groups are identified as significant in the literature. Two resources given particular attention are economic resource (including resources of labour) and ideologies of 'legitimacy' (Jessop 1990; Matthews 1990; Abbott 1996). Interest groups that have access to the former have an obvious political resource available to them. Ideologies of legitimacy, however, are also used as a political resource by government and interest groups themselves. The legitimacy of an interest may be claimed via the representational ability of the interest group, or an interest may have a particular moral connection to a current state project, or it may rest on the cultural or social significance of an interest in society (Matthews 1990; Abbott 1996).

As an aspect of the notion of legitimacy Bennett (1989: 2–3) identifies the idea of 'special aura', which is applied to interests perceived to hold a 'special place' or an emotional appeal. Although Bennett (1989) develops his argument in the context of Australia his argument is relevant also to North America. He suggests that the idea of special aura has particular relevance in understanding the 'legitimacy' given, and at times withheld by government, to Indigenous interests. He notes that government has often invoked an idea of 'special aura' in publicly legitimizing policy development with respect to Aboriginal populations. As part of this process Bennett (1989: 13–15) argues that expert knowledge (or what he refers to as 'white-norms') about Aboriginal people is often used in defining this 'special aura' and in developing policy and legislation (see also Attwood 1989). Hunt's concept of 'regulatory knowledge' comes into play here, and Indigenous interests become an object of governance through the social and political relations of the state. In addition, the effects of archaeological expertise are thus identified as having a material effect not only through the regulatory role of legislation (Hunt 1993), but also through the relational interplay between interests (Jessop 1990).

Conclusion

This chapter does not make grandiose claims for a fully rounded theory. Nor am I trying to make absurd claims about the universal importance of archaeology or CRM. In this chapter, I have, however, tried to draw on this diverse material from the wider social sciences as an archaeologist who is looking at archaeology and CRM, to examine how, in history, a relatively minor area of science came to claim some form of 'stewardship' over the material culture of other cultures and societies. I want to discuss how, in twentieth and twenty-first century post-colonial contexts, a more explicitly scientific (in a modern sense) form of archaeology, has amongst other forms of knowledge and expertise (anthropology, law, management, history, architecture, etc.) played a unique, and influential, role in managing Indigenous peoples' claims not only to material culture, but also to the interpretation of that material culture and the pre-colonial past more generally.

The idea of governmentality, coupled with critical realist theories of the state, provides a more adequate framework for an analysis of archaeology and CRM than currently supplied within processual or postprocessual theory. This framework will be applied in the following chapters. The next chapter re-examines the history of both American and Australian archaeology in the light of this framework, and argues for an understanding of archaeology as a technology of government. Specifically it is CRM that allows a mobilization of archaeological knowledge and expertise in the governing of Indigenous material culture. Through the construction of material culture as 'heritage', issues of identity are thus governed by the regulation of material culture through archaeological knowledge. Further, that knowledge is deployed in legislation and policy, and in the identification and construction of legitimate interests by executive governments and state institutions. Chapter 6 will also examine the implications of this process, and consider the role of archaeological knowledge, discourse and expertise, by tracing the development of the idea of archaeological 'significance' as a key policy discourse in determining the management and meaning of heritage items.

5
ARCHAEOLOGICAL STEWARDSHIP
The rise of cultural resource management and the 'scientific professional' archaeologist

This chapter examines the history of Anglophone archaeological discourse about material culture. The 'governing' role archaeological knowledge came to play in disputes about material culture will be analysed, with emphasis on how this was applied in America and Australia. It argues that American and Australian archaeology reached its fullest extent as a technology of government, via CRM, during the late 1960s and 1970s, and examines *how* this came about by identifying the preconditions and disciplinary attributes that made this possible. A detailed history of the discipline is not intended. Rather the aim is to develop an argument about archaeological governance, in the context of the discipline's history, by locating the conditions of emergence of an 'archaeological' discourse on material culture which was able to make itself useful in a political sense by arbitrating aspects of conflicts over material culture.

According to theorists of governmentality, academic disciplines, their knowledge base and practitioners were initially mobilized with the rise of liberalism to 'govern' subject populations, as power/knowledge relations became more important than the exercise of 'sovereign' power. Early liberal governance stressed a desire to 'guide' and educate populations into becoming 'good' citizens, and intellectual knowledge became important in this process (Dean 1999). In late liberalism (in the latter part of the twentieth century), disciplines are more explicitly mobilized as technologies of government to deal with particular social problems or issues. The literature also connects the rise of liberalism, and its desire to create 'good' citizens, with the rise of science, as disciplines begin to incorporate liberal welfare values. Further, the rise of professionalism and 'modern' notions of science, and knowledge-power-truth strategies, are also identified as the triggering factors in the mobilization of disciplines in the governance of populations or specific social problems. These strategies were also important in colonial contexts where Indigenous populations were 'governed' and reconstructed as colonized populations (see Markus 1990; Jaimes 1992; Robbins 1992; Finch 1993).

To what extent does archaeology possess the attributes necessary to be mobilized within strategies of governance? Three attributes are identified in American and Australian archaeology as facilitating this mobilization. First, a discourse that emphasizes the 'stewardship' of the past and the material culture that represents that past; second, a conceptual link between 'identity' and material culture came to assume significance within the discipline; and third, the development of 'scientific' processual theory and its power/knowledge implications for the discipline.

First, the discourse of 'stewardship' creates a sense that the discipline is a 'protector' of the past, a spokesperson or interpreter of the past, due to its 'right' as an intellectual and scientific pursuit to make pronouncements about the meaning of the past. This liberal sense of stewardship intensifies as the past in question becomes more distant from the present, in that it becomes less 'knowable' by the average member of the public, and can thus only be really understood through expert scrutiny.

For example, this sense of 'stewardship' is displayed in the persistent debates in American and Australian archaeology around the rhetorical question 'who owns the past?', which is often used to frame debates about the repatriation of human remains and cultural artefacts. In these debates absolute 'ownership' of the Indigenous past and its heritage was deemed by many archaeological commentators not to lie with either Indigenous people or archaeologists (e.g. Frankel 1984; Mulvaney 1985; Meighan 1992; Murray 1993a; Jones and Harris 1997). Rather a sense emerges in ownership debates that archaeology should play an important role in 'protecting' the past and its material culture from destruction by development and amateur collectors (e.g. Johnson 1966; Mulvaney 1970, 1981b, 1989; Davis 1982; Fagan 1993; Jelks 2000[1988]). An 'educative' role is also identified for archaeology because, as Sullivan (1985: 148) notes, it 'has had a positive effect on the general public's view of [Indigenous] society' and thus the discipline 'has a lot to offer' Indigenous cultures (see also Mulvaney 1981b, 1989, 1991; King 1983; Frankel 1993a; McManamon 1991; Herscher and McManamon 2000 who make similar points). Rather than 'ownership' the idea of custodianship or stewardship was put forward in this debate as 'it allows for the concept of universal culture' (Mulvaney 1985: 96). This term also incorporates the idea that the material culture of the past is part of the heritage of all humanity (Mulvaney 1985: 90; SAA 1996; Lynott and Wylie 2000: 36). As McGuire (1992) points out, this universalizing tendency places scientific experts (in this case archaeologists) as those most able to care for and interpret the universal meaning and significance of the past.

This idea of stewardship is so deeply embedded in the discipline that it has been made a foundation stone in the re-development of the SAA principles and ethics (Lynott and Wylie 2000: 35). It is used specifically to reaffirm the archaeological commitment to conservation, and to remind archaeologists that we hold the 'archaeological record' in 'public trust' (Lynott and Wylie 2000: 36). In terms of stewardship, Lynott and Wylie (2000: 35) state that archaeologists must be advocates for the protection of the past, as no one else will, nor does anyone else have the 'knowledge and credibility to be leaders in convincing local, state, and national governments to adopt laws and policies to protect archaeological resources'. This sense of stewardship is also clearly tied together, as Lynott and

Wylie assert (2000: 35), with an idea of archaeological 'best practice', which must be 'most rigorously scientific'. As both Zimmerman (2000a: 72–3) and McGuire (1998: 83) caution, the ideas of science and stewardship advocated by the SAA tend to exclude non-scientific values and knowledge about the past. Moreover, as Zimmerman (2000a: 72–3) contends, and as is argued in this chapter, the discourse is about establishing and justifying archaeological professional access and control over what the discourse also defines as the '*archaeological* resource'.

The second attribute, which is closely related to ideas of stewardship, is the link between archaeology and issues of identity. A growing literature within the wider Anglophone discipline has revealed the extent to which the development of 'a professional academic discipline' (Kohl and Fawcett 1995a: 11) emerged in Europe and America during the nineteenth century, and was integrally linked to developing notions of nationalism and national identity (see for example, D. Fowler 1987; Durrans 1989; Trigger 1989, 1995; Kohl and Fawcett 1995b). This connection helped the discipline's claims to be the 'protectors' of the past and heritage, and facilitated the development of the discipline's role, both in America and Australia, within CRM. This is particularly important in the context of archaeology's mobilization as a technology of government in the late 1960s and 1970s.

During this period, Indigenous political activism became more public, and gained increasing media attention. Subsequently, governments used notions of Indigenous identity in attempts to arbitrate over the political legitimacy of Indigenous interests. Conversely, Indigenous people were concerned in the 1960s and 1970s to recapture a pride in their identity, and were actively reshaping their identities as part of a politicized cultural revival (Miller 1986: 192f; Durham 1992; Robbins 1992). Cultural heritage was identified as important in symbolizing and providing material links with Australian Aboriginal and American Indian cultural identity (see Langford 1983; Ah Kit 1995; Pullar 1994; Gulliford 2000). Issues of 'identity' became central to negotiations with government over the legitimacy of Indigenous claims. Further, the adherence to group identity, especially in the face of policies like cultural assimilation, was an important political and cultural strategy for survival (see Chapter 2). Anthropological and archaeological interpretations of Aboriginal and American Indian culture and 'prehistory' helped governments and policy makers to understand (or in Bauman's terms, interpret) the claims of Indigenous people. As well, 'expert' interpretations of Native American and Aboriginal identity via interpretations of Indigenous culture and prehistory were used by governments to judge the legitimacy of Indigenous claims, especially claims to land, religious freedom and sovereignty. The archaeological discipline's link with issues of identity provided some utility for archaeology to be mobilized by governments in dealing with issues of identity and their representation in 'heritage'.

The third attribute that facilitated American and Australian archaeology's mobilization as a technology of government was the development of processual theory, which stressed the scientific credentials of the discipline. The ability of archaeology to make 'truth'-claims through the discursive strategies offered by logical positivist epistemology and the ideology of 'objectivity' were important in promoting the power/knowledge nexus.

The discourse of stewardship, the linking of archaeology to issues of 'identity', and processual theory, all have histories within the wider context of Anglophone archaeology. This chapter makes brief excursions into these histories and first examines the growth of archaeological discourses of stewardship and its links to issues of identity in the context of the growth of liberalism. This is important as it provides an historical context for the colonial tendencies in American and Australian archaeology that facilitated their mobilization as a technology of government. Although much of the literature drawn on here is American, its relevance to Australia is that it was *directly* and explicitly incorporated into Australian archaeology. Sullivan (1973) and Bowdler (1981, 1983) incorporated processual debates about how and why heritage should be managed into Australian archaeological and CRM literature, while US management practices and ideas were also directly incorporated into CRM policy and practice (Buchan 1979).

The emergence of 'archaeological' discourses on material culture: 'stewardship' and 'national character'

Archaeology and the rise of liberalism

How can archaeology, a self-avowed 'value free science' of the material remains of the past, be seen as a human science that played a constitutive role in the rise of liberalism? What are the 'jurisdictions and interventions' (Watts 1994: 125) that the emergent discipline of archaeology carved out for itself?

First, the nascent discipline of archaeology mobilized knowledge claims to scientific expertise regarding material culture that lay at the heart of the liberal problematic of rule. Central issues such as science and rationality, evolution, 'social improvement' of citizens, and the proper disposition and government of the 'native' peoples of the colonies, were all brought together by archaeology's claims to act as interpreter of and steward to 'material culture'.

Nor was this an innocent exercise. Lubbock, English author of the first popular work of prehistory, *Prehistoric Times* published in 1872, and champion of the *Ancient Monuments Protection Act* of 1882, was a Liberal politician, zealous in turning the claims of science over material culture to the creation of the virtuous citizen – 'Gladstonian liberalism with a time dimension added' (Carman 1993: 40). Although, the legislation he promoted could be seen as a typical piece of social improvement, it also rested on the power of the new discipline of archaeology to make authoritative statements on the disposition of the material remains of the past, and to have these statements taken up and recognized by state institutions. An important factor here is the ability of archaeology to distinguish itself from antiquarianism – glorified grave-robbing and classicist curiosity about the past – and shoulder the mantle of 'Science' to become the 'steward' of the past.

It has been widely argued in the archaeological literature that the collection of antiquities prior to the twentieth century was clearly linked to expressions of nationalism, formation of emerging middle-class identities, and struggles within the European aristocracy to maintain power and social status (e.g. Murray 1989; Trigger 1989; Sherratt 1993; Schnapp 1996). However, as Byrne (1991: 269) points out, many historical analyses of archaeology have tended to simply portray the discipline as one open to manipulation by social and political concerns with little consideration of how archaeology may actually be constituted within these concerns. In a departure from this trend Trigger (1989) charts the intellectual history of archaeology through a close examination of the social, political and colonial contexts in which the discipline operates. Further, he illustrates how these contexts have both influenced and have been influenced by archaeological interpretations and narratives. Trigger's work examines how imperial countries like Britain and the USA have endeavoured to impose their brand of archaeology on other countries (1984a; see also Gidiri 1974), and how American archaeology has influenced normative perceptions of American Indians (1980, 1983, 1985, 1986a, 1991c). He also links the development of archaeological theory to debates and political negotiations over class, and national and colonial identity (1989, 1995). As Diaz-Andreu (1995: 54) argues, the past has a close legitimizing relationship with the formation of national identities. This argument is mirrored by Murray (1996a: 74), who states that one of the core claims of archaeology is that 'race, language and culture are intimately linked', and that without this link the European past would have been 'unintelligible' and 'the claims of nations and ethnic groups' would have been weakened. These arguments subvert the idea of the intellectual development of the discipline as simply mirroring wider social and political debates and agendas. Rather their work suggests a more interactive relation between archaeology and its socio-political context.

During the nineteenth century museums established themselves as the 'stewards' of the past for the 'public', with the aim to 'educate' the public and, consequently, promote national and cultural identity (Bennett 1995). This was part of the liberal education movement, which perceived a moral responsibility to emphasize the 'communal roots of the population', to counter revolution through stressing a sense of community, and to provide social stability during the increasing urbanization of the nineteenth century (Cunliffe 1981: 192). The archaeologist Pitt-Rivers, who established a museum at Oxford to house materials he had excavated, was prominent in this movement (Daniel 1978: 169–74; Chapman 1989). Daniel reports that Pitt-Rivers adopted a deliberate policy to interest and educate the public in prehistory (1978: 174), and notes that Pitt-Rivers had 'sensed a shift of power to the educated masses and insisted that they must be educated aright' (1978: 174). In Pitt-Rivers' own words 'they must learn the links between the past and the present' (quoted in Daniel 1978: 174). Alongside these developments the collection of material culture extended in the nineteenth century to *explicitly* include studies of non-Europeans (Trigger 1981, 1984a, 1989; Byrne 1991; Sherratt 1993; Gamble 1993).

What occurred with the development of 'professional' public museums (as opposed to private antiquarian collections) was an explicit commentary by museum curators on *other* cultural, class, social and historical identities. Archaeological curators, like Pitt-Rivers, attempted to govern ideas about nationalism through the brute presence of physical objects, which the archaeological discourse held to be objective repositories of knowledge, adding authoritative weight to pronouncements about the past and the nature of other cultures (Merriman 1991; Walsh 1992). The physical nature of material objects lends tangibility and authenticity to interpretations of the past, and reinforces the authority of interpretations of intellectuals associated with their collection, curation and interpretation (McGuire 1992; Buchli 1995). Museums in Europe and the USA became actively engaged in the collection of material culture from Indigenous cultures, defining and cataloguing these peoples and thus rendering them 'understandable' to Western audiences (Ferguson 1996; McGuire 1998).

The growth of public museums, and the increasing role of intellectuals in pronouncing on the past, drew on the emerging moral authority of 'Science', and its supposed ability to help make 'good' citizens. It was archaeology's close relationship with evolutionary theory, however, that gave it its greatest impetus in establishing claims to material culture (Trigger 1989; Gamble 1993; Griffiths 1996). Darwinian evolutionary theory provided intellectuals with the framework to develop a sense of national identity based on communal associations, as well as providing an account of social disruption in the face of 'progress' (Cunliffe 1981; Gamble 1993). It also provided archaeology with the authority and disciplinary identity of 'science'. As Piggott (1981: 21) illustrates, antiquities, like fossils, were seen as part of the landscape and, therefore, more appropriately treated as scientific data rather than as the subject of the discipline of history. This was also helped by the antiquarian association with natural history research that allowed the emergent discipline to 'break out of the straight jacket of history' (Chippendale 1989: 76). This perception of material culture found synergy within Darwinian evolutionary theory, and the link between material culture and perceptions of identity was further strengthened through the authority of objective science.

As Trigger (1989: 80f) argues, notions of cultural evolution and seriation that had been developed in Scandinavia in the early nineteenth century were caught up in the revolution offered by evolutionary theory. Seriation incorporated the concepts that cultures 'progressed' through time, and that this progression could be reflected in the development of material culture. Concepts of cultural evolution became inextricably tied to those of physical evolution, and cultural development and change were firmly linked with the scientific search for the origins of humanity. 'Cultural development' was conceived as having some form of physical basis in that it was reflected in artefacts and the archaeological record, and alongside 'national character' was linked, at this time, to environmental influences and perceptions of racial characteristics (Gamble 1993: 46). In effect, notions of cultural identity were conceived as both having physical representations in material culture and being influenced by physical attributes defined by race and environment. This was to have disastrous results for Indigenous people in colonial and ex-colonial countries like Australia and America. Not only could people be classified as 'primitive' based on the racial characteristics and skeletal morphology, but their 'primitiveness' could also be identified, defined and illustrated by their material culture. Moreover, the legacy of this intellectual history continues to influence, as demonstrated in later chapters in relation to both the Kennewick and Tasmanian cases, the ways in which Indigenous identity is constructed and understood by archaeological knowledge and discourse.

Lubbock and his colonial contemporaries, such as Lewis H. Morgan in America, had a profound effect on studies of Indigenous people (Trigger 1989; Mulvaney 1990a; Fowler 1992; McGuire 1998). The role of anthropology in providing colonial governments with cultural classification systems that facilitated the governance and colonization of Indigenous peoples has been well documented (for instance Kuper 1978, 1988; Cowlishaw 1987; Markus 1990; Biolsi 1998). Archaeology, in constituting as its domain the material culture of the past, provided a material underpinning to liberal programmes of social improvement. In both America and Australia, as early attempts to 'civilize' Indigenous people failed or were given up for political and colonial expediency, Indians and Aboriginal people increasingly became the subject of research designed to place them within an evolutionary context (Mulvaney 1958, 1993b; Attwood 1989; McGuire 1992, 1998; V. Deloria 1998). This process was reinforced by the conceptual links forged in the nineteenth century between culture, race, language and their expression in material culture.

Twentieth-century archaeological 'stewardship' and the governance of identity

Culture history

The 'culture history' phase of archaeology is widely seen as the twentieth-century successor to the scientism of evolutionary theory of the nineteenth century (Trigger 1989; Johnson 1999). The various aspects, attributes and theoretical shifts and developments of this phase will not be rehearsed here. However, both Trigger (1989) and Murray (1989, 1996a) equate the development of the culture history approach with Europe's preoccupation in the late nineteenth and early twentieth centuries with issues of nationalism. Evolutionary theory, concerned with the broad issues of human development, was not effective in singling out specific histories or identifying the development of particular 'cultures' and populations (Trigger 1989). Culture history, however, with its aims of identifying, documenting and tracing through time and space the development of specific 'cultures', Trigger and Murray argue, has been more useful than evolutionary theory for European nationalistic debates, struggles for self-determination and the promotion of national unity in the early twentieth century.

Gordon Childe and other advocates of 'culture history' developed the intellectual frameworks that allowed the identification, classification and naming of 'cultures' in the past. The cultural ancestors of European populations and nations could be revealed by the specific and distinguishing attributes and characteristics of the material culture they produced (Trigger 1989). The idea of 'material culture' developed in this period was derived from Childe's Marxist-inspired arguments that human behaviour, thoughts and ideas have a material expression (Trigger 1989; Sherratt 1990). This argument combined with the identification of cultures by the reoccurrence through time and space of particular artefacts, or particular forms or styles of artefacts, again cemented the link between archaeology and perceptions of identity.

The development of processual theory (New Archaeology)

In post-colonial contexts where archaeologists study the past of other cultures, culture history was found to be problematic. In the US the association of archaeology with nationalism through culture history could be, and was, seen as a political corruption of research (Trigger 1989: 314). In his 1973 article, revealingly entitled 'Archaeology Serving Humanity', Ford warned against the use of archaeology for supporting nationalistic agendas, arguing instead for a more universal, and thus objective, approach that would better serve humanity generally. In particular, he warned against the emerging notion of American Indian 'nationalism' which he saw as affecting the political neutrality of archaeology by involving it in land claims or in preventing archaeological research (1973: 86). He cautioned that asserting cultural intuitions as fact, or uncritically extrapolating the present into the past, creates problems for the objectivity of the discipline 'especially when [these intuitions were] conveyed to an unassuming public' (1973: 86). Ford (1973: 89), therefore, argues that archaeology must 'transcend national boundaries' and examine universal issues. In his desire to 'serve' humanity, and by emphasizing the rationality of archaeological knowledge, Ford was staking a claim to the archaeological 'stewardship' of American Indian history.

The positivism of processual theory challenged the existing power structures in the US academy by insisting that the logic and persuasiveness of argument and research would ensure individual academic prestige, rather than the social position of an archaeologist (Patterson 1986a). This perceived effect of processual theory is considered one of the movement's most positive contributions (Redman 1991). It was processual theory's apparent ability to subvert the US discipline's power structures, to incorporate itself into wider generalizing trends in the social sciences, and to render the Indigenous past useful to understanding European behaviour, that was the foundation of the 'relevance' discourse discussed in Chapter 3. The scientistic discourse of a 'New' Archaeology also meant that the discipline was able to distance itself from European antiquarianism, antiquarian colonial legacies and amateurism. These factors, as Trigger (1989: 312) argues, are what helped to make the appeal of processual theory so powerful to the new generation of US archaeologists in the 1960s and 1970s.

The development of 'heritage' as a Western social and political problem

The development of 'heritage' as a public issue in Western countries was contemporaneous with the emergence of processualism in the USA. Although legislation to protect antiquities and ancient monuments was enacted in many European countries during the nineteenth century, and in 1906 in the US, it was not until the 1960s and 1970s that the conservation and preservation of material culture took on a new and significant urgency as a public issue (Lowenthal 1990). Existing legislation was more actively policed or expanded, new legislation developed, and formal policy and procedures implemented in many Western countries, in particular America and Australia. This phenomenon was reinforced by the enactment of numerous conventions during the 1960s and 1970s by UNESCO and ICOMOS, in particular the Venice Charter of 1964, which aimed to internationally regulate the management of cultural heritage (Cleere 1993b).

During these decades, there was an increase in public debate about the effect of urban and rural development on the environment, and archaeologists in many Western countries were lobbying governments for more adequate legislative and policy controls over heritage (King *et al.* 1977; Saunders 1983; McBryde 1986; Mulvaney 1989; King 1998). In addition, archaeologists increasingly became *publicly* concerned with conservation and preservation issues. These included warnings against the antiquities black market (e.g. Clewlow *et al.* 1971; Arnold 1978; Cockrell 1980); the unlawful and unethical salvaging of sites by 'amateurs' (e.g. Mulvaney 1964, 1970; McGimsey 1972; Deetz 1977; Davis 1972; Arnold 1978; Cockrell 1980; Fowler 1982; B. Jones 1984; Cleere 1986); and the threats to archaeological data of universal 'relevance' by demands for the repatriation of artefacts and collections like the Elgin marbles (see, for example, Greenfield 1989; House 1989) to note but a few issues. In addition, Indigenous peoples were demanding control over their heritage; demands that were often encapsulated in calls for the reburial, and later in terms of repatriation, of Indigenous skeletal remains (see Chapter 2).

The development of an archaeological role in American CRM

In the face of increased public interest in material culture as 'heritage', there was a move in the 1960s and 1970s by archaeologists to publicly and institutionally claim material culture as an 'archaeological resource'. American, and some British archaeologists, writing in the 1970s and early 1980s state that a 'crisis' was upon archaeology (e.g. Clewlow *et al.* 1971; King 1971; Davis 1972; McGimsey 1972; Gumerman 1977; McGimsey and Davis 1977; Fowler 1981; amongst others). They noted with growing alarm the destruction of sites and places by development and/or the uncontrolled collection of sites by amateurs. This sense of alarm mirrored similar concerns and debates in America in the lead up to the *Antiquities Act* of 1906 (Hewett 1906; Lee 1970). As then, the concern in the 1970s was not only about saving the database, but was also concerned with differentiating archaeological claims to the resource from other claims. This was done, in part, through a discourse that publicly reconstituted material culture as archaeological data. Many academic and public archaeological publications in the 1970s quite clearly talk about and discuss an *archaeological* resource (e.g. McGimsey 1972; McGimsey and Davis 1977; Dixon 1977; Glassow 1977; McKinlay and Jones 1979). This discourse was exercised within the newly defined arena of 'public archaeology'. In identifying a public face or frontier for archaeology, the discipline reasserted its role as educator, not only about the past and what this means for the future, but also in terms of its development of a 'conservation ethic'.

The development of 'public archaeology', in which archaeology's educative role became publicly explicit, was expressed in an increased interest and debate over the 'public image' of archaeology. Numerous commentators argued for the need to challenge the popular myth of the archaeological 'hairy-chinned' adventurer identified by Kidder in 1949 (see Ascher 1960) and to stress the scientific nature and aims of the discipline (e.g. Ford 1973; Fritz 1973; Fowler 1977; Christenson 1979; Cockrell 1980; Bray 1981; Cunliffe 1981; Coutts 1984a). Others argued that the discipline needed to explicitly identify and develop sets of 'ethics' and professional 'responsibilities' to 'the past' generally, to archaeological sites in particular, and to the public (Smith 1974; Boylan 1976; Johnson 1973; Plog 1980; Raab *et al.* 1980; Rosen 1980; King 1983; Green 1984). A liberal sense of archaeological 'duty' to the past, linked to a sense of responsibility for public education, also emerges in this literature (for instance, Allen 1970; McGimsey 1972; Fowler 1977; Christenson 1979; Mulvaney 1981c; Cunliffe 1981; Coutts 1982a, 1982c; Sullivan 1984a; Cleere 1988; McManamon 1991; and more recently Moe 2000; Jameson 2000; Watkins *et al.* 2000). CRM is characterized as existing for the 'collective good' of the public (McGimsey and Davis 1977: 18) through its responsibilities to conserve, protect and educate. Underlying the identification of these responsibilities was a sense of liberal welfare pretensions: for instance Fowler, in a popular book which discusses the nature and goals of archaeology, and which is aimed at 'school boys' and undergraduates, notes: 'the past, like the poor, is always with us' (1977: 14).

Several American authors have noted that many of the theoretical positions of the New Archaeology were incorporated directly into US heritage legislation and management practice (King 1977; Dunnell 1979; Schiffer 1979; Tainter and Lucus 1983; Redman 1991; Leone and Potter 1992). These authors argue that the new emphasis on systematic field methodologies like site survey, detailed recording of sites, attention to environmental contexts, and concern with the development of regional rather than site specific studies, helped the development of CRM in America. It was also argued that CRM studies could be used to refine, through data collection, archaeological models and hypotheses and thus aid research (e.g. Schiffer and Gumerman 1977; Schiffer and House 1977a; Butler 1978; Schiffer 1979; Adovasio and Carlisle 1988). Concerns with general behavioural and cultural processes, that required regional rather than site-specific studies, found synergy with the managerial need to develop regional inventories in the face of changing land uses. The development of rigorous field methodologies and the concern for the development of regional databases and research questions were incorporated neatly into the management and bureaucratic structures of the 1970s.

The archaeological discourse which stresses objectivity, rigour and politically neutral interpretations of the past was readily embedded into bureaucracies and state institutions, and helped to de-politicize 'heritage' issues. It also ensured the priority of archaeological access to sites over public and Indigenous peoples' access through the authority invoked by the use of archaeological scientific discourse. As Dunnell ironically notes, the US heritage legislation developed at this time protects sites and places from everyone 'other than archaeologists' (1984: 64).

The imperialist tendencies of a world-oriented archaeology provided by US processual theory (Trigger 1984a, 1986b) has found, as Byrne has demonstrated (1991, 1993), an ally in the development of CRM. As in America, processual theory clearly underlines CRM practice and ethics in a number of Western countries (Saunders 1983; Renfrew 1983; Redman 1991; Hodder 1993; Wylie 2000b). The utility and power of processual discourse, tied to a powerful 'conservation ethic' within CRM, has helped the spread of processual theory from the US to other Western centres of archaeology, and ensured that it became, and has remained, the dominant theoretical position in those countries.

The development of an archaeological 'conservation ethic' also helped underline the concept of stewardship. Given that much of archaeological research, or archaeological research as it was traditionally viewed in the 1970s and 1980s, was and is destructive, the ideal of archaeological 'conservation' becomes problematic. Discussions about the protection and preservation of material culture are contradictory given that excavation, by its nature, destroys or disturbs cultural sites. Although Frankel (1993a) eloquently argues that research archaeologists 'create' the past and give it meaning rather than destroying it through their excavations, this argument is based on Western assumptions about the utility and universality of archaeological research. Certainly, those groups who regarded 'heritage' as 'inheritable' objects, things that should be protected and not destroyed or disturbed, may view excavation as destruction. Indigenous people in calling for community consultation in archaeological research consistently make this point (see, for example, Langford 1983; Zimmerman 1987, 1989a; Turner 1989; Creamer 1990; V. Deloria 1992a, 1998; White Deer 1997; Watkins 2001a). However, archaeological stewardship, and the ability of scientific archaeology to provide significant scientific information of 'universal' value, manages to obscure any contradictions between destructive research and 'conservation'.

A further area of archaeological debate and discourse that worked to stress, and was underlined by, ideas of archaeological stewardship was that concerning the 'professionalization' of archaeology. In the context of the increase in public and Indigenous interest in heritage, archaeological discourse began to stress issues of the 'professional' nature of archaeology. In the US, UK and Australia a discourse was established that identified 'amateur' and 'professional' archaeologists (e.g. Clewlow *et al.* 1971; Fowler 1977; Arnold 1978; McCarthy 1970b; Murray and

White 1981; Davis 1982; Cleere 1986). The technical skills and proficiency required by archaeologists working within CRM was also stressed as an aspect of archaeological professionalism. Emphasis was placed on the need to 'professionally' train archaeologists to work within CRM, a discourse that continues today (e.g. McGimsey 1972; Butler 1978; King 1979; Mulvaney 1979, 1981b; Raab et al. 1980; Sullivan 1984a; Fowler 1982; McGimsey and Davis 1984; Cleere 1988; Jelks 2000 [1988]; Elia 1993; SAA 1996; and more recently Wylie 2000b). Archaeology is not a 'profession' in the strict meaning of the term; however, the use of a discourse that stresses 'professionalism' actively makes appeals to and reinforces claims to intellectual prestige and expertise. The ability to demonstrate expertise through a discourse that identified and stressed 'professional' conduct has facilitated the discipline's mobilization as a technology of government.

Summary

The long history of archaeological claims to 'stewardship', and the linkages between cultural expression, 'national character' and cultural identity that had become an intrinsic part of the discipline, together with the ability of processual theory to activate the power/knowledge dyad found synergy within CRM. As 'heritage' became a public issue, and was claimed by Indigenous peoples in post-colonial countries, archaeological access to the database became a significant disciplinary issue. Issues of stewardship, and the claim of archaeological 'rights' of access to data, based on the discipline's scientific credentials, became institutionalized within CRM philosophy and practice.

McGuire (1992: 817) agrees that archaeologists in their stand on the preservation of material culture 'have become stewards of the past'. He further argues that the idea of 'vanishing Indians' allowed space for the identification of spokespersons for these vanishing people, and for the incorporation of American Indian history into white perceptions of American national identity. As Mulvaney (1981a) documents Aboriginal Australians were also characterized as a vanishing people. As in America, this made room for archaeologists to claim the status of spokespersons for Aboriginal prehistory. McGuire sees these processes as occurring throughout the colonial history of America; however, he argues that the reconstruction of American Indian sites as 'archaeological resources' under CRM cemented this process into law. Both he and Trigger (1980, 1984b, 1986a) argue that this trend, and the processual emphasis on discovering universal laws, have worked to alienate Indigenous peoples from their own pasts. As Rivera (1989: 13) suggests, when he poses the question 'do we [American Indians] have to be dead and dug up from the ground to be worthy of respect and preservation?', contemporary Indigenous culture and politics were constructed as separate from their past. This alienation has increased, as McGuire and Trigger argue, the distrust of Indigenous people for archaeologists, particularly as it impedes moves to self-determination through a denial of Indigenous peoples' sense of their own history (see also Friedman 1992; Ferguson 1996).

This distrust, however, is founded on more than just differences over the interpretation of the past. As Fung and Allen (1984: 218) state, heritage legislation and CRM do not exist because governments recognize an intrinsic value in archaeological research. Rather, the past and its material culture are important for the creation of a national ethos. Archaeology, in claiming a pastoral role over material culture though discourses of 'professionalism' and 'stewardship', has carved out a role that influences the development of national identity. The consequences of archaeological knowledge and the degree to which it is mobilized in governing perceptions of identity draw archaeology into the network of state and institutional relations concerned with the governance of nationhood. As Purvis (1996) notes, governments are not comfortable with Indigenous claims about their identities, as they challenge state sovereignty. The management of heritage, as McGuire (1992) argues, is tied to the development of national identity. In the US, debates over the meanings of American Indian history have been utilized in political struggles over the perception of the American nation and Indigenous attempts to reconstitute themselves as 'a first nation'. Archaeology, offering itself up as possessing scientific and technical expertise in managing heritage, renders 'heritage' issues, via CRM, as a series of technical problems about preservation and conservation, and thus allows the use of archaeological knowledge in regulating and de-politicizing issues of identity.

The spread of the American model of CRM to Australia and other countries was due, in part, to the imperialist tendencies of US archaeology and Western CRM as identified by Trigger (1984a) and Byrne (1991, 1993). This process was also helped by active advocacy of the US model as the 'best' and most ethically justifiable (e.g. Schiffer and House 1977b; Schiffer 1979). However, the model of CRM developed in the US offered certain advantages when dealing with Indigenous people in post-colonial contexts. The powerful synergy of processual theory and CRM that occurred in the US, and its ability to deal with competing claims to material culture, had a significant impact both on the nature of Australian archaeology and the discipline's relations with Aboriginal people.

Archaeology and technologies of government in southeastern Australia

The discourse of 'Cambridge in the bush' and the development of a scientific Australian archaeology

The emergence of an Australian scientific discourse of 'stewardship' over the past was influenced by, and has to some extent mirrored, the American synergy between CRM and processual theory. This section outlines the background to the importation of processual theory to Australia, and the rise of an Australian scientific archaeological discourse as part of the first step toward the mobilization of archaeology as a technology of government. The utility of processual theory in a post-colonial context is illustrated by the way it was neatly incorporated into the governance of the politics of Indigenous cultural identity.

The modern (or professional) discipline of Australian archaeology is generally argued to have developed suddenly in Australia with the arrival of a cohort of Cambridge trained archaeologists in the 1960s (see for example, Jones 1968a; Murray and White 1981; Golson 1986; McBryde 1986; Mulvaney 1993a; Moser 1995b). Mulvaney, an Australian trained in Cambridge, took up a university position in 1953 (Murray and White 1981: 256), and offered the first course in 'Pacific Prehistory' in 1957 (Mulvaney 1993b: 19). Megaw (1966: 306) describes 1961 as the *annus mirabili* for Australian archaeology, as not only was this the year that the Australian Institute of Aboriginal Studies (AIAS) was mooted, and funding granted for its formation, but full university courses in Australian archaeology commenced, and research priorities and agendas were clearly developed at the AIAS 'foundational conference' (see also Mulvaney 1971a, 1989; Murray 1992b). The formal establishment of AIAS in 1964 added further impetus to the development of Australian archaeology (Jones and Meehan 2000).

Mulvaney describes intellectual concerns with the Aboriginal past – or prehistory – that he encountered in the 1950s as a remnant form of antiquarianism, in which Social Darwinism was still manifest (1958, 1964). The pervasive intellectual opinion that Aboriginal culture was unchanging, and thus uninteresting, ensured that Australian archaeology was of little significance or interest to the rest of the world (Mulvaney 1964, 1971b, 1977; Murray and White 1981; Murray 1992b, 1993a; Jones 1993). Mulvaney has stated that it was important to establish the dynamic nature of Aboriginal culture, and to challenge the ideas of recent occupation, to assert the value and significance of Australian archaeology publicly and internationally (1979: 218). It was important for the new Cambridge arrivals to distance themselves from the antiquarian history of Australian research due to, what Mulvaney identified as, the 'cultural bias' of preceding anthropological and 'amateur' archaeological research (1993b: 112).

From the 1960s to the present, there has been a strong tendency to clearly separate the pre-1960s 'amateur' archaeology from 'professional' research-orientated archaeology undertaken after Mulvaney's return from Cambridge. This distinction has been seen as meaningless by many Aboriginal critics of archaeology, who see no significant differences in the practice of archaeology in terms of the consequences it has for them (Langford 1983: 2–3). However, the discourse that separated the Cambridge trained archaeologists from preceding colonial research had two important effects. First, during the 1960s it allowed the developing Australian discipline to carve out its own identity as a scientific, neutral and objective pursuit. The discourse of the 'New Archaeology' was obviously palatable to those asserting the uniqueness and infancy of Australian archaeology, despite their British connections. Further, it helped to develop and emphasize the international significance of Australian archaeology and the revelations of Pleistocene occupation at Lake Mungo and elsewhere throughout the 1960s and 1970s. These major discoveries were made by professionally trained archaeologists whose objectivity, and adherence to principles of universal knowledge, clearly proclaimed the 'relevance' of the research. Second, as public Aboriginal criticism of archaeology increased, it became expedient to maintain a distance from the obvious 'cultural bias' of preceding research. Correspondingly, the need for 'professional' archaeologists, who could maintain that professionalism in the face of Aboriginal politics, was discussed in the archaeological literature (e.g. Coutts 1982a, 1984a; Mulvaney 1981b, 1985; Wright 1986).

The 'professional' discourse also tends to emphasize the need for rigorous methodology and 'objective fieldwork' undertaken by well-trained 'experts' (see for example Mulvaney 1964, 1971b, 1979; Megaw 1966; Jones 1968a; Coutts 1978b, 1982a, 1984a; Wright 1986). For instance, Mulvaney in an early article in which he poses research agendas for the newly developed discipline, warns about increasing public interest in the past and states:

> If archaeology is not to degenerate into a combination of antiquarianism and vandalism, the experts must keep posing problems and suggesting avenues of research, and the interested amateur must be willing to listen and discipline his own activities. Many crimes are committed in the name of science, but few as commonly as those involving the destruction of archaeological evidence.
>
> (Mulvaney 1964: 42)

In this instance, expertise and professionalism will separate the discipline from the theoretical sterility of pre-1960s antiquarianism. The development of problem-oriented scientific research assumes a moral dimension, as it is only this type of research that will prevent what Mulvaney terms 'scientific vandalism' (1970: 115) and loss of archaeological knowledge. As in America, the Australian discourse about 'professionalism' found a certain synergy with processual scientific discourse. Together these discourses have facilitated the naturalization, in Bhaskar's (1989a) terms, of the objects of archaeological research and the position of archaeologists as 'stewards' of the past. These unproblematized assumptions also helped to naturalize processual theory and reinforced the power/knowledge position of the discipline in contests over the control of material culture.

Cultural resource management as a social and political problem in southeastern Australia

The processual scientific discourse in Australia was both influenced by and influential in the development of cultural heritage as a social and political problem in Australia during the 1960s and 1970s. Archaeological discourse during this period also began to emphasize archaeologists as spokespersons and stewards for 'vanishing' Aboriginal populations and their 'lost' ties to material culture. There was also a *simultaneous* appropriation of the Australian prehistoric past, which took on a new significance in human experience and Australian identity generally (Nicholson and Sykes 1994). Ultimately this past was appropriated as 'universal' in the form of 'World Heritage' when in 1974 Australia became a signatory of the *Convention of the Protection of World Cultural and Natural Heritage 1972* (Pearson and Sullivan 1995: 40). Since then several places have been put on the World Heritage List, due, in large part, to the Aboriginal cultural material they contain. The development of the discourse of archaeological science and stewardship represents the second stage in establishing the preconditions for the mobilization of archaeology as a technology of government.

Commensurate with the development of a 'professional' and 'scientific' archaeology was an increasing concern over the management of archaeological 'resources'. Before the 1950s no legislation to manage artifacts, sites or places existed (Bowdler 1983; Ross 1996). It was not until the late 1960s and early 1970s that legislation was developed in southeastern Australia (see Chapter 7).

The lobbying for legislation by archaeologists during the 1960s and 1970s was actively undertaken for a variety of explicit reasons. These included the desire to protect a vanishing past and its international scientific significance; to promote public education about the need for preservation; to protect the archaeological database; and specifically to promote a sense of Australian cultural identity (e.g. Mulvaney 1964, 1970, 1981b, 1981c, 1990b; Megaw 1966; Moore 1975; McBryde 1986; Allen 1987; Davison 1991). Of particular concern, however, was the prevention of 'amateur plundering of sites' (Mulvaney 1990b: 1 [1963]). This discourse was underlined by a sense of the 'rights' of stewardship of archaeological science over Aboriginal material culture. Mulvaney argued for the need to preserve Aboriginal sites, and was at pains to point out the 'morality' of leaving the investigation of sites to the professionally trained (1968: 1; sentiments echoed by Megaw 1966, Jones 1968a, and Allen 1970).

The appropriateness of archaeological care of the past is also emphasized in the literature in arguments about the need to adopt systematic theory to interpret the results of excavation (e.g. Megaw 1966; Jones 1968a; Mulvaney 1968; Coutts 1977). A grasp of theory, particularly rigorous scientific theory, was argued to be outside the capacity of most amateurs.

It was argued that archaeologists had a moral right to access material culture due to the ethical status of their scientific training, and they clearly believed that they had a 'responsibility' as spokespersons for the past and a vanishing people. In 1968, a conference was called by the AIAS to lobby for and develop legislation (Anon. 1973; Edwards 1973). McCarthy in the preface to the publication issuing from this conference stated:

> The Aborigines should be encouraged to maintain their rock engravings, stone arrangements, graves and other relics in proper order as they did before the coming of the whites, and to take a pride in what they and their ancestors have produced.
>
> (McCarthy 1970a: II)

The sense of the pastoral care of Aboriginal culture in this statement is also reflected in a 1977 radio broadcast by Coutts about the role of archaeology: 'as recent colonists, we have inherited an Indigenous legacy, and we are ... morally obliged to accept, understand and perpetuate it' (1977: 75). Moreover, 'to take our legacy seriously an understanding of Aboriginal history can only be achieved through excavation of Aboriginal sites' (1977: 76).

This idea that Aboriginal culture was part of white Australian heritage and should thus be preserved was a significant one in the archaeological literature at this time (Megaw 1966, 1980; Golson 1975; Moore 1975; Stockton 1975; Coutts 1977; Mulvaney 1981b, 1985). The conservation of the Aboriginal past was seen as important in the context of ongoing Australian public debate about an 'Australian identity'. Certainly, appropriation of the Aboriginal past as part of national identity has been well documented (e.g. Allen 1988a; Attwood 1989; Fourmile 1989b; Byrne 1993; Nicholson and Sykes 1994). As Byrne (1993: 143f) and McBryde (1995) note, discoveries at Lake Mungo during the late 1960s and early 1970s had pushed dates for Australian occupation back to 40,000 years ago and this sense of antiquity had been used to give Australian identity a sense of uniqueness and age. During the 1970s Aboriginal 'prehistory' and culture were incorporated into the 'new nationalism' that was encouraged by the then Federal Labor Government and its promotion of Australia as a pluralist society (White 1992). The consequences of archaeology's involvement, through CRM, in this appropriation, are significant not only for Aboriginal interests, but also for the discipline itself. It was specifically archaeological knowledge about the age, cultural complexity and uniqueness of the Aboriginal past and sites such as Lake Mungo, rather than Aboriginal knowledge, that was incorporated into Australian national identity.

A sense of archaeological stewardship was thus important in ensuring that an increase in public and 'amateur' interest did not damage archaeological sites. This sense of stewardship was also underlaid by the idea that the Aboriginal past belonged to all 'mankind'. The idea was given strength by the discoveries at Lake Mungo, which established the international significance of Australian archaeology due to the great antiquity of Aboriginal occupation (see Mulvaney 1989). Processual science, as Bowdler (1988) and Byrne (1991) point out, provided the framework for constructing the universal significance, and stewardship, of the Aboriginal past.

Aboriginal heritage as a social and political problem in southeastern Australia

The stewardship of the Aboriginal past also became an important issue in Aboriginal criticisms about the relevance of archaeological research to Aboriginal people, and the apparent lack of respect afforded to Aboriginal culture (see Williams 1975; Fesl 1983; Mansell 1985; Willmot 1985). Mulvaney, in response to Aboriginal criticisms argues:

I am also an Australian and I regard with pride the cultural achievements during the remote past of this continent and wish to study and analyze it as part of the inheritance of all Australians. Testimony to the excesses of mystical claims to folk monopoly of truth and research is provided by the Aryan racial intolerance of Hitlerite Germany. Past social intolerance by white Australians does not justify reciprocity now.

(Mulvaney 1981b: 20)

Mulvaney's attempts to dismiss Aboriginal truth claims about the past as 'mystical' or folklore are important in identifying the attributes of the discipline that facilitated its mobilization as a technology of government. In dismissing Aboriginal knowledge about the past as mythology, Mulvaney was staking a claim to the rationality of archaeological stewardship of the past. The consequences of these claims are considerable if the wider political context in which they were made is understood.

Alongside the development of a 'professional' and 'scientific' Australian archaeological discipline and CRM was the development of Aboriginal activism that challenged and hung on perceptions of both Aboriginal identity and Australian nationalism (see Chapter 2). By the 1970s, Aboriginal activists were explicitly challenging received ideas about Australian history. New references to 'invasion' rather than 'peaceful settlement' jeopardized general Australian perceptions of history and national identity, while arguments about Aboriginal sovereignty and identity questioned the idea of a unified nation. A politicized Aboriginality that called on the Aboriginal past as a way of defining the political legitimacy of Aboriginal interests had become an important political resource for Aboriginal people by the 1970s. However, the use of the Aboriginal past in constructing and defining political legitimacy and interest was almost immediately made more complex for the Aboriginal Land Rights Movement by the development of heritage legislation which legally recognized the legitimacy of archaeologists and other experts (e.g. anthropologists, historians) in interpreting the Aboriginal past. That Aboriginal people had no input into the development of legislation at this time in southeastern Australia has been well documented in the literature (S. Sullivan 1983; Coutts 1984a; Fourmile 1989a; NPWS 1989; Ellis 1994; Brown 1995; Smith 2000). At the same time that Aboriginal people were increasingly lobbying government and state institutions for political recognition, archaeologists were asserting their pastoral role over material culture and lobbying for heritage legislation. This lobbying, moreover, successfully stressed the archaeological stewardship of material culture through appeals to scientific morals and responsibility and the archaeological ability to universalize the Aboriginal past.

Aboriginal identity had become a political resource, and had to be both understood by governments and 'governed', so that governments and policy makers could arbitrate on the political legitimacy of Aboriginal interests. Archaeological claims to stewardship of the remote past, and attempts to universalize that past as part of wider debates about Australian nationalism, helped governments to 'make sense' of Aboriginal claims and to measure the legitimacy of these claims against the pronouncements of 'objective' experts.

The point Fung and Allen (1984: 218) make, that governments do not recognize an intrinsic value in archaeological research, and that heritage legislation and CRM policy are enacted because the past plays a role in the creation of a national ethos, is important here. Archaeological research during the 1960s and 1970s was challenging the view of Aboriginal culture as unchanging, and had made discoveries like that at Lake Mungo, which had captured public attention. Further, the discipline had become 'professional' and scientific, and could thus provide knowledge about the past that supposedly contained no 'cultural bias'. Archaeological research was not only playing a role in the creation of a 'national ethos', it was also helping to make sense of Aboriginal claims. Archaeological claims to scientific neutrality also helped to de-politicize claims made by Aboriginal people about the past. The successful lobbying of archaeologists for legislation to protect Aboriginal sites and the development of CRM policy institutionalized the power/knowledge claims of the discipline. The enactment of heritage legislation provided the technical and material means by which Aboriginal claims to identity could be 'governed'.

Perhaps the most politically significant reflection of this process is the degree to which land claims were arbitrated, supported or overturned using archaeological information (as well as other expertise) in the Northern Territory under the *Aboriginal Land Rights (Northern Territory) Act 1976* (Cwlth). As Coutts (1984a: 213) stated, Aboriginal claims to land 'often have to rely heavily on non-Aboriginal specialists' to verify claims. Ucko (1983: 16), in commenting on the history of Australian archaeology during the 1970s, noted that this Act gave purpose to archaeology (see also 1986). He suggested that Aboriginal criticism and opposition during the 1970s had paralyzed archaeological research, and that it was archaeo-logical support of land claims in the Northern Territory that gave renewed impetus to research by demonstrating support for Aboriginal people. The significance, however, was not so much that archaeology supported land claims, but that it was *used* – archaeology gained a role as translator and arbitrator of Aboriginal claims about the past and their culture – it took on a governmental role. The demonstration of cultural ties to the land, via archaeological and anthropological expertise, helped to defuse political agendas concerning the granting of land. Thus the legitimacy of Aboriginal claims was defined as resting on 'traditional' cultural connections, rather than on contemporary culture. Any impetus given to archaeology by this Act was not, as Ucko (1983) argues, due to archaeological support of land claims, and thus Aboriginal acknowledgement of archaeology's value, but rather because archaeological research could be incorporated and used in public debates to deal with social problems.

The observation made by Ucko, that archaeological research into the Indigenous past has worked to support Indigenous cultural revival, provided Indigenous people with a history, or challenged prejudice and racist misconceptions and thus encouraged public support for Indigenous self-determination, has been echoed time and again in the American and Australian literature, and is often pointed to as a justification for research (e.g. Mulvaney 1971a, 1981c; Creamer 1975;

Golson 1975; Wright 1986; Allen 1987; Ubelaker and Grant 1989; Goldstein and Kintigh 1990; Davidson 1991b; Meighan 1996). However, what is said about the past is not always as important as who is saying it or how it is said. Take, for instance, the following statement addressing the importance of Australian archaeology to public awareness of Aboriginal issues:

> Archaeologists in Australia have a very strong case in support of their work. What we are doing is of world importance, but it is of particular importance to Aborigines, because it is establishing their long antiquity in and possession of the Australian continent. It reinforces their claim to land, increases their stature and identity as a people, and will ultimately establish their place in the brotherhood of man. The point that must be strongly made is that our work can only be to the ultimate advantage of the Aborigines themselves.
>
> (Moore 1975: 9)

He is correct, archaeological research into Aboriginal origins, particularly at Lake Mungo, has strengthened Aboriginal demands for cultural respect by white Australia. However, in arguing for the justification of research because of the benefits it offers Aboriginal people, Moore manages all at once to 'legitimate' Aboriginal cultural claims; appropriate Aboriginal history as part of the 'brotherhood of man'; assert archaeological rights of access to the data by alluding to the universal significance (and thus scientific validity) of research; and, overall, to invoke a sense of archaeological pastoral care. By locating the ability to construct 'authentic' knowledge within a professional expert population and not with Indigenous (non-technical) experts, the state legitimates a new form of power over Indigenous people, and new forms of Indigenous disempowerment.

Consequences for the discipline of archaeology as a technology of government

The use of archaeological discourse and knowledge as a technology of government has consequences for the definition of, and relations between, Indigenous interests and the institutions that govern claims to land and other resources. It also has consequences for the development of knowledge and debate within the discipline. One of these consequences is the degree to which processual theory is maintained as the 'natural', unquestioned, underpinning philosophy of the discipline, and another is the degree to which attempts are made to de-politicize debates within the discipline. For instance, initial reaction in the 1970s and 1980s to Indigenous demands for the reburial of skeletal material were often met (although not uniformly) with a discourse that argued for the scientific right of access to data and warned against the political use of the past (see for example, Buikstra 1981; Meighan 1984; Duncan 1984a, 1984b; Stannard 1988; and for an overview on this Ubelaker and Grant 1989). The dominant archaeological response during the 1970s and much of the 1980s to Indigenous criticisms, reburial, demands for consultation and so forth, is perhaps best summarized by the following extract from an academic overview of Aboriginal and archaeological relations during the 1970s and 1980s:

> One value of extracting the information from the cultural materials of the past is specifically to guard against such misuses [i.e. political uses] in their symbolic guise ... the durability of objects from the past give them independence from the humans who make and use them and thus their objectivity stands against human subjectivity. It seems to me that here is one direction and purpose of archaeology in a university: in keeping with the general principles of scholarship which demand the freedom to pursue knowledge and make scientific inquiry without undue political restraint, academic archaeologists have the ability to protect us from the political misuse of the past. While we all recognize that no research is done in a cultural vacuum, and that all researchers are culturally biased to some degree, the relative objectivity of academic research is always open to scrutiny.
>
> (Allen 1987: 6)

This position, clearly underpinned by positivism, empiricism and processualism, also stresses the morality of the processual claim that it is the scholarship, rational persuasiveness, logic and objectivity of archaeologists' interpretations and arguments, rather than their social or political position, that ensures the validity of their interpretations. This is married with archaeological stewardship that represents the discipline as the final and authentic arbitrator of the past due to claims to 'scholarship' and rational 'objectivity'. Power/knowledge is maintained by the claims to objectivity and the ability to 'protect us' from the political misuse of the past. Subsequently, not only is material culture protected both from destruction and inauthentic interpretation, but academic archaeologists also protect 'us' (presumably the discipline, the public or more generally perhaps, non-Indigenous Americans and Australians) from the political 'misuse' of the past. Thus archaeology, as perceived by Allen, has a role in governing the past and the extent to which it is politicized. This role can only be maintained if archaeological research continues to adhere to scientific principles and demand scientific rigour. Any characterization of Indigenous people as 'external' to issues surrounding the interpretation of the past is a claim to maintain the position of the discipline in making authoritative and authentic pronouncements on the past by excluding Indigenous interests.

The processes of CRM are where archaeologists explicitly encountered Indigenous 'political misuse of the past', and where archaeologists had to deal directly with competing claims to the 'resource'. Rather than engage directly with politicized issues, however, the archaeological CRM literature of the 1970s and 1980s tended to stress the need for technical expertise in maintaining, caring for, preserving and interpreting Indigenous culture. Political issues were defused not only for governments, but also for and by the discipline, in reducing 'heritage' issues to technical issues of conservation, salvage and recording. The unproblem-atized acceptance of processual theory demonstrates the success of the discursive mobilization of positivist claims in the power/knowledge strategy of the discipline. The development of CRM was not accompanied by rigorous academic debate on the philosophy it should embody. These debates were not required as the power/knowledge authority provided by processual theory and archaeological claims to stewardship were transposed into, and were embedded and institu-tionalized within CRM policy, practice and legislation.

The consequence of institutionalization has meant that the development of CRM not only facilitated the mobilization of archaeology as a technology of government, but also institutionalized it in heritage bureaucracies and law. Institutionalization within CRM policy and practice reinforces the 'naturalization' of processual theory within the discipline generally. Any questioning of processual theory jeopardizes the power/knowledge strategies of the discipline and the role archaeology assumes within CRM.

More recently, some archaeologists (e.g. Lewis and Rose 1985; Bowdler 1988, 1992; Zimmerman 1989a, 2000a, 2000b; Pardoe 1990, 1991, 1992; Ferguson 1996; McGuire 1998) have encouraged an acceptance of the political and cultural concerns of Indigenous people. In both America and Australia, policies of community consultation have been implemented (Ferguson 1984; Murray 1986; Jonas 1991; Carter 1997; Field et al. 2000). In Australia a code of ethics was adopted in 1991 that recognized the custodianship of Aboriginal people over Indigenous material culture, and which made consultation with communities prior to and during research compulsory. The act of consultation is often viewed within the discipline as evidence that it is highly politicized. However, it is the practice of consultation that gives archaeology, in its own eyes, political credibility (Lahn 1996). Very little discussion has, so far, occurred in the literature about the implications of consultation for *power/knowledge* relations. However, what the emerging literature does illustrate is how consultation that does more than just 'tell people' about research, and which enters into negotiation, will mean that research directions are reconsidered and altered in the light of Indigenous knowledge and concerns (K. Mulvaney 1993; Davidson *et al.* 1995; Swidler *et al.* 1997; Anyon *et al.* 2000; Derry and Malloy 2003).

However, archaeological consultation often does not necessarily entail 'negotiation' (Deloria 1992a), and very little work has actually dealt with the problematics of how to incorporate non-scientific knowledge systems into research. Although NAGPRA has facilitated recent debate within the US about the relationship between oral traditions or oral histories and archaeology, this debate is still firmly framed with an insistence that oral traditions must be 'tested' or at some level verified by archaeological or other scientific knowledge (see Anyon et al. 1997; Echo-Hawk 1997, 2000; Mason 2000; Whiteley 2002). While I am by no means suggesting that archaeologists must uncritically accept any or all orally transmitted knowledge as legitimate, what does emerge from this debate is a hesitation in the acceptance that a knowledge system may exist as externally legitimate to that of archaeological knowledge and theory. If archaeologists are to work towards accepting and incorporating Indigenous knowledge into the discipline, in a way that is more than simply appropriation or verification, then the positivism and rationality of processual theory must be successfully challenged. Any assessment of the legitimacy of Indigenous knowledge using current processual theory will result in the appropriation of that knowledge through the established power/knowledge strategies of the discipline. If appropriation is to be avoided, the political desires of archaeologists to incorporate non-positivistic Indigenous knowledge will have to be acknowledged. If the positivism of the discipline is successfully questioned, the discipline runs the risk of reducing or compromising the authority of archaeological knowledge as a technology of government. If archaeology becomes less of an 'objective' science through incorporating the non-scientific values it has guarded against since the 1960s, it loses its usefulness in arbitrating on the disposition of material culture. In short, its position of technical expertise within CRM is jeopardized because its ability to reduce political issues to technical problems would become impaired.

Conclusion

The discourses which encapsulate archaeological claims to 'stewardship' of the past, the scientific credentials established by processual theory, and the conceptual links between 'identity' and material culture that have become an intrinsic part of the discipline's conceptual apparatus, have all facilitated the development of archaeology as a technology of government relevant to social 'problems' in late liberalism. Through CRM the discipline plays a role in governing and regulating social and political problems that intersect with or centre on heritage issues. Archaeology governs the meanings and claims made about the past, which in turn help to regulate Indigenous identity and political interests. While establishing that archaeology in America and Australia has the attributes to participate in strategies of governance, and that these attributes have antecedents in the wider Anglophone discipline, several issues remain to be explored.

First, while this chapter has identified the philosophical and ideological underpinnings that made it possible for archaeology to enter into strategies of governance, the mechanism of how these are translated into, or articulated within CRM is yet to be identified. The nexus between archaeological ideology, discourse and knowledge on the one hand, and CRM policy and practice on the other, needs to be identified so as to offer a more complete picture of the relative position archaeology occupies within negotiations and relations between governments and Indigenous interests. The identification of this nexus will also illustrate how this relationship is negotiated within CRM on a day-to-day level.

Indigenous resistance to archaeological expertise has also raised further issues, including how resistance is negotiated between governments, Indigenous peoples and archaeologists, and what consequences it has for the relationships between these three groups. While the issue of resistance will be discussed and documented in more depth in later chapters, the point around which Indigenous interests, governments and archaeologists negotiate power/knowledge within CRM needs to be identified so that the impact of these negotiations can be understood.

These negotiations are often played out within CRM during assessments of the 'significance' of cultural resources, as it is the 'significance' of the resource that, according to CRM policy, will determine its management and thus its meaning. The concept of significance, as the next chapter will demonstrate, also incorporates archaeological discourse, ideology and knowledge into these negotiations and into the day-to-day practices of CRM.

6

SIGNIFICANCE CONCEPTS AND THE EMBEDDING OF PROCESSUAL DISCOURSE IN CULTURAL RESOURCE MANAGEMENT

This chapter examines the implications of the theoretical issues developed in the preceding three chapters, and illustrates how CRM and the discourse of archaeological theory intersect. It also provides an example of how the disciplinary attributes that facilitate the mobilization of archaeology as a technology of government are articulated within CRM. The chapter deals explicitly with the 1970s and 1980s literature concerned with the definition and development of the concept of archaeological 'significance', a term that had, and continues to hold, a central role in Australian and American CRM practice and policy. It is argued that ideas about archaeological 'significance' developed in these decades are underpinned by processual theory, and that it was the discourse of archaeological significance that explicitly facilitated the development of archaeology as a technology of government within CRM during this time.

As Purvis and Hunt (1993) argue, all discourse may have an ideological content. In the case of the discourse of archaeological significance, its ideological content revolves around the value of 'science' and the power and authority it conveys. The political consequences of this ideological content are to render conflicts over access to and the interpretation of material culture as technical issues of management. This has implications in public policy responses to conflicts over managing material culture. The discourse of significance, underpinned by archaeological science, plays a crucial role in the cultural resource or heritage legislation (discussed in Chapter 7), and in the management practices and processes of state agencies. The concept of significance dominates the practice of archaeology in state agencies, and the practices of the network of consultants who help administer heritage legislation. The assessment of the significance of material culture is held to be the point from which all management decisions and practices should, ideally, derive (ICOMOS 1964). The ability of the archaeological discourse of significance to render conflicts as technical management issues, and its central role in archaeological and CRM practice, are key to archaeology's usefulness in the governance of material culture.

The significance assessment process is where negotiations over the meanings of the past are carried out, because the value of the 'resource' under assessment will reflect and influence its meaning. It is also where power relations and the positioning of interests in management decisions are played out. The privileging of certain 'significances' or values in the assessment of a resource will, in turn, privilege those who associate with or claim those values as their own.

While it is explicitly acknowledged in CRM that material culture may have different values (or different significance) for different groups in society, it is argued below that the *archaeological* significance of Indigenous heritage has been given a privileged role in the governance of the meanings given to, and the management of, Indigenous heritage. As significance assessments have a pivotal role in CRM, archaeological discourse, and the theoretical and ideological assumptions embedded in archaeological significance criteria, become institutionalized within public policy and bureaucratic practices of heritage management.

Indigenous people, and other interest groups such as those of developers, tourist operators, mining and forestry, have, on occasion, successfully contested the archaeological significance given to a particular site or place. However, this contestation is often played out in the significance assessment process defined below. The positioning of the archaeological discourse of significance in this process ensures that any negotiation and debate is undertaken within parameters set by archaeological theoretical discourse – and thus, archaeological governance of Indigenous heritage is operationalized.

Significance assessments in CRM

The assessment of the 'significance' of an artefact, site or place, is internationally held to be the most fundamental and important step in the management of heritage (see Schiffer and Gumerman 1977; Pearson and Sullivan 1995; King 2000). This means that what is significant about a place (site, place, monument and etc.) should determine how it is managed and protected. Ideally, no decision made about the use of a site or place by any heritage manager or agency should conflict with or alter the values attributed to that site or place. This is a fundamental philosophy of CRM that was established internationally by the *Venice Charter* (ICOMOS 1964), and reinforced in Australia by the *Burra Charter* (ICOMOS 1979), and underlies the NHPA Section 106 process in the US (King 2000). The various values attributed to material culture both by archaeologists and various interests, including Indigenous interests, are assessed by managers and archaeologists, and other 'professionals' as part of the management process, and are described in formal assessments of the resource's 'significance'.

Overall the process of CRM may be summarized into various 'stages', which in order comprise: recording and documentation; significance assessment; the development of management policies and actions; the implementation of these policies and actions; and the monitoring and re-evaluation of policies and practices (see Pearson and Sullivan 1995: 8–9; King 1998). Experts inevitably complete the first stage. In the case of Australian Indigenous sites generally and American Indian sites on public lands, it is almost always archaeologists who undertake this work for either a state authority or as consultants. The second stage is completed by the various groups identified by government agencies (often on the advice of archaeologists) as having a stake in the management of the site or place, and is overseen and co-ordinated by either consultant archaeologists or archaeologists within the relevant heritage authority. The final stages are conducted or overseen by archaeologists and/or other heritage experts again employed within the relevant heritage authority or as consultants.

As the first stage in this process, the recording and documentation of sites and places is important in defining and classifying the site or place to be assessed. This stage works to set not only the physical boundaries of the site or place for management, but also the conceptual boundaries. The way a site is recorded, its definition and classification as a particular *type* of site, the identification of physical boundaries and so forth will influence the meanings given to the site and subsequently the assessment of its significance. For instance, in defining a site as an 'occupation' site particular values and expectations are formulated – not only that the site unquestionably *is* an occupation site, but that certain types of data of particular value and meaning will inherently occur within this site. As Byrne (1993: 211–12) has argued, the classifications used by archaeologists to define material culture in CRM help constrain the way material culture is perceived, and constitute and constrain the arena of debate over the potential range of meanings and values that might be attributed to material culture. For example, in defining a site as an occupation site in the first stage of the CRM process, little conceptual space is allowed for non-experts to contest the meaning of the site as an 'occupation' site or not. This then has implications for the significance assessment as the assessment will be made on the site's classification as an 'occupation' site, this assessment then determines the management of the site, which must then work to reinforce the site's significance, and thus its range of potential meanings. Subsequently, the boundaries of any debate about the significance of the site, its management and so forth, will have been constrained by the 'objective' classification of a site by an 'expert'.

Material culture has a physical existence, and its social construction as 'archaeological sites', 'archaeological data' or as part of the 'archaeological record' has direct political consequences. The positivism and empiricism of processual theory often assume that objects from the past are inherently 'archaeological' in that they are 'data' or part of an objective 'archaeological record'. The positivist epistemology of processualism conflates the signifier with the signified, and in doing so archaeologists represent, with an authority conferred on them by their professional status, a view that the objects *are* the label rather than described by the label.

Subsequently, 'archaeological' descriptors take on force and authority as representing the 'reality' or substance of material culture. In the recording and classifying processes of CRM, 'material culture', in being labelled 'archaeological', takes on an identity as 'archaeological data'. This reinforces the claims of archaeologists to material culture, and reinforces the authority of 'archaeological' meanings attributed to the past. Moreover, any debates about the meaning that a site or place, and the past it represents, may have to the present are bounded and constrained by this assessment process. Thus, wider debates about the meaning of the past to Indigenous communities are often reduced to debates about 'ownership' or control over individual sites and places (Smith and van der Meer 2001).

The development of an American processual discourse on significance

The concept of significance is one that has been important in archaeological research. As Schiffer and House (1977a) point out, archaeologists have chosen sites for research based on the significance of the sites to their research topic. It was incorporated from research archaeology into management when it became necessary to choose which sites should be preserved and conserved, and which allowed to be destroyed (Fowler 1982; Butler 1987). During the 1970s processual archaeologists engaged in extensive debates in the pages of *American Antiquity* and other influential publications, about the criteria that should be used to determine which aspects of the cultural resource should be preserved (Fowler 1982). Much of this debate, as Trigger (1986a: 203) points out, drew on those dealing with the nature of science and the role of archaeology in US society. In a sense, these debates played out tensions between the emerging processual theory and its rise to become the mainstream position in archaeology, and the discipline's assertion of its position as the 'steward' of 'mankind's heritage'.

The development of a discourse on significance is intermingled with that of 'stewardship' discussed in Chapter 5. This latter discourse, that emphasized the need to educate the public about the past for the 'collective good' (McGimsey and Davis 1977: 18), staked out the intellectual authority of archaeology in CRM and thus facilitated archaeological access to its database. Within this discourse public values or special interests are derided, and replaced with universalistic claims through 'archaeology' – with no sense of irony that there are no such things as archaeological 'objects' or 'data', but rather the discourse and special pleadings of archaeologists. The discourse of 'significance' continued this process by ensuring that the conceptualization and interpretation of material culture was defined by archaeological vocabulary, concepts and values. Conceptual access to the 'data' was maintained by the incorporation of 'archaeological' concepts of value – in particular that material culture was valuable as data – into formal significance assessment processes as part of CRM policy and practice.

Also interlinked with the development of the discourse of significance was the idea of a 'conservation ethic'. As argued in Chapter 5 the desirability of maintaining access to the resource through claims to stewardship highlighted an apparent contradiction between the destructive nature of archaeological research and philosophies of 'preservation'.

The apparent contradiction was successfully obscured in US archaeological debates during the 1970s over what Fowler (1982) characterizes as 'salvage vs. conservation'. Debate hinged on whether sites should, in the face of development and other destructive processes, simply be excavated for all the data they contained, that is 'salvaged', or whether sites should be chosen for preservation and thus set aside for future research. At issue here was the need, on the one hand, to preserve sites for future reference and research, which would include destructive research, while, on the other hand, to foster ideas about archaeological 'conservation' and stewardship. Concerns that archaeologists were seen by developers and governments as conducting excavation only for monetary gain were canvassed in the literature, and used to emphasize the need for scientific objectivity and the professionalism of archaeologists (e.g. King 1979; Raab *et al.* 1980).

These concerns over criticisms that archaeologists were primarily concerned about monetary issues also threatened archaeological claims to stewardship, and aspirations to a 'conservation ethic', by threatening the image of the 'purity' and 'selflessness' of scientific aims. As McGimsey and Davis (1977: 29f) argued, conservation was important as it ensured the existence of future data, but also provided archaeology with a role in the long-term management of sites by offering preservation as an alternative to simple salvage. Following from this debate, the question of how to choose sites for conservation and preservation became an important issue. One of the important criteria stressed early in debate was the value of sites for research (Fowler 1982). Any contradictions between 'preservation' and destructive research became abstracted in debates about defining criteria for assessing the future research value of sites.

Research values

One of the most active debates in the US during the 1970s was the use of 'research designs' in guiding archaeological research and archaeological work in CRM (Fowler 1982). Another major concern of the US archaeological literature in the 1970s, which focused debate about the desirability of the use of research designs in CRM, was the threat of CRM to archaeology's new status as a science (Fowler 1982). King argued that the New Archaeology's call for deductive research, which he saw as deriving out of its emphasis on the explicit generation of research questions from theory, was at odds with the way CRM was being practised in the 1960s and 1970s (1971, 1977). He argued that CRM agencies assumed archaeology was an inductive science that resulted in an emphasis on the salvage of information as an end in itself (1977). He suggested that authorities should reorganize to include academic advisors, and to develop long range and large-scale deductive research programmes (1971: 260–1). These research programmes would include surveys to develop site inventories, which would also help with the identification of a sample of sites to be preserved for research, and allow the development of hypotheses and research questions that would regulate archaeological work and research within CRM (1971, 1977). As King argued, the incorporation of deductive research into CRM would make salvage 'relevant' to scientific archaeology (1977: 92).

Raab *et al.* (1980: 540–1) also warned that archaeological work within CRM was becoming too 'client-oriented' and so threatened the status of archaeology as a science. That is, survey work which determined the existence and value of sites and the impacts of development, as well as making recommendations for their management, was becoming too technical: 'CO [client-oriented] studies can be distinguished by their emphasis on providing a *technical* as opposed to a *research* service' (Raab et al. 1980: 540, emphasis in original). They further argued that this approach impaired 'scientific performance' by devaluing research, calling on archaeologists to make technical evaluations when the body of data and information about the archaeological record was too little known and understood, and compromised archaeological professionalism by undermining archaeological control over practice and procedure (1980: 541–2). The development of the Society of Professional Archaeologists (SOPA) in 1979 was viewed as helping to alleviate the latter problem of control over the professional performance of archaeologists by promulgating a 'Code of Ethics and Standards of Research Performance' (1980: 542; Davis 1982; McGimsey and Davis 1984: 122). However, this organization could not 'ensure that science is practised', a problem Raab *et al.* saw as stemming from archaeologists' and management agencies' lack of 'commitment to a research ethic' (1980: 542). They saw CRM as weakening archaeological controls on research due to the ambiguity of archaeological significance criteria, lack of publication of scientific data, and the failure of CRM to ensure peer reviews of the archaeological work undertaken within it. The solutions they offered to these problems were: to ensure archaeologists were trained as 'researchers'; to lobby for the employment of government archaeologists; to develop a stronger understanding of professionalism, and expand this concept to include contract archaeologists; to develop codes of ethics to control conduct; and to ensure the public and Indigenous Americans benefited from archaeological research by conveying to them the results of research (1980: 547–9). They particularly emphasized the need for ethical debate and the development of a code of conduct to ensure that archaeology maintained its scientific standards.

They also argued that the archaeological response to developmental pressures prior to the revision of US legislation and policy in the 1970s was inevitably salvage, and that 'salvage' had been embedded in the discipline as the legitimate archaeological response to pressure on the resource (see also chapter 7). Archaeologists had to break out of this conceptual constraint as it further reduced archaeology to a technical response (1980: 545–6). Instead they advocated that archaeology pay more attention to other interests:

> Archaeology in the public domain serves many clients at once: the archaeological profession, science, public and private agencies, taxpayers, and segments of the public with cultural ties to archaeological resources.
>
> (Raab *et al.* 1980: 547)

The way these interests would be 'served' was through an adherence to research values, which would ensure that knowledge about the past was obtained and made available to the public. This point was made repeatedly in the literature, and particular stress was often placed on the ethics of providing 'the public' with research results to ensure public support (e.g. McGimsey 1972; Schiffer and Gumerman 1977; King 1979, 1983; Knudson 1982). This pastoral sense of service was also linked with the concept of 'stewardship' identified in Chapter 5 as underpinning the authority of archaeology in CRM. In this instance the discourse is specifically ensuring that archaeological 'research' is privileged, and that archaeological scientific concerns are not compromised.

Others advocating the use of research values stressed that their use would lead to the preservation of sites that were relevant to research, and thus a more meaningful database would be preserved than if sites were preserved for ad hoc and unspecified reasons (King 1971, 1977; Gumerman 1977; Goodyear *et al.* 1978; Raab and Klinger 1977, 1979; Schiffer and Gumerman 1977; Lynott 1980). Further, the use of research designs would, it was argued, provide frameworks for the assessment of scientific or research significance (Raab and Klinger 1977).

In stressing research and its regulation in archaeological professional and ethical debates, US archaeologists in the 1970s were ensuring that the identity of archaeology as a 'science' was maintained within CRM. The 'technical' process identified by Raab *et al.* (1980) works to de-politicize heritage issues. However, this 'technologizing' of archaeology was not one that could, or can be reversed, by the solutions offered by Raab et al. (1980). Rather, the 'technologizing' of archaeology in CRM has actually helped to maintain archaeology's identity as a 'science' by stressing archaeological objectivity through technical responses, and thus its suitability in regulating conflicts over material culture. In addition, the arguments advocated and supported by Raab *et al.* also helped to reinforce the professional and ethical fibre of the discipline, which reinforces the 'technologizing' of archaeology as the most 'appropriate' and 'relevant' 'professional' body to mitigate conflicting interests over heritage.

Indeed, Schiffer (1979) has argued that CRM has ensured that archaeology has maintained scientific research, facilitating the incorporation of research values into significance criteria. In reviewing the results of a questionnaire sent to a sample of 500 US archaeologists, he notes that CRM has forced archaeologists to plan and design their research in advance; it has forced archaeologists to more frequently analyse their excavated material and write up their results; and it has made large-scale surveys possible and economically feasible (1979: 8–9). He also stated that CRM had increased archaeological concerns about the social and public significance of their work and had lead to 'many more attempts at making the findings of archaeology relevant to modern society' (1979: 10). These achievements derive from processual positivistic concepts of science, which include an emphasis on maintaining methodically technical standards in research and writing, and in ensuring the results are disseminated both within and outside the discipline (see Gibbon 1989: 10f).

Schiffer and House (1977b) argued that the scientific significance of cultural resources should rest on their ability to provide data on substantive theoretical issues and theory. These arguments were echoed ten years later by Butler, who argued that scientific significance should rest on 'the theoretical and substantive knowledge of the discipline' (1987: 820). Although what constitutes theoretical and substantive knowledge has never been clearly defined in the discipline, this discourse, nonetheless, delineates the importance of scientific research and material culture's role in that research. The use of research designs in directing assessments of research significance works to help regulate archaeological values and ideology. Goodyear *et al.* (1978: 168) advocated the use of research designs including their use in the assessment of a site's research values. They argued that research designs would 'make' archaeologists consider the archaeological significance of sites, 'force' archaeologists to think about the 'meaningfulness of archaeology to a wider range of audiences', and consider whether or not they were maintaining 'public support' for projects (1978: 168). Research designs were being advocated as more than simply a way of directing research. Within CRM, they were also advocated as a way of maintaining values and ethics, regulating archaeological professionalism and drawing archaeological attention to certain issues – such as ensuring public approval. Research designs became a 'code of conduct', ensuring the appropriateness of archaeological association with material culture and its disposition.

Schaafsma (1989: 40) has speculated that the American emphasis on research designs, and the stress on developing hypotheses before data is gathered, may have been an archaeological response to fears of being labelled 'treasure hunters'. The emphasis on scientific credibility and professionalism in debates about research value reinforces, as Tainter and Lucus (1983: 711) point out, popular concepts of science held in many Western countries. The discourse on 'research designs' was part of processual power/knowledge strategies that reinforced archaeological claims to scientific credentials and, subsequently, privileged archaeological access to data. This discourse also facilitated access to data in relation to American Indian protest and attempts to deny archaeologists access to sites. As Winter (1980: 124) notes, the significance criteria used in the 1970s to assess sites on the US National Register reflected scientific values which tended to result in the exclusion of American Indian values. In the American literature, as in the Australian (see Chapter 9), McGuire (1992) identifies that it is often the unquestioned value and authority of scientific research and knowledge that archaeologists cite as the key element in defence of their access to Indigenous sites and places. In Britain too, the ideological position that archaeology is a 'scholarly', 'intellectual' discipline is often stressed in arguments about archaeological rights of access versus those of an often ill-defined, monolithic and ignorant public (see Fowler 1981, 1986). For instance, Fowler notes (1981: 68) 'a sense of the past may require an intellectually sophisticated frame of mind'. As Tilley (1989b) and Hill (1992: 810) argue the notion of archaeological 'science' and 'objectivity' are self-legitimating political concepts that invalidate alternative ways of viewing the past.

Representativeness

The use of research designs in assessing significance came under criticism for too 'narrowly' defining research value. US government archaeologists argued that it could not be concluded that a site that did not fit a current research problem was lacking in significance, either to archaeology or to other interested peoples (Sharrock and Grayson 1979; Barnes *et al.* 1980). According to this criticism, research value, while supported by government archaeologists, was not, in itself, sufficient for dealing with or incorporating 'other' values. It did not provide a solution to conflict over access to material culture and its interpretation. Others felt that research designs developed their own bias, and that it was only certain research problems that would be considered to be important enough in assessing sites (Dixon 1977; Dunnell 1984: 71).

Advocates of 'research designs' agreed that assessing a site's significance on its potential to answer current theoretical and research questions would not allow for the preservation of sites that may have the potential to answer future research questions (Raab and Klinger 1979). However, to overcome the complex and fluid nature of research significance the notion of 'representativeness' was advocated (most notably by Lipe 1974, 1977; Dixon 1977; Glassow 1977; Raab and Klinger 1979).

Lipe (1974, 1977) and Glassow (1977) argued that a typology representing the 'main varieties' of site types needed to be established so that sites of different varieties could be preserved for future research. As well, sites from different environmental contexts, sites representing different ethnic groups, with varying densities and ranges of artefacts, and sites with varying stratigraphical and spatial properties, and so forth, should also be saved as 'representative samples' (Lipe 1974; Glassow 1977; Hickman 1977). Klinger and Raab (1980) emphasized the need for archaeologists to make these assessments as they could provide meaning to, and ensure the consistency of, assessments. The idea of representativeness also incorporates a sense that its application will ensure that not only sites of significance and potential significance to archaeologists, but also sites of significance to other groups and disciplines as well will be saved (see Dixon 1977).

It was at this point in the American debate, that the concept of representativeness was incorporated into the Australian literature (Bowdler 1981, 1984). Although the debate on 'research designs' has not been as significant in the Australian literature, the associated idea that 'research value' should be a measure of archaeological significance has been important in influencing the development of significance criteria in Australia (Flood 1993).

Australian significance discourse

Incorporation of US concepts

The developing Australian discipline of archaeology explicitly incorporated the American debate on significance in preference to other approaches. This is because the American literature had utility in terms of the problems occurring in Australia.

In Australia, like the US, archaeologists faced a similar degree of scrutiny from community interests that included Indigenous critics and local communities concerned with development. Although the UK literature, like the US, discussed the need to deal with increasing developmental pressure (e.g. Lynch 1972; Cormack 1978; Groube 1978; Lowenthal 1979; Hareven and Langenback 1981; Groube and Bowden 1982; Cleere 1984a; Wainwright 1984) and discussed the need to increase public recognition of expertise (e.g. Fowler 1977, 1981; Cleere 1984a, 1986, 1988), the issue of the contestation of the past was less marked in the British than in the American literature.

The US discourse, and its incorporation into CRM, had utility for Australian archaeologists in terms of providing a rationale for a 'conservation ethic' to deal with developmental pressures, and in providing scientific authority through its scientistic and technical discourse. The authority of science, together with the idea that 'representativeness' could incorporate 'other' values, provided both a defence and a partial solution to Indigenous criticisms. The US processual discourse on significance structured its object of study as primarily 'archaeological' and thus accessible, both physically and conceptually, to archaeologists. This construction ensured the utility of the American processual discourse in CRM, especially in the face of conflicts over heritage issues. The mechanisms for the adoption of this discourse in Australia included its incorporation into ICOMOS conventions (in particular ICOMOS 1979, 1990, 1999) which remain central in influencing CRM policy and practice; visits by Australian archaeologists to the US to study American policy and practice (Sullivan 1973); and the explicit use of American CRM literature to inform Australian policy (see Sullivan 1973; Buchan 1979). The teaching of processual theory in Australian universities and its incorporation into research practices (Huchet 1991; Moser 1995b) also facilitated the incorporation of the American discourse.

Professional standards and the need for 'rational' assessments

One of the earliest Australian published systematic considerations of how archaeological significance should be measured was developed by Coutts et al. (1976). This study noted that the research potential or scientific value of a site was hard to quantify and measure, although various attributes such as a site's content, type and so forth were proposed as useful measures of significance. This system was only cautiously recommended later by one of its authors who was concerned to point out that it 'needs to be thoroughly *tested* before it can be accepted' (Coutts 1979: 42, emphasis added). The need to test its suitability and, as is implied by Coutts (1979), its objectivity, reveals an interesting assumption about the nature of archaeological values held by Coutts *et al.* (1976). They assume that values could be empirically quantified and measured or tested against a constant. This processual assumption about the inherent nature of value has led, as it will be argued later in the chapter, to some internal contradictions in the later development of archaeological significance concepts. However, the failure to adequately theorize concepts of value and distinguish them from physical attributes underlies the development of the following discussions on significance. The assumption that archaeological values are inherent worked to reinforce archaeological power/knowledge claims about the value and meaning of Aboriginal heritage.

Other early Australian discussions of significance and CRM occurred at ANZAAS conferences in the late 1970s and early 1980s (Sullivan 1984b). Some of these discussions were published in the landmark McKinlay and Jones (1979) volume and others as individual papers (Bickford 1981; Bowdler 1981; Hammond 1981). Bowdler's papers on this issue (1981, 1983, 1984) are the most widely cited, and perhaps the most influential in setting the intellectual framework of the significance concept still used in Australia today. She explicitly outlines the American significance criteria and use of research designs, and argues for their usefulness in 'raising the [research] standard of contract archaeology', and ensuring site management was 'carried out according to the most vigorous scientific principles' (1981: 131).

The proceedings of the 1981 Australian Archaeological Association symposium on significance and survey methodology were published a few years later (Sullivan and Bowdler 1984). This publication is an important record of the debate on the topic of significance, and the involvement of both influential academics (e.g. Bowdler) and senior government-employed archaeological managers. For example, Sullivan (Head, Aboriginal Relics Section NSW NPWS), Pearson (NSW NPWS), Coutts (Head, VAS), and Flood (AHC) were all archaeologists and high-ranking public servants in State and Federal heritage authorities and their papers reflect policy development as well as academic debate.

The need for detailed and considered significance criteria had become important in the late 1970s as planning legislation enacted in NSW and Victoria at this time (see Chapter 7) had significantly increased the amount of survey work requiring archaeological input (S. Sullivan 1983; Bowdler 1984). Environmental impact assessments (EIAs), in which archaeologists were required to justify recommendations to State authorities about the management of sites, required the development of rigorous and uniform criteria (M. Sullivan 1983; Flood 1987). Marjorie Sullivan (at that time an archaeologist employed by the NSW NPWS) also called for consideration of significance issues as, she argued, the recommendations about sites made by consultant archaeologists during EIA work very often became the decision of the determining authority. This meant that a 'high level of professionalism amongst the advisors [consultants]' was needed, and this included 'rational' significance assessments (M. Sullivan 1983: 361, 360).

In practical terms, discussions about the need for professional standards manifested themselves in the formation of the Australian Association of Consulting Archaeologists (AACA) in 1979. This self-styled professional organization (as with SOPA) has worked to ensure the 'professionalization' of consultants, standardized work practices, including the significance assessment process, and has developed a code of ethics (see Haglund 1984). Control of conduct is rigorous, at least on paper. The AACA also lobbies government departments, and in policing conduct has facilitated the recognition of archaeological expertise both in and out of state institutions, and has subsequently facilitated the technologizing of the discipline.

Australian significance concepts – underlying assumptions

Bowdler, in leading the discussion on significance, argued that standardized and systematic significance criteria were necessary. She considered it important that archaeologists, faced with assessing sites that they may have no research interest in, be supplied with criteria that would allow for informed and objective assessments (1981). One of the most important points Bowdler (1984) emphasized was that the values attributed to sites and places change. This was a point brought home by the experiences of archaeological managers (Snelson and Sullivan 1982). Bowdler also argued that as archaeological knowledge developed, what was perceived to be archaeologically important would change as new research questions were developed and explored (1984: 7). To preserve only those sites of value to archaeologists in the present would stifle the development of new and important research questions in the future.

Bowdler thus proposed two broad criteria for the measurement of archaeological significance: research significance and representativeness (1981: 129, 1984: 1). The assessment of research significance would be undertaken in relation to 'timely and specific research questions' (Bowdler 1984: 1). Bowdler and Bickford developed a set of questions that should be asked in measuring the research value of a site:

1 Can this site contribute knowledge which no other site can?
2 Can this site contribute knowledge which no other resource … can?
3 Is this knowledge relevant to specific or general questions about human history or behaviour or some other substantive subject?
     (Bowdler 1984: 1–2; also in Bickford and Sullivan 1984: 23–4)

This discourse tends to imply that value or information is something that can be possessed by the site. Bickford (1981, 1985) at least, in contradiction to this assumption, implicitly argues that value is something that is attributed to sites, arguing that sites may be used to challenge or to reinforce the cultural and historical perceptions of people historically associated with particular sites. Although she personally may argue from this position, the discourse constructed by the above questions employs the language used in the wider archaeological community, which reflects the positivist philosophy that perceives meaning and value as inherent in an object.

Research values – setting agendas in CRM

Discussions on research significance were clearly linked to wider archaeological discussions about the value, social role and importance of Australian archaeological research. The general desire to emphasize the maturity, scientific significance and importance of Australian research has been remarked upon in Chapter 5. This phenomenon also found expression in the archaeological discourse on CRM and significance assessments. It did so in two ways: first, through calls to save valuable sites for archaeological research in the future; and second, through attempts to publicly reinforce the social and scientific value of archaeological research. Most notable amongst these was the decision to not dam the Franklin River due, in large part, to the presence of the Kutikina Cave Pleistocene site (see Chapter 9), and public discussion about the world heritage listing of Lake Mungo. In addition, the scientific importance of Australian archaeology was reinforced through the incorporation of 'research significance' as part of the formal policy for assessing the value of sites and places. As published policy statements reveal, 'scientific/ archaeological' significance was an important part of the significance assessment process during the 1970s and 1980s (Buchan 1979; Flood 1979, 1984; Coutts 1982a, 1982c; AHC 1985), and is still maintained today (see Pearson and Sullivan 1995; Colley 2002).

Frankel and Gaughwin (1984: 222) argued that CRM had brought dramatic changes to the 'archaeological community'. In arguments reminiscent of US processual concerns about CRM's effects on the status of science in the discipline, they argue for the desirability of using 'research values' to underpin the CRM process. Further, they argue that universities must be involved in training archaeologists in contract work so that professional standards and values could be maintained as 'it is the "pure" prehistory which both justifies and underpins … the scientific assessment of cultural remains' (Frankel and Gaughwin 1984: 222).

Appeals to 'pure' research, and associated processual values, are reflected in Coutts' (1977: 77) discussion of the desirability of educating the public about the research value of sites in order that they may be saved for future archaeologists. The educational value of sites has been closely linked to their research value, so that it is often archaeologists who, in the CRM assessment process, assess the educational value of sites, or whose knowledge or research values are used in assessing educational significance. As Coutts (1984a: 212) notes 'the motivation for protecting Aboriginal sites is essentially derived from their potential scientific and educational value'. This point is reinforced by Jones (1985: 301) in his discussion of the management of sites in Kakadu: 'Preservation of this resource for potential intensive archaeological attention a century or more ahead must be a prime management goal'. As part of the processual conceptual baggage, 'scientific' education of the public about the past plays an important role in maintaining the scientific value and identity of the discipline.

The educative role of archaeology, and the public attention archaeology has gained because of its role in CRM, has helped to reinforce the identity of the discipline and the value of archaeological research. This educative role is reinforced on a small, but not insignificant scale, in the use of archaeological information to interpret individual sites for the public and tourists. Archaeology through CRM maintains an interpretive and regulatory role over the past by defining Aboriginal political discourse and interests. The assessment process in CRM, however, enables archaeology to make 'legislative' statements about the value of the past and its material culture. In emphasizing the research, and thus scientific, value of material culture, the archaeological discourse's legislative authority as a governmental technology reinforces its interpretive role in negotiations over Aboriginal political interests.

This is not to say, however, that archaeological values are not challenged by other interests, such as those of Aboriginal people and developers, who have a stake in the management of sites. There are also archaeologists and other heritage experts who have argued that Aboriginal values and other cultural or social values are as important or more important than archaeological and other 'scientific' values (e.g. Sullivan 1985, 1993; Johnston 1992; Organ 1994). However, the power/knowledge of archaeological science, the use of archaeological experts to catalogue and define heritage as 'sites', and the recognition of the role and value of that expertise in documents such as the original *Burra Charter* (ICOMOS 1979), work to define the arena (albeit contested) of debate and to privilege scientific values.

The position of scientific values in the significance assessment process not only works to apply legislative authority to negotiations over interests, it also provides legislative authority to archaeological claims about the importance of research. As outlined in Chapter 5, establishing the value of archaeological research to domestic and international audiences has been a significant concern in the Australian discipline. For instance, the scientific importance and international significance of research often explicitly preface accounts of Australian archaeology (e.g. Mulvaney 1961: 58–60; White 1974: 28; Golson 1975: 7; Moore 1975: 9; Jones 1968b: 189, 1990: 290). Murray (1992c) confirms that discussions of Australian archaeology, particularly of Tasmanian archaeology, have often linked the significance of research to European archaeological concepts or made comparisons to European research. He argues that this is part of a process that emphasizes the value of Australian research to the discipline internationally. The institutionalization of 'research value' within State bureaucracies and institutional policies reinforces claims about the 'scientific value' of research and its legislative authority to both the academy and Australian society generally.

The concept of research significance is used in contemporary assessments of the value of Aboriginal sites to archaeologists (see, for example, Rhoads 1992; Dunnett and Feary 1994; Pearson and Sullivan 1995). In recent years, however, there has been a gradual change in the assessment of archaeological research value. Assessments based on the questions advocated by Bowdler and Bickford, and applied by Attenbrow and Negerevich (1984) are not carried out as systematically as Bowdler (1984) advocated. In practice research value is often expressed simply in terms of whether or not a site is disturbed (Byrne and Smith 1987; Smith

1989, 1991a). If *in situ* material is considered to occur in a site, then it is assumed that the site has the potential to answer present or future research questions. If a site can be shown to have relevance to specific research questions, this is taken as enhancing a site's archaeological value. This change in emphasis does not appear to have come about through an active debate over the nature of research values, but rather because specific research questions often have not been clearly defined in many areas of Australia, due to the lack of preceding systematic archaeological work. The lack of regional archaeological research has been commented on as hindering the development of regional or site-specific assessment criteria (Hiscock and Mitchell 1993). Thus, the use of research designs or specific questions or problems has often been found to be too difficult to implement in the Australian CRM context. However, the point is that the ideal is still adhered to and advocated (e.g. Pearson and Sullivan 1995).

Representativeness – 'technologizing' and excluding

Because it was recognized that research questions may change over time, Bowdler considered that it was also important to preserve a representative sample of sites (1981, 1983). This sample would contain both rare sites and sites which were common (Bowdler 1983, 1984; Sullivan 1984a, 1984b). Paralleling the American arguments she suggested that the sample would provide the resources from which new research questions could be developed and explored (Bowdler 1981; see also Coutts and Fullagar 1982; Pearson 1984). Clegg (1984) argued that while rare sites were important, as Bowdler and Bickford's questions quoted above allowed, common sites were also important for research. Representative samples would thus provide a cross-section of potential data.

The importance of representativeness in Australian CRM at this time is illustrated by the Australian Heritage Commission and various southeastern State site authorities, which commissioned studies to help determine useful criteria for defining common and rare types of sites and establishing 'site type profiles' for both Aboriginal and non-Aboriginal sites, including middens, open campsites, quarries etc. (e.g. Brown 1986; Ellender 1990; Rich 1990; du Cros 1989, 1990; Smith 1989, 1991a, 1991b; Smith *et al.* 1990; Hiscock and Mitchell 1993). However, the concept of representativeness did garner some criticism. My own experience (Smith 1989, 1991a), and that of Hiscock and Mitchell (1993), in attempting to define representative criteria for groups of sites, led us to the conclusion that it is difficult, if not impossible, to define representative criteria. Attempts to define criteria have tended to be based on unstructured analyses of a sample of sites, in which site attributes are compared to determine if patterned variation occurs within a practical site type. Attributes may then be identified which can be used to distinguish between 'rare' or 'common' categories of sites in a region or amongst a given type of site. In these analyses, unsurprisingly, it was found that every site was different in some respect. Structuring any analysis through research values was vital if representative types were to be recognizable. The representativeness of particular sites effectively depends on the research questions asked about those sites.

In using the concept of representativeness to incorporate both the changing nature of research values and the non-research values of other interests, the idea that research value is mutable and other interests may have significantly different values to those of archaeologists is effectively obscured. Assessments about the value and significance of sites are reduced to mere technical assessments of representative criteria, and critical scrutiny of the degree of difference between, for instance, Indigenous and archaeological values is deflected. Allen (1988b) makes a similar point, and argues that the identification of specific physical attributes with which to assess the representativeness of sites derives from a 'natural science' approach. The classification of sites based on similar features is one that is used in natural resource management to define ecosystems and other land system categories for management. The application of rigid criteria based on physical attributes leaves little room for community involvement in management decisions. This is because values, which are perceived by government policy makers as 'cultural' or 'social', are treated as intangible. These may be rendered less valid than scientific values that are assumed to have physical expressions. Decisions, as Allen argues, tend to be 'technocratic-managerial' in nature (1988b: 146), which reinforces the exclusion of community involvement.

Governing values

The *Burra Charter* has an important role in underpinning and guiding Australian CRM policy and practice. The version of this Charter that was used in Australia up until its radical rewrite in 1999 reinforced the sense of the tangibility of scientific values. The perception that meaning is inherent in the fabric of a place is embedded in the original version of the *Burra Charter*:

> *Conservation* is based on a respect for the existing *fabric* and should involve the least possible physical intervention. It should not distort the evidence provided by the *fabric*.
> (ICOMOS 1979, Article 3, emphasis in original)[1]

As Marquis-Kyle and Walker (1992: 15) state, one of the principles on which the *Burra Charter* of 1979 is based is that 'the *cultural significance* of a *place* is embodied in its *fabric*' (emphasis in original). Hence, the meanings, the significance of material culture, are perceived to exist in its physical characteristics. The *Burra Charter* also explicitly acknowledges that archaeology, and other areas of expertise, provide the technical skills to care for, record and preserve the information and meanings contained within a site or place's fabric (ICOMOS 1979: Articles 23–5). Both the *Burra Charter* of 1979, and Marquis-Kyle and Walker's (1992) interpretation of it, stress the need to use professionals in the management of material culture. Marquis-Kyle and Walker (1992: 18) define such a person as someone who 'has to act on behalf of the community, and ensure that different views are taken into account'. Thus, not only do experts work to protect a community's heritage, they also have a pastoral role, or in Bauman's (1987) terms, an interpretive role, over 'different views'.

The emphasis on expertise, together with the stress placed on the importance of the fabric (the physical attributes of a site), creates a sense that the 'best', if not the most ethical, way to deal with material culture is through the technical processes of recording and conservation. Further, it is the physicality of material culture that allows it to be 'governed' and regulated, and it is 'experts' who have the technical and intellectual knowledge to protect the fabric of a heritage place and to authenticate its value.

Sullivan (1993) discusses what she terms the cultural imperialism of archaeology and CRM, which rests on its ability to appropriate or override Aboriginal values and concerns. She has suggested that the significance assessment process is important in handing back Aboriginal custodianship (1993: 54). The implication is that by giving priority to Aboriginal values in significance assessments more control by Aboriginal people will be achieved. This sentiment also underlines the AAA 1991 code of ethics that recognizes the rights of Aboriginal people to veto research, and the AACA code of ethics that requires consultation with Aboriginal people on management issues. The point here is that significance assessments are seen, and have been used, to ensure increased Aboriginal involvement in archaeology and CRM. For example, the then AIAS, in a move to encourage archaeological consultation with Aboriginal people, and to increase Aboriginal involvement in CRM, financed the 'sites of significance recording programme' in 1973 (Moser 1995a: 160).

This programme was in part a response, as Moser (1995a: 160) argues, to lobbying by leading archaeologists for government support in recording Aboriginal sites. It was also a response to Aboriginal agitation, which was exemplified in 1974 by the 'Eaglehawk and Crow document', an open letter to the AIAS demanding that the Institute concern itself with contemporary Aboriginal issues (cited in Moser 1995a: 153). The letter stated that the AIAS 'has largely functioned as a fellowship of academics who supported each other to further their careers' and that concerns for Aboriginal people were 'at best, secondary' (Widders *et al.* 1974, cited in Moser 1995a: 153). As part of the AIAS response, a number of State heritage agencies were funded to employ Aboriginal people and archaeologists to survey for sites of traditional and sacred significance (Creamer 1975; Kelly 1975; Moser 1995a).

Kelly, in defending the NSW stage of the programme, and his role as an Aboriginal person in it, noted that he had been accused by Aboriginal people of being an 'Uncle Tom' and warned that:

> If these sites are only recorded for academic values and not protected for the Aboriginal people, then once again the Aboriginal values will be cast aside.

> (Kelly 1980: 80)

The need for such a warning indicates that the status of Aboriginal values in the programme was insecure, despite the politicized efforts of archaeologists and anthropologists, like Ucko and Creamer, who were involved in the programme. The apparent insecurity of Aboriginal values in this programme, despite stated intentions of ensuring greater Aboriginal participation in CRM and archaeology (Creamer 1975, 1980; Ucko 1983; see also Moser 1995a), may have been caused by several factors. First, and most obviously, the programme in defining 'sites of significance to Aborigines' as 'traditional' or 'sacred' implies that other types of sites, such as secular sites (largely not included in the programme), or sites of historical or cultural importance, are not of significance to Aboriginal people. They thus remain 'archaeological sites', that is sites within the domain of archaeologists rather than the Aboriginal domain.

Second, the recording of sites and their registration in site registers, as is the practice in Australia, ultimately constructs sites as 'archaeological' (Byrne 1993). The archaeological recording of sites, or their recording on site forms designed either by archaeologists, or (in the case of the NSW sites of significance programme) for inclusion in a site register managed by archaeologists, redefines the sites as 'archaeological'. It does so, as Sullivan (1993: 56) suggests, by reducing sites to their physical characteristics and thus obscuring other values. Further, Aboriginal values that are defined, as they were in the 1970s and 1980s, by site register classification systems as 'mythological' (as in 'mythological site'), devalue, due to the Eurocentric assumptions embedded in them, non-scientific values as 'primitive'. Further, Aboriginal values are treated as culturally specific and, in comparison to the 'universal' values of archaeological science, relegated to a lower rung on the hierarchy of values.

Third, archaeologists also gain advantages by using significance assessments as a means to increase Aboriginal participation in site management. Ucko, in comments made about a number of AIAS programmes, including the sites of significance programme, illustrates the subtle benefits that can be accrued:

> The Institute will have failed if, over the next year, it does not manage to place Aboriginal Studies in its rightful position within the world context of the study of human societies. We can only achieve this aim, a vital one for the understanding of the peaceful co-existence of different populations and social groups, if we adapt to the changing situation in Australia and if we can convince those in power that research and Aboriginal Indigenous activity are intimately connected, and inextricably bound together.
>
> (Ucko 1974, cited in Moser 1995a: 156)

The binding together of 'Aboriginal Indigenous activity' with 'research' (and, what is more, research of international value) provides a veneer of political credibility and ensures an 'interpretive' role for archaeology. This interpretive role is again reinforced by the legislative and regulatory role of intellectual knowledge in state institutions through the formal significance assessment processes.

As argued in Chapter 5 the technologizing of archaeology through CRM not only regulates the interpretation and value of material culture, and contributes to the interpretation and value placed on the political identities of populations associated with material culture, it also regulates the conduct and discourse of archaeologists themselves. Paradoxically, CRM has been an important site for the rise of feminist awareness in Australian archaeology (see Beck and Head 1990; du Cros and Smith 1993; Smith and du Cros 1994; Smith 1995b). This phenomenon may in part derive from a reaction to a strongly held perception in the Australian discipline that CRM is 'women's work'. This perception is reinforced by an archaeological discourse, identified by Clarke (1993), which links 'management' to nurturing images and housework, while research archaeology invokes a discourse of 'cowboy' masculinity. Despite the activities of self-identified feminist archaeologists, such as Sharon Sullivan, Anne Bickford and Jeannette Hope in CRM, the ability of feminists to alter the positivist discourse of archaeology in CRM has, to date, been limited. As Sullivan (1992) and Hope (1993) point out, discourse or practice which deviates from the 'scientific' to incorporate 'humanistic' concerns, whether increased Aboriginal participation in management or feminist issues, is marginalized within management agencies. These agencies require, as Allen (1988b: 146) points out, 'technocratic-managerial' decisions, which do not easily incorporate the non-technical aspirations of either feminists or Aboriginal people.

Conclusion

Archaeological knowledge and discourse, in defining the nature of material culture, tends to covertly set the boundaries of conflict over the values, and subsequently the meanings, given to material culture. Not only does archaeology have a privileged role in CRM through its constitution in processual science, but, in defining material culture as physical data, it also defines the area of conflict. Conflict over material culture becomes conflict over how *fabric* is preserved and conserved. As Sullivan (1993: 58) argues, in conceiving material culture as purely physical, it is separated from its historical and social values and contexts. Any conflict over interpretation and meaning subsequently becomes obscured within technical conservation issues about physical preservation.

How material culture is assessed for its value or significance has important consequences for both archaeologists and non-archaeologists. The way in which resources are managed and chosen for destruction or preservation will effect the types of research questions that archaeologists of the future can ask about the past and about human culture and behaviour. Whether Indigenous material culture is valued in the assessment process and managed will impact upon debates about the cultural and historical identity of the American and Australian nations as a whole, and Indigenous communities in particular. It is in the assessment process that archaeology negotiates its position in the governance of perceptions of the past and cultural identity. As will be demonstrated in the following chapters a consequence of this is that archaeological discourse, theory and practice also become governed and regulated. This happens both via the need of archaeology to maintain the discourses of processual science and values to maintain access to data through CRM, and also by the processes of regulation and negotiation of cultural and political legitimacy that the discipline subsequently gets caught within.

As the concept of significance is integral in defining what it is that is saved, and in constituting debates over what is saved, the concept of significance provides a useful focus for examining the specifics of the mobilization of archaeology as a technology of government. Further, the integral role of archaeological significance in CRM provides a useful focus for any analysis of the consequences of archaeological discourse and ideologies, particularly within debates on cultural identity. The consequences to the discipline and Indigenous people of the mobilization of archaeology as a technology of government, and the role of significance in this mobilization will be examined with reference to specific cases in Chapters 8 and 9. These chapters, in focusing on debates from particular regions about material culture and its management, undertake a specific and concrete examination of the consequences of archaeological discourse and its use within CRM. However, Chapter 7 will examine in detail how archaeological discourse and knowledge has become incorporated into cultural resource legislation. The embedding of archaeological ideology and perceptions into legislation provides concrete support and reinforcement for the mobilization of archaeology as a technology of government through the concept of 'significance'. Archaeological discourse on material culture and its significance has developed a particular relationship and role with cultural resource law.

7

THE ROLE OF LEGISLATION IN THE GOVERNANCE OF MATERIAL CULTURE IN AMERICA AND AUSTRALIA

This chapter analyses how archaeological knowledge and discourse were incorporated into, privileged by, and then contested within, legislation to protect 'archaeological resources' in both the USA and southeastern Australia. The analysis is not simply concerned with historical, legal or policy developments, but will also examine how one particular form of expert knowledge (amongst others) came to play a governmental role in particular social conflicts and how that role became formalized and institutionalized in the development of CRM legislation. The previous chapters have examined the rise of a professional and scientific discourse and the ways in which this discourse became embedded within and framed debates about the nature of CRM and its various practices. In discussing the history of CRM legislation this chapter identifies the ways in which a particular discourse became explicitly mobilized in the framing of key pieces of legislation.

The chapter reveals the extent to which the claims of scientific expertise of archaeology both in late nineteenth century liberal modernity, and then later under the guise of the 'New Archaeology', were utilized and incorporated within the legislative framework of CRM. The chapter starts with an analysis of the US legislation and the *Antiquities Act* 1906 (PL 59–209). This Act, as other commentators have noted (McManamon 1996: 20; McGuire 1998), established some of the basic parameters of archaeological, government and Indigenous relations that were ultimately built upon and reinforced in the development of a range of acts in the 1960s and 1970s. This Act also, as the second half of the chapter reveals, had some influence on the development of CRM legislation in Australia. However, the chapter also argues that the process of establishing CRM legislation contained the seeds for the challenges to the authority of archaeology made by Indigenous peoples. In the US, the political and cultural renegotiations that followed this challenge also became embedded in legislation. The *Native American Graves Protection and Repatriation Act* 1990 (PL 101–601) institutionalized and formalized these negotiations and thus paradoxically reinforced the role of archaeology as a technology of government while at the same time provided a formal framework through which to regulate and govern the Indigenous process of contest and challenge.

The role of legislation in CRM

Legislation plays a key role in the management of Indigenous material culture, as it not only stipulates which government departments have the responsibility for protection and management, but it establishes the need for management procedures and processes. As Bates (1992: 74) points out, the administrative structure of the state is contained in legislation as only specific Acts can authorize agencies to undertake actions. Cultural resource legislation subsequently provides procedural guidelines by stipulating certain requirements, for instance, a permit system for destructive archaeological research, or disturbance or destruction of sites by developers (Ward 1983; King 1998). The existence of such legislation also stimulates policy development not only with respect to how sites are to be protected, but also in relation to determining which sites should be protected and for what reasons. As was shown in Chapter 6, this latter issue will often revolve around the 'significance' of sites determined in a formal assessment process (Pearson and Sullivan 1995; King 2000).

Further, the Acts define who will manage Indigenous material culture. This is done overtly through the nomination of specific government departments or agencies, and covertly, by incorporating discourses which, in framing the field of debate, influence the development of policy and procedure. In effect, the incorporation of specific vocabulary, language and concepts into legislation works to privilege or exclude certain groups. For instance, the use of the term 'relic' in the Australian Acts or 'archaeological resources' in many of the American Acts tends, as Indigenous people have argued, to locate Indigenous material culture in the past and disassociate it from contemporary Indigenous values and perceptions of significance (NPWS 1989; Geering and Roberts 1992; Tsosie 1997; Riding In 2000). This discourse and its embedding in legislation also formally defines the subject of management. It does this in an overt sense by clearly defining what constitutes, for instance, a 'resource' or a 'relic' for the purposes of the Act in question. It also does this, again in a more subtle way, by incorporating certain discourses and concepts in its definitions that set the parameters of policy debate and influence the interpretation of each Act. Archaeological resources, become precisely that, *archaeological* rather than Indigenous.

In terms of the tripartite set of relations established by CRM, the legislation also defines the parameters within which archaeologists, Indigenous people and governments interact. It determines the parameters of acceptable management practice. It also, in effect, determines the scope of policy debate, and influences the way in which debate is conducted between the three actors. The importance of this cannot be stressed enough; in the USA there is considerable cultural significance placed on the legislative process. Americans legislate to an extent that many other cultures do not, and place great emphasis on this process as a means to justify and legitimize a range of actions and positions (Chaudhuri 1985: 16). This is both expressed in and reinforced by the discourse of 'compliance' that is prominent in American CRM. As King (1998: 10) observes, this simply means 'doing what the various laws require an agency to do to manage its impacts on the cultural environment'. However, as King goes on to argue, compliance is equated with 'good management', and 'good management should put an agency in compliance with the law' (1998: 11). In Australia, the legislative culture is less pronounced and heritage agencies may actively use policy to extend their activities outside the scope of the legislation (McGowan 1992, 1996). This was particularly the case, for instance, with Indigenous consultation in southeastern Australia, which was often required, but nonetheless an enforceable requirement, based on agency policy rather than legislation. The significance of these different attitudes toward legislation has had an impact on the ways in which archaeologists in each country have attempted to deal with the Indigenous critique, a point I will revisit in Chapter 10. However, the point for now is that legislation and the role it plays in framing CRM together with its incorporation of expert discourses, works to underpin the position of expertise in the CRM process, while also defining the terms and scope of Indigenous contestation of that expertise. In effect, legislation provides governments and bureaucracies with terms, concepts and guidelines against which competing claims to material culture may be assessed and regulated.

The development of cultural resource legislation in the USA

The *Antiquities Act* 1906 (PL 59–209) protects what the Act identifies as both 'antiquities' and 'archaeological sites' (16 U.S.C. 431–3) on public lands. It requires that all excavation of antiquities on public land be undertaken under a permit obtained from the Secretary of the Interior. The Act was placed under the administration of the US National Park Service (NPS), after their establishment in 1916, as an organization charged with the care of both natural and cultural resources (Glass 1990). The character of this Act and many of the principles it establishes and incorporates were defined by the emergence of a number of movements and processes. Active support for the Act came both from professional quarters and from the American preservation movement (Lee 1970; Murtagh 1997).

The preservation movement has a long history in the USA and can be traced back to the decade before the Civil War (Hosmer 1965: 299; Murtagh 1997). It was a movement that is defined as developing spontaneously and organically throughout America and was a concern not only of professional, but what Hosmer also identifies as amateur, activity (1965: 21–2). This movement has been characterized as inherently patriotic and explicitly concerned with actively defining and preserving a sense of American identity (Lee 1970). Unsurprisingly then, it was primarily concerned throughout most of its history with the preservation of great houses and other buildings for their association with great men and their deeds (Whitehill 1983: 138). Although an interest in archaeology and a concern for archaeological or Indigenous heritage was not a significant aspect of this movement (Murtagh 1997: 147), preservationists were alerted in the late nineteenth century to the vandalism of Pueblo sites in the southwest by pot-hunters (Glass 1990). Their concern for such sites corresponds with the preservation movement's increasing concern to cement the aims of educationalists and reformists as central to the movement's platform of social reform (Hosmer 1965: 299). Those involved with the preservation movement believed that preservation would lead to American cultural maturity and many 'thought that old buildings might prove to be an important tool for the Americanization of immigrant children' (Hosmer 1965: 299–300).

In 1882 the New England Genealogical Society was moved by the threat to Pueblos in Arizona and New Mexico to petition Congress for the protection of these sites 'as they furnish invaluable data for the ethnological studies now engaging the attention of our most learned scientific, antiquarian and historical students' (Congressional Record 1882: 3777). Although this petition was unsuccessful as legislators were concerned about the ability to police such an act, a range of newly developed learned bodies and organizations continued, as Lee (1970) documents, to lobby the Federal government. Underwriting this lobbying was a desire to protect what many considered to be the material record of a vanishing people. A major force in this lobbying process was the Smithsonian Institution's Bureau of American Ethnology charged in 1879 with acquiring data and artefacts in the hope of recording some of the vestiges of the vanishing way of life of American Indians (King *et al.* 1977: 15; McManamon 2000a: 41–2). This body not only lent the weight of scientific authority to the lobbying process, but also underwrote the sense that the resulting Antiquities Act was built upon the myth of vanishing Indians. As McGuire (1998: 63) argues, this myth worked to alienate American Indians from their pasts while at the same time persuaded archaeologists that they were the legitimate stewards for that past. The 1882 petition simultaneously incorporates an idea of a past disassociated from contemporary culures, while affirming a sense of stewardship:

> the remnants of very ancient races in North America, whose origin and history lie yet unknown in their decayed and decaying antiquities, that many of their towns have been abandoned by the decay and extinction of their inhabitants; that many of their relics have already perished and so made the study of American ethnology vastly more difficult; that the question of the origin of those Pueblos, and the age of their decayed cities, and the use of some of their buildings ... constitutes one of the leading and most interesting problems of the antiquary and historian of the present age.
>
> (Congressional Record 1882: 3777)

In 1899, the American Association for the Advancement of Science also began lobbying Congress for the preservation of objects of 'archaeological interest' (Lee 1970: 47). The lobbying process then gained further force in 1902 when a range of learned organizations merged to form the American Anthropological Association (Anon 1906: 442). The passage of the *Antiquities Act* was stormy, with many professional societies and organizations presenting competing drafts of the bills they desired, but as Lee (1970: 69–75) reports, archaeologists from the American Anthropological Association finally helped formulate the successful draft of the bill.

Of major concern to those lobbying for the legislation was the degree to which pot-hunters and other 'amateurs' were destroying sites and endangering the nascent discipline of archaeology (Hewett 1906). Significant in the campaigning for this Act were fervent calls to regulate the activities of amateur collectors on public land:

> In the early days, before the problems connected with these ruins had become clear and definite, the simple collection of pottery and other utensils was natural and not without justification. But it is now evident that to gather or exhume specimens – even though these be destined to grace a World's Fair or a noted museum – without at the same time carefully, systematically, and completely studying the ruins from which they are derived, with full records, measurements, and photographs, is to risk the permanent loss of much valuable data and to sacrifice science for the sake of plunder.
>
> (T.M. Pruden 1903, quoted in Lee 1970: 38)

Clearly, what is emerging here is a sense that the natural curiosity of the antiquarian must now give way to the development of systematic and regulated activities. At this time, the emerging American discipline was starting to define itself both as a 'science' and as a 'professional' body of expertise (Wylie 2000b). In focusing the lobbying for legislation on the need to protect American Indian sites from amateur collection, as much of it did (Lee 1970), the newly emerging discipline of archaeology was staking out an identity for itself as a systematic and scientific pursuit. This was not insignificant, as McManamon notes, the Federal government through the *Antiquities Act* effectively 'supported the professionalization of the young discipline of archaeology' (1996: 21; see also Riding In 2000: 114). The Act, through the permit system it initiated, had the ability to regulate activity on sites within public land by requiring all work to be carried out by those 'properly qualified to conduct such examination, excavation, or gathering' (16 U.S.C. 432). What is important about this Act is not so much that it preserved 'archaeological sites', but that it recognized the rights of access to what was now defined as *archaeological* to those who could guarantee their conduct would be guided by their expertise and professional affiliations. In protecting sites from commercial and amateur interest the Act must regulate and define what constitutes appropriate scientific conduct and practices. Moreover, the Act also establishes that any investigation into sites be undertaken for the benefit of the public and their education (16 U.S.C. 432). In other words, this Act establishes four important elements. First, it initiates the ability of policy makers to regulate archaeological conduct. Second, it defines an identity for the new discipline as centred on systematic and controlled research for public benefit.

Further, the Act ensures that adherence to this identity would be rewarded by access to certain public resources. Third, it establishes a stewardship role for archaeology in not only preserving a 'dead' past, but in ensuring that that past could be utilized for public benefit. Because of archaeological lobbying, the Act repositions Indigenous heritage as the property of the Federal government, under the custodianship of archaeological expertise (Moore 1989: 202–3; Riding In 2000). Fourth, in redefining Indigenous heritage as archaeological and in institutionalizing the myth of vanishing cultures, the Act firmly repositions Indigenous material culture as part of collective American history. That is, it enshrines a sense of universal value by institutionalizing the principle that material culture has a value to the general public (McManamon 1996: 20). In the context of the intersection of the interest of the preservation movement and the establishment of archaeological stewardship rights, this Act also shifts the sense of 'ownership' of the past into the wider American public domain. In terms of emerging postcolonial tensions about what constitutes American identity, this was important. As Philip Deloria (1998) notes, images of Indians have always played a part in the construction of American identity; however, what this Act does is anchor the ambiguity of that image to place. McManamon in discussing the value of a National Historic Landmarks study comments:

> Most Americans do not need a cultural connection to make this heritage [American Indian sites] their own. An anchor to the past – in this case embedded in place rather than culture – helps balance modern life through reflection on the times that came before.
>
> (McManamon 2000b: 5)

The *Antiquities Act* was drafted at a time when American liberal governance was asserting itself and governments were requiring access to expertise that could help them to define and thus regulate the disparate nature of the American population (Cawley and Chaloupka 1997; Hannah 2000). As McManamon (1996: 19) states, this Act was developed through the influence of the Progressive Movement in which 'politicians asserted new ways of looking after the public good within a federal system staffed by professional civil servants able to provide technical assistance'. This new system of liberal government could easily recognize the pleas of the educationalist tendencies of the preservation movement and the cries of self-styled scientific and professional advocates to not only establish, but to protect their access to the resources needed for the education of the public and the regulation of public conduct. This is not to say that the Act was seen by legislators as a major tool in public regulation or governance, indeed the Senate debate over this Act was largely focused on whether it set an unwanted precedent for locking up public lands from commercial interests (Congressional Record 1906: 7888). However, what this Act does do is establish a sense of archaeological stewardship, and sets the precedent for the later, more explicit incorporation of archaeological technical assistance in dealing with Indigenous conduct and cultural claims in the 1960s and beyond.

During the Great Depression a number of architectural and archaeological works programmes were initiated; their aim was not only to survey and record structures and sites, but also to employ unemployed professionals (Bullock 1983; Glass 1990; Murtagh 1997). Many of these programmes were administered by the NPS; the *Historic Sites Act* 1935 (PL 74–292) subsequently authorized the NPS to continue these programmes as well as to acquire and manage places of historic national significance (King 1998: 14; McManamon 2000a: 42). This Act, like the *Antiquities Act* before it, continued to define historic resources as Federal property held in trust for 'the benefit of the people of the United States' (16 U.S.C. 461–7). Significantly, this Act saw the employment of archaeologists, as well as architects and historians, within the NPS (Murtagh 1997: 60). Recognition of the legitimacy and authority of archaeological expertise had thus progressed a further step.

However, a more pronounced boost to the development of American archaeology and CRM was the River Basin Surveys (Jennings 1985: 281). In the face of a massive national programme of post-War reservoir construction, archaeologists as well as personnel from within the Bureau of Reclamation, the NPS and the Army Corps of Engineers lobbied the Federal government to salvage, through excavation and recording, sites in regions that were to be flooded (Brew *et al.* 1947). In 1945 a number of archaeological bodies including the SAA and the American Anthropological Association formed an independent Committee for the Recovery of Archaeological Remains (CRAR), the purpose of which was to assist in planning the nationwide salvage programme (Roberts 1948: 13). The aim was to salvage and preserve archaeological data both through excavation and publication (Brew *et al.* 1947: 213). Although the work was administered by a number of government agencies under the sponsorship of the NPS and with the assistance of the Smithsonian Institution's Bureau of American Ethnology (Johnson 1951: 30, 1966: 1595; see also Roberts 1952, 1961), the CRAR had a significant policy input (Wendorf and Thompson 2002).

The nationwide salvage programme and the development and activities of CRAR helped establish a self-confident identity for the American discipline. Brew, a member of CRAR, while lamenting the need to implement the programme saw it as nonetheless serendipitous for the discipline, and importantly because of 'salvage archaeology':

> An esoteric humanistic discipline which has never before had prominence expect in realms of the imagination and as a very minor subject in academic halls, now finds itself of concern to the board rooms of great construction companies, to the world's most august legislative assemblies, to the cabinets of nations, and even to heads of state.
>
> (Brew 1961: 1)

The exuberance of this statement underlines what Jennings (1985: 281) identifies as the self-conscious posture of CRM that was one of the legacies of the River Basin Surveys. Further, CRAR and the survey programme itself, helped to establish and reinforce certain archaeological principles of conservation. As Wendorf and Thompson (2002: 321) document, CRAR in not wanting to be seen as sitting in opposition to dam construction emphasized the idea of the 'recovery' of data rather than conservation. While Wendorf and Thompson (2002: 321) argue that this emphasis gave credibility to archaeological preservation, what it does do is emphasize the significance of archaeological knowledge and information above that of the preservation of material culture as such. While this emphasis may give credibility to archaeological claims to expertise and the authority of archaeological knowledge, the emphasis on the informational value of heritage may de-legitimize the material sense of place that many non-archaeological groups, such as American Indians, value. Effectively the River Basin Surveys established not only a national archaeological presence, but they also reinforced a sense of archaeological expertise and emphasized the significance of archaeological knowledge by identifying it as the focus of salvage and thus value. The *Reservoir Salvage Act* 1960 (PL 86–523) authorized the NPS role in funding the continuation of reservoir salvage archaeology, an Act that Moore (1989: 204) characterizes as continuing the alienation of American Indian heritage while legitimizing and financing the looting of Indian sites by the professional archaeological community.

The *National Historic Preservation Act* (NHPA), 1966 (PL 89–665), while a significant Act in American CRM (King 1998, 2000), was an Act that developed out of the lobbying of the preservation movement rather than lobbying by archaeologists (Rains *et al.* [1966] 1983; Glass 1990). Archaeologists were not involved in the lobbying for, nor were they aware of the significance of, the passing of the *National Environmental Policy Act* 1969 (PL 91–190), which was to ultimately provide archaeologists with CRM work in terms of environmental impact assessments and public service positions (King *et al.* 1977: 35; Wendorf and Thompson 2002: 327). NHPA developed out of a study undertaken by a Special Committee on Historic Preservation sponsored by the US Conference of Mayors (House Report 1966; Glass 1990: 10). The Committee's report (Rains *et al.* [1966] 1983) recommended the development of a national preservation programme. The recommended programme had the support of both President Johnson and the first lady, Lady Bird Johnson (Johnson [1966] 1983), and these recommendations were quickly developed into legislation (King 1998: 15). In nominating archaeology as one of the disciplines to be consulted in determining the significance of historic properties, this Act did raise the profile of archaeological values (Murtagh 1997: 147; see also ACHP 1976a). The Act also incorporated and broadened the statements of public policy on protection and preservation incorporated in the preceding acts (McManamon 2000a: 43). NHPA cemented a national concern for the protection of what the Act terms 'historic properties' through the establishment of a register of culturally significant sites at local, State and national levels (King 1998: 15). It also created the Advisory Council on Historic

Preservation (ACHP), supposedly a panel of experts, to advise Congress on preservation matters.

The discourse embedded in NHPA, and in particular the use of the term 'historic properties', largely reflects the values and concerns of the preservation movement and the architects and historians who were instrumental in lobbying for it (see Rains *et al.* [1966] 1983; Congressional Record 1966; Senate Report 1966). This discourse tended to obscure the value of this Act for archaeology and the ACHP reported that archaeologists had begun lobbying them during the 1970s, asserting that NHPA overlooked archaeological concerns (ACHP 1976b, 1976c). The early 1970s marked an increase in archaeological lobbying activity for legislation to protect archaeological resources, a process reported to have been sparked by increasing concern about environmental degradation and development (King *et al.* 1977). However, lobbying also appears to have been galvanized by a concern that archaeological interests were not clearly articulated in NHPA and that protection through the '106 process' was not, at this time, useful to archaeologists as it related only to properties already included on the National Register and thus unregistered sites could be ignored in Federal developments (King 2000: 19).

In 1968, a conference on the Mississippi Alluvial valley work led to the nationwide circulation of the pamphlet *Stewards of the Past* that warned archaeologists and the Federal government and its agencies about the continuing threat to the sites posed by Federal developments (Committee on Interior Affairs 1973: 93; McGimsey 1985). The SAA also became increasingly assertive in lobbying for legislation while at the same time defining and developing ethical codes of practice, a process that helped to provide a sense of political coherency and constituency for the archaeological community (Knudson 1984: 251; Garza and Powell 2001). Archaeologists Charles McGimsey and Carl Chapman drafted what became known as the Moss-Bennett Bill after the Senator and Congressman who sponsored it (King *et al.* 1977; McGimsey 1985). This Bill became the *Archaeological and Historic Preservation Act* (AHPA) of 1974 (PL 93–291) and built upon and extended the 1960 Act (Senate Report 1971; Congressional Record 1973). As with the preceding Act, AHPA emphasized the preservation of scientific and archaeological data. AHPA requires all Federal government agencies to consider the impact of their actions on 'significant scientific, prehistorical, historical, or archaeological data' and for these agencies to fund any salvage of this data (16 U.S.C. 469–469c).

The importance of AHPA is that it corrects the vagaries of NHPA toward archaeological sites and draws Federal attention to the importance of archaeological data and information. It also institutionalizes a number of assumptions about the nature of the resource being protected. Throughout the lobbying process and debates about this Act, both legislators and archaeologists emphasized the scientific value of archaeological data (see Congressional Record 1973: 16378; Committee on Interior Affairs 1973). One of the concerns expressed about the passing of this Act was that it would hold up or otherwise impede Federal or Federally funded developments. The archaeologists who were questioned on the possibility of such impediments during House of Representative hearings were at pains to emphasize that the preservation of archaeological data was best achieved through salvage (Committee on Interior Affairs 1973: 108f). Once again, this emphasis privileges the attainment of archaeological information above the preservation of heritage places and derives from a privileging of scientific values. This position simply reflects the archaeological academic and professional debates of the times, which stress the inherent and immutable scientific and research values of material culture. It was not until after the passage of this Act that debates centred on the idea of 'representativeness' began to incorporate the idea of the mutability of research values (see Lipe 1974, 1984; Sharrock and Grayson 1979; Chapter 6).

As with the *Antiquities Act*, AHPA also stressed the universal relevance of the Indigenous past and repositioned this heritage as a national heritage belonging to all American citizens: 'Modern people learn much from early predecessors … Knowledge of the past is part of everyone's basic heritage' (Congressman Johnson in Committee on Interior Affairs 1973: 14). Moreover, a strong sense emerges from the debates over AHPA that the preservation of archaeological data was important for providing cultural maturity and understanding in the present (Committee on Interior Affairs 1973: 13–32). As Congressman Clausen opined, 'the study of [archaeological] information can bring the past alive for us and for all future generations' (Committee on Interior Affairs 1973: 15). Further, a sense also emerges that it is only the rigour and objectivity of archaeological expertise that can work to translate an otherwise unknowable past into a knowledge system understandable by the American public. As McGimsey pointed out to the Committee on Interior Affairs, American Indian culture had all but vanished leaving archaeologists with the responsibility of recording the material culture before all was lost (1972: 91–2). The idea of archaeological stewardship that incorporates a sense of 'public service' clearly underpins the rationale for this Act. For instance, Professor Charles Cleland saw the act as enhancing the capacity of archaeologists to 'continue to serve the public for the preservation of their cultural heritage' (Committee on Interior Affairs 1973: 91). What the discourse under-pinning this Act does is firmly embed in the minds of legislators and policy makers that while this past may be important for a sense of American cultural maturity, it is only archaeology, with its combined adherence to the values of science and public service, that may make this 'vanishing' past meaningful and relevant.

A key Act in terms of the protection of 'archaeological resources' is the *Archaeological Resources Protection Act* (ARPA) of 1979 (PL 96–95). This Act protects what it terms 'archaeological resources' over 100 years old (16 U.S.C. 470bb) on Federal, public and Indian lands and regulates collection and excavation under a permit system (16 U.S.C. 470cc). The Act was developed in response to intensive archaeological lobbying following the inability of the *Antiquities Act* to adequately prosecute looters (Knudson 1984: 260). In 1974, in *United States* v. *Diaz* it was held that the penalty provisions and definitions of 'antiquities' in the

Antiquities Act were unconstitutionally vague (cited in House Report 1979; King 1998: 19). The failure to achieve significant prosecutions together with increasing concern about the looting of archaeological sites saw the SAA combine with a number of other archaeological organizations, including the newly formed Society of Professional Archaeologists (SOPA), to lobby for new legislation, a process that had broad support throughout the American discipline (Knudson 1984: 260–1; Jelks 2000 [1988]). The Bill, drafted by archaeologists, was built upon and reaffirmed the basic assumptions, underpinnings and structure of the *Antiquities Act* while both extending it and tightening its provisions.

Counter lobbying for the Bill was undertaken by commercial collectors, amateur collecting enthusiasts, and the metal detector industry amongst others, while debate on the Bill questioned the impact it would have on hobby arrowhead and bottle collectors (Congressional Record 1979; Knudson 1984: 206). While legislators were very sympathetic about the archaeological aspiration to protect sites from commercial looting they were nonetheless concerned that collectors of arrowheads, bullets, bottles and similar items should not be prosecuted. In large part this was because the practice was seen as not only too widespread to effectively prohibit, but more to the point, it was seen as a process whereby citizens affirmed their connection to American history, and, moreover, the then American president was himself cited as engaged in arrowhead collecting (Congressional Record 1979: 28117). Amendments were subsequently made to the Bill, as Knudson (1984: 260) reports, that included the alteration of the definition of 'archaeological resource' to exclude materials less than 100 years old rather than the 50 years originally drafted, removal of the surface collection of arrowheads as a prohibited activity, and exclusion of the idea of 'context' in defining archaeological resources (see also Congressional Record 1979: 28116). Although the Bill was drafted without consultation with American Indians (Gulliford 2000: 102), a further amendment to the Bill included the requirement for consultation with American Indians over the issuing of permits on Indian lands (House Report 1979: 24). Although this provision has been legitimately critiqued as offering lip service only to American Indian concerns (Tsosie 1997: 69), it does mark the beginning of legislative acknowledgement of extant Indigenous cultural values in relation to 'archaeological resources'. Nonetheless, the dominant concern of both archaeologists and legislators in developing this Act was the preservation of scientific values and the Act was considered to provide 'a reasonable procedure for responsible persons to request permission to scientifically and systematically excavate archaeological sites' (Congressional Record 1979: 17393).

ARPA, as with preceding Acts, again reaffirmed and privileged the archaeological value of Indigenous material, and reaffirmed that while this heritage was the property of the American state it nonetheless was placed into the custodianship of professional archaeologists. As with the *Antiquities Act*, ARPA also regulates the conduct of archaeologists with the inclusion of a permit system to regulate archaeological activity on public lands. That the permit system was expanded upon and tightened under an Act to control looting is important. ARPA, like the

Antiquities Act, regulates archaeological conduct and identity by defining and regulating professional archaeological activities in opposition to commercial and amateur activities. This Act thus reaffirms and institutionalizes the scientific values that underpin American disciplinary identity by regulating access to resources to those that 'comply', through the permit process, with those values. The ethos expressed by Jelks (2000: 19 [1988]) that 'the public's well-being demands that an appropriate measure of control be exercised over the practitioners of certain professions' and that 'only practitioners possessing specialized knowledge and skills acquired through formal education ... can adequately perform the field's functions' had become more firmly institutionalized with ARPA.

NAGPRA and the technologizing of conflict

What this history of American cultural resource legislation reveals is that the late nineteenth and early twentieth-century values about the nature of archaeological science and its database have been institutionalized and maintained through the cycles of legislative history. That archaeology was able to gain prominence in the development of cultural resource legislation as it did in the 1970s was due not only to the lobbying activities of individual archaeologists and prominent organizations, but it was as much due to the utility of the discourse of archaeo-logical science that they employed. This discourse gained maturity and definition in the 1960s and grew to prominence within the discipline by the early 1970s. It stressed the values of scientific neutrality and objectivity together with a professional sense of liberal 'duty' to 'the public' that not only found synergy with modern governance, but also echoed the legacy of archaeological stewardship established in 1906. Moreover, this discourse reinforced the usefulness of archaeological science in both making sense of, and de-politicizing, a past that was increasingly being used by American Indians during the 1970s to underpin the cultural politics of identity claims (see Chapter 2). This is not to say that ARPA and its predecessors came into existence explicitly or *only* because of archaeology's usefulness as a technology of government. However, the cultural and political context of the times helped to facilitate the development of this legislation by providing a context in which policy makers would more readily appreciate archaeological claims to scientific neutrality.

However, the fact that key cultural resource legislation was developed at the time of increasing American Indian political and cultural activism meant that the discipline of archaeology had been positioned as a legitimate and necessary target for American Indians in their negotiations with governments for recognition of their political and cultural legitimacy. ARPA and AHPA were developed, in part, specifically to deal with Indigenous material culture after the limitations of NHPA to protect such material had been recognized. These Acts, and NHPA itself, gave ownership of Indian material culture on Federal land to the American state. Even though archaeology only has direct access to archaeological material on public land, the legislative framework, by incorporating the discourse used in archaeological lobbying for them, institutionalizes a range of meanings and ideas about the significance and nature of archaeological data. Archaeological knowledge is mobilized by the Acts not only in terms of the governance of particular material culture found on public lands, but in establishing the discursive field within which archaeological knowledge must operate in general to retain its relevance and utility as a technology of government. CRM, its legislative base, together with its principles and practices, establishes and maintains the primary relevance of archaeological knowledge in understanding the entirety of the American past. In effect, embedded within the Acts are referents to the knowledge base, dominant ideas and values that underpin the discipline at a particular point in time. Thus, one of the consequences of the Acts has been to redefine American Indian material culture as archaeological – a labelling process of some symbolic significance. In defining Indian material culture as 'archaeological' any non-archaeological claims to know the significance and meaning of the pasts and histories this material represents are immediately undermined and called into question. This then permits governments and their policy makers to, if they so choose, dismiss or de-legitimize non-archaeological claims about the role of material culture in supporting claims to certain cultural affiliations and traditions and thus land.

This situation is reflected in the critiques of archaeology offered by American Indians who have consistently questioned the ability of archaeological research to provide anything constructive for American Indians (Turner 1989: 193; Mihesuah 2000: 97). As Tsosie (1997: 69) observes, ARPA 'epitomizes the essential differences in values and beliefs about the past between Native Americans and Euroamericans'. Moreover, she goes on to argue that both the permit process that recognizes only 'qualified people' and the ethos that Indian heritage is managed 'in the public interest' only work to further reinforce Euroamerican values at the expense of Indigenous values (1997: 69). This in turn works to reinforce the dominant Euroamerican assumption identified by Deloria (1992a: 595) that 'only scholars have the credentials to define and explain American Indians and that their word should be regarded as definitive and conclusive'. This sense of expertise and the relationships it creates between archaeologists and American Indians is institutionalized, as Tsosie (1997: 73) forcefully argues, in the Federal statutes. Thus, as Riding In (2000: 110) observes, archaeological investigations not only infringe on Indian beliefs, but ultimately and significantly on Indian sovereignty.

In response to Indigenous lobbying, amendments were made in 1992 to NHPA. Tribal Historic Preservation Officers (THPOs) were recognized, allowing tribes more active participation in the '106 process', that is, reviewing Federal impacts on cultural resources (King 1998: 23). While THPOs have the potential to give tribes greater responsibility over heritage management, some tribes are concerned about the need to adhere to NPS rules in undertaking their duties under NHPA (Stapp and Burney 2002: 63). Thus, it is yet unclear as to what extent THPOs will be able to legitimize Indigenous knowledge and values.

The Federal government also faced vigorous lobbying by Indigenous organizations over the reburial and repatriation of American Indian human remains. As part of the wider Indigenous political movement, the rights of archaeologists to speak for Indigenous peoples were also disputed (Hammil and Cruz 1989: 197). Symbolic of this challenge was the debate over reburial. During the 1980s American Indians became increasingly vocal and active in the pursuit for control over their ancestral remains, and effectively made the conflict a public issue by seeking the support of the wider American public (Zimmerman 1998a, 2000b). By the late 1980s there was, to the surprise of many archaeologists, widespread public sympathy for reburial (Zimmerman 1997, 2000b). Public support was expressed in terms of both a general empathy for reburial aspirations and more specifically the rights of American Indians to observe their religious practices (see for instance, Hill 1988; Preston 1989).

Meanwhile, archaeologists publicly appeared obstinate and immovable in their opposition to reburial and repatriation (Zimmerman 1989a, 2000b: 295). The SAA (1986) passed a policy opposing 'universal or indiscriminate reburial', which only helped to polarize the conflict (Hammil and Cruz 1989: 197). Effectively, archaeology as a technology of government had failed to de-politicize the conflict and prevent it from becoming a social and public issue. Although this conflict is often portrayed as one between science and religion, as was argued in Chapter 2, this conflict was and is much more than that. Debates over reburial and repatriation are part of wider negotiations for the control of the rights to define cultural identity and sovereignty. At stake in this debate is not only the appropriate treatment of the dead, but the ability to define who your ancestors are and to control the appropriate disposition of their remains. These abilities are important symbolic statements and have a material consequence in negotiations with governments over defining and assessing political legitimacy (see Chapter 4). The failure of archaeology to regulate and govern this conflict, and its attendant cultural and social issues, meant that policy makers had to intervene. Consequently, the *Native American Graves Protection and Repatriation Act* (NAGPRA) of 1990 (PL 101–601) was enacted.[1]

This Act, in summary, requires the repatriation of human remains and certain cultural items to Federally recognized tribes and Native Hawaiian communities in such situations where those groups can demonstrate cultural affiliation with the remains and items. It regulates the excavation of human remains on Federal or Indian land through the implementation of the permit provisions of ARPA and the subsequent disposition of those remains (McManamon 1999a). As well it requires Federal agencies and public museums to inventory their collections of human remains and funerary objects and other related items. NAGPRA also includes provisions to suspend, for a given minimum period, any earthmoving work on Federal land that inadvertently uncovers human remains (King 1998).

Commentators on the history of NAGPRA have unanimously stressed that its development was offered as an act of compromise between the archaeological and American Indian positions (McManamon 1999a; Gulliford 2000; Zimmerman 2000b; Haas 2001). The response to NAGPRA by both archaeologists and American Indians has been mixed. Some see it as a positive piece of legislation that offers an ethical and promising compromise between archaeological and American Indian interests (for instance, Rose *et al.* 1996; Carter 1997;White Deer 1997; Dongoske 2000; Hubert and Fforde 2002), while some American Indian commentators suggest it has not gone far enough (for instance, Tsosie 1997; Killion 2001: 149, who comments on this), and other archaeologists argue that it has perhaps gone too far in restricting archaeological practice (for instance, Meighan 1992; Bonnichsen 1999; Clark 1999; Owsley 1999).

Certainly, the dominant view that arises from the American archaeological and Indigenous literature on the Act is a tentative but positive perception that NAGPRA provides a reasonable compromise between the two competing value systems. Despite this sense of compromise, what NAGPRA actually does is to define more firmly the parameters in which archaeology may be mobilized as a technology of government to regulate and arbitrate on the issue of Indigenous cultural identity. This Act, rather than watering down, compromising or devaluing archaeological values and knowledge in the face of the American discipline's failure to govern the social issues embedded in the reburial debate, actually reinforces archaeological scientific values. It does so in a way that may be opaque to many archaeologists, but to public policy makers who may wish to mobilize archaeo-logical knowledge to help arbitrate or regulate certain issues the Act provides a clear and more structured framework in which to do so. NAGPRA, as with the legislation discussed above, institutionalizes archaeological scientific values; however, it also institutionalizes more tightly and specifically the frameworks that define the relations and negotiations between archaeologists, Indigenous peoples and government. In doing so the social problems that intersect with definitions of Indigenous cultural identity are more effectively regulated and governed under NAGPRA. This does not mean that these problems are necessarily 'solved' or even resolved, but rather that they are regulated and governed – or, more simply, these problems become more manageable and understandable by policy makers. For this to have happened the role of archaeological values and knowledge in the governance of cultural identity had to be more clearly defined, and that is precisely what NAGPRA does.

The drafting of NAGPRA was initiated primarily through the lobbying activities of American Indians, and accelerated in the late 1980s following public debates about the extent of American Indian remains held by the Smithsonian Institution (Bray and Killion 1994; Rose *et al.* 1996). In 1988 the Senate Select Committee on Indian Affairs convened a hearing on legislation to provide for the repatriation of American Indian remains (House Report 1990: 10). At the request of witnesses to this hearing, the hearings were suspended so that a panel could be formed to facilitate dialogue between the museum and Indigenous communities. What became a year-long dialogue, hosted by the Heard Museum in Arizona, saw the collaboration of American Indian representatives, museum professionals, archaeologists, and anthropologists. This resulted in the drafting of a report with a sequence of recommendations for the development of legislation (House Report 1990; see also Trope and Echo-Hawk 2000). While the majority of the panel believed that 'respect for Native human rights is the paramount principle that should govern resolution of the issue when a claim is made', the panel was nonetheless split on what to do about human remains which were not culturally identifiable (quoted in House Report 1990: 10–11). Some members maintained that such remains should be repatriated while others that scientific and educational needs should predominate (House Report 1990: 11).

The legislative hearing on the Bill took testimony from a range of lobby groups and interests. The House Report (1990: 13) summarized the Indian testimony as centring on their inalienable rights to their ancestral human remains and the religious significance of these remains. It was also noted that unearthed non-Indian remains were treated very differently to those of American Indians. This point appears to have forcefully struck Senator Inouye, sponsor for the Bill and chair of the Select Committee on Indian Affairs, as he stressed the inequitable treatment of American Indian remains in Congressional debates on the Bill (Congressional Record 1990: 35678).

The scientific community, on the other hand, stressed the scientific values of human remains and warned that there would be a loss to science when new technologies for retrieving information were developed in a future when remains would be out of reach for research (House Report 1990: 13). This is a point that has been continually stressed in much of the pre- and post-NAGPRA archaeological literature (for instance, Buikstra 1981; Cheek and Keel 1984; Meighan 1984, 1992; Bonnichsen 1999; Landau and Steel 2000; Baker et al. 2001; and Mihesuah 2000 who comments on this). However, as a position on which to lobby it is, in terms of public policy immediacy, not particularly convincing as it rests on an appeal to unknowable and intangible qualities. Looting was also an issue raised by the scientific community – an ironic point in this context given that many American Indian activists were making the same point about archaeological excavation (see Zimmerman 1989b; Goldstein 2000). Nor was this point necessarily effective in the context of the NAGPRA Bill, as ARPA had been enacted to address this issue. The House Report (1990: 13) also notes that private art dealers were also active in lobbying government about the Bill and that they were concerned that American Indians not be the sole conservators of Indian cultural items as this was shared American history. This issue of the universal applicability of the American Indian past and culture is of course one that also underwrites the dominant archaeological perceptions of the significance of this past. NAGPRA does not significantly question that assumption as Senator McCain, in introducing the Bill to Congress, stated that the proposed legislation would maintain 'our rich cultural heritage, the heritage of all American peoples' (Congressional Record 1990: 35677).

On the face of it this lobbying history does, as Trope and Echo-Hawk (2000) point out, recognize American Indian values above those of archaeological science. Certainly archaeological and other scientific lobbying does not appear to have been as effective here as in previous Acts dealing with material culture. However, a number of government agencies, and in particular the DOI, who ultimately are responsible for administering much of the cultural resource legislation via NPS, were reticent about the Bill (House Report 1990: 23–33). The DOI successfully sought amendments so that the Federal government maintained its 'stewardship role' over unaffiliated remains, and ensured that provisions for the use of archaeological and other expertise in the determination of affiliation were tightened (House Report 1990: 31–32).

The inclusion of American Indian values in NAGPRA has prompted early commentators on the Act to proclaim that it is 'human rights legislation' (Trope and Echo-Hawk 2000: 139 [1992]). While the Act 'is about human rights' and attempts to redress the 'civil rights of America's first citizens' as Senator Inouye attested (Congressional Record 1990: 35678), its status as human rights legislation as such is questionable. One of the significant limitations of NAGPRA is that it applies only to Federally recognized tribes, that is those tribes that stand in what is termed a 'government to government' relation with the American state. Consequently, NAGPRA is not applicable to all American Indian communities, a practicality that restricts its claims to embodying human rights. Also, in only applying to Federally recognized tribes NAGPRA regulates the cultural conflicts of those tribes whose formal relations with the Federal government makes the negotiations over their political legitimacy not only more fraught for the American state, but more significant in terms of the need for the state to regulate and govern those relations. Further, in terms of its regulatory abilities, NAGPRA does not abandon the colonialist claims of the American state to a sense of stewardship or even 'ownership' of the Indigenous past, nor does it abandon archaeological scientific values. Senator Inouye stated in Congress that:

> When we visit museums and look at the remnants of past civilizations, we are really learning about ourselves, and how our societies and civilizations have evolved. Museums enhance our quality of life. As enlightened people, we welcome scientific inquiry and the opportunity to know more about ourselves. Accordingly, we welcome the preservation and scientific purposes that museums fulfill.
>
> (Congressional Record 1990: 35678)

The Senator, in stating his support of scientific and educational values, is using revealing discourse. Not only is his statement embedded with an Enlightenment sense of rationality, this statement re-invokes a colonialist discourse that claims the Indigenous past for the American Nation while also incorporating ideas of vanishing Indians when he invokes the image of 'past civilizations'. This invocation raises and acknowledges the spectre of archaeological and anthropological stewardship over the American Indian past and, by association, cultural identity. The Senator's statement also incorporates a discourse of cultural evolution – a discourse that is still embedded in Western archaeological theory and is intimately tied to archaeological assumptions about the nature of race that are important in this Act. Not only does NAGPRA not abandon scientific values, despite the apparent inadequacies of archaeological lobbying, in this case those values reflected in Senator Inouye's statement are actually employed in a significant way within the Act.

One of the sticking points in the drafting of NAGPRA was the disposition of culturally unaffiliated human remains (House Report 1990). It is around the definition of 'cultural affiliation', and the utilization of evidence to determine this, that NAGPRA re-institutionalizes archaeology as a technology of government. In order to determine cultural affiliation archaeological research, as well as other expert testimony, are required under the Act (McManamon 1999a: 143–4). Indeed the Act specifically identifies archaeological evidence as one of the specified types of evidence that should be used in determining cultural affiliation, and allows access to disputed remains that are 'indispensable for completion of a specific scientific study' judged to have 'major benefits to the United States' (25 U.S.C. 3005). While evidence of cultural affiliation also includes oral tradition, folkloric and other non-traditional areas of knowledge, and while a preponderance of the evidence only needs to be identified, archaeological and/or other 'expert opinion' of some sort is still required to contribute to the balance of evidence (25 U.S.C. 3005). Indeed the DOI stressed the need to ensure the use of expert information to allow 'correct determination of affinity' (House Report 1990: 31–2). The point here is that scientific expertise is being utilized to verify and augment American Indian knowledge about their past and the history and nature of their cultural identity. It does not matter that this information may support Indian knowledge claims, the important point is that it is being *used* and thus American Indian knowledge is being regulated. NAGPRA simply does not accept American Indian knowledge about their past and their sense of identity on its own terms, and requires that this knowledge be arbitrated and ultimately governed by expert opinion. This is significant, and illustrates the degree to which Indigenous knowledge and values are open to governance in the 'government to government' relations between Indian tribes and the American state. It also illustrates that the door is open for the mobilization of archaeological and other expert knowledge in the governance of those relations.

In addition, the definition of cultural affiliation is a concept that carries the baggage of American colonialism and works also to facilitate the governance of identity issues. The definition of cultural affiliation as used in NAGPRA is complex. In demonstrating cultural affiliation, one of the areas of evidence that is nominated is biological affiliation. Although only one of several areas of evidence, this issue has been a focus of heated public discussion. The inclusion of biological evidence allows for an intersection with an evolutionary idea of human culture, as it is a definition underpinned by the idea of 'race' as a significant element in the determination of cultural identity. In the debates surrounding the implementation of NAGPRA the idea that cultural affiliation can be, and indeed should be, demonstrated by direct biological links through osteological or bioarchaeological studies has been important; this had been particularly stressed in the very public and ongoing legal debate over the disposition of the Kennewick human remains (see Chapter 8). Archaeologists have raised the possibility of using DNA tests to link remains with living populations to demonstrate cultural affiliation, and skeletal morphological attributes have been, and continue to be, utilized to define affiliation. This sense of cultural identity that has been included within NAGPRA incorporates the common sense assumption about race that is dominant in American culture and still has some currency in archaeology (Stiffarm and Lane 1992; Lieberman and Jackson 1995; P. Deloria 1998: 5). While this definition of identity and cultural affiliation may be one that has cultural relevance to the American nation, and indeed to American Indians themselves, it is, nonetheless, a definition embedded with the colonial politics and history of population classification and governance. The great *stress* that is placed in the debates over the implementation of NAGPRA on the importance of biological affiliation is the issue here. While some sense of biological link is often, but not always, important in informing a sense of kinship or familial association, the degree to which biological links are stressed in these debates is significant – as this stress is not far removed from the colonial blood quantum definitions previously used by government policies to define American Indians.

NAGPRA is a complex and difficult piece of legislation and the issues raised here are further explored in Chapter 8 and its examination of the Kennewick human remains case. In summary, however, the cultural resource Acts that preceded NAGPRA established and institutionalized the role of archaeology in the governance of material culture, and thus the social and cultural issues associated with that material; NAGPRA in turn institutionalized the processes through which that role is itself regulated and governed.

The development of Aboriginal heritage legislation in southeastern Australia

As with the American cultural resource legislation the development of heritage legislation in southeastern Australia was influenced by similar archaeological concerns and aspirations. It too became embedded with certain scientific archaeological values and set the parameters for the mobilization of archaeological knowledge and expertise as a technology of government. Despite the broad similarities in the lobbying and legislative history between the two countries, there are a number of important differences. First, it is legislation at State, rather than the Federal level, that is key in the provision of legal frameworks for the protection of Aboriginal material culture. Federal legislation may only be called into play at State level in certain carefully defined circumstances and then infrequently (see Bates 1992). Second, a fundamental difference in Australian legal attitudes to land ownership means that in all Australian States Aboriginal heritage legislation is applicable to all forms of land tenure. In the American system legislation tends to protect or manage cultural resources found on Federal or Indian lands; in Australia all Acts to protect and/or manage Indigenous material culture will apply equally to privately owned (i.e. freehold) and publicly owned land.

Heritage legislation in Australia is relatively recent. The first key Act dealing with the protection of Aboriginal material culture in southeastern Australia was the *NSW National Parks and Wildlife Act 1967*, which was later re-enacted as the current *NSW National Parks and Wildlife Act 1974*.[2] This latter Act was more comprehensive than previous Acts in other States, and was used by some States as a model on which to base their own legislation. In southeastern Australia the lobbying activities of archaeologists concerned about 'vanishing Aboriginal culture', and the destruction of sites by development and amateur activities were significant in initiating legislation.

Embedding processual assumptions in southeast Australia

The earliest attempts to get the NSW government to legislate to protect Aboriginal material culture occurred in the 1930s and 1940s. In 1938 Fred McCarthy, who at that time was assistant curator in ethnology at the Australian Museum, put forward proposals for legislation to protect Aboriginal material culture. McCarthy, was very active in archaeological fieldwork and in 1964 was made foundation Principal of the AIAS, retiring in 1971. He served on various international committees (including UNESCO) concerned with the preservation of prehistoric sites (Khan 1993a). McCarthy's contributions to Australian archaeological and anthropological research were considerable (Khan 1993b; Specht 1993; Moser 1994), and were marked by an honorary doctorate from the Australian National University in 1980 (Khan 1993a). His proposals for legislation were based, in part, on the American *Antiquities Act* of 1906, a model he preferred as it provided blanket protection of sites, rather than requiring, as in Great Britain, that the value of sites be shown before their declaration as protected monuments (McCarthy 1938: 123). He argued for the development of legislation to protect Aboriginal sites and artefacts, not only to advance scientific study and educate people as to the significance of 'our archaeological deposits' (1938: 121), but also because he considered that cultural information was vanishing with the 'disappearance' of Aboriginal people and customs:

> The study of the material culture of the Australian aborigines [*sic*] has been advanced considerably in recent years by research workers ... A serious drawback to final conclusions being reached is that scant information is available about the customs, weapons, domestic gear and ceremonial paraphernalia of the tribes which inhabited those parts of Australia first settled ... Similar remarks apply to all other parts of Australia, even where the natives are still living in semi-primitive condition and in their untouched nomadic state, because the spread of

the activities of miners and other Europeans in the interior ... is rapidly breaking down the old customs of the natives.

(McCarthy 1938: 123–4)

He also argued that legislation was important if 'Australian archaeology was to have world significance', and that sites had to be protected from 'treasure hunters' so that they could be used by 'trained specialists' (1938: 123). McCarthy and Shellshear (Professor of Anatomy, University of Sydney) together drafted the text for an Act based on McCarthy's 1938 proposals, which was unsuccessfully submitted to the NSW government in 1939 by the Australian Museum (McCarthy 1970e: 153). The draft was resubmitted by the Anthropological Society of NSW in 1945 (McCarthy 1970c: 23; McKinlay 1973). The proposals were considered by government to be too costly to administer and were again rejected (McCarthy 1970e: 153).

However, in 1966, the NSW conservative Liberal government reconsidered due to continuing pressure from academics, the Museum and AIAS and established in that year an Advisory Committee on Aboriginal Relics to the NSW Minister for Lands, Tom Lewis, to, amongst other things, advise on the development of heritage legislation (McCarthy 1970e: 153). The Committee consisted of eminent anthropologists and archaeologists from the University of Sydney and the Australian Museum, and representatives from the Lands Department, Geological Survey and the National Trust (Anon 1969: 7; McCarthy 1970c; Sullivan 1972, 1975a; Carr 1970). The Minister for Lands was responsible for establishing the NSW National Parks and Wildlife Service (NPWS) and developing its legislation. Prior to the release of the Advisory Committee's recommendations the NPWS was established under the *National Parks and Wildlife Act 1967*, which also contained limited provisions to protect declared 'Historic Sites' (NSW, Legislative Assembly 1966: 3053; Sullivan 1975b).

The Minister for Lands favoured the American national park model, and to this end employed a senior officer from the US Park Service, Mr Samuel P. Weems, in 1966 to help establish the NPWS – a situation which members of the Labor Opposition criticized as an attempt to 'Yankify' Australian national parks (see NSW, Legislative Assembly 1966: 3052; NSW, Legislative Council 1974: 905). Weems is reported as defining his brief as setting aside 'primitive areas' as National Parks (*SMH* 1967). The construction of National Parks as 'primitive areas' would have created no conceptual difficulties for the inclusion of Aboriginal material culture within the NPWS Act, as Aboriginal 'primitiveness' was a popularly held perception of the times (see Mulvaney 1958). A point which McCarthy himself approved, nominating national parks as appropriate for the preservation of 'primitive' areas and Aboriginal 'antiquities' (1970b: xii–xiii).

In September 1967 the Advisory Committee to the Minister for Lands resubmitted a revision of the text drafted in 1939 by McCarthy and Shellshear. This revision was finally incorporated into the *National Parks and Wildlife*

(Amendment) Act 1969, gazetted in April 1970 (McCarthy 1970e: 153; Sullivan 1975a: 10, 1975c: 28), which then formed the basis of the provisions of the *National Parks and Wildlife Act* 1974 (Sullivan 1975c). The 1969 Amendment Act made provision for the protection of what the Act termed archaeological, anthropological and Aboriginal 'relics', and all relics became the property of the Crown under this Act (Anon 1969). The existing Advisory Committee became the Aboriginal Relics Advisory Committee to the Minister of Lands and the Director of the NPWS (McKinlay 1973; Sullivan 1975a). This Committee was to advise on any matter relating to the management and preservation of relics (Anon 1969).

There is a very real sense that archaeologists in the 1960s perceived themselves as dealing with a 'fossilized' past. As McCarthy (1970d: 53) opined, 'in most of eastern Australia the relics *in situ* exist as prehistoric antiquities because the Aboriginal culture no longer exists in most of this region'. Aboriginal culture was not only being relegated as part of NSW natural history by the inclusion of heritage provisions within a national parks Act, but that culture was also clearly being redefined as existing within a vacuum. The perception of a 'vanished' people is embedded in the use of the term 'relics' and 'antiquities', specifically as they imply that Aboriginal heritage no longer exists within contemporary cultural and social contexts. The use of the term relic has been consistently criticized by Aboriginal authors; as Fourmile (1989a: 50) states, the term has a 'strong connotation that items of Aboriginal cultural property so defined have no connection or significance to Aboriginal people today, that they belong to a dead past' (see also NPWS 1989; Geering and Roberts 1992).

Aboriginal people had no input into the development of the NSW Act (S. Sullivan 1983). It is 1960s archaeological assumptions about the 'relict' nature of Aboriginal culture, and assumptions about the ability of archaeological science to offer pastoral care over a dead past that became embedded within the Act. The term relic in emphasizing the physicality of Aboriginal heritage, also denies non-material aspects of cultural heritage. What ultimately is being protected by these Acts is archaeological *data* and not Aboriginal 'heritage' as such.

In Victoria the *Archaeological and Aboriginal Relics Preservation Act* 1972 (Vic) was originally administered by the National Museum of Victoria, then in 1973 the Victorian Relics Office was established under the directorship of the archaeologist Peter Coutts (Coutts 1975). In 1976 it became the Victoria Archaeological Survey or VAS (until Aboriginal heritage came under the auspices of Aboriginal Affairs Victoria in 1993). Lobbying for this legislation came from the National Museum of Victoria, AIAS, and individual archaeologists (McCarthy 1970b, 1970e). However, notably in this State, lobbying also came from amateur archaeologists as represented by the then Victorian Archaeological Society and the Victorian Naturalists Club (Coutts n.d.[a]).

Under the Victorian Act the definition of relic also includes Aboriginal 'skeletal remains' older than 1834, the date of European 'settlement' of Victoria (s.2). Archaeologists working in Victoria at this time argued that not only was Aboriginal culture extinct in that State, but that skeletal remains 'should be valued and scientifically collected with all possible data' (Gill 1970: 27). Quite explicitly in this Act is embedded the idea that human remains are simply to be understood as data, and part of the archaeological province. Further, inclusion of the date of colonization as the cut off point for the inclusion of human remains under this Act implies that contemporary Aboriginal identity and culture has been effectively colonized and is now divorced from its past. The discourse embedded in this Act reinforces notions that contemporary Aboriginal people either are not 'real' Aborigines, as they are not living a hunter-gatherer lifestyle (see Chapter 2), or that they do not exist.

In Tasmania, the embedding of processual science in the Aboriginal legislation appears to have been quite explicitly undertaken by legislators in a conscious attempt to de-politicize the cultural claims by Tasmanian Aboriginal people. The Tasmanian conservative Liberal government adopted the NSW model (Sims 1975) and placed the authority for the management of relics with what is now the Parks and Wildlife Service (PWS – then the Tasmanian National Parks and Wildlife Service). Originally, provisions to protect Aboriginal relics were to be incorporated into the 1974 amendments to the *National Parks and Wildlife Act* 1970 (Tas), but in the end they were relegated to the *Aboriginal Relics Act* 1975. The Tasmanian government was subject from the mid-1960s to the 1970s to persistent rigorous lobbying about the need for legislation from individual archaeologists, the Tasmanian Museum, the Department of Anatomy at the University of Tasmania, the AIAS and natural historians (McCarthy 1970a; Edwards 1975). The lobby documents stress the need to preserve sites from the impact of tourism, to control research, to protect sites from amateur excavators and black market collectors, and for the government to include provisions in the legislation for opportunities and resources to educate the public about the importance of Aboriginal prehistory (see for instance PWS n.d.[a]; Stockton n.d.; Lourandos in Minute Paper 1968; Memo 1968; Sims 1971, 1972, 1974; Gregg 1972, 1974; Jones and Mulvaney cited in Sims 1975).

Provisions advocated by Murrell (1973), Director of the Tasmanian Parks Service, included the need to protect 'aboriginal [sic] relics of archaeological importance', and to control the movement of 'relics of archaeological significance'. The assumption that the legislators were dealing with a 'dead' culture is embedded in discussions of the importance of the Act, and its implications for the protection of 'archaeological resources' and 'Tasmania's heritage' (PWS n.d.[a]).

The degree to which the legislators and archaeologists wished to believe they were dealing with a dead Aboriginal past and culture that they could claim stewardship over is revealed in two interlinked debates that were sparked over the drafting of the legislation. These were over the definition of 'Aboriginal relic' and the protection of skeletal remains. The definition of 'relic' in the Act includes all aspects of Aboriginal material culture made before 1876 and 'the remains of the body of such an original inhabitant or of a descendant of such an inhabitant who died before the year 1876' (s.2).

The year Truganini died, 1876, was deemed, by policy makers and the Tasmanian non-Indigenous population generally, to be the year in which Aboriginal culture ceased to exist as Truganini was popularly represented as 'the last Tasmanian Aboriginal', and believed to have been the last so-called 'full-blood' Indigenous Tasmanian (Ryan 1981; Maykutenner 1995). At the time of drafting of this Act the Tasmanian Aboriginal community were forcefully and publicly demanding the reburial of Truganini's remains (Hubert 1989: 150f). As with the Victorian Act, the definition of 'relic' in the Tasmanian Act effectively denies the continuing culture of Aboriginal people (Brown 1995; TALC 1996). Despite this apparent legal denial, policy makers and legislators were keenly aware of people they termed 'Aboriginal descendants' (PWS n.d.[a]; Murrell 1974). At the time the legislation was being developed the Aboriginal Information Centre had been established (c. 1972/3) and was lobbying government about Tasmanian Aboriginal land rights (see PWS n.d.[b]; McGrath 1995c; Maykutenner 1995). However, the cultural and political legitimacy of Tasmanian Aboriginal people (or Pallawah) is actively denied by the Act and its underlying assumption that cultural identity is tied to racial definitions and blood quantum. The decision to exclude post-1876 material culture from the Act was actively taken by the Director of PWS:

> The reason for the definition of 'aboriginal' in section 30a [current s.2(3)a] is to ensure that the bill does not apply to present day persons of aboriginal [sic] descent. Without this definition it could be held that such persons are covered.
>
> (Murrell 1974)

The drafting of the Act to appease archaeological, AIAS and other lobby groups, meant that it was clearly concerned with preserving 'archaeologically' significant material. It subsequently enshrined in legislation politically meaningful and, for the government at the time, useful definitions of cultural identity.

The inclusion of human remains in the Act had come from lobby pressure from the Department of Anatomy, University of Tasmania (Wendell-Smith 1974; Wallace n.d.). This was supported by PWS (Chief Management Officer 1974), but was queried by the Crown Counsel. Originally, it was considered the inclusion of human remains was not necessary, as they would be protected under the criminal code. However, Allan Wallace from the University of Tasmania, in discussing the matter with the Solicitor-General, appears to have raised the issue of what would happen under the criminal code if archaeologists were to excavate and study Aboriginal skeletons, and was concerned that these researchers could be prosecuted. Wallace reports that the Solicitor-General 'seemed appalled at the prospect of having the Crown prosecute a scientist for committing an indignity to a fossil' (Wallace n.d.). He goes on to report that:

in order that Truganini should not be the stumbling block, it was felt that the term 'skeletal remains' might be qualified by some clause as 'interred prior to 1875'.

(Wallace n.d.)

Under the *Relics Act*, pre-1876 Aboriginal remains were not protected under the criminal code along with other human remains so that archaeologists and anatomists could have access to them. Their inclusion is not so much for their protection per se, but for their protection from development, amateurs and the like so that they could be reserved for, and studied by, 'scientists'. Their removal from protection under the criminal code also sets aside these remains as 'different' to the ancestral remains of non-Indigenous Tasmanians, and their identity as 'fossils', which are the subject of scientific stewardship and control, becomes institutionalized.

Regulation of archaeological professionalism in southeastern Australia

As in America the Acts in southeastern Australia also established provisions for the regulation of archaeological professionalism and the governance of archaeological scientific values. The 1974 NSW Act saw the introduction of a permit system that controlled the collection of artefacts (s.86[b], s.87). The regulation of destructive research, such as excavation, by permits or Ministerial consent is also a key feature in the Tasmanian (s.9, s.13[1,2], s.14) and Victorian (s.22) Acts, while in Victoria notice of intent to survey areas is also a requirement under a 1980 amendment to the Act (s.22[a]). The control of destructive and non-destructive research by permit systems is a significant reflection of one of the main themes developed in Australian archaeological lobbying for legislation. Although archaeologists at this time were concerned for the protection of sites from increased development, of equal or greater concern was the destruction of sites by uncontrolled amateur collection and research. John Mulvaney, one of Australia's pre-eminent archaeologists, was at pains to publicly argue for the need to protect against amateur disturbance of sites while stressing that research should rest with the trained professional:

'Scientific' vandalism, committed in the name of science, is, in my opinion, a more serious problem. We are familiar with the implement collector or fossicker whose sole purpose is the amassing of a private cabinet collection.

(Mulvaney 1970: 115; see also 1968)

Concerns over amateur activity also arise repeatedly in archived lobbying submissions to the three State governments from archaeologists (for instance, Coutts n.d.[b]; PWS n.d.[a]; West n.d.; Anon 1969; McCarthy 1970c). The processual discourse which stressed the professionalism and neutrality of archaeological experts was important here in convincing policy makers of the importance of regulating archaeological research through permits. As in America the lobbying of legislators in Australia about uncontrolled access to sites by amateurs found synergy with wider archaeological debates of the 1960s and 1970s which had been stressing the need to distance the new 'professional' and modern period of archaeology from the 'amateur' past.

Provisions also existed in these Acts for archaeologists and other persons to report their research results or the location of sites within certain periods. D.P. Landa (Labor Opposition) also commented, during debate on the NSW Act, that the requirement that relics be reported 'within a reasonable time … places an enormous responsibility on the experts … It cannot be expected that experts, even with the best intention in the world, must go around notifying the director every time they find a relic' (NSW, Legislative Council 1974: 2277). The incorporation of these clauses reflects archaeological concerns of the 1960s, that scientific researchers were ethically and professionally obliged to report their findings within reasonable periods. The inclusion of these provisions not only regulates archaeological scientific conduct, it also aims (somewhat naïvely perhaps) to ensure that information held by non-archaeologists would be revealed.

Through the permit process professional standards are effectively regulated by archaeologists employed in agencies responsible for the administration of the Acts. As in America, Australian archaeologists were, at their own behest, ensuring that their conduct as archaeologists could be governed. This regulation ensured archaeological access to data while limiting undue amateur access. In Victoria, however, the regulation of archaeological conduct is less obvious as amateur archaeologists were one of the principal lobby groups for legislation in that State. As a consequence it is legal to collect surface artefacts under the 1972 Act, although it is a requirement that all information about collections be reported to the agency (s.27). Also, unlike in NSW and Tasmania, only those relics located within proclaimed archaeological areas are legally the property of the Crown (s.20). Mulvaney, in reviewing the Victorian Act shortly after its enactment, deplored the extent of amateur influence on the Act (cited in West n.d.). However, despite amateur influence in the development of the Act, it does work to regulate amateur activities, by providing provisions for their archaeological education and harnessing amateur enthusiasm into a system of wardens appointed to police sites and their visitors (s.9, ss.11–14). The requirements that collections be reported and provenanced ensure that these collections are not only 'useful' to archaeological research, but also accessible to archaeologists.

The influence of amateur lobbyists in Victoria quickly declined with the removal of the administration of the Act in 1973 from the Museum to the Victorian Relics Office (and thence the VAS) under the directorship of the archaeologist Peter Coutts. Coutts appears to have explicitly used a list of tenets clearly drawn from processual assumptions about the nature of archaeological science in VAS policy from 1973 (Coutts n.d.[c], [d], 1983) and was keen to promote professional activities via his administration of VAS and the Act (Coutts 1974, 1978a, 1980).

The Victorian Act also nominates the development of education programmes as a function of the agency administering the Act (s.4, s.10). Coutts in fulfilling this aim of the Act developed an extensive educational programme designed to regulate amateurs and turn them into professional archaeologists. He established the Summer School programme in 1975 in which interested persons went through a complex series of accreditation and examinations to earn the 'right' to record and excavate sites in that State (Coutts 1978b). In NSW, the Sydney and Illawarra Prehistory Groups were also given instruction on site recording by NPWS archaeologists (Sullivan 1975a). Both these programmes grew out of the intentions of both Acts, which was to regulate material culture as an 'archaeological' resource, and to limit access to that resource to people who held and understood archaeological and scientific values and ethics.

Another significant result of the stress on the control of amateur behaviour in archaeological lobbying for heritage legislation was the inclusion of 'ignorance' clauses in the three acts. A key carry-over provision from the NSW 1969 Act to the 1974 one was that:

> A person who, without first obtaining the written consent of the Director, knowingly destroys, defaces or damages a relic or Aboriginal place is guilty of an offence against this Act.
>
> (s.90[1]; section 33 in 1969 Act)

Ignorance is a defence under all three Acts (Tasmania s.21[3]; Victorian s.21; see also Bird 1988). Amateurs who could be deemed to 'know' what a relic looks like could be policed under these Acts, while the ignorance provisions would have mollified the concerns of land developers. Although Aboriginal heritage was a significant social problem in the 1960s and 1970s, heritage legislation was not seen as being of critical importance to legislators (a point noted by Landa in NSW, Legislative Council 1974: 2276–7). Nor was the management of relics necessarily seen as a priority within some of the bureaucracies responsible for them (see Sullivan 1992; McGowan 1992; Hope 1993). Rather the development of legislation by governments and their policy makers was simply part of a process to de-politicize the claims of Aboriginal activists by reducing heritage issues to legal issues of management overseen by archaeological professionals – professionals whose own conduct could be assured by the administration of the various heritage Acts.

As Kate Sullivan (1986) notes, the NSW legislation would probably never have been passed if parliament had been aware of quite how many sites there actually were in the State. Archaeologists themselves believed that as Aboriginal people were nomadic hunters and gatherers they would have left relatively little behind in the way of material culture (Mulvaney 1963: 34). The legal fiction of *terra nullius*, under which the British Crown claimed Australia, is important here. This was the fiction that Australia was unoccupied at time of European 'discovery', and is similar to fallacies used in the colonization of the Americas (Stiffarm and Lane 1992: 28). The legacy of *terra nullius* may have also influenced the erroneous perception by legislators that Aboriginal people would leave little material culture behind them (see NSW, Legislative Council 1974: 2154 on the issue of site numbers in NSW). Legislators clearly had little indication of exactly what the consequences would be of protecting relics within each of the three States. However, the inclusion of the 'ignorance' clauses in the Acts is revealing here. It is through the inclusion of these clauses that we get close to the primary aims of the Acts – that is the protection of archaeological access to data and regulation of archaeological/amateur conduct and professionalism rather than the policing of public and developer behaviour and relic protection. The fact that the Acts are as effective as they have been rests, in part, with the later development of planning Acts that required the inclusion of site assessments in environmental impact assessments. With this inclusion developers were required to employ archaeologists, governed by the permit systems of each State Act, to undertake not only surveys, but salvage or other mitigation work where necessary and thus the legal framework for CRM was established. It also meant that through the formal impact assessment process developers could be deemed to have been informed about the existence of sites and relics.

Challenges to archaeological authority and stewardship

All three Acts have come under sustained criticism by Aboriginal commentators for the lack of Aboriginal consultation on the development and implementation of the Acts and the failure of the Acts to recognize Indigenous values (for instance, Fourmile 1989a; NPWS 1989; Geering and Roberts 1992; Organ 1994; Brown 1995; TALC 1996). Aboriginal people have lobbied all three State governments for legislative change, and in NSW recent amendments to the 1974 Act have seen the removal of the term 'relic' and its replacement with 'object' and 'place', and greater inclusion of Aboriginal participation in the implementation of the Act. While in 1984 a review of the Victorian Act, undertaken by that State's Cain Labor government in response to Aboriginal lobbying (Thorpe n.d.), resulted in substantive changes.

During the 1970s Victorian Aboriginal people were increasing their political profile and resurrecting and controlling their cultural identity (Broome 1995). During the 1970s the term Koori was increasingly used instead of 'Aboriginal' to redefine identity, and to oppose the received views on the nature and history of Victorian Aboriginal culture (Broome 1995: 153). In the early 1980s the newly formed Koori Information Centre (KIC) presented the Victorian government with a 'Koori Heritage Charter' which demanded that 'control and ownership of heritage' rest with Aboriginal people, and called for the establishment of a Heritage Council comprised of Aboriginal people to manage the State's Koori heritage (KIC n.d.). The VAS response to these criticisms under Coutts' leadership seems to have been relatively slow or minimal during the late 1970s and early 1980s. Coutts (1976, 1984b) was certainly hesitant to get involved in the issue of Aboriginal participation in the management of the Act.

Increasing Aboriginal frustration in general and Aboriginal community anger over the apparent failure of VAS and the 1979 Alcoa Environmental Effects Statement (EES) to protect sites were the triggers for the review (Bird 1988). The important point about Aboriginal opposition to the initial Alcoa EES was that they argued that the archaeologists' professionalism had been compromised by the failure to survey the entire proposed development area, and that there were inaccuracies and contradictions in the scientific assessment of the sites (Rose and Rimmer 1979). Further, the VAS was portrayed by the Aboriginal community as having failed to protect potential culturally and historically significant sites, which Rose and Rimmer (1979) were at pains to point out were also significant and important to non-Aboriginal people. It was precisely this challenge to the professionalism of archaeology that triggered a review of the Act (Jim Kennan, Minister for Aboriginal Affairs in 1984, pers. comm. 1995).

It is important that this trigger was not just Aboriginal disgruntlement over a lack of consultation, but that archaeological professionalism and stewardship was demonstrated to have been inadequate. The Alcoa case provided an opportunity for Victorian Aboriginal people to *explicitly* undermine archaeological claims to stewardship, and thus undermine the authority of archaeological knowledge as a technology of government. Archaeological expertise, in the Alcoa case, could not only be argued to have failed to provide 'stewardship', it moreover had not worked to de-politicize Aboriginal claims – particularly at the end of a decade which had seen a Victorian Aboriginal cultural and political resurgence (Broome 1995: 152f).

Aboriginal control over heritage management was a feature of a Bill drafted by the Review Committee (Bird 1988: 75). A submission by the Australian Archaeological Association criticized this Bill for not mentioning archaeology explicitly enough, for removing formal management structures, and for endangering research by requiring that research results be vetted by Aboriginal organizations (Gaughwin 1986). This Bill was blocked by the conservative Liberal Opposition in 1986 because, as John Cain (the then Premier of Victoria, pers. comm. 1995) reports, the Liberal Opposition were worried by the implications the Labor Bill would have for the recognition of Aboriginal sovereignty. The Victorian Labor government then requested the intervention of the Federal Labor Government to deal with the legal stalemate.

At the same time that the Victorian government was attempting its legislative change, the Commonwealth was in the process of reviewing the *Aboriginal and Torres Strait Islander Heritage (Interim Protection) Act 1984* (Cwlth). A two-year sunset clause had been included in the Commonwealth Act requiring that it be reviewed or repealed in 1986 (Ward 1985). In redrafting this Act, and in response to the Victorian government's request, the Victorian amendment Bill was incorporated, largely unchanged (Cain pers. comm. 1995), into Part IIA of the *Aboriginal and Torres Strait Islander Heritage (Amendment) Act 1987*. This Act now works in tandem with the early Victorian 1972 Act, and means that Aboriginal people have greater control over their heritage in this State. It was under these new provisions that the Kow Swamp collection of human remains was reburied in 1990 (see Mulvaney 1991). Importantly in this Act, unlike in NAGPRA, it was Aboriginal knowledge only that was utilized to determine the affiliation of the remains that were between 9,000 and 15,000 years old. However, the new provisions aim to preserve Aboriginal 'traditions' and deals primarily with human remains and sacred material. While Aboriginal communities in Victoria have a significant role to play in the administration of the Act, it is still archaeological knowledge that plays a primary regulatory role in the management of the bulk of Aboriginal heritage in that State.

Conclusion

The legislation discussed in this chapter establishes the frameworks that structure CRM in both America and southeastern Australia. In doing so, however, the legislation also provides the conceptual frameworks that must govern debates within CRM. The processual and general scientific discourse embedded in the Acts works to ensure debates about the disposition of material culture are framed by scientific values. These values thus become basic reference points in almost all debates and processes regulated by these Acts.

If we accept that material culture plays a symbolic role in the production and negotiation of cultural and other identities, then the way this material is managed will have a consequence for social and public debates that intersect with or call upon certain understandings of the past. These understandings, and the meaning and values given to heritage items, are regulated through the governance of material culture. This governance is achieved through CRM and the Acts that underpin and structure that process. It is through the implementation and administration of cultural resource law that archaeology may be directly and explicitly mobilized to govern and regulate specific social and cultural values, issues and debates. This occurs no matter the intention of individual archaeologists, because the values that underwrite archaeological knowledge have become institutionalized, and themselves governed by cultural resource agencies and Federal and State governments through their application in legislation.

In effect, these Acts institutionalize and regulate the role of the discipline as a technology of government. This does not mean to say that governments and their bureaucracies must always use archaeology as part of the governance of certain social problems. It does, however, mean that it *can* be used if a need is perceived. Nor does it mean that this use of archaeology must always be negative, and that archaeology cannot be used to support the aspirations of Indigenous populations. In Australia during the early 1970s, the then Whitlam Federal Labor Government used the new discoveries at Lake Mungo in western NSW to garner public support for controversial land rights legislation. This government used the newly archaeologically documented discovery that Aboriginal occupation of the continent was as much as 40,000 years old to invoke an aura of special cultural and thus political legitimacy of land rights claims. The point here, however, is that archaeological knowledge was used to regulate (whatever the outcome)

Indigenous knowledge and cultural claims. Subsequently archaeology becomes a legitimate target for Indigenous people wishing to validate Indigenous knowledge and cultural values in negotiations with governments and policy makers.

The parallel legislative developments in both America and Australia illustrate the effectiveness and utility of archaeological scientific discourse in this history. It is significant that the *Antiquities Act* helped to inspire early legislation in Australia, but that it was not until the introduction of processual discourse into Australia in the 1960s and 1970s that legislation was finally developed. The American solution found synergy with the Australian context in its ability to provide a process to de-politicize Indigenous public debate in the context of constructing a post-colonial identity for the two nations. That these processes were challenged was inevitable; the next two chapters examine how archaeologists and policy makers in each country were able to respond to those challenges.

8

NAGPRA AND KENNEWICK
Contesting archaeological governance in America

The previous chapters have argued that archaeological knowledge and practice, as a form of expertise, may be taken up and utilized by governments, their bureaucracies and policy makers to help them get things done (Dean 1999). In particular, archaeological knowledge and practice may be used to help governments understand, interpret and arbitrate over a range of often competing cultural and other claims made based on an understanding of 'the past'. These claims are often consequential in assessing the political legitimacy in negotiations between governments and other interests.

As the previous chapters have demonstrated this process has developed out of social problems that rest, in part, on certain claims about the past and its use in underpinning identity claims, the historical development of certain discourses within archaeology that have stressed archaeological expertise and professionalism, and the embedding of these discourses in the practices of CRM and in cultural resource legislation. Both this and the following chapter aim to illustrate this process in action by analysing particular heritage conflicts. The examples discussed in these chapters demonstrate how archaeology works to govern identity claims, and the consequences that this can have for negotiations between interest groups, government bureaucracies and their policy makers. Further, the way in which archaeological knowledge and practice, and ultimately archaeological theory itself, become subject to regulation is revealed. In this process the identity claims of the discipline of archaeology – in particular its claims to the status of a 'science' – are themselves subjected to regulation and governance. Both chapters concern themselves with examples that centre on conflict between archaeological and Indigenous interests; this is because in conflicts the resources of power and negotiations over its deployment are revealed. This is important for understanding not only the nature of the relations between archaeology, government bureaucracies and Indigenous interests, but also in understanding how those relations change and fluctuate, and the consequences of those changes for both archaeology and Indigenous interests.

The so called 'Kennewick Man' conflict has been very publicly debated in the US since the accidental discovery in 1996 of human remains dated to be between 8500–9500 years old. Archaeological challenges to NAGPRA and its perceived constraint of archaeological practice have played a crucial role in this conflict. The importance of the case to American archaeology, and the fact that it has wider political implications beyond the boundaries of the discipline, has been acknowledged in the archaeological literature (for instance, Crawford 2000; Thomas 2000). In part, this dispute has been about contesting archaeology's own governance and regulation under NAGPRA. The ongoing conflict is therefore particularly useful in revealing how archaeology operates as a technology of government, but also in revealing how archaeological disciplinary claims to professionalism, objective neutrality and expertise are as much cultural claims tied to identity issues as are the cultural claims of the Indian groups seeking the reburial of the Kennewick remains.

American archaeology as a technology of government

Before examining the history of the Kennewick case, it is useful to briefly review the character and nature of American archaeological governance. In 1979, with the implementation of ARPA, American archaeology became firmly cemented as a technology of government. As such American State and Federal governments and their policy makers used archaeological knowledge to make sense of and de-politicize the American past – to make it of 'universal relevance', managed for the 'public benefit'. This was important in the context of post-colonial American culture, which had developed new, and very public, tensions in the post 1960s/ 1970s as American Indian political activism challenged the dominant assumptions about the nature of American nationhood and identity. Archaeological claims to professional objectivity and neutrality found synergy with the need of policy makers to understand the politically charged claims made by American Indians about the nature of the past, and subsequently the present.

Under ARPA, and the preceding cultural resource Acts, archaeologists became established as the stewards of the 'archaeological' past, at least as it occurs on public lands. What is very clear in the lobbying documents for these Acts, and in the statements of the senators and congressmen who introduced and championed these Bills through Congress and the Senate, is that they are protecting a 'scientific resource' for the betterment of 'mankind'. Archaeologists are identified in these documents as best placed not only to protect this heritage, but also to make it 'relevant' and 'meaningful' to the rest of America. This heritage is identified as 'American heritage', and archaeologists as scientists are the 'experts' who have established a prior ethical 'responsibility' to look after this material, which is institutionalized by the legislation. What these Acts effectively do in protecting archaeological resources is to render Indigenous heritage as archaeological data, subject to the regulation of archaeological knowledge and meaning. Even though archaeology only has direct access to archaeological material on public land, the legislative framework, by incorporating the discourse used in archaeological lobbying for them, institutionalizes a range of meanings and ideas about the significance and nature of archaeological data, practice and research that have wider implications beyond the management of resources on public lands. In effect, embedded within the Acts are referents to the knowledge base, dominant ideas and values that underpin the discipline at a particular point in time. Public policy makers and their bureaucracies, in arbitrating on or regulating the disputes that fall under the auspices of the Acts, then use these referents. The Acts, along with the more easily mutable public policy documents, are the instruments that mobilize archaeology as a technology of government, as well as on a more pragmatic level providing jobs for archaeological practitioners. Archaeological knowledge is mobilized by the Acts not only in terms of the governance of particular material culture found on public lands, but in establishing the discursive field within which archaeological knowledge must operate. CRM, its legislative base together with its principles and practices, establishes and maintains the primary relevance of archaeological knowledge in understanding the entirety of the American past. Moreover, it establishes and maintains the discursive field within which archaeological practices are framed and thus regulated to ensure their relevance and utility as a technology of government.

Thus, it is with the establishment of CRM and its legislative base that archaeology became a technology of government. This is not to say, however, that archaeology was the only, or necessarily the primary, form of expertise thus mobilized. In terms of both Indigenous and non-Indigenous American heritage, other fields of expertise such as law, the wider discipline of anthropology, history, architecture, sociology and so forth were also significant. However, it is understanding the role of archaeology in this process that is the focus of this argument. What archaeology gained through its mobilization as a technology of government was not only access to certain resources and employment established and guaranteed by various cultural resource laws, but also a public underlining of the authority and power of archaeological knowledge. In Bauman's (1987) terms, the legislative and interpretative authority of archaeological knowledge was institutionally recognized and maintained through the processes and practices of CRM. However, this does not mean that the archaeological discipline and its knowledge base are all powerful. Archaeological knowledge is often marginalized within the CRM process by more powerful economic concerns associated with land development, tourism and other enterprises or even by natural resource management concerns and interests. What CRM does, however, is establish the framework of relations, and the discourses within which those relations must operate. Further, CRM also identifies the resources of power that various interests or groups may legitimately draw upon. This is an important point; in any negotiation over a particular management conflict CRM not only governs the conduct of interests in the conflict, but also governs and regulates the deployment and negotiations over resources of power. The power/knowledge claims of archaeology may often in such negotiations be subsumed by more powerful economic interests, while on the other hand being invested with more authority and power than the knowledge claims of 'non-expert' interests, such as Indigenous interests.

This is the point to which the governmentality thesis, developed out of the later work of Foucault, takes the analysis: the establishment of archaeology as a technology of government situated within a network of power/knowledge claims. However, as a number of commentators have pointed out, the governmentality thesis has, as yet, little to say beyond this point as it sees these relations of power as largely static (Curtis 1995; Smith and Campbell 1998). As any casual glance at American CRM will illustrate these power relations are not static; for instance, archaeological concerns do not *always* lose out to economic interests, and archaeological knowledge claims do not *always* dominate Indigenous interests. What CRM does do, in facilitating the mobilization of archaeology as a technology of government, is establish the frameworks in which conflicts are mitigated and regulated and in which power and authority are negotiated. By linking the technologizing of archaeology into the context of the bureaucratic framework and practices of CRM a conceptual space is made for understanding first, that expert knowledge is open to challenge; second, how expertise must itself become governed and regulated by its role as a technology of government through such challenges; third, how expertise may at times be subsumed by Indigenous knowledge claims; and fourth, that these negotiations, occurring within the context of state sanctioned processes, have a material consequence for the deployment of the resources of power outside the confines of CRM. This is crucial for understanding the nature of NAGPRA and the consequences of the conflict over the disposition of the Kennewick human remains.

NAGPRA and the governance of the power/knowledge nexus

Almost at the same time that archaeology was established as a technology of government American Indians increased their opposition to archaeological practices and research. A particular focus of criticism was the archaeological study and collection of human remains. As was argued in Chapter 2 this was because human remains are of religious significance but also because they are an important political resource in and of themselves. They are particularly important in the context of the uneasy relations between Indigenous peoples and modern post-colonial states and societies. For instance, as various commentators have noted, the image of the 'Indian body' has been significant in American iconography (Trigger 1980, 1983, 1985; P. Deloria 1998; Churchill 1998; Crawford 2000). It has been used to define and redefine post-colonial American identity from the Boston Tea Party to backyard games of cowboys and Indians (P. Deloria 1998). Anthropological classifications of skeletal morphology have also been central to debates about Indian identity, and at times the nature of their humanity. Control over the Indian body in terms of dress and hairstyle was used to identify the 'culturally assimilated' (Hoxie 1995). The cultural and religious need for Indigenous peoples to control heritage, and in this case ancestral remains, is underlined by the need to control knowledge and meaning about what it means to be Indian.

As discussed in Chapter 7, an aspect of Indigenous negotiations with governments about the legitimacy of Indian identity was Indigenous criticisms of
archaeological resource Acts. Indigenous groups who lobbied for legislation to
protect their own interests have challenged many of these Acts. One piece of
legislation enacted in response to Indigenous lobbying was the *American Indian
Religious Freedom Joint Resolution*, 1978 (PL 95–341). However, as Vine Deloria
(2000: 176) notes, this Act is limited, as the US constitution means that the
Federal Government cannot champion, support or otherwise legitimize religious
groups. However, amendments did occur to archaeological Acts, particularly
ARPA, requiring consultation with local Indian tribes (King 1998).

These amendments, however, were not enough to de-politicize Indian cultural
politics and demands for the custodianship of their ancestral human remains.
During the 1980s, a range of Indian organizations increasingly demanded
legislation to repatriate human remains. The Federal government, on this occasion,
acceded to Indian requests. Indigenous lobbying to mobilize public sympathy
was very successful, while the use of archaeology as a technology of government
failed to de-politicize the social problem posed by Indigenous activism. It becomes
clear in congressional debates that archaeologists, in the form of the SAA and
other professional organizations, were not seen by policy makers to be offering
sufficient compromises in the reburial debate. Indeed, it has been reported by
Zimmerman (1998a: 105) that Democratic Senator Inouye, sponsor of NAGPRA,
made a statement to the effect that 'if the professional community couldn't solve
the problem on its own, the compromise would be legislated'. However,
archaeology as a discipline cannot offer the compromises required by American
Indians. Under the current discursive frameworks regulated by CRM any such
compromise would jeopardize not only archaeological identity as a scientific
enterprise, but also undermine the position of archaeological knowledge as a
technology of government, and the privileges and powers that flow from this.
What is revealing is that the prevailing discourse inevitably brought to bear on
repatriation debates by individual archaeologists, and by the SAA and other
organizations, is that of the scientific importance of human remains. This 'missed
the boat' with NAGPRA – as public sympathy was perceived to be with the
Indians. As discussed in Chapter 7, the idea that these remains are scientifically
valuable misunderstood the social context in which policy makers were being
required to develop policy and legislation.

US archaeology in the late 1980s was not blind to these debates, and a
significant element in the US archaeological community, led by people like Larry
Zimmerman, Randall McGuire and others, had recognized the need to compromise and negotiate with Indigenous communities on the use of human remains
in archaeological research. The dominance of the processual discourse that stressed
the value-free nature of archaeological science cannot, however, readily allow the
legitimacy of these humanistic compromises. It cannot do so because if the
processual discourse was to surrender its emphasis on objectivity and technical
rigour its position as a technology of government, access to data and the very

identity of the discipline itself, all become compromised. It is simply ironical that in the reburial/repatriation debate the political negotiations of Indigenous activists and organizations did successfully challenge the utility of archaeology as a technology of government – despite the fact it maintained its discourse as a scientific and professional discipline. NAGPRA was subsequently offered as a compromise between both Indigenous and archaeological interests.

While NAGPRA recognizes the rights of Native Americans to reclaim their ancestors it does so under very specific circumstances. As argued in Chapter 7, the Act tends to apply only to those Indian tribes that have been Federally recognized; in addition 'scientific' evidence is given a privileged position in determining the cultural affiliation of human remains. Although oral traditions may be used as evidence, it is only one class of information among many, which together must form a 'preponderance of evidence'. Oral tradition was clearly added to the law to make Indians believe their knowledge would be treated equally with science, but in fact, the more 'scientific' forms often outweigh it. The weight given to scientific forms of expertise in NAGPRA means that the Act explicitly recognizes the utility of archaeological knowledge as a technology of government. What we see embedded in NAGPRA are, not only the archaeological values and knowledge that were dominant at the time of the Act's drafting, but also the forms and processes of negotiations and the political resources used by archaeologists and Indigenous groups that were in place in the late 1980s. Archaeological knowledge is put head to head with Indigenous knowledge and traditions under this Act, and the frameworks of CRM that regulate and govern the conduct of negotiations become more firmly and explicitly institutionalized here. Thus, what NAGPRA does, in institutionalizing, or in McGuire's (1998: 82) terms 'bureaucratizing', heritage conflicts, is provide a tight framework for playing out and governing negotiations over knowledge claims that have wider material consequences in state negotiations about the current political legitimacy of Indigenous cultural claims. With the Kennewick case, these negotiations became particularly fraught and *very* public. As this case is disputed precisely on the issue of the relative legitimacy of archaeological and Indigenous knowledge claims over the remains, it offers a useful and revealing study on the ways in which archaeological governance is contested, and the consequences this has for archaeological knowledge and theory and for the cultural politics of Indigenous interests.

Kennewick: a case study in the governance and regulation of power/knowledge

The Kennewick conflict has been described as the case that 'will determine the course of American archaeology' (Preston 1997: 72). It is a conflict, as both Crawford (2000: 228) and Thomas (2000: xxv) identify, about the control of the meanings given to the past and the rights of certain groups to 'authenticate' Indian identity. Since the inadvertent discovery of human remains in July 1996 by members of the public near Kennewick in Washington State, the conflict over disposition of the remains has attracted significant public attention. It has been the focus of continuous media and intense academic scrutiny and commentary, and the subject of several popular and academic volumes (for instance, Downey 2000; Thomas 2000; Chatters 2001; Benedict 2003), while the case has also been the subject of various academic conference sessions and formal debates and resolutions, and statements from a range of anthropological and archaeological organizations have been made (SAA 2000; AAPA 2000; WAC 2003). Internet sites such as 'kennewick-man.com' have been established to trace and archive newspaper and other media commentaries, and other websites, such as the *Friends of America's Past* were established to advance the 'rights of scientists and the public to learn about America's past' (FOAP 1998). Television documentaries and interviews have been filmed (for instance, MacNeil/Lehrer Productions 1997, 2001; RDF 1998); it has been the subject of radio talk back (Preston 1997) and of class debates amongst school children (Lee 1998; Lord 2003); and finally the find spot has even become a tourist destination (AP 1998; Anon. 1998).

Upon the discovery of human bones eroding out of a bank of the Columbia River, the local county coroner enlisted the help of forensic anthropologist James Chatters to identify and classify the morphology of the skeleton. The initial assessment by Chatters, who had a record of archaeological research interest in the Columbia region, was that the bones were relatively recent. This assessment was due to what he defined as the 'European characteristics' of the skull (Chatters 2001: 31). Initially, he thought he was dealing with the remains of an early male settler. The events that followed are complex in their detail and have been reported elsewhere (for instance, Downey 2000; Thomas 2000; Chatters 2001). The aim here is not to rehearse the minutiae of this case, but to examine its overarching themes and consequences. However, the event that then triggered both academic and public interest in the remains was the identification, by Chatters, of a stone spear point embedded in the pelvis; an artefact identified through CT scans as a fragment of a Cascade Point, a type of implement dated as occurring in the archaeological record between 8000–5000 BP (Chatters 2000: 298). A radiocarbon date from bone collagen of 8410 +/– 60 BP was obtained and was calibrated to 8340–9200 calendar years ago (Taylor *et al.* 1998). This date was later confirmed by DOI archaeological investigations (McManamon 2000d; Jelderks 2002: 15), and has popularly been disseminated as a date of '9000 years'.

As the remains were found on Federal land, archaeological investigation of them fell under the auspices of ARPA. However, with the dating of the remains the Army Corps of Engineers (COE), who administered the lands on which the remains were found, moved under the provisions of NAGPRA to take the remains into their direct control. The COE moved swiftly to claim their responsibility and forcefully removed the remains from Chatters' possession. The COE announced in September of 1996 that the remains would be returned to local Indian communities (Egan 1996; Preston 1997). The COE took responsibility for the remains as required under NAGPRA and were operating on the clear assumption that these remains were Indian, and thus subject to NAGPRA, due to their radiocarbon age.

In a sequence of public statements about the archaeological significance of the remains it was emphasized by Chatters that the remains were morphologically unlike modern Indian populations, and that they were only one of a few specimens dating from the early Holocene in the US (reported in Egan 1996; Miller 1997; Preston 1997; Slayman 1997). The forced removal of the remains from Chatters swiftly became the focus of widespread media attention. The media readily accepted the archaeological significance of the remains, latching onto the idea that these remains were somehow 'different' from modern Indians. Reports that these remains were 'Caucasoid' or even 'European' were widespread in the American and International media (for example, Egan 1996; Geranios 1997; Miller 1997; Morell 1998; Radford 1998; O'Meara 1999; Gugliotta 1999; Biel 2003). Chatters and fellow physical anthropologist Catherine MacMillan were reported as identifying the remains as 'Caucasoid' (Egan 1996; Preston 1997: 70; Slayman 1997: 17; RDF1998), while Chatters was reported as evocatively stating that 'I've got a white guy with a stone point in him' and that 'that's pretty exciting. I thought we had a pioneer' (quoted in Egan 1996; quoted also in Slayman 1997: 16). Chatters has since clarified that he initially referred to the remains as 'Caucasoid like', and had not meant to suggest that Kennewick was a member of 'some European group' (2000: 306). Chatters has since concluded, alongside DOI bioarchaeological investigations, that the remains are craniometrically most similar to populations from the south Pacific, Polynesia and the Ainu of Japan, but remain significantly dissimilar to modern local Indian populations (Powell and Rose 1999; Chatters 2000). Chatters has suggested that this dissimilarity in morphology has important consequences for the archaeological understanding of the peopling of the Americas (2000: 311–12).

The public and academic dissemination of the idea that the Kennewick remains were possibly 'white', or at least morphologically dissimilar to modern Indian populations, had implications for two simmering issues. The first, centred on archaeological concerns about the restrictions placed upon research by NAGPRA, while the second concerned post-colonial tensions about American identity. Kennewick immediately became characterized as a test case through which the restrictions on archaeological research imposed by NAGPRA could be challenged. Eight physical anthropologists/archaeologists sued to gain access to the remains by questioning the applicability of NAGPRA to this case. As Downey (2000: 48) argues, a significant asset possessed by the plaintiffs was their 'sheer eminence in science', an assist that was continually reinforced by media and literature references to 'prominent scientists' (for instance, Miller 1997: 3; Thomas 2000: xxi; Custred 2002: 5). The plaintiffs' argument in the lawsuit, *Bonnichsen et al.* v. *United States of America*, asserts that the removal of the bones by the COE under NAGPRA violated their 'first amendment rights' (Barran and Schneider 2001). As the narration in the RDF documentary stated, scientists 'made their stand [against NAGPRA] with Kennewick Man'. Physical anthropologist Grover Krantz is reported to have stated on examining the remains prior to their removal by the COE, that 'this skeleton cannot be racially or culturally associated with any existing American Indian group' and that 'the Native Repatriation Act [sic] has no more applicability to this skeleton than it would if an early Chinese expedition had left one of its members there' (quoted in Preston 1997: 72). The conflict over Kennewick became characterized by Bonnichsen, one of the plaintiffs in the lawsuit, as 'a battle over who controls America's past', suggesting also that the term paleo-Indian used to describe people from the north American ancient past was 'wrong' and that 'maybe some of these guys were really just paleo-American' (quoted in Egan 1996). The public nature of the archaeological debates about the origins of the Kennewick remains fuelled post-colonial tensions about American nationhood and the place of Indigenous peoples in American national identity.

A reconstruction of the Kennewick skull was undertaken from casts, and this reconstruction was widely published by the media. Chatters was quoted in the *New Yorker* (Preston 1997: 73) as saying that while watching television one night he had spotted Kennewick Man in the form of Shakespearean actor Patrick Stewart who had gained wider public fame in *Star Trek*. Pictures of both Stewart and the Kennewick reconstruction were publicly disseminated and compared (see Egan 1998, 1999; Miller 1997: 2; Henderson 1998a amongst others). The statement that Kennewick could have been 'white' and the public association of the reconstructed skull with an identifiable modern figure struck a public chord. Kennewick Man was both heroic and noble and, moreover, possessed a transatlantic accent. This association had resonance to a number of American constructions of postcolonial identity. Here the Indian past was once again being appropriated and made not only universally applicable, but also *directly* applicable to Euroamericans. Ideas of the 'authentic Indian', which have played an important role in the construction of American identity, could be more explicitly appropriated and made meaningful because, as Crawford ironically remarks, 'the real Indians are now white folks' (2000: 223). Crawford (2000: 222–3) argues that 'the wisdom and strength' associated with prehistoric America not only has an important place in American mythologies, but that Kennewick also confirmed that these values could only be restored to American society by scientists and their study of the archaeological past.

Archaeological speculation that Kennewick may be evidence of a prior Euro-Asian or even European migration or presence in America before American Indian occupation fostered claims that American Indians were not 'Indigenous' and may have wiped out a prior European population (reported in Preston 1997: 80; Egan 1998; O'Hagan 1998; May 2001). For instance, the Asatru Folk Assembly, a Nordic pagan sect with neo-Nazi connections (Goodman 1998), laid claim to the remains, stating that this person was possibly an ancestor of theirs and an early Nordic settler to the Americas (AFA 1997; Egan 1998, 1999; Watkins 2001a). A lawyer for this group is reported to have stated that 'Kennewick Man is a threat to the Indians because he jeopardizes their moral authority and argument that they were the victims of Europeans which succeeded them' (quoted in Egan 1998). Thus, the colonial tensions and themes underlying the moundbuilder myth were resurrected (Crawford 2000: 219–20). Archaeological pronouncements about the morphology of the Kennewick skeleton were used to explicitly question the rights of Native Americans to their cultural sovereignty and land rights.

Under NAGPRA, a coalition of tribes under the Confederated Tribes of the Umatilla Reservation had claimed the remains. Their claim was based on their knowledge that they had always occupied the Kennewick region, which remained their traditional homeland as recognized under their 1855 Treaty (Minthorn 1996: 1). In opposition to archaeological and media speculation over the origins of the remains, Armand Minthorn, spokesperson for the Umatilla, emphasized that the Umatilla had a cultural and religious custodial duty to ensure that the remains were given due respect and reburial stating that:

> If this individual is truly over 9000 years old, that only substantiates our belief that he is Native American. From our oral histories, we know that our people have been part of this land since the beginning of time. We do not believe that our people migrated here from another continent, as the scientists do.
>
> We also do not agree with the notion that this individual is Caucasian. Scientists say that because the individual's head measurement does not match ours, he is not Native American. We believe that humans and animals change over time to adapt to their environment. And, our elders have told us that Indian people did not always look the way we look today.
>
> (Minthorn 1996: 1–2)

Following an inter-agency agreement the DOI was assigned responsibility to determine, under the provisions of NAGPRA, if the remains were American Indian and, if so, their specific cultural affiliation (McManamon 1999b). The court case was suspended while the DOI investigations were carried out, and in 1998, the remains were sent to the Burke Museum of Natural History and Culture in Seattle. In 1999, they were examined by physical anthropologists and bioarchaeologists contracted by the NPS (McManamon 1999b; Powell and Rose 1999; Hackenberger 2000). In addition to these studies, geomorphological and sedimentological investigations of the find spot were undertaken and linguistic and archaeological analyses were initiated (Huckleberry and Stein 1999; Ames 2000; Boxberger 2000; Hunn 2000). The DOI in considering its case called in expert archaeological, linguistic and anthropological witnesses and heard the evidence of oral traditions from the Confederated Tribes of the Umatilla (McManamon *et al.* 2000). As part of this determination further testing of the remains were undertaken, the date was confirmed and DNA analyses were undertaken, although reliable DNA samples were unable to be extracted (Merriwether *et al.* 2000; Smith *et al.* 2000).

In 2000 the then Secretary for the Interior, Bruce Babbitt, determined that the remains were Indian and that their cultural affiliation lay with the Confederated Tribes of the Umatilla, and moved to have the remains repatriated to them. The identification of the remains as Indian was 'based upon chronological information supplied by the radiocarbon analysis' (Babbitt 2000: 1; see also McManamon 2000c). It was noted that the archaeological, linguistic and anthropological evidence was not able to trace an unbroken cultural connection of the present communities back as far as 8500–9500 years ago (Babbitt 2000). However, it was acknowledged that oral traditions did claim a timeless cultural affiliation and geographical association with the region in which the remains occurred, and thus that the DOI considered the geographical association and the oral tradition 'establishes a reasonable link between these remains and the present-day Indian tribe claimants' (Babbitt 2000: 4). Babbitt's determination was based, first, on legal advice that NAGPRA was 'Indian legislation' and that in the case of doubt or ambiguity the course of action best in keeping with the nature of the Act was to find in favour of Native American interests (Babbitt 2000: 2; Leshy n.d.: 2). Second, that he accepted that the preponderance of evidence supports the Umatilla claims of affiliation (Babbitt 2000: 5). What he does not say, but what clearly underlines his determination, is that he accepted the evidential legitimacy of the oral traditions of the Indian claimants. What his determination did by interpreting NAGPRA in favour of Indian interests was to implicitly legitimize their cultural knowledge, while downplaying archaeological values. Responses in the US archaeological literature to this determination were mixed, but certainly, a sense of fear emerges in some quarters that this determination does indeed undermine the legitimacy of archaeological science. For instance, the SAA while supporting the determination that the remains were Native American disagreed with the conclusions made about cultural affiliation and argued that this determination upset 'the balance struck by Congress in NAGPRA' between scientific and Indian interests (2000: 1). The American Association of Physical Anthropologists (AAPA) also questioned the determination of cultural affiliation and expressed its puzzlement as to why Babbitt appeared to be ignoring physical anthropological evidence in this case while such evidence had been cited in other cases (2000: 2–3). What both the SAA and the AAPA are identifying here is the process, bureaucratized by NAGPRA and CRM, whereby political legitimacy is both conferred and withheld.

In making his determination, Babbitt acknowledges that while the archaeological and other expert research and testimony does not unequivocally support the oral traditions, for instance, it does suggest some cultural discontinuities may have occurred, this does not overturn the oral traditions (Babbitt 2000: 5). The archaeological study of cultural affiliation undertaken as part of the DOI investigation is interesting in that it is clearly a culture historical study. The report, like many similar investigations under NAGPRA, attempts to define cultural identity through tracing the similarities in the material culture record through time (Ames 2000). Despite the embedding of processual discourse and values in both CRM and NAGPRA, when archaeology is asked to pronounce on issues of identity archaeological practice reverts to the dictates of culture history. Trigger (1989) has argued that culture history was in part overturned as the dominant discourse in America due to its preoccupation with issues of cultural identity. While these found synergy in wider European social and cultural debates about nationalism and nationhood, the post-colonial tensions in the modern American state found them problematic. As Trigger (1989) argues, processualism de-emphasized identity issues and placed the Indigenous past into a framework of universal relevance and significance, which spoke with more utility to the wider social and cultural agendas of the USA in the 1960s and 1970s. NAGPRA in initiating this sort of archaeological practice tells us one of two things. Either that despite the hegemony of processual discourse archaeology has failed to put theory into practice. That is, while the discipline may invoke processual scientistic discourse the science that is done is bad science. Or, more simply, that in dealing with issues of identity it is culture history, rather than processual archaeology, that must be invoked.

Babbitt's determination was immediately contested by the reactivated legal case brought by the eight anthropologists/archaeologists. At this stage in the history of the Kennewick case, the remains had been extensively studied by DOI archaeologists/anthropologists, and Chatters (2000) had published his report on his study of the remains. Yet, the plaintiffs who submitted their own research programme (FOAP n.d.) to the court saw this work as insufficient. While there may be archaeologically valid grounds for verification of existing work and for undertaking additional research, the political and symbolic importance of access to the remains by the plaintiffs cannot be underestimated. The court case became vital, in the wake of the Babbitt decision, in repositioning the public and political legitimacy of archaeological knowledge and in reasserting the authority of archaeological science. Further, in pursuing the court case the plaintiffs were also challenging the governance of archaeological knowledge and practice, and asserting their own claims about the nature of archaeological disciplinary identity and values.

Babbitt's determination not only repositioned power relations in the tripartite relations established by CRM between archaeologists, Indigenous interests and the state, it also revealed the extent to which archaeological knowledge and practice had themselves become governed and regulated by this relation. What is revealing here is Babbitt's determination that the remains are indeed Indian. In the late 1980s, when NAGPRA was drafted, the dominant and publicly accepted archaeological thesis about Indian occupation of the Americas was that it had occurred no earlier than 12,000 years ago (Meltzer 1989: 471). One of the dominant assumptions was that there had been a single migration involving a homogenous population, and that the Indian cultures encountered by European colonizers had developed from the Clovis Paleo-Indian culture (Meltzer 1989: 472; Steel and Powell 1999: 109). Implicit in this is that modern American Indians are Indigenous and were descendent from peoples who arrived in the Americas

12,000 years ago. Certainly, NAGPRA incorporates this model as 'Native Americans' are defined as indigenes (25 U.S.C. 3001(9)), that is, all those peoples occupying America before colonization (McManamon 2000c). In the 1990s, however, this model alters in that occupation was pushed back at least to 17 000 years ago. Subsequently, the idea of a 'pre-Clovis' culture was actively debated alongside multiple migration theories, and Kennewick joined a growing population of remains that were argued to be morphologically dissimilar to modern Indian populations (Steel and Powell 1992, 1999; Grumet and Brose 2000). Archaeological speculation about what all this may mean to models not only about 'when', but as Bonnichsen (1999: 3) puts it, 'who' peopled America increased during the 1990s. Further, as Bonnichsen (1999: 3) notes, the hitherto neglected field of bioarchaeology was gaining in importance in First American studies by providing insights into 'who were the First Americans'. The Kennewick remains' archaeological value to the changing archaeological knowledge base is explicitly pronounced in this context. It is also important to note that a number of key leaders in the new debates about the peopling of the Americas are also the plaintiffs in *Bonnichsen et al.* v. *United States of America*.

In his determination, Babbitt drew upon 1980s archaeological knowledge when he identified the remains as American Indian. The archaeological significance of Kennewick, or at least its value to 1990s bioarchaeological debates, was inadvertently negated in Babbitt's determination. It is inadvert as Babbitt was drawing on the archaeological knowledge and values on which NAGPRA was built, and thus not allowing for change to them. It is revealing that Owsley, one of the plaintiffs, and an outspoken critic of NAGPRA (see Owsley 1999), is reported to have commented that the lawsuit was about 'the rights to ask questions of the past and challenge what's in the archaeology books' (quoted in Smith 2002). Thus, the lawsuit was as much about repositioning the legitimacy of archaeological knowledge, as it was about contesting its governance and the place of so-called 'new research initiatives' in American archaeology.

Judge Jelderks, who heard the case in the Oregon District Court, argued in his decision of 2002 that Babbitt's determination was faulty on two grounds. The first was that the definition of Native American used by the DOI and by Babbitt was intellectually and anthropologically flawed. Indeed Jelderks states that Babbitt erred in assuming that all remains that pre-dated colonization were Native American (2002: 29). Jelderks infers (2002: 27) that Congress had intended the definition of 'Native American' under NAGPRA to 'require some relationship between remains or other cultural items and an existing tribe, people, or culture that is indigenous' and says that the DOI had not demonstrated that the remains were ancestral to modern American Indians. Jelderks thus considered that Babbitt 'did not have sufficient evidence to conclude that the Kennewick Man remains are "Native American" under NAGPRA' (2002: 31). In effect, Jelderks is questioning the validity of the 1980s' archaeological knowledge base on which Babbitt's determination was made, as it is not supported by the archaeological knowledge that is privileged and espoused by the eight plaintiffs. Thus, in this case, archaeological knowledge becomes directly subject to regulation and governance, and certain values about the nature of archaeological science and the role of bioarchaeology in American archaeology are publicly affirmed and validated. Bonnichsen (1999: 15) has asserted that 'scientific study offers the only objective way of reconstructing America's cultural and biological heritage', and certainly Jelderks' decision not only reaffirms the authority of archaeological pronouncements about American Indian cultural identity, but specifically identifies the particular archaeological values, assumptions and knowledge base on which pronouncements should be based.

This legal decision, and the archaeological knowledge it draws upon, is based on the assumption that skeletal morphology is revealing of race and that race is a biologically significant concept. Moreover, it explicitly assumes that race is a determining feature of cultural identity. Lieberman and Jackson (1995) have argued that although these ideas of race are debated and contested within anthropology, they are nonetheless prevalent in American anthropology and in wider American popular culture. The key assumption is that skeletal morphology has linkages to cultural identity. This assumption underlines Chatters' original pronouncements about the nature and significance of the remains, the subsequent media attention to the idea that these remains were not Native American, and the claims that there was a prior 'European' presence in the Americas. This assumption is also a legacy of American colonial history, and shares, perhaps unwittingly, the same discursive space as a range of quite explicitly racist assumptions that centre on the unsustainable idea that culture, and more specifically cultural identity, is an expression of biology. Archaeological speculation about a 'prior presence' has led some to proclaim that the indigenous and sovereign rights of American Indians should be overturned and that land claims, and rights to fishing and hunting and other resources, should be revoked (reported in Preston 1997: 81; Egan 1998; May 2001). These claims highlight what is at stake in this conflict for the American Indigenous community. As Tsosie, an American Indian academic, is reported to have observed, 'It would be only too convenient to find that Native Americans are merely another "immigrant" group with no special claim to lands within the United States' (quoted in Lee 1999a; see also Lee 1999d; May 2001). Indeed one non-Indian academic is reported in the media to have opined that Indian attempts to oppose further study of the remains were based on the idea that Kennewick had the potential to undermine the political legitimacy of Indian claims: 'if it turned out that the Indians weren't the first Americans after all; that Europeans may have been here before them; or that Indians, like Europeans who followed, may have come to America as colonizers to find a racially different aboriginal population, which they eventually replaced' (quoted in Seldon 2001).

The various claims that have been made based on the racial identification of the Kennewick remains, and many of Chatters' original claims, have been heavily and publicly criticized by a range of physical anthropologists and archaeologists (see reports in Egan 1998; Henderson 1998b; Lee 1999b, 1999d; see also Goodman 1998; Thomas 2000; Zimmerman 2000b). Despite these criticisms, however, the discipline of archaeology has gained a great deal of public attention in this process. For instance, under the headline 'Archaeology becoming popular science' one reporter asserted that 'Thanks in large part to Kennewick Man and the questions it raises about the New World's first inhabitants American archaeology is becoming an increasingly popular science' (Lee 1999c). Certainly, the Kennewick case appears to mark a shift in public support for archaeological studies of the remote past, including the study of ancient human remains. In addition, some politicians have publicly criticized NAGPRA because of the Kennewick case, and have suggested its remit should be narrowed (Egan 2000; Seldon 2001). The degree to which debates about the identity of the Kennewick remains sparked media and public debate illustrates not only the degree of authority given to archaeological and scientific pronouncements, but also the way they can and do feed into wider cultural issues and anxieties. This authority and the ability to maintain it is, of course, what the conflict over Kennewick is ultimately about.

Jelderks' second point was that the evidence for cultural affiliation was insufficient and that Babbitt's 'determination of cultural affiliation could not be sustained' (2002: 38). That is, Jelderks effectively de-privileges the evidential legitimacy of the oral traditions. Quite specifically he notes that, in this case, the oral traditions are highly problematic due to the lengthy passage of time and thus cannot be relied upon, while also questioning their objectivity (2002: 52). As the evidence offered by the oral traditions could not be verified archaeologically, anthropologically or linguistically it was given little legitimacy in Jelderks' decision, and he states that Babbitt 'reached a conclusion that is not supported by the reasonable conclusions of the Secretary's experts' (2002: 38). What this legal decision then does is not only de-legitimize the Umatilla knowledge, but more importantly subjects all Indigenous knowledge to the arbitration of expert witnesses. Jelderks has not only reaffirmed the role of archaeology as a technology of government in the NAGPRA legislation, but has also removed any ambiguity about this role under what some had identified as 'Indian legislation'. Indeed, he found that NAGPRA did not apply in this situation, although ARPA did, and that the eight scientists should be granted permits under this Act to study the remains (2002: 70, 73). In making this ruling Jelderks notes that research undertaken under ARPA must be 'undertaken for the purpose of furthering archaeological knowledge in the public interest' (16 U.S.C. 470cc(2) quoted in Jelderks 2002: 71).

The Confederated Tribes of the Umatilla have appealed this decision; the appeal will be heard at circuit court level, although it is likely that the process of appeal will take it to the Supreme Court (McCall 2002; AP 2003; Cary 2003). If the appeal is denied, Jelderks' decision may stand as an important legal precedent, which will underwrite the privileged position of archaeological expertise.[1] However, if the appeal is granted there may, once again, be a shift in the negotiations of power and legitimacy. However, it is likely that the prevailing political climate in the USA will be a major influence on the outcome of the case, as it has long-term implications for the political legitimacy of a range of interests. Certainly the identification by Babbitt that the remains were subject to NAGPRA has been 'identified' by some in the media as part of a range of Clinton governmental 'cover ups' (West 2001; Custred 2002). It has been asserted that Babbitt and Clinton have attempted to cover up the rights of 'free enquiry', and more importantly have attempted to avoid debate over North America's first inhabitants and the possibility that they were not American Indians (West 2001). The widely quoted statement by Alan Schneider and Paula Barran, the attorneys for the plaintiffs, on the *Friends of America's Past* web pages proclaimed that: 'the scientists view the court's decision as confirmation of their contentions that the American past is the common heritage of all Americans, and that it should be open to legitimate scientific research' (Schneider and Barran 2002); it has significant implications for ongoing public debates about the origins and nature of the American past. These in turn have implications for the ways in which current and later American Federal governments perceive public support for archaeological and Indigenous interests, and how they negotiate and confer or withhold political legitimacy to those interests.

Chatters' response to Jelderks' decision was to note that 'taking a stance for science ... had been the right thing to do', while the President of SAA noted that this would 'go a long way toward restoring the balance between the interests of science and those of the Native Americans' (both quoted in Lepper 2002: 3–4). Certainly the case has been hailed as 'a victory of sound science over identity politics' and 'a thorough rebuke of the Clinton administration' (Miller 2002: 1). Responses from the Indigenous community have also identified a shift in power relations; Riding In has observed that the Jelderks decision 'has the effect of keeping large pools of remains for the privilege of science' (quoted in Mulick 2002) and John Echohawk identifies that 'NAGPRA itself is under attack by the scientific community' (quoted in King 2003). Certainly, Minthorn has noted that conflict over Kennewick has eroded the 'intent of NAGPRA making repatriation more difficult' (n.d.: 1). He observes that DNA testing on the Kennewick remains by the DOI was undertaken against the wishes of the Umatilla, and the other claimant tribes, and that this had undermined the consultation process required by NAGPRA (n.d.: 1–2). Further, the attempt by the DOI to examine DNA to show cultural affiliation had set an alarming precedent and had been 'constructed as an open invitation to all federal agencies and museums to allow such testing on their collections' (Minthorn n.d.: 2). The decision by Jelderks must further substantiate the legitimacy of this precedent and all it implies. Further, the apparent victory of the plaintiffs in the case so far has implications for the validation of a range of issues raised by the Kennewick case. Great stress has been placed in this case on the nature and meaning of cultural identity, both in terms in which the lawsuit was pursued, and the ways in which the entire Kennewick conflict has been defined and debated in the media. The Jelderks decision in explicitly recognizing the authority of archaeological science also validates, however unintentionally, the wider public debates that latched onto, otherwise intersected, or aligned with archaeological pronouncements about North America's past. Certainly, the popular cultural view that biology is a determining factor in cultural identity and expression has been worryingly validated in this case. At the same time, the case to date has also devalued the need to consult and consider Indigenous cultural knowledge on its own terms.

Shown Harjo (2002) has observed that 'body snatching is substituting for land-grabs and scientific right replaces divine right of kings'. She has also noted that the Jelderks family have had significant land holdings in Oregon for over 100 years and has thus questioned Jelderks' wider motivation (Shown Harjo 2002). While this criticism of Jelderks has been characterized as simply 'spiteful innuendo' (Lepper 2002: 4), it does have a valid point. One of the things that archaeological knowledge does outside the academy, and which is well illustrated in the Kennewick case, is arbitrate on the cultural politics of identity, which in the case of Indigenous identity will ultimately impact on sovereignty issues and attendant rights to land.

Conclusion

What the Kennewick case does is map out the political and cultural negotiations within which archaeological knowledge and discourse unwittingly finds itself positioned. The significance of this case for archaeology is that the analysis reveals the wider discursive and political fields within which archaeology must operate, and the interrelation of these on the expression and construction of archaeological theory and practice. The significance for the governmentality thesis is that this case reveals that expertise and technologies of government are open to and can be challenged and contested, while the consequences of this for the discipline involved can be dramatic.

In the Kennewick case, NAGPRA was perceived by some of the archaeologists who involved themselves in the conflict as presenting a significant challenge to archaeological authority. In the case to date, the challenges to archaeological 'science' were perceived to derive from the Indigenous critique from the 1980s reburial and repatriation debate which eventually initiated the development of NAGPRA. Although NAGPRA may not, as argued in Chapter 7, inherently privilege Indian values over archaeological ones, it did allow Babbitt an opportunity to express the legitimacy that his government was, in 2000, affording to Indigenous interests. Babbitt's 2000 determination both acknowledged and affirmed the legitimacy of Indigenous oral knowledge and history, and in doing so was perceived to have de-legitimized not only archaeological knowledge, but also the discipline's identity as an objective and authoritative science. It is important that it was archaeologists and anthropologists who quite specifically saw themselves as objective scientists that answered the challenge. Babbitt's determination had the potential to remove an archaeologically significant piece of 'data' from archaeo-logical access, and by doing so deny the scientific value of the remains. Thus, this determination directly jeopardized the identity of archaeology as a 'science' by publicly supporting non-empirical oral traditions. Any confrontation to disciplinary identity challenges not only the public authority of archaeological practitioners to make binding statements about the past, but also the status of various internal disciplinary values. More specifically, public challenges to archaeological science must also tackle the hegemony of processual theory and discourse within the discipline. Jelderks' final decision not only very publicly repositions the authority of archaeology under NAGPRA, but also reaffirms the authority of archaeological claims to *be* an objective science. In addition, the relatively new field of 'bioarchaeology' is publicly identified and affirmed as an important element in understanding the past. The values and belief systems that underpin the discourse of archaeological science are given material weight and substance through the symbolism of Jelderks' recommendation that archaeological access to the Kennewick remains be granted to the plaintiffs under ARPA (even though that access has currently been postponed due to the Umatilla appeal). Thus, not only does the discipline gain reaffirmation of its disciplinary identity through gaining symbolic control over the archaeological heritage as represented by the Kennewick remains, it also reaffirms the central place of processual theory and its values within the archaeological discipline.

In this case the human remains became a resource of power and symbolic of not only the cultural identity of American Indians, and post-colonial American nationalism, but also the disciplinary identity of archaeology as a science. What is highlighted in the claims of archaeological scientists for possession of the Kennewick remains is that these claims are *cultural*, and that disciplinary identity is created through linking identity to objects in much the same way as objects are linked to cultural identity for Indigenous people. In effect, the authority of archaeological knowledge and discourse is given tangibility by disciplinary control and possession of material culture and its identification as archaeological 'data'. The values and perspectives of archaeological positivistic science are also reaffirmed by the symbolism of possession. The processual conceptualization of the nature of archaeological knowledge and research practices is continually reaffirmed through its success at ensuring archaeological possession and access to material culture. This symbolism and the material power of processual scientific values and discourse are reinforced daily through the practices and legal underpinnings of CRM, although, from time to time, they may become modified, weakened, strengthened or simply reaffirmed in specific heritage conflicts.

9

THE 'DEATH OF ARCHAEOLOGY'

Contesting archaeological governance in Australia

This chapter examines the history of archaeology in the State of Tasmania. Because of the very public nature of the conflicts that have occurred in this State the history of Tasmanian archaeology, and challenges to it by Aboriginal people, provides a good example of the changing relationship between archaeology, Aboriginal people and government, and changes to State heritage strategies. This example is particularly significant, as it had profound consequences for archaeological practice and ethical debates in the rest of Australia (Colley 2002; du Cros 2002). This chapter argues that Tasmanian archaeological knowledge and research was, during the 1970s, mobilized as a technology of government by Tasmanian State institutions, and by the Federal government during its 1983 intervention in the Franklin Dam heritage conflict. However, as Aboriginal political agitation continued during the 1980s and 1990s, the post-Franklin Dam era of interactions has resulted in significant changes in the relationship between archaeologists, Indigenous people and heritage bureaucracies. As policy makers gave Aboriginal political interests more legitimacy, the degree to which archaeology as a technology of government was implemented, and the nature of that implementation, changed.

The changes in relationships between archaeologists, Aboriginal people and governments occurred as Aboriginal people challenged popular assumptions about their demise in southeastern Australia, and asserted the political legitimacy of their cultural identities. In Tasmania, archaeology moved away from its 1970s proclamations that the 'last of the Tasmanian Aborigines' had died in 1876, to provide reinterpretations of the past that were used to support public recognition of Tasmanian Aboriginal identity. The relationship altered to such an extent that the Tasmanian Minister for Aboriginal Affairs supported the Tasmanian Aboriginal Land Council's (TALC) demands for the return of material excavated from the southwest of the State by archaeologists based at La Trobe University in the State of Victoria. The return of this material signalled such a significant change in power relations between archaeologists, Aboriginal people and governments, that some archaeologists declared that it was the 'death' or 'end of archaeology' in Tasmania, while also issuing 'warnings' about the threats posed nationally to archaeological 'science' and research (see Allen 1995b; Maslen 1995a, 1995b; Morell 1995; Murray 1995; Wright 1995).

As with the Kennewick case (Chapter 8), this event provides an opportunity to examine the consequences for the discipline of the regulation of archaeological knowledge in CRM legislation, policy and practices. Certain power/knowledge strategies have been institutionalized in CRM policy and legislation (Chapters 5–7), and Aboriginal interests contest these. Archaeological responses to these challenges become constrained by archaeology's own regulation as a technology of government. The reaction by some archaeologists to the recognition of Aboriginal interests by State policy makers and institutions in this particular conflict have been constrained by the role of archaeology as a technology of government. This was established in Tasmania during the 1970s, and institutionalized and regulated by the development of heritage legislation in 1975. This reaction is constrained by an adherence to positivistic concepts contained within the Australian version of processualism, and a philosophy of science that has been embedded in heritage legislation and the regulatory practices of archaeologists. An adherence to this philosophy has been made necessary and desirable through the legislative authority given to the discipline by its position as a technology of government. To effectively challenge this philosophy is to undermine the authority of the discipline within CRM, and thus its usefulness in arbitrating on and regulating the meanings given to, and conflicts over, material culture. The 'paradox' faced by archaeology is that while this relationship provides authority for the discipline, this relationship is also being contested and altered because of the working out of the 'politics' of CRM.

Archaeological accounts of Tasmanian 'prehistory'

'The Tasmanian paradox'

In the nineteenth century, Tasmanian Aborigines were regarded as Darwin's missing link between humans and apes, and were seen to be more 'primitive' and 'wretched' than mainland Aboriginal people (for commentary on this see Mulvaney 1958, 1971a, 1981a; Ryan 1981; R. Jones 1984, 1987a, 1992b; Murray 1992c). The construction of Tasmanians by nineteenth-century evolutionary science, and European evolutionists like Lubbock and E.B. Taylor, as examples of Palaeolithic 'survivors' went hand in hand with the robbing of new graves to secure 'scientific' specimens for study (see Mulvaney 1981a; Reynolds 1995; Jones 1992b, 1993; Pilger 1989; Pybus 1991). The construction of Australian Aboriginal, and Tasmanian people in particular, as 'primitive' by intellectuals was part of colonial governing strategies of domination and subjugation (Kuper 1988; Murray 1992c; Chapter 2).

These 'scientific' constructions corresponded with, and justified to some, the attempted genocide of Tasmanian Aboriginal people that ended with the death of Truganini in 1876, purported to have been the last 'full blooded' Tasmanian Aboriginal (see Ryan 1981; Pilger 1989; Pybus 1991; Reynolds 1995 for accounts of this history). Although white Tasmanians believed that Aboriginal culture and people had ceased to exist with Truganini's death, as Ryan (1981) has documented, and as the existence of the Tasmanian Aboriginal Centre (TAC) and TALC attest, Aboriginal communities and culture continued. These communities resisted attempts by white administrators to assimilate them into white culture, and have continually fought for recognition of their identity and cultural continuity (see Ryan 1981; Birmingham 1993; Reynolds 1995; McGrath 1995c; Maykutenner 1995). The challenge to white assumptions that denied the existence of Tasmanian Aboriginal identity will be discussed in the next section.

However, the colonial history of Tasmanian Aboriginal study has complicated Aboriginal and archaeological relations (Bowdler 1980; Murray 1992c). Bowdler (1980) has argued that this legacy, together with Social Darwinism, saw expression in Rhys Jones' study of Tasmanian archaeology during the 1960s and 1970s (see also Thomas 1981: 168). Certainly, some of the assumptions underlying the construction of Jones' interpretation of Tasmanian archaeology reflect wider assumptions and normative perceptions of the time about the so-called 'primitiveness' of Tasmanian culture.

The Tasmanian archaeological record was held by Jones to represent a cultural 'paradox', to be 'bizarre' and an 'aberration' (Jones 1977a: 189, 1978a: 42). Jones believed this was due to a simplification in the late Holocene of the Tasmanian material assemblage, and what he assumed was a corresponding 'slow strangulation of the mind' brought about by isolation from the mainland (Jones 1977a: 203). Jones, the first of the new 'professional' archaeologists to work in Tasmania, commenced field work in 1963, undertaking survey and excavation work in the northwest (Jones 1965, 1966, 1968b, 1971a).

Jones established his research agenda in his 1966 paper stating that:

> It would be interesting to see, in the archaeological record, what cultural changes occurred in response to the new conditions and also what were the effects, if any, of isolation on prehistoric man [sic] and his cultures on the island.
>
> (Jones 1966: 1)

Documenting and hypothesizing about the effects of Tasmanian isolation from the mainland characterized Jones' work in Tasmania into the 1980s (Bowdler 1980, 1982). Tasmania was thought to have been separated from the mainland about 12 000 years ago by rising post-glacial seas, with the Bass Strait forming a 250 km barrier which was swept by the 'Roaring Forties' – winds from Antarctica (Jones 1977a, 1987a, 1993; Porch and Allen 1995). Jones' work drew heavily on ethnographic information which documented that the Tasmanians did not eat fish, had minimal water craft (none in the northeast), and possessed a stone tool kit different and, as the literature implies, 'simpler' than that of the mainland Aboriginal people (Mulvaney 1961; Jones 1966, 1971a, 1971b, 1977a, 1977b, 1978a). Ethnographically, the Tasmanians were reported to lack bone tools, edge-ground axes, the boomerang, and the barbed spear head (Jones 1971a, 1971b,

1977b, 1978a; Bowdler 1980). Jones speculated that these differences were caused by the isolation of Tasmania from the mainland and, lacking the stimulus of mainland contact, the Tasmanian tool kit had remained static (1966, 1977a). Using a metaphor once employed by the Darwinist Lubbock (Trigger 1989: 115) about the Tasmanians, Jones suggested that Tasmania presented 'a perfect laboratory situation' against which change and development on the mainland could be measured (1977a: 189). He repeated this suggestion (1971b: 271, 273) with respect to the information and comparisons the Tasmanians and their material culture offered to Palaeolithic and Neolithic Europe (see also R. Jones 1984: 56).

However, through his excavations in northwest Tasmania Jones uncovered what he considered a remarkable 'paradox' – rather than technological progression or stasis Jones argued that he had found degeneration and maladaptation (e.g. 1971a, 1971b, 1977a, 1977b, 1978a). Jones' work identified an 8000-year occupation sequence for the northwest which was characterized by the disappearance of scaled fish and bone tools from the archaeological record at c. 3500 BP (Jones 1978a). Jones characterized the Tasmanian tool kit as the 'simplest tool kit in the world', far 'simpler' than that on the mainland (1977a: 196–7; see also 1971a: 28, 1978a: 21) and notes that on Tasmania 'people made their living through the medium of a technology, so simple in the number and elaboration of elements as to stagger the imagination' (1977a: 197).

Then, as Jones documents, aspects of this tool kit disappear through time. This observation confronted the notions of Enlightenment 'progression' that Bowdler (1980) and Murray (1992c) identify as underlying both Jones' Tasmanian work and the Australian discipline generally. For Jones the answer to this 'enigma' was isolation of a relatively small population on a small island, large sections of which he argued were not, and could not, be occupied. He calculated that the total Aboriginal population of Tasmania was in order of between 3000 and 5000 people confined to the coastal regions (1971a, 1971b). He also concluded that the southwest of the island was unoccupied due to the ruggedness of the terrain and the extreme density of vegetation cover during the Holocene (Jones 1968b, 1971b; see also Lourandos 1970, 1977). This proposition was supported by ethnographic evidence that reported that the Tasmanian inland was unoccupied at contact. These conclusions later played a role in the Tasmanian Hydro-Electric Commission's (HEC) arguments in the Franklin Dam dispute that the hinterland was unoccupied (discussed below).

For Jones, the changes in the Tasmanian tool kit and economy are best summarized by the following, often quoted (both by Jones and others), passage:

> Consider the trauma which the severance of the Bassian Bridge delivered to the society isolated there. Like a blow above the heart, it took a long time to take effect, but slowly but surely there was a simplification in the tool kit, a diminution in the range of foods eaten, perhaps a squeezing of intellectuality ... The world's longest isolation, the world's simplest

technology. Were 4000 people enough to propel forever the cultural inheritance of Late Pleistocene Australia? Even if Abel Tasman had not sailed the winds of the Roaring Forties in 1642, were they in fact doomed – doomed to a slow strangulation of the mind?

(Jones 1977a: 202–3)

Jones' interpretation of the changes he observed in the archaeological record have been popularly taken to suggest that the Tasmanians were dying out prior to the arrival of the Europeans, who simply hastened their death – an assumption Bowdler argues is implicit in Jones' work (1980: 335). Certainly Jones' juxtaposition of arguments about a 'Tasmanian population collapse' with the success of the occupying European 'farmers' (1971b) works to reinforce perceptions that Jones' work supported normative assumptions about Tasmanian 'primitiveness', and assumptions about their status as 'Palaeolithic survivors' who were unable to cope with and survive against a superior European culture and technology. Jones has argued that his work has been misinterpreted, and that his interpretations of the Tasmanian past have been parodied as putting forward a 'dying race' theory (1992b: 59). He denies ever saying that the demise of the Tasmanian Aborigines was inevitable, and therefore Europeans should feel no guilt 'at the extirpation' (1992b: 59). Rather, he suggests that the misunderstanding derives from his use of the word 'doom'. Certainly, Jones' interpretations and theories had a considerable public impact, which will be discussed below. However, as Hunt (1993: 317) points out, and as occurred with the Kennewick case, regulatory knowledge can often take on 'a life of its own'.

The archaeology of southwest Tasmania

By the late 1970s, the southwest was characterized as being unoccupied, except for the presence of small bands that were thought to have made hunting excursions into the hinterland (P. Murray *et al.* 1980: 150; also Jones 1979: 455). The proposal to build the Franklin Dam resulted in surveys for archaeological sites in the southwest, which were questioned by Jones for their adequacy (1982). These surveys, conducted by the Tasmanian Hydro-Electric Commission (HEC), took Jones' map of the ethnographically known distribution of tribes to support contentions that no sites, or at least none of significance, would be found in the southwest (Jones 1982, 1984).

However, in 1977, the geomorphologist Kiernan identified several caves, one of which, F34 Fraser Cave (later renamed Kutikina by TAC), he recorded as containing dense bone deposits (Kiernan et al. 1983; Jones 1987b). This site, re-examined and test excavated in 1981, was found to contain extremely dense stone, hearth and animal bone deposits sealed by a layer of soft stalagmite (Jones 1982, 1987b, 1990). Occupation at Kutikina cave was dated to between 14 840 ±930 and 19 770 ±850 BP, its occupation corresponding to the height of the last glaciation when the hinterland was, as new geomorphological discoveries revealed, not densely vegetated but instead covered in heathland (Jones 1982; Kiernan *et al.* 1983). Occupation ceased at this site at the end of the last glaciation, when dense forest closed in (Kiernan *et al.* 1983; Jones 1990).

The identification of this site was met with considerable media attention, not only because of its archaeological significance, but also because it was threatened by the construction of the Franklin Dam. The archaeological significance of the site was argued to rest on the fact that this site overthrew previous theories about the initial occupation of Tasmania, and the so-called 'primitiveness' of its people. Rather, the Tasmanians were now proclaimed as the 'southernmost people in the world', capable of dealing with harsh climates (Jones 1982: 102).

Jones and others reproduced this image of the 'southernmost humans' in numerous publications, public interviews and television documentaries (e.g. 1981, 1983, 1984, 1987b, 1990; Jones in Butt 1984; see also Mulvaney quote in the *Launceston Examiner* 1982a; Porch and Allen 1995) – an image that is the antithesis of his 'slow strangulation of the mind' scenario. The significance of the site in throwing light on human survival in a harsh climate was emphasized, and the site was characterized as 'one of the richest archaeological sites ever found in Australia' (Jones 1981: 55; see also Dingle n.d.; *TWS* 1981). The site's uniqueness and its international importance to 'mankind' were all publicly stressed (e.g. Kiernan 1981; *TWS* 1981; *The Mercury* 1982a; *Launceston Examiner* 1982a; Jones 1981, 1982, 1983). The discovery of Kutikina, and subsequently several other Pleistocene Tasmanian sites, corresponded to a decrease in the active consideration of the so-called Tasmanian 'paradox' and fish eating debate. As Jones himself notes, he had stopped 'comparing Palaeolithic European man to ethnographic Tasmanians', but 'had come full circle in comparing Palaeolithic Tasmania with Palaeolithic Europe' (1984: 56).

By 1993 over 50 occupation shelters and caves had been found in the southwest and those that have been excavated range in age from 35 000 to 10 250 BP (McGowan *et al.* 1993). The excavated sites have revealed rich deposits of a density and range of material not usually found in other Australian or overseas Pleistocene sites (Allen 1993: 147; McNiven *et al.* 1993; McNiven 1994). La Trobe University researchers had investigated many of these sites as part of the Department of Archaeology's 'Southern Forests Archaeological Project' (SFAP), which commenced in 1988 and followed on from the Gordon-Franklin River surveys of the early 1980s (McNiven *et al.* 1993). The initial aims of the project were to examine 'an apparent paradox' (yet another!) of why Pleistocene sites appeared to be occurring in the southwest but not the southeast (McNiven *et al.* 1993: 213; also Allen 1993: 148).

This dichotomy was overthrown when sites were found in the southeast and the aims of the project altered to determine the spatial and temporal boundaries of the distribution of Tasmanian Pleistocene occupation, and to uncover and test inter-site variability (McNiven *et al.* 1993; Porch and Allen 1995). This project has resulted in an archaeologically significant body of research data, and has developed a convincing picture of the nature and scope of Pleistocene and late

Holocene occupation in the southwest of the State. The details of this research will not be discussed here (but see McNiven *et al.* 1993; Porch and Allen 1995 for overviews).

In summary, the Pleistocene data suggested that humans in this period adopted a 'fluid and adaptable strategy' in dealing with a changing environment during the Last Glacial Maximum (Porch and Allen 1995: 721). Unlike in other areas of the globe, Porch and Allen (1995) argue, the Tasmanian response to changing environmental conditions did not follow a single trajectory toward 'intensification'. Rather, the socioeconomic systems developed varied significantly, ending with abandonment of the southwest after 13 000/12 000 BP. Porch and Allen offer two possible explanations, based on the notion of Tasmanian isolation after 12 000 BP, for both abandonment and the lack of a 'single trajectory' of development into the Holocene. They suggest that either the lack of contact with outside people, ideas and technology, or the constrictive nature of the environment did not allow for a significant population increase, which they argue has been seen in other parts of the world as a trigger for intensification (1995: 729). The idea of Pleistocene Tasmanians as 'flexible and adaptable' has yet to be rationalized against Jones' Holocene model – although the assumptions about isolation underlying Porch and Allen's interpretations do not lay to rest the ghosts of previous archaeological and popular assumptions about Aboriginal 'primitiveness' and the universality of Enlightenment 'progress'.

The constant comparison of Kutikina to the European Palaeolithic as well as the French Magdalenian (e.g. Jones 1981; Kiernan 1981) reinforced its international significance – as the *SMH* (1981) reported: 'Find hailed as Tutankhamen of Tasmanian cave archaeology'. As further Pleistocene sites were found during the 1980s, the international significance of the region was confirmed. This significance reinforced the authority of archaeological knowledge and discourse as a technology of government. However, this authority was successfully challenged and renegotiated during the late 1990s. Paradoxically, this challenge was successful precisely because of the very nature of the history of archaeology that had established archaeological authority in Tasmania in the first place.

Contestation and the governing of Tasmanian material culture

'The Last Tasmanian': filming the 'paradox' and the 'governing' of identity

The development of archaeological knowledge about the Aboriginal past of Tasmania has had significant consequences on public and policy perceptions of Tasmanian Aboriginal identity, and has met with stiff Aboriginal opposition. One of the most public Tasmanian conflicts over the interpretation of Aboriginal material culture occurred over the 1978 documentary film *The Last Tasmanian*, made by Tom Haydon and based on research by Jones and Jim Allen (Haydon 1978; ARTIS 1978; Jones 1992a).

This film, telling the story of Tasmanian 'prehistory' and European occupation, incorporated, and was based in part on, 1970s archaeological knowledge, incorporating Jones' interpretations about the 'Tasmanian paradox' and Jones' theories about the maladaptive effects of cultural isolation (Jones 1978b: 21). The film met with extensive and variable critical attention. One review of the film reported that audiences were 'stunned and horrified' by the revelation of what the film terms 'the most complete case of genocide of a whole race in recorded history' (quoted in Daniels and Murnane 1978). It won a prestigious Logie award in 1979 for the best documentary (Jones 1992a), and critical acclaim in the British (Raven 1978) and Australian media (ARTIS 1978).

However, TAC criticized the film for denying the existence of twentieth-century Tasmanian Aboriginal people and staged demonstrations outside cinemas where it was shown (Daniels and Murnane 1978; Bickford 1979). The archaeologist Bickford (1979: 11–12) argued that the film was a 'racist fantasy' for not only denying the existence of contemporary Tasmanian Aboriginal people, but for also portraying Aboriginal people as non-adaptive and perpetuating the dying race myth (see also Sykes 1979: 13).

Aboriginal people and archaeologists opposed to the film's content also initiated a campaign of plastering posters advertising the film with the message: 'Racist! This film denies Tasmanian Aborigines their Land Rights' (Bickford 1979: 11). Tasmanian Aboriginal people argued that in denying their existence the film, and the archaeological knowledge it was based on, denied them political identity and undermined Tasmanian claims for land rights (Daniels and Murnane 1978). Land rights claims in Tasmania were being made with increasing frequency during the 1970s (McGrath 1995c), with a petition being sent to the Tasmanian government in 1977 (PWS n.d.[b]). The release of the film corresponded with an increased Aboriginal political public profile in Tasmania – archaeological science in the form of a popular documentary film jeopardized Aboriginal political recognition and legitimacy. The film became a powerful medium through which archaeological knowledge was mobilized in a public arena, and gave support and credibility to public and policy perceptions that Tasmanian Aboriginal people did not exist.

Haydon and Jones vigorously defended the film. For Haydon, the film told the story 'of white-black conflict in Tasmania last century, and though it deliberately tries to be cool and fair, the whites hardly come out as the heroes' (1979: 12). For Jones, the film told the story of the Tasmanian archaeological record and provided a global warning tale about the effects of 'closed systems' and the over-use of 'energy and other resources' (1978b: 21). Here the processual rhetoric of 'relevance' was invoked. As illustrated in Chapter 3, one of the concerns of the New Archaeology was to make archaeological research more relevant to modern concerns, including if possible the drawing of lessons for the present and future from the past. In defending the film, Jones stressed the archaeological data, and reiterated its meanings – offering no argument against criticisms that his interpretations may be seen as justifying European colonization (1978b). There is a sense in Jones' response that the data objectively tells its own story – and that the data cannot be argued with.

Both Jones and Haydon recognized the existence of what they both termed 'Aboriginal descendants' or 'straitsmen' – people they describe as descended from Aboriginal women taken to Bass Strait islands by sealers (Haydon 1979; Jones 1978b). In an episode of the nationally broadcast current affairs programme, *Monday Conference* (ABC 1979), Haydon debated the film with the Tasmanian Aboriginal activist Michael Mansell and a studio audience in part comprised of self-identified Tasmanian Aboriginal people. In the debate Haydon, although confronted by Tasmanian Aboriginal people, continued to assert that they were not Aboriginal, but rather descendants. He also offered the term 'straitsman' as a 'better' alternative, as for him at least it invoked a proud and unique heritage. He argued that 'straitsmen', while not Aboriginal, had survived within geographically, but not culturally, coherent communities. He argued that Mansell and members of the audience were not Aboriginal because archaeological and historical 'evidence' revealed that they were not. Throughout the debate Haydon is obviously bewildered (an observation also made by Bickford 1979) by the failure of Mansell and members of the audience to accept the 'evidence' – he appeared not to understand how scientific evidence could be questioned.

As discussions about the development of Tasmanian heritage legislation in Chapter 7 revealed, the Tasmanian government accepted the archaeological 'evidence' that supported wider assumptions about Aboriginal identity, writing into the *Aboriginal Relics Act 1975* the definition that an Aboriginal relic could not be made after 1876. This then implies that Aboriginal culture ceased after this date – a move publicly supported a few years later by the film. As Lehman (1991) reports, the film also gave popular support to the denial of land rights, and implied that Aboriginal culture was an 'invention of the present':

> In this way, the invaders have not only stolen our land, but also seek to claim Aboriginal heritage as theirs: a scientific resource which becomes the property of the researcher.
>
> (Lehman 1991)

Archaeological knowledge therefore not only gave scientific authority and evidence to popular white assumptions about the identity of present day Tasmanian Aboriginal people – it also reinforced archaeological claims and access to material culture. This occurred through claims to archaeological scientific objectivity and the assumed inherent international scientific values of Jones' data. Archaeological knowledge was both allowing itself to be used by policy makers and government, and simultaneously constituting itself as the authority responsible for the stewardship of a material culture. Defining that material culture as no longer existing within an ongoing cultural context did this. However, the use of archaeological knowledge to deny the existence of Aboriginal people failed to help de-politicize Aboriginal interests and conflicts over the disposal and management of Aboriginal heritage. This is because the very public profile of the film and its message served to reinforce Aboriginal activism and claims to controlling their identity. As Lehman (1991) notes: 'Aboriginal community outrage at this film launched a new offensive for regaining control of our heritage', which together with the confusing role archaeological knowledge was to play in the Franklin Dam case, helped to alter the authority and role of archaeology as a technology of government and its ability to offer regulatory knowledge in Tasmania.

The Franklin Dam decision

In 1979, the HEC recommended the construction of the Gordon-below-Franklin Dam to help meet the power needs of Tasmania. The proposed flooding of the Franklin River met with stiff opposition from environmentalists, and turned into an Australia-wide conflict between environmental conservationists, development interests and sympathetic State governments (Bates 1992). In 1980, the Australian Heritage Commission listed the southwest on the Register of the National Estate, and the Wild Rivers National Park, which included the Franklin, was created. Attempts to prevent the construction of the dam rested on claims about the significance of the natural heritage of the area, particularly its 'wilderness' values; values which stressed the lack of disturbance and occupation of the area by humans (Griffiths 1991).

In February 1981, this changed with the discovery of Kutikina Cave, its Pleistocene occupation challenging the concepts of 'wilderness' values, although its considerable scientific importance bolstered the 'no dams' movement's arguments for the need to prevent the flooding of the Franklin. As Allen (1983) and Griffiths (1991) point out, the discovery of Kutikina produced an uneasy alliance between environmentalists, archaeologists and Aboriginal people, because of their conflicting views on 'wilderness' and prior Aboriginal occupation, which were further complicated by the role archaeological knowledge had played in denying the existence of contemporary Aboriginal people. Conflicts between Aboriginal groups and some environmentalists occurred when environmentalists used the existence of early Aboriginal occupation to support their claims but hesitated in actively supporting land rights claims, especially as these claims jeopardized the 'wilderness' argument (Griffiths 1991).

In July 1981 the Tasmanian government passed the *Gordon River Hydro-Electric Power Development Act* 1982 (Tas), and a few months later large tracts of land were revoked from the Wild Rivers National Park. A Federal Senate Select Committee was established in 1981 to examine the power needs of Tasmania, and found that no new power scheme was necessary. In response, the Tasmanian government invoked 'States' rights' arguments, protesting against the 'right' of the Federal government to intervene in State issues. At the end of 1981, the conservative Fraser Federal government agreed that it would not intervene to stop the dam, while at the same time the World Heritage Committee meeting in

Paris listed the Tasmanian Wilderness National Parks on the World Heritage List (*Launceston Examiner* 1982b; *The Mercury* 1982b).

In December 1982 the Australian Democrats had their *World Heritage Protection Bill* passed through the Senate, and the Tasmanian Wilderness Society started blockading the development site. The Federal elections in 1983 brought the Hawke Labor government to office, with an election promise to intervene in the Franklin Dam issue. The Federal government then passed the *World Heritage Properties Conservation Act 1983* with regulations prohibiting construction work in the southwest World Heritage Area without the consent of the appropriate Federal minister (Bates 1992: 53). The Act was then challenged in the High Court by the Tasmanian government. The High Court, in *Commonwealth v. Tasmania* 1983, found that s.109 of the Constitution applied, and upheld the validity of the Commonwealth Act while rendering the Tasmanian Development Act inoperable (Bates 1992). Under s.109 of the Constitution, in any conflict between a State Act and a Commonwealth Act, the Commonwealth Act is deemed to prevail.

The archaeological 'significance' of Kutikina cave, and other southwest Pleistocene sites, was an important element in the Australian High Court's decision. Justice Murphy of the High Court himself nominated it as the most important consideration in the decision. The archaeological values of Kutikina were assessed by the former Liberal Prime Minister Malcolm Fraser as important in bringing down a decision in favour of preservation (cited in Allen 1987: 9). Some archaeologists have seen the Franklin Dam decision as highly significant for the discipline as it raised the public and political profile of archaeology (e.g. Mulvaney 1983, 1985b, 1988; Coutts 1984a; Allen 1987; Flood 1987; Murray 1992c).

The Franklin Dam case brought national and international attention to archaeology and highlighted, according to Flood (1987, 1989), the role of CRM in preserving archaeologically significant sites. At this point, the role of archaeology as a technology of government seems clear. In effect, archaeological significance assessments and knowledge were successfully used in arbitrating a highly political decision by the Federal government and High Court. The scientific values, although called into question by the HEC (Allen 1987), allowed the High Court to make an 'objective' technical and legal decision that was Federally, at least, *highly* politically expedient.

However, at the State level the use of archaeology in supporting Tasmanian government and HEC claims that Tasmanian Aborigines were 'extinct' did not achieve its ends, and only heightened Aboriginal political opposition to the Tasmanian government and its policies. Because of Aboriginal contestation of archaeological knowledge and political activism, archaeology as a technology of government failed in Tasmania to defuse and de-politicize cultural claims about the material culture of the southwest. Nor was archaeology so visible in Tasmania as some archaeologists have assumed. A random survey of 500 Tasmanians completed by Hocking in 1994 revealed that while 80 per cent of those surveyed knew about the Franklin case, of these only one per cent knew about or had heard about Kutikina Cave, its archaeological values, and the role it played in the High Court decision (Hocking 1994). Tasmanian newspaper reports about the lead up to, and the actual 1983 High Court decision also tended to play down, if they mentioned it at all, the 'importance' of Kutikina Cave in the saving of the Franklin.

The Tasmanian government and HEC argued in the High Court that the Tasmanian Aborigines were 'extinct' and, therefore, any arguments that Kutikina was a spiritually or culturally significant place to contemporary Tasmanian Aboriginal people were irrelevant (*Launceston Examiner* 1982c, 1983; *The Mercury* 1983; Terry 1983). This was an important point in arguments put by the Tasmanian government in an attempt to play down the significance of the southwest material culture. Kutikina Cave was held by the Aboriginal community to be significant to them as it provided contact with past Aboriginal people and culture, and as Michael Mansell stated in referring to Kutikina Cave, 'it was like coming home', 'the most important cultural thing that's ever happened to us' (quoted in Griffiths 1991: 96). Further: 'It took nearly 200 years for us to find something with real meaning, and now they're going to take it away, destroy it, just like that' (quoted in Allen 1987: 4).

In addition, the cave was an important 'spanner in the works' (Jim Everett – Tasmanian Aboriginal – quoted in Griffiths 1991: 96) for the environmentalists' claims about 'wilderness', as it supported the long occupation of Tasmania by Aboriginal people, which also lent further political and cultural legitimacy to land claims (see also Langton 1995). Indeed, in 1985 the Tasmanian Aboriginal community added Kutikina Cave to the list of areas that were the subjects of continuing land claims since the 1970s (Fulton 1985; PWS n.d.[b], 1992). It was thus important for the Tasmanian government to defuse the political legitimacy of the Aboriginal values given to Kutikina, not only for the dam project, but also for wider issues concerning the political legitimacy of Aboriginal interests in Tasmania and future land claims. Kutikina, as both Allen (1987) and Griffiths (1991) document, had become a political and cultural symbol for Tasmanian Aboriginal activism – 'a sacred symbol of identity for the Tasmanian Aborigines' (Allen 1987: 9). This point was reinforced by the Aboriginal activist Ros Langford's threats to take legal action to protect Kutikina from destruction (*Launceston Examiner* 1982c). Allen argued that Kutikina was important for providing political unity within the Tasmanian Aboriginal community, as well as unity with mainland Aboriginality through the Pleistocene history of Kutikina, which linked Tasmanian history back to mainland Australia. However, he warned (1987: 9) that 'Aboriginal ownership, if conceded, would likely prevent the excavation of Kutikina ... and might impede other access to the region by both scientists and the general public'. A prophetic warning as it turned out, but the important point here is that the 'ownership' of Kutikina Cave was important not only to the Tasmanian government, the HEC, and the Aboriginal community, but also to archaeologists.

The Tasmanian government's case was that the Commonwealth had no constitutional powers to implement the World Heritage Act, as the Commonwealth could only pass laws to exercise its functions on a national level. The Commonwealth successfully responded that it could enact domestic legislation in relation to 'external affairs' if the subject of the legislation was of 'international concern', or if the legislation was enacted for the purposes of meeting an international treaty – in this case the UNESCO Convention for the Protection of the World's Cultural and Natural Heritage (James and Halliday 1990; Bates 1992: 55). The Commonwealth also responded, as Terry reports in the *Aboriginal Law Bulletin*, that under s.51(xxvi) of the Constitution it had the power to legislate with respect to 'the people of any race for whom it is deemed necessary to make special laws' (1983: 2). The 1967 referendum having deleted the words 'other than people of the Aboriginal race in any State' from this clause, it was argued that the World Heritage Act could be considered a 'special law' for the purposes of protecting Aboriginal heritage (Terry 1983). Significantly the High Court rejected the Tasmanian government's argument that Tasmanian Aborigines were extinct (Terry 1983) – an argument which could not be sustained in the face of Aboriginal media claims that the Tasmanian government, although maintaining that Aborigines were extinct, had taken and spent Federal funding for Aboriginal welfare projects (*Launceston Examiner* 1982c; *The Mercury* 1983; *ALB* 1983).

A minority of the High Court accepted the Tasmanian government's arguments that as the site was of international significance, and as the artefacts in the site were so old, its significance was universal and thus the law was not a 'special law' (Terry 1983). In effect, the Tasmanian government was using notions of archaeological scientific significance to exclude or defuse the political legitimacy of other values. However, the majority of the High Court, although noting that in contemporary usage the word 'race' was hard to define, accepted that Aborigines were a 'race' for the purposes of the Constitution due to their adherence to a common identity and culture (Terry 1983). Further, the majority of the Court found that 'the cultural heritage of a people is so much a characteristic or property of the people to whom it belongs that it is inseparably connected with them' (Terry 1983: 3). Justice Murphy argued that the World Heritage Act would help to strengthen the common understanding and tolerance of Aboriginal identity and, as Terry summarizes: 'A law aimed at the preservation or uncovering of evidence about the history of the Aboriginal people was therefore a special law' (1983: 3). The *Aboriginal Law Bulletin* editorial team, however, argued that this judgment was more likely to have been made for political expediency than for any real concern for Aboriginal people (*ALB* 1983: 3). Regardless of the motivation, the judgment explicitly recognizes the existence of contemporary Aboriginal people in Tasmania, and the value the community held for Kutikina Cave.

In response to this decision and continuing Aboriginal activism, a certain 'goal creep' (McGowan 1996: 303) has occurred with respect to Aboriginal heritage policies. Throughout the 1980s and early 1990s, following this judgment and in the face of continued and sustained Aboriginal agitation that ensured heritage issues remained in the public view, the PWS policies on Aboriginal consultation and 'ownership' of heritage changed. PWS policy changes attempted to address Aboriginal demands about increased consultation and more Aboriginal input into decision-making in the CRM process. By the mid-1990s changes in PWS CRM policies had resulted in a situation whereby policy had extended the boundaries of practice set by legislative requirements (McGowan 1992, 1996).

'The death of archaeology' in the southwest

The Southern Forest Archaeological Project (SFAP) conducted by La Trobe University academics, postgraduate and honours students has generated a significant amount of research in the form of honours and Ph.D. theses, reports and publications through excavation and survey work (see, for example, Allen 1989; Cosgrove *et al.* 1990; Webb and Allen 1990; Freslov 1993; McNiven *et al.* 1993; Murray 1993b; Stern and Marshall 1993; I. Thomas 1993; McNiven 1994; Holdaway and Porch 1995; Porch and Allen 1995 and their bibliographies). However, in a series of newspaper and television interviews in 1995, Jim Allen and Tim Murray, leading and supervising academics of this project, announced that this research had been jeopardized – if not ended (e.g. Maslen 1995a). They went further to suggest that archaeology in Australia as a whole was under threat due to the actions of PWS cultural heritage managers, John Cleary (the then Tasmanian Minster for Environment and Land Management), and the TALC over an application to extend research permits (Hawes 1995a; Maslen 1995a, 1995b; Morell 1995; Murray 1995; Murray and Allen 1995).

Permits were held variously by Allen and Murray to excavate, analyse and remove material interstate from four sites – Bone Cave, Warreen, Pallawa Trounta and Warragarra – as part of the SFAP and these expired in 1991 and 1992 (Allen 1995a; Olney 1995). Unsuccessful applications were made by Allen to extend these permits in 1993 (Allen 1995a; Murray 1996b).

Following PWS policy, TALC was asked to comment on the application for renewal and, according to documents quoted in Allen's (1995a) summary of events, advised that the permits should not be extended, ostensibly because they had had long enough to analyse the material and the permits had expired some time previously (see also Hawes 1995b; Murray 1996b). Darby considers that TALC saw this as an opportunity to make the Tasmanian government comply with promises to return control over heritage to Aboriginal people (1995a).

Allen also reports that PWS archaeologists suggested that he carry out consultations with TALC about the permits, which he reports that he and Murray did, citing not only meetings with TALC members, but also the employment of Aboriginal people on the excavations who could 'close any excavation which turned up human skeletal material' (Murray and Allen 1995: 872; see also, Allen 1995a, 1995b; Maslen 1995b; TV9 1995). However, TALC (1996) and TAC members (Mansell 1995) have questioned this consultation process and characterized archaeological attitudes to consultation as obtaining 'a rubber stamp'.

Pearse, the Acting Director of PWS, advised the Minister to deny the permit extensions, on the apparent basis that this would encourage Allen to re-open consultations with TALC (Pearse 1994, reproduced in Allen 1995a: 44). Certainly, perceptions of the legitimacy of archaeological claims by PWS appear to have changed as statements made by Pearse in the media further indicate:

> Does it mean that the scientific view must prevail? If the Aboriginal community sees it differently, then perhaps their view is entitled to prevail. The days are long past when what archaeologists regard as good scientific practice is the sole factor determining how they do their work.
>
> (Pearse quoted in Maslen 1995b: 53)

This is an interesting sentiment from a non-archaeologist and senior public servant in an institution that had previously used archaeological knowledge to regulate access to, and the meanings given to, Aboriginal material culture. Pearse was calling the regulatory practices and knowledge provided by archaeology into question, and the role of archaeology as a technology of government in Tasmania was shifting. However, Pearse's motivations and aims quickly became a moot point, as TALC took legal action to have the material returned to Tasmania. The matter, heard in the State of Victoria, went before Justice Olney who on 28 July 1995 ordered the material be sent to the Victorian Museum (Olney 1995). Olney's decision also encouraged Cleary to intervene, and subsequently Cleary directed that the material be returned to Tasmania, a move that finalized the litigation (Auty 1995; Dubdale 1995). Olney was less than complimentary in his decision about the respondents' willingness to comply with the permits (1995).

Following the judgment, a lot of media attention was given to the issue, with polemic not only about the 'death of archaeology', but also the threat to archaeo-logical science. Allen characterized the return of the material as 'the greatest act of scientific and cultural vandalism yet seen in this country' (Allen 1995b). Then Australian Archaeological Association president Anne Ross was reported in *The Weekend Australian* as stating that the disposal of the artefacts before full analysis would 'result in the effective vandalism of these highly significant sites and destruction of extremely important and valuable archaeological information' and described the court ruling as a 'serious' one for science (quoted in Hawes 1995a).

Much of the archaeological response in the media and the literature to these developments is clearly underlain by processual theoretical assumptions about the nature of 'science'. Not only is the 'interference' of non-scientists (bureaucrats and Aboriginal people) seen as a threat and an act of 'vandalism' against science, but also one of the arguments against the return of the material (and one widely circulated in the media) was that the material belongs to all 'mankind'. For instance, Allen was reported as stating that the 'sites represent part of the universal history of humans and as such should be a source of history and pride to all Australia, Aboriginal and non-Aboriginal alike' (Allen quoted in Maslen 1995a: 31). Murray considered that the excavated material was 'the most significant collection of ice-age material in Australia and one of the best in the world' (Murray quoted in Braund 1995; see also Akerman 1995; Darby 1995b; Ferguson 1995; Gregory 1995; Hawes 1995a, 1995b; *Launceston Examiner* 1995a, 1995b).

Various commentators have argued that the universal and international value of the material overrides the value of the material to contemporary Aboriginal people (Akerman 1995; Allen 1995b; Darby 1995a; *Launceston Examiner* 1995a; Maslen 1995a; Murray 1995; Murray and Allen 1995). The literature implies also that contemporary Aboriginal people have little legitimate claim to the material as it was abandoned by Aborigines over 13,000–12,000 years ago (Allen 1995b; Darby 1995a; Gough 1995; Maslen 1995a; TV9 1995). Murray and Allen also claimed that all Australians had, through current processes of reconciliation, claimed Aboriginal history as their own history (1995: 873; see also editorial in *Launceston Examiner* 1995a). This is an invocation of an old argument in Australian archaeology, in which the long period of time was seen as a barrier to the claims of connection and ancestry by contemporary Aboriginal people, yet allows Aboriginal heritage to be claimed as part of all Australians' history (see Frankel 1993b). Frankel (1993b) asserts that this argument had been seen as a fallacy in Australian archaeology as the discipline recognizes that Aboriginal people do not draw a distinction between a 'recent' and an 'older' past and that there had been an acceptance that Aboriginal people viewed time very differently to Europeans (see Swain 1993). As TALC (1996) argued in response to assertions in the media that they could not be seen as custodians of the sites due to their abandonment:

> We know that the people living in the Southwest Tasmanian caves during the ice age are our ancestors. Our ancestors are not just our genetic forebears. They have a spiritual dimension which incorporates those past Aboriginal people who are a creative force in our culture and heritage (for example, Trukanini [Truganini] had no children, but she is one of our ancestors). You as a profession know that these people are not your ancestors. It is because the people who lived in these caves are our ancestors that we, as a community, are the legitimate owners and custodians of these sites.
>
> (TALC 1996: 295; see also Brown in TV9 1995)

In terms of the repatriation of the Lake Mungo Woman and other ancient human remains, these arguments had been accepted (see Bowdler 1988; Pardoe 1992; Horton 1993). The ongoing debate in Australia over 'who owns the past' had previously been carried out with reference to specific cases of reburial, or control over religious and/or sacred material. However, in Tasmania these arguments were being brought to bear on secular cultural material. As Darby states 'there has never been such a contest over material that is neither human nor sacred but simply cultural' (1995a: 11). Allen and Murray both argued that the material was 'garbage' – the remains of day-to-day activities and not sacred – and they continuously emphasized in the media that no human remains occurred amongst the material (ABC 1995; Akerman 1995; Allen 1995b; Darby 1995a; Maslen 1995a, 1995b; Murray and Allen 1995). The implication is that this material is only significant to science – a position opposed by TALC (1996), who argue that the proclamations about the scientific significance and universal importance of the material works only to deny their cultural custodianship and any values they hold for the material.

Maslen (1995a: 7) also commented that archaeology had 'empowered Aboriginal communities', and helped to increase their 'assertiveness' and the 'widespread acceptance among white Australians of the Mabo land rights legislation' (views also echoed in Darby 1995a; Gough 1995; Murray 1995). These views, which suggest that Aboriginal history will become silent if archaeological values do not prevail, appear to be a response to the threat to the stewardship of archaeological science. Although Hughes, a spokesperson for TALC, has stated that the material excavated by La Trobe University 'is significant for us because it tells us about our past' (quoted in Ferguson 1995), this significance, and its apparent privileging by the Tasmanian government, is seen by sections of the media as jeopardizing the status of science:

> Scientists the world over are appalled by the decision to remove control of the material from the archaeologists who excavated it and award it to a group of untrained and unskilled lay people before all scientific research is complete.
>
> (Akerman 1995: 14)

The threat to archaeological stewardship posed by Aboriginal demands to control the material is emphasized in this case because it is secular material – the basic data of archaeology. The Minister acknowledged that his act was politically motivated in the favour of the Aboriginal community and stated that 'there is a movement towards enfranchising Aboriginal communities with respect to their heritage and which requires consultation with the Aboriginal community by archaeologists' (Cleary 1995).

Clearly, the use of archaeological knowledge by governments in reducing heritage issues to technical issues to restrict Aboriginal autonomy was overturned in this case. Rather, a technical issue of law (the expiry of permits) was used by Minister Pearse, and later by Olney, to attempt to regulate the consultation practices of Allen and Murray. By acting on a technical point, the Minister appears to have hoped to defuse the tension between the archaeologists and TALC. Allen and Murray's contestation of the Minister's refusal to renew the permits, however, inflamed rather than defused the situation, as did TALC's recourse to legal action. In this situation, Murray and Allen become paradoxically 'governed' by the instrumentality – the Relics Act – that set the parameters for the governance and regulation of material culture.

The discipline's public reaction to the TALC/La Trobe conflict has been mixed

– some supportive of Murray/Allen (e.g. Gait 1995; Wright 1995), others critical (e.g. Hope 1995). Concern has been raised over 'what would happen to Australian archaeology' after this affair and close attention has been given to the assertion that Australian archaeologists were deserting research in Aboriginal archaeology and going overseas or turning to historical archaeology (for example, Feary and Smith 1995; Maslen 1995a; Murray 1995; Wright 1995).

These perceptions, and the degree of attention they have received, reveal a significant undercurrent of unease in Australian archaeology over events in Tasmania. This is not simply because of specific contingencies in the situation, but because the affair signals a wider change in relationships between Aboriginal people, archaeologists, politicians, courts and bureaucracies. In Tasmania, the balance of power has shifted away from archaeological science, jeopardizing its authority. The arguments put forward by Murray and Allen and others about the 'rights' and authority of science publicly 'failed' to prevent the disruption of research.

Murray and Allen were also constrained in the arguments they could make. Both Murray and Allen had written previously on the political aspects of Aboriginal and archaeological relations within CRM, and had supported the Aboriginal cultural value of archaeological work (e.g. Allen 1983, 1987; Murray 1992a, 1993a, 1996a). In the light of their previous contribution, it is surprising that they became so embroiled; feeling the need to resort to arguments about 'access', 'scientific' 'rights' and other discourses underpinned by rigid positivism. Similar arguments had previously failed in Australia to stop the reburial of the Kow Swamp remains, the return of the Murray Black collection and the return of the Mungo Woman – but they were still invoked in this affair.

The use of these arguments again in the Tasmanian case suggests that the underlying theoretical position of processual theory has not been overthrown, and that it continues to provide philosophical and ideological underpinnings for the discipline. It also suggests that it remains an important source of arguments to be drawn on in the discipline's defence. More importantly, however, arguments about the universality and 'rights' of science have become the logical, and in some ways inevitable, arguments applied by archaeologists within CRM debates. This is because the parameters for any debate on heritage issues were set by the earlier embedding of processual philosophy within heritage legislation, archaeological regulatory practices, and archaeological perceptions about the nature and aims of CRM. Thus, in a certain sense, bureaucracies and governments *expect* that archaeologists will respond in certain ways, and it is reasonable that archaeologists will respond to those expectations. The institutionalization of archaeology as a technology of government, and sustaining the discipline's role in this process, requires that archaeologists invoke the authority of a positivist science previously privileged in the legislation – which is precisely what Murray and Allen attempted to do. If they had not evoked this discourse, their arguments would have been *openly* political. Openly political arguments, for instance those that might be put by postprocessualists, would have had little legitimacy given the intellectual confines set for archaeology by its position as a technology of government. That, on this occasion, appeals to science failed, reflects the changing relations and nature of Aboriginal politics, particularly in the wake of the 1992 Native Title decision. This decision ruled that Australian common law did recognize native title where it had not been legally extinguished and challenged the notion of *terra nullius* (Bartlett 1993; Butt and Eagleson 1993; also see Chapter 2).

The usefulness of archaeological knowledge in governing Aboriginal identity through material culture has decreased in Tasmania. The decline in usefulness cannot be surprising given the results of the Franklin Dam case for the Tasmanian government, the extent of Aboriginal lobbying of government, and the enactment of the *Native Title Act 1993* (Cwlth). These developments have made the regulation of Aboriginal identity more complex throughout Australia.

In relation to consultation issues and archaeological and Aboriginal relations generally TALC has put forward a clear challenge to the discipline:

> By accepting our role in analysis and interpretation, you [archaeologists] may find that new questions are identified and the interpretations acquire a relevance that extends beyond the confines of your discipline.
>
> We suggest that our exclusion from analysis and interpretation is just another way in which you strive to maintain control over our past. It allows you to write the 'authoritative' account of our past. But your authoritative account is based on the exclusion of the authority of our custody of heritage. It is also one of the reasons that you have problems with our community.
>
> (TALC 1996: 298)

The mobilization of archaeology as a technology of government has previously rested on the authority of archaeological science at the expense of non-scientific knowledge about the past, and the exclusion or marginalization of other knowledge systems. In response to Aboriginal contestation of archaeology's role in 'governing' material culture, most archaeologists have developed pragmatic responses to expectations of consultations. The discipline has been slow in matching this pragmatic response with a philosophical and theoretical response that could 'deal with' and incorporate competing and non-scientific claims to knowledge about the past. This hesitation is evident in the accusations of 'censorship' by some archaeologists concerned that TALC, following its victory, would require research proposals and interpretations to be altered (Gait 1995; Wright 1995). TALC (1996) quite rightly argues that the alteration of academic research designs already occurs as a result of peer reviews, ethics committees, and the demands of funding bodies and that this is not called 'censorship', whereas a non-scientific body's attempt at input into the research process is. The failure of some La Trobe University archaeologists to perceive consultation with TALC and TAC as more than just a 'rubber stamp' (TALC 1996: 295–6), and the lack of theoretical tools to deal with competing knowledge claims did not occur because Murray and

Allen did not adhere to 'better practices'. Rather the range of discourses that could be drawn on in the conflict was constrained by the institutionalization of archaeology as a technology of government.

Conclusion

The interaction of interests concerned with the management of Aboriginal heritage in Tasmania illustrates how archaeological knowledge is used, maintained and contested as a technology of government. The 'professionalization' of Tasmanian archaeology, its claims to status as positivistic science, and its accumulation of information and knowledge about the Tasmanian past allowed its mobilization by policy makers. Claims to, and the discourse about, the scientific significance of Tasmanian Aboriginal sites ensured that archaeological knowledge developed a privileged position in conflicts over the management of Aboriginal heritage up until and including the Franklin Dam debate.

The highly public use of archaeological knowledge in governing Aboriginal identity in Tasmania, particularly in the Franklin Dam case, saw archaeology's role in governing material culture change. Aboriginal activism, and claims to their material culture, always particularly strong, vocal and politically astute in Tasmania, were ensured a greater public and popular audience due to the debate over the film *The Last Tasmanian*. As Lehman (1991) states, this film and the archaeological knowledge and advice it drew on, marked an increasingly successful Aboriginal contestation of archaeological knowledge and claims.

The extent of public Aboriginal demands for control over their heritage and identity ensured a continuous political profile for the Tasmanian Aboriginal community in relation to heritage issues. The High Court decision over the Franklin Dam again saw, at least at an interstate and international level, critical attention given to Aboriginal cultural values. In addition, the Tasmanian government itself suffered a political loss at a State level due to the High Court's use of the archaeological values ascribed to Kutikina Cave, and public recognition of the existence of the Tasmanian Aboriginal community. With this decision Tasmanian Aboriginal cultural and heritage values and claims could no longer, in Matthews (1990) terms, not be 'listened to' by policy makers and government. In other words, the political legitimacy of Aboriginal interests had to be more directly engaged with by Tasmanian governments and institutions, and in particular the political legitimacy of their cultural and heritage values.

As McGowan (1996) argues, changing heritage policy within the PWS to meet Aboriginal demands resulted in a shift away from the archaeological scientific values embedded in the Relics Act. Unlike in America with the Kennewick case, policy was able to extend the parameters of practice beyond those set by the relevant Act. Archaeological knowledge lost some of its authority and political legitimacy gained in its role as a technology of government. Instead archaeology itself became, in this case, just another interest that needed to be actively regulated by the Tasmanian government. Although always regulated through legislation, its legitimacy in this interaction was decreased in favour of Aboriginal interests. It is ironic that archaeologists in this encounter had the legitimacy of their claims questioned by the implementation of the Relics Act – the very Act that had previously ensured archaeological knowledge was privileged over the legitimacy of claims made by Aboriginal interests.

Archaeological responses to competing Aboriginal claims invoked well-established processual arguments about the 'significance' of archaeological research, scientific rights of access, and claims to reassert archaeological stewardship. They did this for two reasons: first, the archaeologists within this conflict failed to recognize the changing political arena and relationships, and second, the regulation of archaeology by the Relics Act and its mobilization by policy makers meant that archaeological responses were constrained. The archaeological arguments employed in this case did not work because Aboriginal political interests over time in Tasmania had successfully questioned the *political* legitimacy of the history of archaeological research and practice in Tasmania. It is important to note that Aboriginal public criticism of archaeology rested largely on the inadequacies of archaeological *practice* (i.e. consultation) rather than actively questioning the legitimacy of their scientific knowledge and pursuits. Thus the political sophistication of archaeology was found wanting, and claims to scientific authority could be marginalized as an irrelevancy in the conflict.

10

CONCLUSION

This book has argued that archaeological discourse, practice, theory and the discipline's sense of its own 'identity' are governed and regulated by the processes of CRM. CRM, which may be defined in Western contexts as the process concerned with the management of material or tangible cultural heritage, is also ultimately about the management and governance of the meanings and values that the material heritage is seen to symbolize or otherwise represent. Those values, and the cultural, historical or social identities that are linked to heritage places and items, become themselves governed and regulated. Archaeological discourse is therefore constitutive of the practice of CRM, which means that it is archaeological knowledge that is explicitly implicated in this governance. Archaeologists therefore become a legitimate and specific target of interests, such as Indigenous peoples, who question the validity of archaeological pronouncements and judgments that influence governmental and bureaucratic perceptions of their cultural identity.

Any conflict over the management and meaning of heritage, such as the Kennewick and Tasmanian disputes, will be particularly fraught due to what is at stake for all parties involved. For Indigenous peoples, for instance, what is often at stake is the right to control a sense of their own identity, which in turn can have vital implications in wider negotiations with governments and their bureaucracies over the political and cultural legitimacy of Indigenous interests. For archaeologists, the stakes may not be as high, but are often nonetheless keenly felt. At one level, the issue will be the maintenance of the privileged position of archaeological expertise in CRM. This position not only helps to ensure both physical and intellectual access to the discipline's database, but also helps to maintain the intellectual legitimacy of the discipline in the eyes of bureaucrats and governments. Further, as with Indigenous peoples, archaeologists also use access to heritage places and items to reaffirm identity – in this case the disciplinary identity of a mature 'science'. This process is continually reaffirmed by the ways in which the processual discourse, particularly that of 'stewardship', 'professionalism' and 'scientific objectivity', is continually rehearsed and ultimately regulated by its inclusion in CRM policy and legislation. Although this has been discussed in terms of Indigenous CRM, it operates nonetheless within all areas of CRM and in disputes over the meaning of such things as class, gender, and ethnic or other social, cultural and historical identities.

This dynamic is encapsulated in the position the discipline occupies as a technology of government. The antecedents to the mobilization of archaeology in the governance of material culture and its meanings began in the late nineteenth century with the beginnings of archaeological discursive claims to intellectual and disciplinary maturity, which found synergy with liberal projects concerned with the development of 'good citizens'. This process accelerated during the latter parts of the twentieth century, with archaeology reaching the zenith of its mobilization as a technology of government from the late 1960s. By the 1990s, however, this position was slightly modified, at least in terms of Indigenous heritage management, in response to sustained and politically sophisticated criticisms by Indigenous peoples worldwide. This modification has allowed the power/ knowledge dynamic to shift, following the fluctuations of governmental political climates and agendas, although it has yet to overthrow the underlying authority of archaeological expertise and its role as a technology of government.

The events that established the discipline as a fully-fledged technology of government within Indigenous CRM were, ultimately, the conjunction of publicly expressed archaeological concerns over the fate of 'archaeological' resources, the discipline's new identity as a maturing 'science', and the development of a politicized Indigenous cultural resurgence. Archaeology was seen by governments to be useful, in so far as it had a concrete policy effect, because of the social claims made by Indigenous peoples in the 1960s and 1970s. Archaeology as an area of expertise could be mobilized to help the state make sense of, and 'govern', Indigenous claims. It could, in Bauman's terms, 'interpret' and regulate Indigenous claims to identity based on expert interpretations of 'the past'. Other disciplines, such as anthropology and history were also mobilized in similar ways; however, the physical focus of archaeological inquiry, which could 'quantify' and empirically 'validate' material culture, proved to have a great utility in conflicts and negotiations over 'identity', and Indigenous land rights and sovereignty claims. This is not to argue that there was an archaeological 'conspiracy' to actively challenge or support Indigenous claims, or to deny access to material culture. Rather, the conjunction of events, together with the development of the discipline's new profile as 'professional', 'objective' and 'scientific', meant that archaeological knowledge could be a useful tool in establishing policy for dealing with Indigenous politics, which was being constructed around perceptions of 'cultural identity' and claims about historical and cultural links to land based on interpretations of material culture.

These events also coincided with public concerns about Indigenous and European heritage, and the conservation of 'natural' environments. During the 1960 and 1970s, Western concerns about conservation increased, and more critical attention was paid to the role of both Indigenous and non-Indigenous heritage in the development of post-colonial national identities. Indigenous claims to prior sovereignty also at this time began to publicly challenge post-colonial perceptions about the Indigenous past, Indigenous and Euroamerican/Euro-australian relations, and perceptions about national identity and nationhood.

These events in turn lead to the development of Indigenous heritage legislation, which embedded processual discourse and values about the nature of 'cultural resources'. The value and 'significance' of material culture helped to define the objects, which in Hunt's terms, were to be 'regulated' by legislative intervention (1993: 318). The various cultural resource or heritage laws in both Australia and America have since played a part in regulating public perceptions about Indigenous cultural identity and political legitimacy. Archaeological discourse, through its regulatory role in legislation, thus plays a part in 'governing' populations and representations of their past. This is not to say that archaeological knowledge is necessarily the only privileged form of intellectual knowledge in this process, certainly legal and bureaucratic knowledge play key roles. However, archaeology has made a particular and unique contribution to the development of both cultural heritage legislation, policy and the overall processes of CRM and in doing so has cemented its claims both to the 'resource' and its claims to intellectual authority and expertise.

So far, I have made specific claims about the interrelationship between CRM, one significant area of archaeological practice, and the development and main-tenance of archaeological discourse and theory, but what are the implications of the insights I offer? Whether, at this point, you agree or disagree with the theory and ideas put forward, my analysis offers a specific challenge to the discipline: it is time to start actively debating questions and observations about what it is that archaeology *does*, and to start to critically engage with the wider contexts and consequences of theoretical development and practice.

The postprocessual push within the discipline drew attention to the under-theorization of archaeological practice, and revealed that the discipline was, and remains, theoretically behind the social sciences. As argued in Chapter 3, the Anglophone discipline has also yet to adequately engage with the cultural, social and political contexts in which theory and practice are developed and utilized – to date archaeological theory has been overly self-referential. This tendency is no longer tenable in the continuing presence of Indigenous criticism of archaeological theory and practice. Moreover, heritage interests and community groups other than Indigenous peoples are now staking claims for direct involvement in heritage management and research (for instance, see Newman and McLean 1998; Marshall 2002, Derry and Malloy 2003; Singleton and Orser 2003). This situation will continue to develop as Western governments start to consider 'community inclusion' issues in CRM more generally. By not engaging with, and attempting to understand, the contexts and consequences of archaeological knowledge and practice the discipline will only continue to rehearse the tired old claims to archaeological authority and expertise. Worse, if you accept the theoretical insights I have offered here, the discipline will continue to unwittingly engage not only in the governance of the identities of various interest groups, but also in its own governance and regulation – and theoretical debate will continue to stagnate.

While my analysis offers a challenge to commence a theoretically engaged debate, it also has a range of other implications and issues for practice and theory. These are premised on the assumption that, either collectively as a discipline or individually, we *do* wish to engage with the wider context and consequences of archaeological knowledge and practice, and deal equitably with different interests and stakeholder groups. Certainly, as discussed in Chapter 2, there is an increasing literature in the discipline that has called for greater community participation in archaeology and recognizes not only a need, but also a desire, to engage with Indigenous criticism. The Australian Archaeological Association and the World Archaeological Congress have both developed codes of ethics that attempt to acknowledge the custodial rights of Indigenous peoples to their heritage, and Australia ICOMOS has rewritten the *Burra Charter* to encourage more community inclusion in CRM and conservation generally (WAC 1990; AAA 1991; ICOMOS 1999).

Any attempt to develop an inclusive or critically engaged practice with Indigenous, or any other interest group, must commence from an acknowledgement and understanding of the power/knowledge dynamic that underpins both the discipline and its place within CRM. It is simply insufficient for archaeologists and cultural resource managers to assume that we occupy an equitable position with all other interest groups. An understanding of the resources of power and the authority of archaeological pronouncements is vital if space is to be made to include the concerns and aspirations of interest groups in CRM and wider archaeological research agendas. Conversely, any understanding of the resources of power and limits of archaeological authority could also become useful in negotiations with those economic interests who often subvert and overrule archaeological values and aspirations within CRM. Subsequently any debate about the nature of archaeological practice and theory cannot afford to neglect identifying and dealing critically and constructively with relations of power and expertise.

This also means that simple consultation with Indigenous and other community or stakeholder groups can no longer be seen as good enough. Without an active understanding of power/knowledge relations, any attempts to incorporate Indigenous or other non-archaeological knowledges and aspirations into archaeological practice will simply end in appropriation by archaeologists, no matter how unintended that may be. Although a lot of stress has been placed in the literature on the utility and desirability of consultation with Indigenous and other community groups, and attempts are made to incorporate Indigenous knowledge and values in CRM, these attempts are still constrained by the dominant technical and scientific discourse of processual science which frames CRM practice. This means that, at the very least, non-positivistic based knowledge and values cannot be incorporated, or that they become appropriated by translation and interpretation by archaeological experts for bureaucratic consumption. Indigenous peoples continue to complain that consultation is often little more than 'rubber stamping' (TALC 1996) or that it is inherently limited (Lippert 1997; Watkins

2001b, 2003). In Australia, despite a genuine commitment to a code of ethics and a practice of informed consultation, these criticisms have not abated. For instance, a 2003 media release by Australian Indigenous archaeologist David Johnson noted that Indigenous participation within heritage management was still insufficient and that archaeological notions and values tended to dominate the management process:

> Australian Federal and State government agencies are not adequately addressing Indigenous cultural values and the ongoing management needs of our cultural heritage. Although more communities are being involved and consulted about archaeological programs, too often archaeological or scientific assessments conflict with the social and cultural values we have for our sites, particularly where political and economic/development interests and pressures are strong … Ministers and the bureaucracy of the various sites' departments ultimately determine whether sites are allowed to be destroyed. In theory their assessments of sites' significance take on board both archaeological significance and Indigenous social values. … Indigenous people need control over our cultural heritage and the decision-making that goes with it. We need recognition of our social values and significance. The archaeological record is only one aspect of what makes an Indigenous place sacred or significant.
>
> (Johnson 2003: 1)

The point that Johnson highlights is that despite the incorporation of Indigenous knowledge through consultation it remains nonetheless subject to the interventions of archaeological interpretation and regulation. Further, archaeological scientific values are understood and utilized by government heritage agencies to mitigate conflict over the fate of heritage sites and places in a way that non-scientific values are not. To start to address the inclusion of Indigenous values a politics of recognition is needed. That is, collectively and individually, archaeologists need to recognize that other interest groups, and Indigenous groups in particular, have different but entirely legitimate knowledge and values about the past. This is not to say that as archaeologists we must adopt or even agree with those values – but simply recognize that they exist legitimately alongside archaeological knowledge and values.

To some extent, this is done in Australia, which may have lessons to offer practice in the USA. As Claire Smith and Heather Burke point out (2003), Australian archaeologists, in handing back to the Indigenous community the 25 000-year-old remains of Mungo Woman in 1992, accepted the legitimacy of Indigenous claims to cultural ties with these remains. Explicit in the management of the Mungo remains was recognition of different cultural values and conceptualizations of kinship. This recognition is an act of respect, and this act, in turn, has meant that future research or access to the remains is open to negotiation (Smith and Burke 2003). The Kennewick conflict, in part, hinges on an inability of the CRM process to accept the legitimacy of Indigenous claims to kinship that could stretch through time as long as 9000 years ago (see Chapter 8). It is difficult in the frameworks offered by American CRM to move beyond the dominant cultural and scientific discourse as the Australians managed to do in the case of Mungo Woman. What the Australian practice does is to offer an explicit recognition or acknowledgement of, first, the existence of different values systems and then, second, the legitimacy of that difference. This is an important point of departure for inclusive practices and associated theoretical debates. However, the Australian attempts at cultural recognition and respect have not entirely resolved the problem of meaningful community inclusion nor have they initiated serious theoretical debate – as witnessed by continuing Indigenous criticism about consultation and the events in Tasmania (Chapter 9). This is because the politics of recognition tend to be divorced from an acknowledgement of the material and institutional realities of inequality.

Nancy Fraser's work on the politics of recognition offers some useful insights here. She recognizes that identity politics can: 'represent genuinely emancipatory responses to serious injustices that cannot be remedied by redistribution alone. Culture, moreover, is a legitimate, even necessary, terrain of struggle, a site of injustice in its own right ...' (2000: 2). However, she goes on to develop a bifocal analysis of the politics of recognition, which she believes has the danger of obfuscating institutional and economic inequalities behind a single-minded emphasis on cultural identity. Her emphasis on redistribution is crucial – by emphasizing the imbrication of the economic and cultural aspects of social justice issues she turns our attention to the material consequences of over-reliance on the value of simply validating identity. She goes on to observe that:

> Properly conceived, struggles for recognition can aid the redistribution of power and wealth ... This means conceptualizing struggles for recognition so that they can be integrated with struggles for redistribution, rather than displacing and undermining them.
>
> (Fraser 2000: 2)

My intention is not to dismiss the good work that many archaeologists have done in 'recognizing' the cultural claims of Indigenous peoples, and in some cases actually acting on them. The point is that though there may be a 'feel good' factor for the discipline at large here, it is often more a politics of gesture than serious recognition. Needless to say archaeology does not have the power to redress, in terms of either restorative or redistributive justice, the wrongs done to Indigenous peoples. However, the role, for example, that land claims have come to play in Australia and the US for Indigenous communities' search for economic independence, or attacks on American Indian rights to casino operation on Indian lands couched in terms of cultural authenticity and continuity, suggest there is a point where the social justice aspects of what archaeology does are not just abstract.[1]

Subsequently, the politics of recognition must exist within a context of critical engagement with archaeological power and authority and its institutionalization within CRM. The analysis I have offered renders unsustainable archaeological complaints that the discipline is powerless. Further, the discipline can no longer pretend to be innocent when the knowledge and discourse that we use 'takes on a life of its own' and is utilized in wider public debates as was done in the Kennewick and Tasmanian cases. The discipline is not innocent here as it draws authority and power from this process. This means that, as Goodman (1998: 1) argues in the Kennewick case, we cannot ignore the sometimes subtle and indirect discursive – and the sometimes not so subtle – connections that are made between archaeological pronouncements and knowledge and wider racist debates and assertions about Indigenous peoples or any other interest group. An unintended consequence of archaeological knowledge is that, at times, it may share discursive spaces with ideas and interests that are extremely problematic. It is indefensible to ignore this. Not only because to do so condones such uses of archaeological knowledge, but also because once again the discipline will draw power and authority from this use. The implication of this is that individually and collectively the discipline has to be politically more aware.

Postprocessual, feminist and Marxist archaeologists have all made similar calls for the discipline to adopt explicit political agendas. I am not necessarily advocating a specific agenda be adopted here (although I clearly have my own). Rather I am suggesting that individually we cannot pretend to be politically neutral or objective. I am suggesting that we need to acknowledge the agendas that we may individually adopt for ourselves and not be shy about it. By self-consciously and honestly acknowledging these agendas, the privileged position of archaeologists and archaeological knowledge within CRM will be jeopardized. However, by not acknowledging them, the discipline will not move on, and consultation practices and attempts at social and community inclusion will continue to be limited. Through CRM the discipline has sustained a long-term commitment to public education and outreach; this programme may perhaps be extended to target bureaucracies and other policy makers. That is, the 'translator' role played by archaeologists within CRM can be actively utilized to explicitly pursue wider policy developments that may facilitate the politics of recognition and thus encourage challenges to the processual discourse that underpins CRM.

This does not mean that by acknowledging and actively using the political nature of CRM, and by adopting explicit agendas, that archaeologists have to uncritically accept Indigenous agendas or those of other interests. It does mean, however, that a recognition and respect of difference needs to include political as well as cultural difference. Honest and 'upfront' debate that acknowledges the values and aspirations of each participant is simply a more constructive position from which to commence debate and negotiations over cultural heritage – especially as such debate has wider cultural and political implications.

In summary, a practice informed by the insights offered in this book rests on an explicit acknowledgement of the power/knowledge relations regulated by CRM and of the political and cultural agendas and assumptions that underpin archaeological knowledge and practice. However, this practice must also be informed by critically engaged theoretical debate. One of the important things revealed in this analysis is that theory and practice are indeed interlinked. Further, that without explicitly challenging the discourse embedded in CRM the theoretical development of the discipline will continue to remain self-referential and practices will subsequently not change. Throughout the later part of the 1980s and much of the 1990s, theoretical debate was stimulated by developments in postprocessual theory and other critical traditions such as feminist and Marxist archaeologies. These debates have failed to move on since the late 1990s, and a significant reason for this stagnation has been the failure to translate a critically informed archaeology into practice.

Another reason for this is the degree to which theoretical debate has ignored CRM. Failure to engage with this important area of practice has meant that the processual values and discourse have remained dominant, and are continually reinforced through the role archaeology plays as a technology of government. In turn, this has meant that theoretical debate has been unable to successfully challenge the mechanisms that regulate and govern the development of discourse, and this in turn has meant that the hegemonic position of processual science within the discipline has not been subverted. Awareness of the interrelation of archaeological theory development and the regulation of archaeological discourse and practice within CRM will be necessary, if theoretical debates are to develop beyond oppositional and polarized positions.

A significant issue confronting theory development and debate is how to recognize Indigenous and other non-positivist knowledge claims within archaeological theory. Given the current power/knowledge relations that the discipline operates within, this is a particularly thorny problem – especially as the issue here is to recognize rather than appropriate. Any attempt to engage with non-positivistic knowledge and values must be informed by a critical practice as discussed above, but it must also be informed by a new way of recognizing and legitimizing knowledge. Zimmerman (2001) offers one way forward with 'ethnocriticism'. In this approach, compromise between Indigenous and archaeological knowledge is not the aim – as any compromise is likely to simply rehearse the dominant value system. Rather a way between objectivism and relativism is sought by working at 'the boundaries of our ways of knowing' (2001: 179). Further, he argues that archaeology can 'still be scientific in ways that are meaningful, by specifying the methods and procedures followed and by indicating the empirical and logical components of arguments' but that claims to a master narrative would be abandoned (2001: 179). This position, as with other critical approaches, is useful, but must engage clearly with analysis of power/knowledge to succeed. My analysis provides an extra dimension to theoretical debates that must take that debate outside the concerns of abstract knowledge construction and focus attention on consequence and practice.

I do not pretend to have all the answers here, nor do I claim to offer a 'better' theoretical and ideological position for the discipline. The analysis does reveal, however, why continual re-examination of, and debate about, the epistemological and ontological underpinnings of the discipline are worthwhile. It lays the theoretical groundwork for conceptualizing the power/knowledge strategies of the discipline and their consequences. The governmentality literature, coupled with a strategic relational understanding of the state, wherein state apparatuses enter into negotiations over the legitimacy of interests, presents a useful framework for contextualizing the development of archaeological discourse and practice. By understanding how the discipline enters into the governance of cultural heritage and associated values and identities, and how subsequently the discipline unwittingly contrives to participate in its own governance, the work also offers the conceptual tools for challenging the hegemony of processual science. At the very least this work demonstrates that the idea of theorizing for the sake of it cannot be sustained, and that an active sense of theory that allows itself to go out and 'do' a critically informed archaeology is required.

NOTES

3 Archaeological theory and the 'politics' of the past

1 I focus on the theoretical debates largely developed in the North American, British and Scandinavian English literature, as it is these debates that ultimately have had an impact, at some level, on archaeological practice in the USA and Australia. For want of a better term 'Anglophone' archaeology refers to this literature. In the rest of this chapter, and the book as a whole, for 'archaeology' read 'Anglophone' archaeology.

2 Processual theory was initially referred to as the 'New Archaeology', Binford (1988: 107–8) claims, as a form of ironic derision by its opponents. However, the rhetoric of a New Archaeology had positive polemical value for its adherents. Once the 'newness' wore off the term 'processual' was adopted to describe what the New Archaeology had become.

3 The name 'prehistoric' archaeology has been rightly criticized by Aboriginal people for denying Aboriginal history prior to European arrival in Australia, and 'Aboriginal Archaeology' or 'Australian Archaeology' are more generally preferred. However, during the period that this book is concerned with the term 'prehistory' was widely used, and is thus used here. The term 'prehistory' tends to privilege archaeologists as spokespersons or stewards for a distant past unconnected to the politics of the present – an idea that is explored in Chapter 5.

4 Research into the public perceptions of archaeology has noted that excavation features as one of the main public images of archaeological research (Ascher 1960; Bray 1981; Cunliffe 1981; Stone 1986; Cleere 1988; Zarmati 1995). Moreover, there is a sense in the discipline that unless you excavate you are not a 'real' archaeologist (e.g. Flannery 1982; see also Woodall and Perricone 1981; Zarmati 1995 who comment on this phenomenon).

5 Some postprocessualists deny association with post-modernism (e.g. Thomas and Tilley 1992; Thomas 1993a), although links are acknowledged by others (Hodder 1985, 1999). Its association is, however, evident in the material that postprocessualists both draw on and actively translate for archaeological consumption (Solli 1992).

6 The issue of Indigenous criticism, as well as the whole 'politicization' issue, was significantly reinforced by the split of the World Archaeological Congress (WAC) from the UNESCO organisation International Union of Prehistoric and Protohistoric Sciences (IUPPS), and by the very public controversies and events leading up to the 1986 WAC Congress (see Ucko 1987; also Champion and Shennan 1986; Hodder 1986b).

7 There has been extensive debate in the UK archaeological literature about the conflict over the different meanings given to this site in which fears have been variously expressed about not only damage to the site but also to its archaeological meanings (see Hawkes 1967; Chippendale 1983, 1986, 1989; P. Fowler 1987; Bintliff 1988; Chippendale *et al.* 1990; Bender 1992; for examples of this debate). Despite these fears the site remains controlled by heritage instrumentalities and it is archaeological technical and interpretive knowledge, and no other interpretation, that is presented at this site.

8   This issue was given added urgency during the 1980s by surveys of museum visitors that measured visitor knowledge about archaeology. The results indicated that there was not much public interest in archaeology (Prince and Schadla-Hall 1987; Stone 1989). Discussion of this survey stresses the need for archaeology to work on its 'public relations' and to make archaeology more 'relevant' and socially responsible to the public (Stone 1986, 1989; Prince and Schadla-Hall 1987; Cleere 1988; DeCicco 1988; McManamon 1991). This issue was of particular interest for Hodder who participated in one of the surveys (Stone 1986: 14). However, what is missing in discussing these surveys is any consideration that 'the public' may not necessarily have an awareness of archaeology as such, but that archaeological knowledge may still be used to affect in museum and other public forums.

4 Archaeology and the context of governance: expertise and the state

1   *Mabo* refers to the court judgment in *Mabo* v. *Queensland*. In 1982 Eddie Mabo and other Meriam people mounted a legal challenge to the annexation of the Murray islands by Queensland in 1879. Mabo claimed that communal native title still existed, and had not been extinguished by 'settlement'. On 3 June 1992 the High Court upheld Mabo's argument, and ruled that native title had not been extinguished on the Murray Islands. This then challenged a previous legal ruling (by the British Privy Council in 1889) that Australia was *terra nullius* – or vacant land – at the time of European 'discovery' of Australia (see Bartlett 1993; Butt and Eagleson 1993; Goot and Rowse 1994).

6 Significance concepts and the embedding of processual discourse in cultural resource management

1   Many of the assumptions identified here in the original version of the Charter have now been challenged by the 1999 version. However, the assumptions that underwrote the original Charter were embedded in CRM discourse and values during the 1980s.

7 The role of legislation in the governance of material culture in America and Australia

1   NAGPRA was enacted alongside its sister Act the *National Museum of the American Indian Act* 1989 (PL 101-185) which requires the repatriation of human remains in the collections of the Smithsonian Institution. For details of the history of this Act see Bray and Killion (1994). It must also be noted that many of the States within the USA were, at this time, also enacting their own reburial laws. The history of these Acts is outside the scope of this volume, but see Price (1991).

2   The Northern Territory introduced the *Native and Historical Objects and Areas Preservation Ordinance* 1955 and South Australia the *Aboriginal and Historic Relics Preservation Act* 1965 (both repealed) (see Edwards 1970; Pretty 1970; McCarthy 1970d for histories of these Acts). Queensland enacted the *Aboriginal Relics Preservation Act 1967* in the same year as NSW introduced limited provisions for the protection of Aboriginal sites in the *National Parks and Wildlife Act* 1967 (see Killoran 1970; McKinlay 1973: 70–4).

8 NAGPRA and Kennewick

1 On 4 February 2004 a three-judge panel of the Ninth US Circuit Court of Appeals in San Francisco upheld the 2002 Oregon District Court decision by Jelderks. Any appeal to this will be heard in the US Supreme Court; at the time of going to press, dates by which an appeal had to be lodged had not been reached.

10 Conclusion

1 I will not belabour the point, but note that the journalist who wrote a book about the Kennewick conflict, supportive of the 'scientific' agenda, has also written another about 'scandals' in American Indian-run casinos (Benedict 2001, 2003).

BIBLIOGRAPHY

AAA (Australian Archaeological Association) (1991) *Code of Ethics*. Available online: http://www.australianarchaeologicalassociation.com.au/codeofethics.html (accessed 15 September 2001).

AAPA (American Association of Physical Anthropologists) (2000) *Statement by the American Association of Physical Anthropologists on the Secretary of the Interior's Letter of 21 September 2000 Regarding Cultural Affiliation of Kennewick Man*. Available online: http://www.physanth.org/positions/kennewick.html (accessed 15 September 2001).

ABC (Australian Broadcasting Commission) (1979) *Monday Conference: The Last Tasmanian Debate*, AIATSIS Film archives no. LV0043.

—— (1995) *Quantum*, screened on ABC, Wednesday 8pm 15 November, M. Jones reporter/interviewer.

Abbott, K. (1996) *Pressure Groups and the Australian Federal Parliament*, Canberra: Australian Government Publishing Service.

ACHP (Advisory Council on Historic Preservation) (1976a), *Report, Compliance Issue*, IV(7), Washington, DC: ACHP.

—— (1976b) 'Survey of local preservation programs', *ACHP Report, Special Issue*, IV(2), Washington, DC: ACHP.

—— (1976c), *Report, Compliance Issue*, IV(5), Washington, DC: ACHP.

Adams, E. (1984) 'Archaeology and the Native American: a case study at Hopi', in E. Green (ed.) *Ethics and Values in Archaeology*, New York: The Free Press.

Adovasio, J.M. and Carlisle, R.C. (1988) 'Some thoughts on cultural resource management in the United States', *Antiquity*, 62: 72–87.

AFA (Asatri Folk Assembly) (1997) 'Kennewick Man – ancient caucasian in North America'. Available online: http://www.runestone.org/km.html (accessed 10 January 2003).

AHC (Australian Heritage Commission) (1985) *Australia's National Estate: The Role of the Commonwealth*, Canberra: Australian Government Publishing Service.

Ah Kit, J. (1995) 'Aboriginal aspirations for heritage conservation', *Historic Environment*, 11(2 and 3): 31–6.

Akerman, P. (1995) 'Bones of contention', *Daily Telegraph-Mirror*, 1st edn, 1 August: 14.

ALB (Aboriginal Law Bulletin) (1983) 'Editorial: commonwealth and responsibility', *Aboriginal Law Bulletin*, 8: 3.

Allen, H. (1988a) 'History matters – a commentary on divergent interpretations of Australian history', *Australian Aboriginal Studies*, 1988/2: 79–89.

—— (1988b) 'Public archaeology: choices for the 1990s', *Archaeology in New Zealand*, 31(3): 142–52.

Allen, J. (1970) 'Early colonial archaeology', in F.D. McCarthy (ed.) *Aboriginal Antiquities in Australia*, Canberra: Australian Institute of Aboriginal Studies.

—— (1983) 'Aborigines and archaeologists in Tasmania, 1983', *Australian Archaeology*, 16: 7–10.

—— (1987) *The Politics of the Past*, Melbourne: La Trobe University Inaugural Address.

—— (1989) 'When did humans first colonize Australia?', *Search*, 20(5): 149–54.

—— (1993) 'Notions of the Pleistocene in Greater Australia', in M. Spriggs, D.E. Yen, W. Ambrose, R. Jones, A. Thorne and A. Andrews (eds) *A Community of Culture*, Canberra: Department of Prehistory, Research School of Pacific Studies, The Australian National University.

—— (1995a) 'A short history of the Tasmanian affair', *Australian Archaeology*, 41: 43–8.

—— (1995b) 'Letters: We find that what's theirs is theirs – but what's ours?', *Weekend Australian*, 2–3 September.

Allen, J. and Jones, R. (1983) 'Facts, figures and folklore', *Australian Archaeology*, 16: 165–7.

Ames, K. (2000) 'Review of the archaeological data', unpublished report to the National Parks Service, Department of the Interior, Washington, DC. Available online: http://www.cr.nps.gov/aad/kennewick/ames.htm (accessed 26 July 2002).

Anawak, J. (1989) 'Inuit perceptions of the past', in R. Layton (ed.) *Who Needs the Past?* London: Unwin Hyman.

Anon. (1906) 'Recent progress in American anthropology: a review of the activities of institutions and individuals from 1902–1906', *American Anthropologist*, 8(3): 441–555.

—— (1969) 'Preservation of antiquities', *Australian Institute of Aboriginal Studies Newsletter*, 2(12): 7–8.

—— (1973) 'National register of Aboriginal sites', *Australian Institute of Aboriginal Studies Newsletter*, 3(6): 13–16.

—— (1998) 'Tour bus may focus on site of Kennewick Man', *The Seattle Times*, 30 December. Available online: http://archives.seattletimes.nwsource.com/ (accessed 25 September 2003).

Antone, C., Benallie, L. Jr., Jenkins, L., Johnson, W., Jojola, T., Ladd, E., Lomawaima, H. (1992) 'Round table: Native American perspectives on archaeological interpretation', unpublished discussion at the third Southwest Symposium, Tucson, Arizona, USA.

Anyon, R. and Ferguson, T. (1995) 'Cultural resources management at the Pueblo of Zuni, New Mexico, USA', *Antiquity*, 69: 913–30.

Anyon, R., Ferguson, T. and Welch, J. (2000) 'Heritage management by American Indian tribes in the southwestern United States', in F. McManamon and A. Hatton (eds) *Cultural Resource Management in Contemporary Society*, London: Routledge.

Anyon, R., Ferguson, T.J., Jackson, L., Lane, L. and Vicenti, P. (1997) 'Native American oral tradition and archaeology: issues of structure, relevance and respect', in N. Swidler, K.E. Dongoske, R. Anyon and A.S. Downer (eds) *Native Americans and Archaeologists: Stepping Stones to Common Ground*, Walnut Creek: AltaMira.

AP (Associated Press) (1998) 'Kennewick Man a big tourist draw', *The Seattle Times*, 16 February. Available online: http://archives.seattletimes.nwsource.com/ (accessed 25 September 2003).

—— (2003) 'Court blocks study of bones pending appeal', *Tri-City Herald*, 21 February. Available online: http://www.kennewick-man.com/kman/news/story/2883302p-2919309c.html (accessed 12 September 2003).

Archer, J. (1991) 'Ambiguity in political ideology: Aboriginality as nationalism', *The Australian Journal of Anthropology*, 2(2): 161–9.

Arnold, J.B. (1978) 'Underwater cultural resources and the antiquities market', *Journal of Field Archaeology*, 5: 232.

ARTIS (1978) Information Package: The Last Tasmanian, unpublished documents released with the film: *The Last Tasmanian*, held in the AIATSIS film archive files.

Ascher, R. (1960) 'Archaeology and the public image', *American Antiquity*, 25(3): 402–3.

Attenbrow, V. and Negerevich, T. (1984) 'The assessment of sites, Lucas Heights waste disposal depot: a case study', in S. Sullivan and S. Bowdler (eds) *Site Surveys and Significance*

Assessments in Australian Archaeology, Canberra: Department of Prehistory, Research School of Pacific Studies, The Australian National University.

Attwood, B. (1989) *The Making of the Aborigines,* Sydney: Allen and Unwin.

—— (1995) 'Aboriginal history', *Australian Journal of Politics and History*, 41: 33–47.

Auty, K. (1995) 'Aboriginal cultural heritage: Tasmania and La Trobe University', *Aboriginal Law Bulletin*, 3(76): 20.

Babbitt, B. (2000) *Letter from Secretary of the Interior to the Hon. L. Caldera, Secretary of the Army*. Available online: http://www.cr.nps.gov/aad/kennewick/bcbb_letter.htm (accessed 26 July 2002).

Baber, Z. (1992) 'Sociology of scientific knowledge: lost in the reflexive funhouse', *Theory and Society*, 21: 105–19.

Baker, B., Varney, T., Wilkinson, R., Anderson, L. and Liston, M. (2001) 'Repatriation and the study of human remains', in T. Bray (ed.) *The Future of the Past*, New York: Garland Publishing.

Baker, F. (1988) 'Archaeology and the heritage industry', *Archaeological Review from Cambridge*, 7(2): 141–4.

—— (1990) 'Archaeology, Habermas and the pathologies of modernity', in F. Baker and J. Thomas (eds) *Writing the Past in the Present*, Lampeter: St David's University College.

Bapty, I. (1989) 'The meaning of things', *Archaeological Review from Cambridge*, 8(2): 175–84.

Bapty, I. and Yates, T. (eds) (1990) *Archaeology After Structuralism*, London: Routledge.

Barnes, M.R., Briggs, A.K. and Neilsen, J.J. (1980) 'A response to Raab and Klinger on archaeological site significance', *American Antiquity*, 45(3): 551–3.

Barran, P.A. and Schneider, A.L. (2001) Plaintiffs' opening brief in *Bonnichsen et al.* v. *United States of America*. Available online: http://www.friendsofpast.org/kennewick-man/court/briefs/416Brief/03brief.html (accessed 21 February 2003).

Bartlett, R.H. (1993) *The Mabo Decision*, Sydney: Butterworths.

Barunga, A. (1975) 'Sacred sites and their protection', in R. Edwards (ed.) *The Preservation of Australia's Aboriginal Heritage*, Canberra: AIAS.

Bates, G.M. (1992) *Environmental Law in Australia*, 3rd edn, Sydney: Butterworths.

Bauman, Z. (1987) *Legislators and Interpreters*, Cambridge: Polity Press.

—— (1992) *Intimations of Postmodernity*, London: Routledge.

Beck, W. and Head, L. (1990) 'Women in Australian prehistory', *Australian Feminist Studies*, 11: 29–48.

Bell, J.A. (1994) *Reconstructing Prehistory*, Philadelphia: Temple.

Bender, B. (1992) 'Theorising landscapes, and the prehistoric landscapes of Stonehenge', *Man*, 27(4): 735–55.

—— (1999) 'Subverting the Western gaze: mapping alternative worlds', in P.J. Ucko and R. Layton (eds) *The Archaeology and Anthropology of Landscape*, London: Routledge.

—— (2001) 'The politics of the past: Emain Macha (Navan), Northern Ireland', in R. Layton, P. Stone and J. Thomas (eds) *Destruction and Conservation of Cultural Property*, London: Routledge.

—— B. (2002) 'Time and landscape', *Current Anthropology*, 43: 103–12.

Bender, B. and Winer, M. (eds) (2001) *Contested Landscapes: Movement, Exile and Place*, Oxford: Berg.

Benedict, J. (2001) *Without Reservation: How a Controversial Indian Tribe Rose to Power and Built the World's Largest Casino*, New York: Harper Collins.

—— (2003) *No Bone Unturned: The Adventures of a Top Smithsonian Forensic Scientist and the Legal Battle for America's Oldest Skeletons*, New York: HarperCollins.

Bennett, S. (1985) 'The 1967 referendum', *Australian Aboriginal Studies*, 1985/2: 26–31.

—— (1989) *Aborigines and Political Power*, Sydney: Allen and Unwin.

Bennett, T. (1995) *The Birth of the Museum: History, Theory, Politics*, London: Routledge.

Berglund, M.H. (2000) 'Consequences of styles of thinking: on the relative and the absolute in archaeology at the end of the twentieth century', *Norwegian Archaeological Review*, 33(2): 105–15.

Best, S. and Kellner, D. (1991) *Postmodern Theory Critical Interrogations*, Basingstoke: Macmillan.

Bhaskar, R.A. (1978) *A Realist Theory of Science*, Hassocks: Harvester Press.

—— (1986) *Scientific Realism and Human Emancipation*, London: Verso.

—— (1989a) *The Possibility of Naturalism*, 2nd edn, Hassocks: Harvester Press.

—— (1989b) *Reclaiming Reality*, London: Verso.

Bickford, A. (1979) '*The Last Tasmanian*: superb documentary or racist fantasy?' *Filmnews*, January: 11–14.

—— (1981) 'The patina of nostalgia', *Australian Archaeology*, 13: 7–13.

—— (1985) 'Disquiet in the warm parlour of the past: material history and historical studies, Calthorpes House Museum, Canberra', *History and Cultural Resources Project: Part 2, Seminar Papers*, Canberra: Committee to Review Australian Studies in Tertiary Education.

—— (1993) 'Women's historic sites', in H. du Cros and L. Smith (eds) *Women in Archaeology: A Feminist Critique*, Canberra: Department of Prehistory, Research School of Pacific Studies, The Australian National University.

Bickford, A. and Sullivan, S. (1984) 'Assessing the research significance of historic sites', in S. Sullivan and S. Bowdler (eds) *Site Surveys and Significance Assessments in Australian Archaeology*, Canberra: Department of Prehistory, Research School of Pacific Studies, The Australian National University.

Biehl, P.F., Gramsch, A. and Marciniak, A. (eds) (2002) *Archäologien Europas/Archaeologies of Europe: Geschichte, Methoden und Theorien/History, Methods and Theories*, Münster: Waxmann.

Biel, M. (2003) 'Der Streit um den Kennewick Man', *P.M. Magazin*, October. Available online: http://www.pm-magazin.de/de/heftartikel/artikel_id746.htm (accessed 30 October 2003).

Binford, L.R. (1962) 'Archaeology as anthropology', *American Antiquity*, 28: 217–25.

—— (1964) 'A consideration of archaeological research design', *American Antiquity*, 29: 425–41.

—— (1968a) 'Some comments on historical versus processual archaeology', *Southwestern Journal of Archaeology*, 24(3): 267–75.

—— (1968b) 'Archaeological perspectives', in S.R. Binford and L.R. Binford (eds) *New Perspectives in Archaeology*, Chicago: Aldine.

—— (1972) *An Archaeological Perspective*, New York: Seminar Press.

—— (1977) 'General introduction', in L.R. Binford (ed.) *For Theory Building in Archaeology*, New York: Academic Press.

—— (1978) 'On covering laws and theories in archaeology', *Current Anthropology*, 19: 631–2.

—— (1986) 'In pursuit of the future', in D.J. Meltzer, D.D. Fowler and J.A. Sabloff (eds) *American Archaeology Past and Future*, Washington, DC: Society for American Archaeology.

—— (1987) 'Data, relativism and archaeological science', *Man*, 22: 391–404.

—— (1988) *In Pursuit of the Past*, London: Thames and Hudson.

—— (1990) 'The "New Archaeology", then and now', in C.C. Lamberg-Karlovsky (ed.) *Archaeological Though in America*, Cambridge: Cambridge University Press.

Bintliff, J. (1988) 'A review of contemporary perspectives on the "meaning" of the past', in J. Bintliff (ed.) *Extracting Meaning from the Past*, Oxford: Oxbow Books.

—— (1991) 'Post-modernism, rhetoric and scholasticism at TAG: the current state of British archaeological theory', *Antiquity*, 65: 274–8.

—— (1993) 'Why Indiana Jones is smarter than the post-processualists', *Norwegian Archaeological Review*, 26(2): 91–100.

Biolsi, T. (1998) 'The anthropological construction of "Indians": Haviland Scudder Mekeel and the search for the primitive in Lakota Country', in T. Biolsi and L.J. Zimmerman (eds) *Indians and Anthropology: Vine Deloria Jr and the Critique of Anthropology*, Tucson: University of Arizona Press.

Bird, G. (1988) *The Process of Law in Australia: Intercultural Perspectives*, Sydney: Butterworths.

Birmingham, J. (1993) 'Engendynamics: women in the archaeological record at Wybalenna, Flinders Island 1835–1840', in H. du Cros and L. Smith (eds) *Women in Archaeology: A Feminist Critique*, Canberra: Department of Prehistory, Research School of Pacific Studies, The Australian National University.

Bocock, R. (1986) *Hegemony*, Chichester: Ellis Horwood.

Bolt, C. (1987) *American Indian Policy and American Reform*, London: Unwin Hyman.

Bonnichsen, R. (1999) 'An introduction to *Who Were the First Americans?*', in R. Bonnichsen (ed.) *Who Were the First Americans? Proceedings of the 58th Annual Biology Colloquium, Oregon State University*, Covallis: Centre for the Study of the First Americans, Oregon State University.

Bordewich, F. (1996) *Killing the White Man's Indian: Reinventing Native Americans at the End of the Twentieth Century*, New York: Doubleday.

Bove, P.A. (1992) *Mastering Discourse*, Durham: Duke University Press.

Bowdler, S. (1980) 'Fish and culture: a Tasmanian polemic', *Mankind*, 12(4): 334–40.

—— (1981) 'Unconsidered trifles? Cultural resource management, environmental impact statements and archaeological research in NSW', *Australian Archaeology*, 12: 123–33.

—— (1982) 'Prehistoric archaeology in Tasmania', in F. Wendorf and A.E. Close (eds) *Advances in World Archaeology*, New York: Academic Press.

—— (1983) *Aboriginal Sites on the Crown-Timber Lands of New South Wales*, Sydney: Forestry Commission of New South Wales.

—— (1984) 'Archaeological significance as a mutable quality', in S. Sullivan and S. Bowdler (eds) *Site Surveys and Significance Assessments in Australian Archaeology*, Canberra: Department of Prehistory, Research School of Pacific Studies, The Australian National University.

—— (1988) 'Repainting Australian rock art', *Antiquity*, 62: 517–23.

—— (1992) 'Unquiet slumbers: the return of the Kow Swamp burials', *Antiquity*, 66: 103–6.

—— (1993) 'Views of the past in Australian prehistory', in M. Spriggs, D.E. Yen, W. Ambrose, R. Jones, A. Thorne and A. Andrews (eds) *A Community of Culture*, Canberra: Department of Prehistory, Research School of Pacific Studies, The Australian National University.

Bower, M. (1995) 'Marketing nostalgia: an exploration of heritage management and its relation to the human consciousness', in M.A. Cooper, A. Firth, J. Carman and D. Wheatley (eds) *Managing Archaeology*, London: Routledge.

Boxberger, D. (2000) 'Review of traditional historical and ethnographic information', unpublished report to the National Parks Service, Department of the Interior, Washington, DC. Available online: http://www.cr.nps.gov/aad/kennewick/boxberger.htm (accessed 26 July 2002).

Boylan, P.J. (1976) 'The ethics of acquisition: the Leicestershire code', *Museums Journal*, 75(4): 169–70.

Bradley, R. (1987) 'Comment on Leone *et al.*', *Current Anthropology*, 28(3): 293.

—— (1993) 'Archaeology: the loss of nerve', in N. Yoffee and A. Sherratt (eds) *Archaeological Theory: Who Sets the Agenda?* Cambridge: Cambridge University Press.

Branigan, K. (1990) 'The heritage industry: whose industry, whose heritage?', in F. Baker and J. Thomas (eds) *Writing the Past in the Present*, Lampeter: St David's University College.

Braund, C. (1995) 'Research to continue on Aboriginal relics', *Launceston Examiner*, 15 November: 16.

Bray, T. (1996) 'Repatriation, power relations and the politics of the past', *Antiquity*, 70: 440–4.

—— (2001) 'American archaeologists and Native Americans: a relationship under construction', in T. Bray (ed.) *The Future of the Past: Archaeologists, Native Americans, and Repatriation*, New York: Garland Publishing.

Bray, T. and Killion, T. (eds) (1994) *Reckoning with the Dead: The Larson Bay Repatriation and the Smithsonian Institution*, Washington, DC: Smithsonian Institution.

Bray, W. (1981) 'Archaeological humor: the private joke and the public image', in J.D. Evans, B. Cunliffe and C. Renfrew (eds) *Antiquity and Man: Essays in Honour of Glyn Daniel*, London: Thames and Hudson.

Brew, J. (1961) 'Emergency archaeology: salvage in advance of technical progress', *Proceedings of the American Philosophical Society*, 105(1): 1–10.

Brew, J. and Strong, W.D., Johnson, F., Kahle, H.E., Roberts, F.H.H., Wedel, W.R, Champe, J.L., Caldwell, J.R. (1947) 'Symposium on river valley archaeology', *American Antiquity*, 12(4): 209–25.

Brock, P. (1995) 'Pastoral stations and reserves in South and Central Australia', in A. McGrath, K. Saunders with J. Huggins (eds) *Aboriginal Workers*, Sydney: The Australian Society for the Study of Labour History, University of Sydney.

Brody, H. (2001) *The Other Side of Eden: Hunter Gathers, Farmers, and the Shaping of the World*, London: Faber and Faber.

Broome, R. (1995) 'Victoria', in A. McGrath (ed.) *Contested Ground*, Sydney: Allen and Unwin.

Brown, K. (1995) 'Tasmania – *Aboriginal Relics Act 1975*', unpublished paper presented at the Australian Heritage Commission workshop on legislation, 15 February 1995.

Brown, S. (1986) *Aboriginal Archaeological Resource in South East Tasmania*, Hobart: National Parks and Wildlife Service, Tasmania, Occasional Paper No. 12.

Brown, W. (1992) 'Finding the man in the state', *Feminist Studies*, 18(1): 7–34.

Buchan, R.A. (1979) 'The significance of land tenure to the management of Aboriginal sites in New South Wales', in J.R. McKinlay and K.L. Jones (eds) *Archaeological Resource Management in Australia and Oceania*, Wellington: New Zealand Historic Houses Trust.

Buchli, V.A. (1995) 'Interpreting material culture', in I. Hodder, M. Shanks, A. Alexandri, V. Buchli, J. Carman, J. Last, and G. Lucas (eds) *Interpreting Archaeology*, London: Routledge.

Buchli, V. and Lucas, G. (eds) (2001a) *Archaeologies of the Contemporary Past*, London: Routledge.

—— (2001b) 'The absent present: archaeologies of the contemporary past', in V. Buchli and G. Lucas (eds) *Archaeologies of the Contemporary Past*, London: Routledge.

Buikstra, J. (1981) 'A specialist in ancient cemetery studies', *Early Man*, 3(3): 26–7.

Bullock, H.D. (1983 [1966]) 'Death mask or living image? The role of the archives of American architecture', in A. Rains, E.S. Muskie, W.B. Widnall, P.H. Hoff, R.R. Tucker, G. Gray and L.G. Henderson (eds) *With Heritage so Rich*, Washington, DC: Landmark Reprint Series, Preservation Press.

Burchell, G. (1991) 'Peculiar interests: civil society and governing the system of natural liberty', in G. Burchell, C. Gordon and P. Miller (eds) *The Foucault Effect*, London: Wheatsheaf Harvester.

Burke, H., Lovell-Jones, C. and Smith, C. (1994) 'Beyond the looking-glass: some thoughts on sociopolitics and reflexivity in Australian archaeology', *Australian Archaeology*, 38: 13–22.

Butler, W.B. (1978) 'Some comments on contracting with the Federal government: types of contracts', *American Antiquity*, 43(4): 741–6.

—— (1987) 'Significance and other frustrations in the CRM process', *American Antiquity*, 52(4): 820–9.

Butt, P. (1984) *Out of Darkness*, producer, director, writer, Peter Butt, Independent Productions P/L and Video Education Australasia, Bendigo.

Butt, P. and Eagleson, R. (1993) *Mabo: What the High Court Said*, Sydney: The Federation Press.

Byrne, D. (1991) 'Western hegemony in archaeological heritage management', *History and Anthropology*, 5: 269–76.

—— (1993) 'The past of others: archaeological heritage management in Thailand and Australia', unpublished Ph.D. thesis, The Australian National University.

Byrne, D. and Smith, L. (1987) 'Survey for Aboriginal archaeological sites in the State Forests of the Eden area', unpublished consultancy report to the Forestry Commission of New South Wales.

Caldwell, J.R. (1959) 'The new American archaeology', *Science*, 129: 303–7.

Cambra, R. (1989) 'Control of ancestral remains', *News from Native California*, 4(1): 15–17.

Cammack, P. (1989) 'Bringing the state back in?', *British Journal of Political Science*, 19(2): 261–90.

Carman, J. (1991) 'Beating the bounds: archaeological heritage management as archaeology, archaeology as social science', *Archaeological Review From Cambridge*, 10(2): 175–84.

—— (1993) 'The P is silent … as in archaeology', *Archaeological Review From Cambridge*, 12(1): 37–53.

Carman, R. (2002) *Archaeology and Heritage: An Introduction*, London: Continuum

Carr, D.A. (1970) 'The National Trusts and antiquities', in F.D. McCarthy (ed.) *Aboriginal Antiquities in Australia*, Canberra: Australian Institute of Aboriginal Studies.

Carroll, J. (ed.) (1992) *Intruders in the Bush*, Melbourne: Oxford University Press.

Carter, C.E. (1997) 'Straight talk and trust', in N. Swidler, K.E. Dongoske, R. Anyon and A.S. Downer (eds) *Native Americans and Archaeologists: Stepping Stones to Common Ground*, Walnut Creek: AltaMira.

Cary, A. (2003) 'Kennewick Man decision passed to new court', *Tri-City Herald*, 11 September. Available online: http://www.kennewick-man.com/kman/news/story/3894093p-3917214c.html (accessed 12 September 2003).

Cash Cash, P. (2001) 'Medicine bundles: an indigenous approach to curation', in T. Bray (ed.) *The Future of the Past: Archaeologists, Native Americans, and Repatriation*, New York: Garland Publishing.

Cawley, M. and Chaloupka, W. (1997) 'American governmentality: Michel Foucault and public administration', *American Behavioral Scientist*, 41(1): 28–42.

Chalmers, A. (1979) *What is This Thing Called Science?* St Lucia: University of Queensland Press.

Champion, T. (1991) 'Theoretical archaeology in Britain', in I. Hodder (ed.) *Archaeological Theory in Europe*, London: Routledge.

Champion, T. and Shennan, T. (1986) 'Why the Congress had to go on', *Archaeological Review from Cambridge*, 5(1): 109–12.

Chapman, W. (1989) 'The organisational contest in the history of archaeology: Pitt Rivers and other British archaeologists in the 1860s', *The Antiquaries Journal*, 69(1): 23–42.

Charlesworth, M. (1984) *The Aboriginal Land Rights Movement*, Richmond: Hodja Educational Resource Cooperative.

Chase, M. and Shaw, C. (1989) 'The dimension of nostalgia', in M. Chase and C. Shaw (eds) *The Imagined Past: History and Nostalgia*, Manchester: Manchester University Press.

Chatters, J. (2000) 'The recovery and first analysis of an early Holocene human skeleton from Kennewick, Washington', *American Antiquity*, 65(2): 291–316.

—— (2001) *Ancient Encounters: Kennewick Man and the First Americans*, New York: Touchstone.

Chaudhuri, J. (1985) 'American Indian policy: an overview', in V. Jr. Deloria (ed.) *American Indian Policy in the Twentieth Century*, Norman: University of Oklahoma Press.

Cheek, A. and Keel, B. (1984) 'Value conflict in osteo-archaeology', in E. Green (ed.) *Ethics and Values in Archaeology*, New York: The Free Press.

Chief Management Officer (1974) Comments on Aboriginal relics, amendments to the Act. Dated 12 June. On PWS File no. 500856, Volume 1.

Chippindale, C. (1983) *Stonehenge Complete*, London: Thames and Hudson.

—— (1985) 'Skeletons rattle down under', *New Scientist*, March: 10–11.

—— (1986) 'Stoned henge: events and issues at the summer solstice, 1985', *World Archaeology*, 18(1): 38–55.

213

—— (1989) 'Philosophical lessons from the history of Stonehenge studies', in V. Pinsky and A. Wylie (eds) *Critical Traditions in Contemporary Archaeology*, Cambridge: Cambridge University Press.

—— (1993) 'Ambition, deference, discrepancy, consumption: the intellectual background to a post-processual archaeology', in N. Yoffee and A. Sherratt (eds) *Archaeological Theory: Who Sets the Agenda?* Cambridge: Cambridge University Press.

Chippindale, C., Devereux, P., Fowler, P., Jones, R. and Sebastian, T. (1990) *Who Owns Stonehenge?* London: B.T. Batsford.

Christenson, A.L. (1979) 'The role of museums in cultural resource management', *American Antiquity*, 44(1): 161–3.

Churchill, W. (1992) 'The earth is our mother: struggles for American Indian land and liberation in the contemporary United States', in M. Jaimes (ed.) *The State of Native America: Genocide, Colonization and Resistance*, Boston: South End Press.

—— (1998) *Fantasies of the Master Race: Literature, Cinema and the Colonisation of American Indians*, San Francisco: City Lights Books.

—— (2003) *Perversions of Justice: Indigenous Peoples and Angloamerican Law*, San Francisco: City Lights.

Churchill, W. and Morris, G. (1992) 'Key Indian laws and cases', in M. Jaimes (ed.) *The State of Native America: Genocide, Colonization and Resistance*, Boston: South End Press.

Clark, G. (1934) 'Archaeology and the state', *Antiquity*, 8: 414–28.

Clark, G.A. (1999) *NAGPRA, Science, and the Demon-Haunted World*. Available online: http://www.findarticles.com (accessed 4 August 2003).

Clarke, A. (1993) 'Cultural resource management as archaeological housework: confining women to the ghetto of management', in H. du Cros and L. Smith (eds) *Women in Archaeology: A Feminist Critique*, Canberra: Department of Prehistory, Research School of Pacific Studies, The Australian National University.

—— (2002) 'The ideal and the real: cultural and personal transformations of archaeological research on Groote Eylandt, northern Australia', *World Archaeology*, 34(2): 249–64.

Clarke, A. and Paterson, A. (eds) (2003) 'Case studies in the archaeology of cross-cultural interaction', *Archaeology in Oceania*, 38(2).

Clarke, D.L. (1968) *Analytical Archaeology*, London: Methuen.

—— (1973) 'Archaeology: the loss of innocence', *Antiquity*, 47: 6–18.

Cleary, J. (Minister for PWS) (1995) 'Letters: lessons of leaving out the Aborigines', *Weekend Australian*, 9–10 September.

Cleere, H. (1984a) 'Great Britain', in H. Cleere (ed.) *Approaches to the Archaeological Heritage*, Cambridge: Cambridge University Press.

—— (1984b) 'World cultural resource management: problems and perspectives', in H. Cleere (ed.) *Approaches to the Archaeological Heritage*, Cambridge: Cambridge University Press.

—— (ed.) (1984c) *Approaches to the Archaeological Heritage*, Cambridge: Cambridge University Press.

—— (1986) 'Amateurs and professionals in British archaeology today', in C. Dobinson and R. Gilchrist (eds) *Archaeology, Politics and the Public*, York: York University, Archaeological Publications No. 5.

—— (1988) 'Whose archaeology is it anyway?', in J. Bintliff (ed.) *Extracting Meaning From the Past*, Oxford: Oxbow Books.

—— (ed.) (1989) *Archaeological Heritage Management in the Modern World*, London: Unwin Hyman.

—— (1993a) 'Managing the archaeological heritage', *Antiquity*, 67: 400–2.

—— (1993b) 'British archaeology in a wider context', in J. Hunter and I. Ralston (ed.) *Archaeological Resource Management in the UK: An Introduction*, Phoenix Mill: Allen Sutton.

Clegg, J. (1984) 'The evaluation of archaeological significance, prehistoric pictures and/or rock art', in S. Sullivan and S. Bowdler (eds) *Site Surveys and Significance Assessments in*

Australian Archaeology, Canberra: Department of Prehistory, Research School of Pacific Studies, The Australian National University.

Clegg, S. (1992) *Frameworks of Power*, London: Sage.

Clewlow, C.W., Hallinan, P.S. and Ambro, R.D. (1971) 'A crisis in archaeology', *American Antiquity*, 36(4): 472–3

Cockrell, W.A. (1980) 'The trouble with treasure – a preservationist view of the controversy', *American Antiquity*, 45(2): 333–44

Colley, S.M. (2002) *Uncovering Australia: Archaeology, Indigenous People and the Public*, Sydney: Allen and Unwin.

Colley, S.M. and Jones, R. (1987) 'New fish bone data from Rocky Cape, north west Tasmania', *Archaeology in Oceania*, 22: 41–67.

Committee on Interior Affairs, US House of Representatives (1973) *Hearing Before the Subcommittee on National Parks and Recreation, 93rd Congress, First Session, on HR296 and Related Bills*, CIS Index No. H441–2.

Congressional Record (1882) *Volume XIII – 23, Senate, Wednesday, 10 May 1882.*

—— (1906) *Volume 40, 59th Congress, 1st Session.*

—— (1966) *Volume 112, 89th Congress, 2nd Session, 7 March.*

—— (1973) *Volume 119, 93rd Congress, 1st Session, 22 May.*

—— (1979) *Volume 125, 96th Congress, 1st Session.*

—— (1990) *Volume 136, 101st Congress, 1st Session, 26 October.*

Connah, G. (1988) *Of the Hut I Builded*, Cambridge: Cambridge University Press.

Cook, W. and Morris, G. (1984) 'Aboriginal involvement in archaeology', in G.K. Ward (ed.) *Archaeology at ANZAAS Canberra*, Canberra: Canberra Archaeological Society.

Cormack, P. (1978) *Heritage in Danger*, London: Quartet Books.

Cornell, S. (1988) *The Return of the Native: American Indian Political Resurgence*, New York: Oxford University Press.

Corner, W. and Harvey, S. (ed.) (1991) *Enterprise and Heritage*, London: Routledge.

Cosgrove, R., Allen, J. and Marshall, B. (1990) 'Palaeo-ecology and Pleistocene human occupation in southcentral Tasmania', *Antiquity*, 64: 59–78.

Coulter, R.T. and Tullberg, S.M. (1984) 'Indian land rights', in S.L. Cadwalader and V. Jr. Deloria (eds) *The Aggressions of Civilization: Federal Indian Policy since the 1980s*, Philadelphia: Temple University Press.

Cousins, M. and Hussain, A. (1984) *Michel Foucault*, Basingstoke: Macmillan.

Coutts, P.J.F (no date [a]) Letter to Miss E. Hawke, re: inquiries about the Victorian relics legislation. AAV file no. 34–5–5 VAS – Archaeological and Aboriginal Relics Preservation Act 1972, Amendments.

—— (no date [b]) Memorandum to Director, re: notes and comments on the act 8273. AAV file no. 34–5–3 VAS – Archaeological and Aboriginal Relics Preservation Act 1972.

—— (no date [c]) Philosophical Tenets of the VAS 1973–1983. AAV file no. 6–3–16 VAS – Role and Structure of the VAS.

—— (no date [d]) Untitled document attached to Philosophical Tenets of the VAS 1973–1983. AAV file no. 6–3–16 VAS – Role and Structure of the VAS.

—— (1974) Memorandum to Under Secretary, Chief Secretary's Department, re: Progress of the Relics Office, 1973/74. Dated 11 June. AAV file no. 6–1–1 VAS – Change of Name from Relics Office to VAS.

—— (1975) 'Victorian Relics Office', *Australian Archaeology*, 2: 32–3.

—— (1976) Memorandum to Secretary, Ministry for Conservation, re: appointment of AIAS representative to Archaeological and Aboriginal Advisory Committee. Dated 9 April. AAV file no. 10–3–1 VAS – Archaeological Relics Advisory Committee.

—— (1977) 'Australia: a new nation with an ancient legacy' (text of an ABC broadcast 29 May 1977)', *Records of the Victorian Archaeological Survey*, 4: 74–9.

—— (1978a) Memorandum to Deputy Director, Ministry for Conservation, re: Amendments to the Archaeological and Aboriginal Relics Preservation Act 1972. Dated 26 June. AAV file no. 34–5–5 VAS – Archaeological and Aboriginal Relics Preservation Act 1972, Amendments.

—— (1978b) 'The Victoria Archaeological Survey activities report', in R. Vanderwal (ed.) *Records of the Victorian Archaeological Survey, Number 8*, Melbourne: Ministry for Conservation.

—— (1979) 'The site recording programmes of the Victoria Archaeological Survey', in J.R. McKinlay and K.L. Jones (eds) *Archaeological Resource Management in Australia and Oceania*, Wellington: New Zealand Historic Places Trust.

—— (1980) 'The Victoria Archaeological Survey activities report 1978–9', *Records of the Victorian Archaeological Survey*, 10(June): 1–39.

—— (1982a) 'Management of the Aboriginal cultural heritage in Victoria', in P.J.F. Coutts (ed.) *Cultural Resource Management in Victoria 1979–1981*, Melbourne: Victoria Archaeological Survey.

—— (1982b) 'Victoria Archaeological Survey activities report 1980–81', in P.J.F. Coutts (ed.) *Cultural Resource Management in Victoria 1979–1981*, Melbourne: Victoria Archaeological Survey.

—— (1982c) 'Victoria Archaeological Survey activities report 1979–80', in P.J.F. Coutts (ed.) *Cultural Resource Management in Victoria 1979–1981*, Melbourne: Victoria Archaeological Survey.

—— (1983) Memorandum to Deputy Secretary, Minister for Planning and Environment, re: philosophical tenets of the VAS 1973–1983. Dated 9 December. AAV file no. 6–3–16 VAS – Role and Structure of the VAS.

—— (1984a) 'A public archaeologist's view of future direction in cultural resource management', in G.K. Ward (ed.) *Archaeology at ANZAAS Canberra*, Canberra: Canberra Archaeological Society.

—— (1984b) Unpublished letter to Professor D.J. Mulvaney, 4 May. AAV file no. 6–3–40 VAS. Aboriginal Consultation Policy, Melbourne: Aboriginal Affairs Victoria.

Coutts, P.J.F. and Fullagar, R.L.K. (1982) 'A matter of significance', in P.J.F. Coutts (ed.) *Cultural Resource Management in Victoria 1979–1981*, Melbourne: Victoria Archaeological Survey.

Coutts, P.J.F., Witter, D.C., Cochrane, R.M. and Patrick, J. (1976) *Sites of Special Scientific Interest in the Victorian Coastal Region*, Melbourne: Victoria Archaeological Survey.

Cowlishaw, G. (1987) 'Colour, culture and the Aboriginalists', *Man*, 22: 221–37.

—— (1992) 'Studying Aborigines: changing canons in anthropology and history', in B. Attwood and J. Arnold (eds) *Power, Knowledge and Aborigines*, Melbourne: La Trobe University Press.

Crawford, S. (2000) '(Re)Constructing bodies: semiotic sovereignty and the debate over Kennewick Man', in D. Mihesuah (ed.) *Repatriation Reader: Who Owns American Indian Remains?* Lincoln: University of Nebraska Press.

Creamer, H. (1975) 'From the "cultural bind" to a solution', *Australian Archaeology*, 2: 17–31.

—— (1980) 'The Aboriginal heritage in New South Wales and the role of the NSW Aboriginal Sites Survey Team', in C. Haigh and W. Goldstein (eds) *The Aborigines of New South Wales*, Sydney: National Parks and Wildlife Service.

—— (1988) 'Aboriginality in New South Wales: beyond the image of cultureless outcasts', in J. Beckett (ed.) *Past and Present*, Canberra: Aboriginal Studies Press.

—— (1990) 'Aboriginal perceptions of the past: the implications for cultural resource management in Australia', in P. Gathercole and D. Lowenthal (eds) *The Politics of the Past*, London: Unwin Hyman.

Cunliffe, B. (1981) 'The public face of the past', in J.D. Evans, B. Cunliffe and C. Renfrew (eds) *Antiquity and Man: Essays in Honour of Glyn Daniel*, London: Thames and Hudson.

Curtis, B. (1995) 'Taking the state back out: Rose and Miller on political power', *British Journal of Sociology*, 46(4): 575–89.

Custred, G. (2002) 'The Kennewick Man Case', *Science Insights*, 7(1). Available online: http://www.nas.org/publications/sci_newslist/7_1/d_kennewick_artic.htm (accessed 21 February 2003).

Daniel, G. (1978) *150 Years of Archaeology*, London: Duckworth.

Daniel, G. and C. Renfrew (1988) *The Idea of Prehistory*, 2nd edn, Edinburgh: Edinburgh University Press.

Daniels, K. and Murnane, M. (1978) 'The last Tasmanians are alive and well', *Nation Review*, 28 July–3 August: 10.

Darby, A. (1995a) 'Wrangle over relics', *The Age*, 26 September: 11.

—— (1995b) 'Aborigines to control ice-age artefacts' *The Age*, 15 November: 7.

Dark, K.R. (1995) *Theoretical Archaeology*, London: Duckworth.

Darvill, T. (1987) *Ancient Monuments in the Countryside: An Archaeological Management Review*, London: English Heritage.

Davidson, A. (1977) *Antonio Gramsci: Towards an Intellectual Biography*, London: Merlin Press.

Davidson, I. (1991a) 'Notes for a code of ethics and Australian Archaeologists working with Aboriginal and Torres Strait Islander Heritage', *Australian Archaeology*, 32: 61–4.

—— (1991b) 'Archaeologists and Aborigines', *The Australian Journal of Anthropology*, 2(2): 247–57.

Davidson, I., Lovell-Jones, C. and Bancroft, R. (eds) (1995) *Archaeologists and Aborigines Working Together*, Armidale: University of New England Press.

Davis, H. (1972) 'The crisis in American archaeology', *Science*, 175: 267–72.

—— (1982) 'Professionalism in archaeology', *American Antiquity*, 47: 158–63.

Davis, W. (1992) 'The deconstruction of intentionality in archaeology', *Antiquity*, 66: 334–47.

Davison, G. (1991) 'The meanings of "heritage"', in G. Davison and C. McConville (eds) *A Heritage Handbook*, Sydney: Allen and Unwin.

Davison, G. and McConville, C. (eds) (1991) *A Heritage Handbook*, Sydney: Allen and Unwin.

Dean, M. (1994) *Critical and Effective Histories: Foucault's Methods and Historical Sociology*, London: Routledge.

—— (1999) *Governmentality: Power and Rule in Modern Society*, London: Sage.

Dean, M. and Hindess, B. (eds) (1998) *Governing Australia*, Cambridge: Cambridge University Press.

DeCicco, G. (1988) 'A public relations primer', *American Antiquity*, 53(4): 840–56.

Deetz, J. (1977) *In Small Things Forgotten*, New York: Anchor Books.

Deloria, P.J. (1998) *Playing Indian*, New Haven: Yale University Press.

Deloria, V. Jr. (1969) *Custer Died for Your Sins: An Indian Manifesto*, London: Macmillan.

—— (1973) *God is Red: A Native View of Religion*, New York: Delta Books.

—— (1992a) 'Indians, archaeologists, and the future', *American Antiquity*, 57(4): 595–8.

—— (1992b) 'Trouble in high places: erosion of American Indian rights to religious freedom in the United States', in M. Jaimes (ed.) *The State of Native America: Genocide, Colonization and Resistance*, Boston: South End Press.

—— (1997) *Red Earth, White Lies: Native Americans and the Myth of Scientific Fact*, Colorado: Fulcrum.

—— (1998) 'Conclusion: Anthros, Indians, and planetary reality', in T. Biolsi and L.J. Zimmerman (eds) *Indians and Anthropologists: Vine Deloria Jr. and the Critique of Anthropology*, Tucson: The University of Arizona Press.

—— (2000) 'Secularism, civil religion, and the religious freedom of American Indians', in D. Mihesuah (ed.) *Repatriation Reader: Who Owns American Indian Remains?* Lincoln: University of Nebraska.

Deloria, V. Jr. and Lytle, C.M. (1998) *The Nations Within: The Past and Future of American Indian Sovereignty*, Austin: University of Texas Press.

—— (2002) *American Indians, American Justice*, Austin: University of Texas Press.

Derry, L. and Malloy, M. (eds) (2003) *Archaeologists and Local Communities: Partners in Exploring the Past*, Washington, DC: Society for American Archaeology.

Diaz-Andreu, M. (1995) 'Archaeology and nationalism in Spain', in P.L. Kohl and C. Fawcett (eds) *Nationalism, Politics and the Practice of Archaeology*, Cambridge: Cambridge University Press.

Dicks, B. (2000) *Heritage, Place and Community*, Cardiff: University of Wales Press.

Dingle, B. (n.d.) 'The discovery that changed history: Fraser Cave and the ice-age Aboriginals', *The Living Australia*, 22–4.

Dippie, B. (1982) *The Vanishing American: White Attitudes and US Indian Policy*, Lawrence: University Press of Kansas.

Dixon, K.A. (1977) 'Applications of archaeological resources: broadening the basis of significance', in M.B. Schiffer and G.J. Gumerman (eds) *Conservation Archaeology*, New York: Academic Press.

Dobres, M.A. and Robb, J.E. (2000) 'Agency in archaeology: paradigm or platitude?' in M.A. Dobres and J.E. Robb (eds) *Agency in Archaeology*, London: Routledge.

Dodson, M. (1994) 'The Wentworth Lecture – the end in the beginning: re(de)fining Aboriginality', *Australian Aboriginal Studies*, 1994/1: 2–13.

DOI, (2000) *Human Culture in the Southeastern Columbia Plateau, 9500–9000 BP and Cultural Affiliation with Present-day Tribes. Final Determination on Kennewick Man*. Available online: http://www.cr.nps.gov/aad/kennewick/encl_3.htm (accessed 26 July 2002).

Dongoske, K.E. (2000) 'NAGPRA: a new beginning, not the end, for osteological analysis – a Hopi perspective', in D. Mihesuah (ed.) *Repatriation Reader: Who Owns American Indian Remains?* Lincoln: University of Nebraska Press.

Dongoske, K.E. and Anyon, R. (1997) 'Federal archaeology: tribes, diatribes, and traditions', in N. Swidler, K.E. Dongoske, R. Anyon and A.S. Downer (eds) *Native Americans and Archaeologists: Stepping Stones to Common Ground*, Walnut Creek: AltaMira.

Dongoske, K.E., Aldenderfer, M. and Doehner, K. (eds) (2000) *Working Together: Native Americans and Archaeologists*, Washington, DC: Society for American Archaeology.

Dornan, J.L. (2002) 'Agency and archaeology: past, present and future directions', *Journal of Archaeological Method and Theory*, 9(4): 303–28.

Downer, A.S. (1997) 'Archaeologists–Native American relations', in N. Swidler, K.E. Dongoske, R. Anyon and A.S. Downer (eds) *Native Americans and Archaeologists: Stepping Stones to Common Ground*, Walnut Creek: AltaMira.

Downey, R. (2000) *Riddle of the Bones: Politics, Science, Race and the Study of Kennewick Man*, New York: Copernicus.

Dubdale, L. (1995) 'Two told to give up old bones', *Herald Sun*, 29 July: 5.

du Cros, H. (1989) *The Western Region: Melbourne Metropolitan Area. An Archaeological Survey*, Melbourne: Victoria Archaeological Survey, Occasional Report Series No. 27.

—— (1990) *The Werribee Corridor: An Archaeological Survey*, Melbourne: Victoria Archaeological Survey, Occasional Report Series No. 39.

—— (2002) *Much More than Stones and Bones: Australian Archaeology in the Late Twentieth Century*, Melbourne: Melbourne University Press.

du Cros, H. and Smith, L. (eds) (1993) *Women in Archaeology: A Feminist Critique*, Canberra: Department of Prehistory, Research School of Pacific Studies, The Australian National University.

Duncan, T. (1984a) '"Bone Rights" now an issue in Tasmania, too', *The Bulletin*, 4: 28.

—— (1984b) 'Aborigines: now it is bone rights', *The Bulletin*, 21: 26–8.

Dunnell, R.C. (1979) 'Trends in current Americanist archaeology', *American Journal of Archaeology*, 83(4): 438–49.

—— (1984) 'The ethics of archaeological significance decisions', in E.L. Green (ed.) *Ethics and Values in Archaeology*, New York: The Free Press.

Dunnett, G. and Feary, S. (eds) (1994) *Representativeness and Aboriginal Archaeological Sites*, Canberra: Australian Heritage Commission.

Durham, J. (1992) 'Cowboys and … notes on art, literature, and American Indians in the modern American mind', in M. Jaimes (ed.) *The State of Native America: Genocide, Colonization and Resistance*, Boston: South End Press.

Durrans, B. (1989) 'Theory, profession, and the political role of archaeology', in S. Shennan (ed.) *Archaeological Approaches to Cultural Identity*, London: Unwin and Hyman.

Eagleton, T. (1991) *Ideology: An Introduction*, London: Verso.

Earle, T.K. and Preucel, R.W. (1987) 'Processual archaeology and the radical critique', *Current Anthropology*, 28(4): 501–38.

Echo-Hawk, R. (2000) 'Ancient history in the New World: integrating oral traditions and the archaeological record', *American Antiquity*, 65(2): 267–90.

Echo-Hawk, W. (1997) 'Forging a new ancient history for Native America', in N. Swidler, K.E. Dongoske, R. Anyon and A.S. Downer (eds) *Native Americans and Archaeologists: Stepping Stones to Common Ground*, Walnut Creek: AltaMira.

Edwards, C. and Read, P. (1989) *The Lost Children*, Sydney: Doubleday.

Edwards, R. (1970) 'Legislation for the preservation of Aboriginal relics in South Australia', in F.D. McCarthy (ed.) *Aboriginal Antiquities in Australia*, Canberra: Australian Institute of Aboriginal Studies.

—— (1973) 'National register of Aboriginal sites', *Aboriginal News*, 1(2): 8–11.

—— (ed.) (1975) *The Preservation of Australia's Aboriginal Heritage*, Canberra: Australian institute of Aboriginal Studies.

Egan, T. (1996) 'Tribe stops study of bones that challenge history', *New York Times*, 30 September. Available online: http://nytimes.com/archive/ (accessed 26 September 2003).

—— (1998) 'Old skull gets white looks, stirring dispute', *New York Times*, 2 April. Available online: http://nytimes.com/archive/ (accessed 26 September 2003).

—— (1999) 'Expert panel recasts origin of fossil man in northwest', *New York Times*, 16 October. Available online: http://nytimes.com/archive/ (accessed 26 September 2003).

—— (2000) 'U.S. takes tribe's side on bones', *New York Times* 26 September. Available online: http://nytimes.com/archive/ (accessed 26 September 2003).

Elia, R.J. (1993) 'US cultural resource management and the ICAHM charter', *Antiquity*, 67: 426–38.

Ellender, I. (1990) *The Plenty Valley Corridor, An Archaeological Survey of Aboriginal Sites*, Victoria Archaeological Survey, Occasional Report Series No. 40.

Ellis, B. (1994) 'Rethinking the paradigm: cultural heritage management in Queensland', *Ngulaig 10*, Monograph Series, Brisbane: Aboriginal and Torres Strait Islander Studies Unit, University of Queensland.

Emerick, K. (2001) 'Use, value and significance in heritage management', in R. Layton, P. Stone and J. Thomas (eds) *Destruction and Conservation of Cultural Property*, London: Routledge.

—— (2003) 'From frozen monuments to fluid landscapes: the conservation and preservation of ancient monuments from 1882 to the present', unpublished Ph.D. thesis, University of York.

Engelstad, E. (1991) 'Images of power and contradiction: feminist theory and post-processual archaeology', *Antiquity*, 60: 502–14.

Fagan, B. (1993) 'The arrogant archaeologist', *Archaeology*, 46(6): 14–16

Fairclough, N. (1993) *Discourse and Social Change*, Cambridge: Polity Press.

Fairclough, N., Jessop, B. and Sayer, A. (2003) 'Critical realism and semiosis', in J. Roberts (ed.) *Critical Realism, Discourse and Deconstruction*, London: Routledge.

Feary, S. and Smith, M. (1995) 'Editorial', *Australian Archaeology*, 41: iii.

Femia, J.V. (1988) *Gramsci's Political Thought*, Oxford: Clarendon.

Ferguson, S. (1995) 'Bones of contention', *Herald Sun*, 1 July: 7.

Ferguson, T. (1984) 'Archaeological ethics and values in a tribal cultural resource management program at the Pueblo of Zuni', in E. Green (ed.) *Ethics and Values in Archaeology*, New York: The Free Press.

—— (1996) 'Native Americans and the practice of archaeology', *Annual Review of Anthropology*, 25: 63–79.

Fesl, E. (1983) 'Communication and communication breakdown', in M. Smith (ed.) *Archaeology at ANZAAS 1983*, Perth: Western Australian Museum.

Fforde, C., Hubert, J. and Turnbull, P. (eds) (2002) *The Dead and Their Possessions: Repatriation in Principle, Policy and Practice*, London: Routledge.

Field, J., Barker, J., Barker, R., Coffey, E., Coffey, L., Crawford, E., Darcy, L., Fields, T., Lord, G., Steadman, B. and Colley, S. (2000) ' "Coming back": Aborigines and archaeologists at Cuddie Springs', *Public Archaeology*, 1: 35–48.

Finch, L. (1993) *The Classing Gaze*, Sydney: Allen and Unwin.

Flannery, K. (1967) 'Culture history versus cultural process: a debate in American archaeology', *Scientific American*, 217(2): 119–22.

—— (1973) 'Archaeology with a capital S', in C.L. Redman (ed.) *Research and Theory in Current Archaeology*, New York: John Wiley and Son.

—— (1982) 'The golden Marshalltown: a parable for the archaeology of the 1980s', *American Anthropologist*, 84(2): 265–78.

Fletcher, R.J. (1981) 'People and space: a case study on material behaviour', in I. Hodder, G. Isaac and N. Hammond (eds) *Pattern of the Past: Studies in Honour of David Clarke*, Cambridge: Cambridge University Press.

Flood, J. (1979) 'The Register of the National Estate: policy and problems', in J.R. McKinlay and K.L. Jones (eds) *Archaeological Resource Management in Australia and Oceania*, Wellington: New Zealand Historic Places Trust.

—— (1984) 'More or less significant, a national perspective on assessing the significance of archaeological sites', in S. Sullivan and S. Bowdler (eds) *Site Surveys and Significance Assessments in Australian Archaeology*, Canberra: Department of Prehistory, Research School of Pacific Studies, The Australian National University.

—— (1987) 'The Australian experience: rescue archaeology down under', in R.L. Wilson (ed.) *Rescue Archaeology: Proceedings of the Second New World Conference on Rescue Archaeology*, Dallas: Southern Methodist University Press.

—— (1989) ' "Tread softly for you tread on my bones": the development of cultural resource management in Australia', in H. Cleere (ed.) *Archaeological Heritage Management in the Modern World*, London: Unwin Hyman.

—— (1993) 'Cultural resource management: the last three decades', in M. Spriggs, D.E. Yen, W. Ambrose, R. Jones, A. Thorne and A. Andrews (eds) *A Community of Culture*, Canberra: Department of Prehistory, Research School of Pacific Studies, The Australian National University.

Flynn, T. (1994) 'Foucault's mapping of history', in G. Gutting (ed.) *The Cambridge Companion to Foucault*, Cambridge: Cambridge University Press.

FOAP (Friends of America's Past) (no date) 'Summary of plaintiffs' study plan', unpublished press release/public statement. Available online: http://www.friendsofpast.org/kennewick-man/press/021126–plan.html (accessed 21 February 2003).

—— (1998) 'About Friends of America's Past'. Available online: http://www.friendsofpast.org/about/ (accessed 26 August 2003).

Fogelson, R.D. (1998) 'Perspectives on Native American identity', in R. Thornton (ed.) *Studying Native America: Problems and Prospects*, Madison: The University of Wisconsin Press.

Ford, R.I. (1973) 'Archaeology serving humanity', in C.L. Redman (ed.) *Research and Theory in Current Archaeology*, New York: John Wiley and Sons.

Forsman, L.A. (1997) 'Straddling the current: a view from the bridge over clear salt water', in N. Swidler, K.E. Dongoske, R. Anyon and A.S. Downer (eds) *Native Americans and Archaeologists: Stepping Stones to Common Ground*, Walnut Creek: AltaMira Press.

Foucault, M. (1972) *The Archaeology of Knowledge*, London: Tavistock.

—— (1973) *The Order of Things: An Archaeology of the Human Sciences*, New York: Vintage Books.

—— (1991a) 'Politics and the study of discourse', in G. Burchell, C. Gordon and P. Miller (eds) *The Foucault Effect*, London: Wheatsheaf Harvester.

—— (1991b) 'Governmentality', in G. Burchell, C. Gordon and P. Miller (eds) *The Foucault Effect*, London: Wheatsheaf Harvester.

Fourmile, H. (1987) 'Museums and Aborigines: a case study in contemporary scientific colonialism', *Praxis M*, 17: 7–11.

—— (1989a) 'Aboriginal heritage legislation and self determination', *Australian Canadian Studies*, 7(1–2): 45–61.

—— (1989b) 'Some background to issues concerning the appropriation of Aboriginal imagery', in S. Cramer (ed.) *Postmodernism: A Consideration of the Appropriation of Aboriginal Imagery*, Brisbane: Institute of Modern Art.

—— (1989c) 'Who owns the past? Aborigines as captives of the archives', *Aboriginal History*, 13: 1–8.

—— (1992) 'The need for an independent National Inquiry into State collections of Aboriginal and Torres Strait Islander cultural heritage', *Aboriginal Law Bulletin*, 2(56): 3–4.

Fowler, D.D. (1982) 'Cultural resource management', in M.B. Schiffer (ed.) *Advances in Archaeological Method and Theory, Volume 5*, New York: Academic Press.

—— (1987) 'Uses of the past: archaeology in the service of the State', *American Antiquity*, 52(2): 229–48.

Fowler, P.J. (1977) *Approaches to Archaeology*, London: Adam and Charles Black.

—— (1981) 'Archaeology, the public and the sense of the past', in D. Lowenthal and M. Binney (eds) *Our Past Before Us, Why do We Save it?* London: Temple Smith.

—— (1986) 'The past in public – roots for all or life with dried tubers?', in C. Dobinson and R. Gilchrist (eds) *Archaeology, Politics and the Public*, York: York University, Archaeological Publications No. 5.

—— (1987) 'What price the man-made heritage?', *Antiquity*, 61: 409–23.

—— (1992) *The Past in Contemporary Society: Then, Now*, London: Routledge.

Frankel, D. (1984) 'Who owns the past?', *Australian Society*, 3(9): 14–15.

—— (1993a) 'The excavator: creator or destroyer?', *Antiquity*, 67: 875–7.

—— (1993b) 'Pleistocene chronological structures and explanations: a challenge', in M.A. Smith, M. Spriggs and B. Fankhauser (eds) *Sahul in Review*, Canberra: Department of Prehistory, Research School of Pacific Studies, The Australian National University.

Frankel, D. and Gaughwin, D. (1984) 'Cultural resource management in a university teaching department', in G.K. Ward (ed.) *Archaeology at ANZAAS Canberra*, Canberra: Canberra Archaeological Society.

Fraser, N. (2000) 'Rethinking recognition', *New Left Review*. Available online: http://www.newleftreview.net/NLR23707.shtml (accessed 12 November 2003).

Freslov, J. (1993) 'The role of open sites in the investigation of Pleistocene phenomena in the inland southwest of Tasmania', in M.A. Smith, M. Spriggs and B. Fankhauser (eds) *Sahul in Review*, Canberra: Department of Prehistory, Research School of Pacific Studies, The Australian National University.

Friedman, J. (1992) 'The past in the future: history and the politics of identity', *American Anthropologist*, 94(4): 837–59.

Fritz, J.M. (1973) 'Relevance, archaeology and subsistence theory', in C.L. Redman (ed.) *Research and Theory in Current Archaeology*, New York: John Wiley and Sons.

Fritz, J.M. and Plog, F. (1970) 'The nature of archaeological explanation', *American Antiquity*, 35: 405–12.

Frow, J. (1991) *What Was Postmodernism?* Sydney: Local Consumption Publications.

—— (1995) *Cultural Studies and Cultural Value*, Clarendon: Oxford.

Fulton, C. (1985) 'Tassie', *Aboriginal Law Bulletin*, 5 October.

Fung, C. and Allen, H. (1984) 'Perceptions of the past and New Zealand archaeology', *New Zealand Archaeological Association Newsletter* 27(4): 209–20.

Gait, P. (1995) 'Letters: excavating under an enforced agenda', *Weekend Australian*, 16–17 September.

Gamble, C. (1993) 'Ancestors and agendas', in N. Yoffee and A. Sherratt (eds) *Archaeological Theory: Who Sets the Agenda?* Cambridge: Cambridge University Press.

Garza, C. and Powell, S. (2001) 'Ethics and the past: reburial and repatriation in American archaeology', in T. Bray (ed.) *The Future of the Past: Archaeologists, Native Americans, and Repatriation*, New York: Garland Publishing.

Gaughwin, D. (1986) President AAA: Comments on Aboriginal Cultural Heritage Victoria: Discussion Paper. Dated 26 February. AAV file 10–1–24 VAS – Relics Act Review Committee.

Geering, K. and Roberts, C. (1992) 'Current limitations on Aboriginal involvement in Aboriginal site management in centralwest and northwest New South Wales', in J. Birckhead, T. DeLacy and L. Smith (eds) *Aboriginal Involvement in Parks and Protected Areas*, Canberra: Aboriginal Studies Press.

Geranios, N.K. (1997) 'Kennewick Man: figure of dispute, mystery – scientists, tribes at odds over prehistoric remains', *The Seattle Times*, 10 August. Available online: http://www.archives.seattletimes.nwsource.com/ (accessed 25 September 2003).

Gibbon, G. (1989) *Explanation in Archaeology*, Oxford: Blackwell.

Gidiri, A. (1974) 'Imperialism and archaeology', *Race*, 15(4): 431–59.

Gill, E.D. (1970) 'Aboriginal antiquities in Victoria', in F.D. McCarthy (ed.) *Aboriginal Antiquities in Australia*, Canberra: Australian Institute of Aboriginal Studies.

Gilman, A. (1987) 'Comment on Earle and Preucel', *Current Anthropology*, 28(4): 515.

Glass, J. (1990) *The Beginnings of a New National Historic Preservation Program, 1957 to 1969*, Nashville: American Association for State and Local History and National Conference of State Historic Preservation Officers.

Glassow, M.A. (1977) 'Issues in evaluating the significance of archaeological resources', *American Antiquity*, 42(3): 413–20.

Goldstein, L. (2000) 'The potential for future relations between archaeologists and Native Americans', in M. Lynott and A. Wylie (eds) *Ethics in American Archaeology*, Washington, DC: Society for American Archaeology.

Goldstein, L. and Kintigh, K. (1990) 'Ethics and the reburial controversy', *American Antiquity*, 55: 589–91.

Golson, J. (1975) 'Archaeology in a changing society', *Australian Archaeology*, 2: 5–8.

—— (1986) 'Old guards and new waves: reflection on antipodean archaeology 1954–1975', *Archaeology in Oceania*, 21(1): 2–12.

Goodall, H. (1995) 'New South Wales', in A. McGrath (ed.) *Contested Ground*, Sydney: Allen and Unwin.

—— (1996) *Invasion to Embassy: Land in Aboriginal Politics in New South Wales, 1770–1972*, Sydney: Allen and Unwin.

Goodman, A.H. (1998) 'The race pit', *Anthropology Newsletter*, May. Available online: http://www.pbs.org/race/000_About/002_04–background-01–10.htm (accessed 24 October 2003).

Goodyear, A.C., Raab, L.M. and Klinger, T.C. (1978) 'The status of archaeological research design in cultural resource management', *American Antiquity*, 43(2): 159–73.

Gordon, C. (1991) 'Governmental rationality: an introduction', in G. Burchell, C. Gordon and P. Miller (eds) *The Foucault Effect*, London: Wheatsheaf Harvester.

Gough, A. (1995) 'Reflection on the La Trobe affair', *The Adelaide Review*, September edn.

Graham, B., Ashworth, G.J. and Tunbridge, J.E. (2000) *A Geography of Heritage: Power, Culture and Economy*, London: Arnold.

Gramsci, A. (1971) *Selections from the Prison Notebooks of Antonio Gramsci*, trans. Hoare, Q. and Smith, G., New York: International Publishers.

Green, E.L. (ed.) (1984) *Ethics and Values in Archaeology*, New York: The Free Press.

Greenfield, J. (1989) *The Return of Cultural Treasures*, Cambridge: Cambridge University Press.

Greer, S. and Henry, R. (1996) 'The politics of heritage: the case of the Kuranda Skyrail', in J. Finlayson and A. Jackson-Nakano (eds) *Heritage and Native Title: Anthropological and Legal Perspectives*, Canberra: Australian Institute of Aboriginal and Torres Strait Islander Studies.

Greer, S., Harrison, R. and McIntyre-Tamway, S. (2002) 'Community-based archaeology in Australia', *World Archaeology*, 32(2): 265–87.

Gregg, D.R. (1972) Memorandum to Museum Trustees, re: legislation to protect Aboriginal sites and relics. Dated 25 September. On PWS File no. 500856, Volume 1.

—— (1974) Letter to P. Murrell, Director, National Parks and Wildlife Service, re: Archaeological and Aboriginal relics bill. Dated 17 December. On PWS File no. 500856, Volume 1.

Gregory, P. (1995) 'Give back artefacts: Aborigines', *The Age*, 25 July: 6.

Griffiths, T. (1991) 'History and natural history: conservation movements in conflict?', in D.J. Mulvaney (ed.) *The Humanities and The Australian Environment: Papers from the Australian Academy of the Humanities Symposium*, Canberra: Australian Academy of the Humanities.

—— (1996) *Hunters and Collectors: The Antiquarian Imagination in Australia*, Cambridge: Cambridge University Press.

Grimes, R. (2000 [1986]) 'Desecration: an interreligious controversy', in T. Bray (ed.) *The Future of the Past: Archaeologists, Native Americans, and Repatriation*, New York: Garland Publishing.

Groube, L.M. (1978) 'Priorities and problems in Dorset archaeology', in T.C. Darvell, M. Parker Pearson, R.W. Smith and R.M. Thomas (eds) *New Approaches to our Past*, Southampton: University of Southampton.

Groube, L.M. and Bowden, M.C.B. (1982) *The Archaeology of Rural Dorset: Past, Present and Future*, Dorset: Dorset Natural History and Archaeological Society, Monograph Series, No. 4.

Grumet, R. and Brose, D. (2000) 'The earliest Americans', *Common Ground*, Spring/Summer: 15–19.

Gugliotta, G. (1999) 'Kennewick Man: no ethnic match – scientists say skull doesn't fit in with traits of modern populations', *The Seattle Times*, 27 July. Available online: http://www.archives.seattletimes.nwsource.com/ (accessed 25 September 2003).

Gulliford, A. (2000) *Sacred Objects and Sacred Places: Preserving Tribal Traditions*, Colorado: University Press of Colorado.

Gumerman, G.J. (1977) 'The reconciliation of theory and method in archaeology', in M.B. Schiffer (ed.) *Advances in Archaeological Method and Theory, Volume 5*, New York: Academic Press.

Haas, J. (2001) 'Sacred under the law: repatriation and religion under the Native American Graves Protection and Repatriation Act (NAGPRA)', in T. Bray (ed.) *The Future of the Past: Archaeologists, Native Americans, and Repatriation*, New York: Garland Publishing.

Hackenberger, S. (2000) 'Cultural affiliation study of the Kennewick human remains: review of bio-archaeological information', unpublished report to the National Parks Service, Department of the Interior, Washington, DC. Available online: http://www.cr.nps.gov/aad/kennewick/hackenberger.htm (accessed 26 July 2002).

Hagland, L. (ed.) (1984) *Checklists and Requirements for Consultants' Reports*, Sydney: The Australian Association of Consulting Archaeologists, Incorporated.

Hall, C.M. and McArthur, S. (eds) (1996) *Heritage Management in New Zealand and Australia*, Auckland: Oxford University Press.

Hall, S. (2001) 'Foucault: power, knowledge and discourse', in M. Wetherell, S. Taylor, and S.J. Yates (eds) *Discourse, Theory and Practice: A Reader*, London: Sage.

Hammil, J. and Cruz, R. (1989) 'Statement of American Indians Against Desecration before the World Archaeological Congress', in R. Layton (ed.) *Conflict in the Archaeology of Living Traditions*, London: Unwin Hyman.

Hammond, G. (1981) 'Aspects of legal significance in archaeology', *Australian Archaeology*, 13: 53–62.

Hannah, M. (2000) *Governmentality and the Mastery of Territory in Nineteenth-Century America*, Cambridge: Cambridge University Press.

Hardy, F. (1968) *The Unlucky Australians*, Sydney: Thomas Nelson.

Hareven, T.K. and Langenbach, R. (1981) 'Living places, work places and historical identity', in D. Lowenthal and M. Binney (eds) *Our Past Before Us, Why do We Save It?* London: Temple Smith.

Harris, S. (1979) *'It's Coming Yet ...' An Aboriginal Treaty within Australia Between Australians*, Canberra: The Aboriginal Treaty Committee.

Hauptman, L.M. (1984) 'The Indian Reorganization Act', in S.L. Cadwalader and V. Jr. Deloria (eds) *The Aggressions of Civilization: Federal Indian Policy Since the 1880s*, Philadelphia: Temple University Press.

Hawes, R. (1995a) 'Court orders uni to return Aboriginal relics', *The Weekend Australian*, 29–30 July.

—— (1995b) 'Aborigines in court battle over relics', *Australian*, 25 July, p. 5.

Hawkes, J. (1967) 'God in the machine', *Antiquity*, 41: 174–80.

Hay, C. (1996) *Re-Stating Social and Political Change*, Milton Keynes: Open University Press.

Haydon, T. (1978) *The Last Tasmanian*, an ARTIS production.

—— (1979) 'A witness to history', *Filmnews*, April: 12–14.

Head, L. (2000) *Cultural Landscapes and Environmental Change*, London: Arnold.

Henderson, D. (1998a) 'Skeleton helps put a new face on the Kennewick Man', *The Seattle Times*, Tuesday, 10 February. Available online: http://www.archives.seattletimes. nwsource.com/ (accessed 25 September 2003).

—— (1998b) 'The Kennewick Man and the man in the middle – Jim Chatters' work on ancient remains draws praise, criticism', *The Seattle Times*, Tuesday, 10 February. Available online: http://www.archives.seattletimes.nwsource.com/ (accessed 25 September 2003).

Herscher, E. and McManamon, F. (2000) 'Public education and outreach: the obligation to educate', in M. Lynott and A. Wylie (eds) *Ethics in American Archaeology*, Washington, DC: Society for American Archaeology.

Hewett, E. (1906) 'Preservation of American antiquities; progress during the last year; needed legislation', *American Anthropologist*, 8: 109–13.

Hewison, R. (1987) *The Heritage Industry*, London: Methuen.

Hiatt, L.R. (1989) 'Aboriginal land tenure and contemporary claims in Australia', in E.N. Wilmsen (ed.) *We Are Here*, Berkeley: University of California Press.

Hickman, P. P. (1977) 'Problems of significance: two case studies of historical sites', in M.B. Schiffer and G.J. Gumerman (eds) *Conservation Archaeology*, New York: Academic Press.

Hill, J.D. (1992) 'Overview: contested pasts and the practice of anthropology', *American Anthropologist*, 94(4): 809–15.

Hill, R. (1988) 'Mining the dead: science, profits and the sacred – despoiling Indian graves', *Christianity and Crisis*, 43: 419–22.

Hill, R.W. (2001) 'Regenerating identity: repatriation and the Indian frame of mind', in T. Bray (ed.) *The Future of the Past: Archaeologists, Native Americans, and Repatriation*, New York: Garland Publishing.

Hindess, B. (1987) *Politics and Class Analysis*, Oxford: Blackwell.

Hinsely, C.J. (2000) 'Digging for identity: reflections on the cultural background of collecting', in D. Mihesuah (ed.) *Repatriation Reader: Who Owns American Indian Remains?* Lincoln: University of Nebraska.

Hiscock, P. and Mitchell, S. (1993) *Stone Artefact Quarries and Reduction Sites in Australia: Towards a Type Profile*, Canberra: Australian Heritage Commission, Technical Publications Series, No. 4.

Hocking, H. (1994) 'World heritage significance and values: a survey of the knowledge of the Tasmanian community', unpublished report to the Parks and Wildlife Service, Tasmania, Hobart.

Hodder, I. (1981) 'Towards a mature archaeology', in I. Hodder, G. Isaac and N. Hammond (eds) *Pattern of the Past: Studies in Honour of David Clarke*, Cambridge: Cambridge University Press.

—— (1984) (ed.) *The Archaeology of Contextual Meanings*, Cambridge: Cambridge University Press.

—— (1985) 'Post-processual archaeology', in M. Schiffer (ed.) *Advances in Archaeological Method and Theory, Volume 8*, New York: Academic Press.

—— (1986a) *Reading the Past*, Cambridge: Cambridge University Press.

—— (1986b) 'Politics and ideology in the World Archaeological Congress 1986', *Archaeological Review from Cambridge*, 5(1): 113–18.

—— (1988) 'Material culture texts and social change: a contextual discussion and some archaeological examples', *Proceedings of the Prehistoric Society*, 44: 67–75.

—— (1989a) 'Post-modernism, post-structuralism and post-processual archaeology', in I. Hodder (ed.) *The Meaning of Things*, London: Unwin Hyman.

—— (1989b) 'This is not an article about material culture as a text', *Journal of Anthropological Archaeology*, 8: 250–69.

—— (1989c) 'Writing archaeology: site reports in context', *Antiquity*, 63: 268–74.

—— (1991a) 'Gender representation and social reality', in D. Wade and N.D. Willows (eds) *The Archaeology of Gender*, Calgary: The University of Calgary Archaeological Association.

—— (1991b) 'Interpretive archaeology and its role', *American Antiquity*, 56(1): 7–18.

——(1991c) 'Archaeological theory in contemporary European societies: the emergence of competing traditions', in I. Hodder (ed.) *Archaeological Theory in Europe*, London: Routledge.

—— (1992) *Theory and Practice in Archaeology*, London: Routledge.

—— (1993) 'Changing configurations: the relationship between theory and practice', in J. Hunter and I. Ralston (eds) *Archaeological Resource Management in the UK: An Introduction*, Phoenix Mill: Allen Sutton.

—— (1998) 'The goddess amd the leopard's den: conflicting interpretations at Çatalhöyük', in M. Casey, D. Donlon, J. Hope, and S. Wellfare (eds) *Redefining Archaeology: Feminist Perspectives*, Canberra: Department of Prehistory, Research School of Pacific Studies, The Australian National University.

—— (1999) *The Archaeological Process: An Introduction*, Oxford: Blackwell.

Hodder, I., Shanks, M., Alexandri, A., Buchli, V., Carman, J., Last, J. and Lucas, G. (eds) (1995) *Interpreting Archaeology*, London: Routledge.

Holdaway, S. and Porch, N. (1995) 'Cyclical patterns in the Pleistocene human occupation of southwest Tasmania', *Archaeology in Oceania*, 30: 47–82.

Hope, J. (1993) 'Double bind: women in the cultural heritage business in NSW', in H. du Cros and L. Smith (eds) *Women in Archaeology: A Feminist Critique*, Canberra: Department of Prehistory, Research School of Pacific Studies, The Australian National University.

—— (1995) 'Letters: *Realpolitik* in archaeology', *Australian*, 4 October.

Horizon (1995) *Bones of Contention*, Horizon Series, London: British Broadcasting Corporation

Horton, D.R. (1993) 'Here be dragons: a view of Australian archaeology', in M.A. Smith, M. Spriggs and B. Fankhauser (eds) *Sahul in Review*, Canberra: Department of Prehistory, Research School of Pacific Studies, The Australian National University.

Hosmer, C.J. (1965) *Presence of the Past*, New York: GP Putnam's Books.

House, M. (1989) 'The plunder of the past', *The Athenian*, July: 23–5

House Report, (1966) *House of Representatives Report 89–1916 Establishing a Program for the Preservation of Additional Historic Properties Throughout the Nation*, 89th Congress, 2nd Session.

—— (1979) *House of Representatives Report 96–311 Protecting Archaeological Resources Owned by the United States, and for Other Purposes*, 96th Congress, 1st Session.

—— (1990) *House of Representatives Report 101–877 Providing for the Protection of Native American Graves, and for other Purposes*, 101st Congress, 2nd Session.

Hoxie, F.E. (1995) *A Final Promise: The Campaign to Assimilate the Indians, 1880–1920*, Cambridge: Cambridge University Press.

Hubert, J. (1989) 'A proper place for the dead: a critical review of the "reburial" debate', in R. Layton (ed.) *Conflict in the Archaeology of Living Traditions*, London: Unwin Hyman.

Hubert, J. and Fforde, C. (2002) 'Introduction: the reburial issue in the 21st century', in C. Fforde, J. Hubert and P. Turnbull (eds) *The Dead and Their Possessions: Repatriation in Principle, Policy and Practice*, London: Routledge.

Huchet, B.M.J. (1991) 'Theories and Australian prehistory: the last three decades', *Australian Archaeology* 33: 44–51.

Huckleberry, G. and Stein, J. (1999) 'Analysis of sediments associated with human remains found at Columbia Park, Kennewick, WA', unpublished report to the National Parks Service, Department of the Interior, Washington, DC. Available online: http://www.cr.nps.gov/aad/kennewick/huck_stein.htm (accessed 26 July 2002).

Hunn, E. (2000) 'Review of linguistic information', unpublished report to the National Parks Service, Department of the Interior, Washington, DC. Available online: http://www.cr. nps.gov/aad/kennewick/hunn.htm (accessed 26 July 2002).

Hunt, A. (1993) *Explorations in Law and Society*, London: Routledge.

Hunter, J. and Ralston, I. (eds) (1993) *Archaeological Resource Management in the UK: An Introduction*, Phoenix Mill: Allen Sutton.

Hunter, M. (1981) 'The preconditions of preservation: a historical perspective', in D. Lowenthal and M. Binney (eds) *Our Past Before Us, Why do We Save It?* London: Temple Smith.

ICOMOS (1964) *International Charter for the Conservation and Restoration of Monuments and Sites (The Venice Charter)*, ICOMOS.

—— (1979) *The Burra Charter*, original version, Australia ICOMOS.

—— (1990) 'The Charter for the Protection and Management of the Archaeological Heritage' (reproduced in 1993), *Antiquity*, 67: 402–5.

—— (1999) *The Burra Charter*, revised, Australia ICOMOS.

Iverson, P. (1998) *'We Are Still Here': American Indians in the Twentieth Century*, Illinois: Harlan Davidson.

Jaimes, M. (1992) 'Federal Indian identification policy: a usurpation of indigenous sovereignty in North America', in M. Jaimes (ed.) *The State of Native America: Genocide, Colonization and Resistance*, Boston: South End Press.

James, P. and Halliday, H. (1990) 'World heritage site protection in Australia', *Heritage Australia*, 9(4): 42–4.

Jameson, J.J. (2000) 'Public interpretation, education and outreach: the growing predominance in American archaeology', in F. McManamon and A. Hatton (eds) *Cultural Resource Management in Contemporary Society*, London: Routledge.

Jelderks, J. (2002) Opinion and Order, Civil No. 96–1481–JE, *Bonnichsen et al. v. United States of America*, Oregon District Court, 30 August.

Jelks, E. (2000 [1988]) 'Professionalism and the Society for Professional Archaeologists', in M. Lynott and A. Wylie (eds) *Ethics in American Archaeology*, Washington DC: Society for American Archaeology.

Jennings, J.D. (1985) 'River basin surveys: origins, operations, and results, 1945–1969', *American Antiquity*, 50(2): 281–96.

—— (1986) 'American archaeology, 1930–1985', in D.J. Meltzer, D.D. Fowler and J.A.

Sabloff (eds) *American Archaeology Past and Future*, Washington, DC: Society for American Archaeology.

Jessop, B. (1983) *The Capitalist State*, Oxford: Martin Robertson.

—— (1990) *State Theory: Putting Capitalist States in their Places*, Cambridge: Polity Press.

—— (2001a) 'Bringing the state back in (yet again): review, revisions, rejections and redirections', *International Review of Sociology*, 11(2): 149–73.

—— (2001b) 'Institutional (re)turns and the strategic-relational approach', *Environment and Planning A*, 33(7): 1213–35.

Johnsen, H. and Olsen, B. (1992) 'Hermeneutics and archaeology', *American Antiquity*, 57(3): 419–36.

Johnson, D. (2003) 'Media release: assessment and management of Indigenous heritage needs improvement', AUSARCH-L. Online posting. Available e-mail: AUSARCH-L@anu.edu.au (10 December 2003).

Johnson, E. (1973) 'Professional responsibilities and the American Indian', *American Antiquity*, 38(2): 129–30.

Johnson, F. (1951) 'The inter-agency archaeological salvage program in the United States', *Archaeology*, Spring: 25–40.

—— (1966) 'Archaeology in an emergency: the Federal government's inter-agency archaeological salvage program is 20 years old', *Science*, 152: 1592–7.

Johnson, L.B. (1983 [1966]) 'Foreword', in A. Rains, E.S. Muskie, W.B. Widnall, P.H. Hoff, R.R.Tucker, G. Gray and L.G. Henderson (eds) *With Heritage so Rich*, Washington, DC: Landmark Reprint Series, Preservation Press.

Johnson, M. (1999) *Archaeological Theory: An Introduction*, Oxford: Blackwell.

Johnson, T. (1993) 'Expertise and the state', in M. Gane and T. Johnson (eds) *Foucault's New Domains*, London: Routledge.

Johnston, C. (1992) *What is Social Value?* Canberra: Australian Heritage Commission, Technical Publication No. 3.

—— (1993) 'Gaps in the record: finding women's places', in H. du Cros and L. Smith (eds) *Women in Archaeology: A Feminist Critique*, Canberra: Department of Prehistory, Research School of Pacific Studies, The Australian National University.

Jonas, W. (1991) *Consultation with Aboriginal People About Aboriginal Heritage*, Canberra: Australian Government Publishing Service.

Jones, B. (1984) *Past Imperfect: The Story of Rescue Archaeology*, London: Heinemann.

Jones, D. and Harris, R. J. (1997) 'Contending for the dead', *Nature*, 386: 15–16.

Jones, R. (1965) 'Archaeological reconnaissance in Tasmania, summer 1963–1964', *Oceania*, 35: 191–201.

—— (1966) 'A speculative archaeological sequence for north-west Tasmania', *Records of the Queen Victoria Museum*, 25: 1–12.

—— (1968a) 'Editorial', *Mankind*, 6(11): 535–6.

—— (1968b) 'The geographical background to the arrival of man in Australia and Tasmania', *Archaeology and Physical Anthropology in Oceania*, 3(3): 186–215.

—— (1971a) 'Rocky Cape and the problem of the Tasmanians', unpublished Ph.D. thesis, University of Sydney.

—— (1971b) 'The demography of hunters and farmers in Tasmania', in D.J. Mulvaney and J. Golson (eds) *Aboriginal Man and Environment in Australia*, Canberra: ANU Press.

—— (1977a) 'The Tasmanian paradox', in R.V.S. Wright (ed.) *Stone Tools as Cultural Markers: Change, Evolution and Complexity*, Canberra: Australian Institute of Aboriginal Studies.

—— (1977b) 'Man as an element of a continental fauna: the case of the sundering of the Bassian bridge', in J. Allen, J. Golson and R. Jones (eds) *Sunda and Sahul*, London: Academic Press.

—— (1978a) 'Why did the Tasmanians stop eating fish?', in R.A. Gould (ed.) *Explorations in Ethno-Archaeology*, Albuquerque: University of New Mexico Press.

—— (1978b) 'The first Tasmanians', *Nation Review* 25–31 August: 21.

—— (1979) 'The fifth continent: problems concerning the human colonization of Australia', *Annual Review of Anthropology*, 8: 445–66.

—— (1981) 'The extreme climatic place: interview with Rhys Jones', *Hemisphere*, 26: 50–5.

—— (1982) 'Submission to the Senate Select Committee on southwest Tasmania: evidence presented at Parliament House', Canberra, Extract from Hansard, 19 March 1982, *Australian Archaeology*, 14: 96–106.

—— (1983) 'Standing where they stood, interview with R. Jones', *Hemisphere*, 28: 58–64.

—— (1984) 'Hunters and history: a case study from western Tasmania', in C. Schrire (ed.) *Past and Present in Hunter Gatherer Studies*, New York: Academic Press.

—— (1985) 'Recommendations for archaeological site management in Kakadu National Park', in R. Jones (ed.) *Archaeological Research in Kakadu National Park*, Canberra: Australian National Parks and Wildlife Service.

—— (1987a) 'Hunting forbears', in M. Roe (ed.) *The Flow of Culture: Tasmanian Studies*, Canberra: Australian Academy of the Humanities.

—— (1987b) 'Ice-Age hunters of the Tasmanian wilderness', *Australian Geographic*, 8: 26–45.

—— (1990) 'From Kakadu to Kutikina: the southern continent at 18,000 years ago', in C. Gamble and O. Soffer (eds) *The World at 18,000 BP, Volume 2 Low Latitudes*, London: Unwin Hyman.

—— (1992a) 'Tom Haydon 1938–1991: film interpreter of Australian archaeology', *Australian Archaeology*, 35: 51–64.

—— (1992b) 'Philosophical time travelers', *Antiquity*, 66: 744–57.

—— (1993) 'A continental reconnaissance: some observation concerning the discovery of the Pleistocene archaeology of Australia', in M. Spriggs, D.E. Yen, W. Ambrose, R. Jones, A. Thorne and A. Andrews (eds) *A Community of Culture*, Canberra: Department of Prehistory, Research School of Pacific Studies, The Australian National University.

Jones, R. and Meehan, B. (2000) 'A crucible of Australian Prehistory: the 1965 Hobart ANZAAS Conference', in A. Anderson and T. Murray (eds) *Australian Archaeologist: Collected Papers in Honour of Jim Allen*, Canberra: ANU.

Keat, R. and Urry, J. (1982) *Social Theory as Science*, 2nd edn, London: Routledge and Kegan Paul.

Keefe, K. (1988) 'Aboriginality: resistance and persistence', *Australian Aboriginal Studies*, 1988/1: 67–81.

Kelly, R. (1975) 'From the "Keeparra" to the cultural bind', *Australian Archaeology*, 2: 13–17.

—— (1979) 'Why we bother: information gathered in Aboriginal site recording in NSW', in J.R. McKinlay and K.L. Jones (eds) *Archaeological Resource Management in Australia and Oceania*, Wellington: New Zealand Historic Houses Trust.

—— (1980) 'A revival of Aboriginal culture', *Parks and Wildlife*, 2(5): 79–80.

Kerr, J.S. (1996) *The Conservation Plan*, 4th edn, Sydney: NSW National Trust.

Khan, K. (1993a) 'Frederick David McCarthy: an appreciation', in J. Specht (ed.) *F.D. McCarthy, Commemorative Papers*, Sydney: Australian Museum.

—— (1993b) 'Frederick David McCarthy: a bibliography', in J. Specht (ed.) *F.D. McCarthy, Commemorative Papers*, Sydney: Australian Museum.

KIC (Koori Information Centre) (no date) Koori Heritage Charter. AAV file 10–1–24 VAS – Relics Act Review Committee.

Kiernan, K. (1981) 'Archaeology in the western river valleys', *Wilderness*, 16: 3–4.

Kiernan, K., Jones, R. and Ranson, D. (1983) 'New evidence from Fraser Cave for a glacial age of man in south-west Tasmania', *Nature*, 301(5895): 1–5.

Killion, T. (2001) 'On the course of repatriation: process, practice and progress at the National Museum of Natural History', in T. Bray (ed.) *The Future of the Past: Archaeologists, Native Americans, and Repatriation*, New York: Garland Publishing.

Killoran, P.J. (1970) '"The Aboriginal Relics Preservation Act of 1967" – Queensland', in F. D. McCarthy (ed.) *Aboriginal Antiquities in Australia*, Canberra: Australian Institute of Aboriginal Studies.

King, P.J. (2003) 'Experience and dedication fuel Native American Rights Fund', *Indian Country Today*, 17 June. Available online: http://www.indiancountry.com/?1055857493 (accessed 10 October 2003).

King, T.F. (1971) 'A conflict of values in American archaeology', *American Antiquity*, 36(3): 255–62.

—— (1977) 'Resolving a conflict of values in American archaeology', in M.B. Schiffer (ed.) *Advances in Archaeological Method and Theory, Volume 5*, New York: Academic Press.

—— (1979) 'The trouble with archaeology', *Journal of Field Archaeology*, 6: 351–60.

—— (1983) 'Professional responsibility in public archaeology', *Annual Review of Anthropology*, 12: 143–64.

—— (1998) *Cultural Resource Laws and Practice: An Introductory Guide*, Walnut Creek: AltaMira Press.

—— (2000) *Federal Planning and Historic Places: The Section 106 Process*, Walnut Creek: AltaMira Press.

King, T.F., Hickman, P. and Berg, G. (1977) *Anthropology in Historic Preservation: Caring for Culture's Clutter*, New York: Academic Press.

Klesert, A.L. (1992) 'A view from Navajoland on the reconciliation of anthropology and Native Americans', *Human Organisation*, 51(1): 17–22.

Klesert, A.L. and Powell, S. (1993) 'A perspective on ethics and the reburial controversy', *American Antiquity*, 58(2): 348–54.

Klinger, T.C. and Raab, L.M. (1980) 'Archaeological significance and the national register: a response to Barnes, Briggs and Neilson', *American Antiquity*, 45(3): 554–7.

Knudson, R. (1982) 'Basic principles of archaeological resource management', *American Antiquity*, 47(1): 163–6.

—— (1984) 'Ethical decision making and participation in the politics of archaeology', in E. Green (ed.) *Ethics and Values in Archaeology*, New York: The Free Press.

Knusel, C. and Roberts, C.A. (1992) ' "Shared principles": the scientists reply', *Antiquity*, 66: 431–3.

Kohl, P.L. (1993) 'Limits to a post-processual archaeology (or, the dangers of a new scholasticism)', in N. Yoffee and A. Sherratt (eds) *Archaeological Theory: Who Sets the Agenda?* Cambridge: Cambridge University Press.

Kohl, P.L. and Fawcett, C. (1995a) 'Archaeology in the service of the state: theoretical considerations', in P.L. Kohl and C. Fawcett (eds) *Nationalism, Politics and the Practice of Archaeology*, Cambridge: Cambridge University Press.

—— (eds) (1995b) *Nationalism, Politics and the Practice of Archaeology*, Cambridge: Cambridge University Press.

Kuper, A. (1978) *Anthropologists and Anthropology*, London: Penguin Books.

—— (1988) *The Invention of Primitive Society*, London: Routledge.

Laclau, E. (1982) *Politics and Ideology in Marxist Theory*, London: New Left Books.

Lacy, M. (1985) 'The United States and American Indians: political relations', in V. Jr. Deloria (ed.) *American Indian Policy in the Twentieth Century*, Norman: University of Oklahoma Press.

Lahn, J. (1996) 'Dressing up the dead: archaeology, the Kow Swamp remains and some related problems with heritage management', in L. Smith and A. Clarke (eds) *Issues in Archaeological Management*, St Lucia: Tempus Publications, University of Queensland.

Landau, P. and Steele, D. (2000) 'Why anthropologists study human remains', in D. Mihesuah (ed.) *Repatriation Reader: Who Owns American Indian Remains?* Lincoln: University of Nebraska.

Langford, R. (1983) 'Our heritage – your playground', *Australian Archaeology*, 16: 1–6.

Langton, M. (1993) *'Well, I Heard it on the Radio and I Saw it on the Television ...'*, North Sydney: Australian Film Commission.

—— (1995) 'What do we mean by wilderness? Wilderness and *terra nullius* in Australian art', unpublished paper given at the Sydney Institute, 12 October.

Larrain, J. (1984) *Marxism and Ideology*, London: Macmillan.

Last, J. (1995) 'The nature of history', in I. Hodder, M. Shanks, A. Alexandri, V. Buchli, J. Carman, J. Last and G. Lucas (eds) *Interpreting Archaeology*, London: Routledge.

—— (1982a) 'Commission condemns power scheme', 6 February. Wilderness Society Newspaper Archives.

—— (1982b) 'S-W is heritage listing choice', 25 January. Wilderness Society Newspaper Archives.

—— (1982c) 'Legal action threatened by Aborigines', 3 March. Wilderness Society Newspaper Archives.

—— (1983) 'Aboriginal or not?' 16 June. Wilderness Society Newspaper Archives.

—— (1995a) 'Editorial: Claims on Aboriginal artefacts', 9 August: 9.

—— (1995b) 'Artefacts wait on Cleary decision', 30 August: 7.

Layton, R., Stone, P. and Thomas, J. (eds) (2001) *Destruction and Conservation of Cultural Property*, London: Routledge.

Leahy, G. (1979) 'One man's meat is another people's poison', *Filmnews*, June: 19–22.

Lee, M. (1998) 'Students use Kennewick Man for class projects', *Tri-City Herald*. Available online: http://www.kennewick-man.com/essays/bellingham.html (accessed 10 January 2003).

—— (1999a) 'New World habitation tricky issue', *Tri-City Herald*, 26 December. Available online: http://www.kennewick-man.com/recasting/story2.html (accessed 10 January 2003).

—— (1999b) 'No turning back on Kennewick Man', *Tri-City Herald*, 28 December. Available online: http://www.kennewick-man.com/recasting/story6.html (accessed 10 January 2003).

—— (1999c) 'Archaeology becoming popular science', *Tri-City Herald*, 27 December. Available online: http://www.kennewick-man.com/recasting/story5.html (accessed 10 January 2003).

—— (1999d) 'Politics of the past', *Tri-City Herald*, 26 December. Available online: http://www.kennewick-man.com/recasting/story1.html (accessed 10 January 2003).

Lee, R.F. (1970) *The Antiquities Act of 1906*, Washington DC: Office of History and Historic Architecture, Eastern Service Centre, National Parks Service.

Lehman, G. (1991) 'The battle for Tasmanian Aboriginal heritage', *Green Left*, April: 10.

Leone, M.P. (1971) 'Review of *New Perspectives in Archaeology* edited by S.R. Binford and L.R. Binford', *American Antiquity*, 36(2): 220–2.

—— (1981) 'Archaeology's relationship to the present and the past', in R. Gould and M. Schiffer (eds) *Modern Material Culture: The Archaeology of Us*, New York: Academic Press.

—— (1984) 'Interpreting ideology in historical archaeology: the William Paca Garden in Annapolis, Maryland', in D. Miller and C. Tilley (eds) *Ideology, Power and Prehistory*, Cambridge: Cambridge University Press.

—— (1986) 'Symbolic, structural and critical archaeology', in D.J. Meltzer, D.D. Fowler, and J.A. Sabloff (eds) *American Archaeology Past and Future*, Washington, DC: Smithsonian Institution Press.

—— (1999) 'Setting some terms for historical archaeologies of capitalism', in M.P. Leone and P.B. Jr. Potter (eds) *Historical Archaeologies of Capitalism*, New York: Kluwer Academic.

Leone, M.P. and Potter, P.B. Jr. (1992) 'Legitimating and the classification of archaeological sites', *American Antiquity*, 57(1): 137–45.

Leone, M.P. and Preucel, R.W. (1992) 'Archaeology in a democratic society: a critical theory perspective', in L. Wandsnider (ed.) *Quandaries and Quests: Visions of Archaeology Future*, Carbondale: Southern Illinois University.

Leone, M.P., Potter, P.B. Jr. and Shackel, P.A. (1987) 'Toward a critical archaeology', *Current Anthropology*, 28(3): 283–302.

Leone, M.P., Mullins, P.R., Creveling, M.C., Hurst, L., Jackson-Nash, B., Jones, L.D., Jopling-Kaiser, H., Logan, G.C. and Warner, M.S. (1995) 'Can an African-American historical archaeology be an alternative voice?', in I. Hodder, M. Shanks, A. Alexandri, V. Buchli, J. Carman, J. Last and G. Lucas (eds) *Interpreting Archaeology*, London: Routledge.

Lepper, B.T. (2002) 'Judge rules scientists can study Kennewick Man', *Mammoth Trumpet*. Available online: http://www.friendsofpast.org/kennewick-man/news/021128–lepper.html (accessed 21 February 2003).

Leshy, J. (no date) Memorandum from Office of the Solicitor to Secretary. Subject NAGPRA and the Disposition of Kennewick Human Remains. Available online: http://www.cr.nps.gov/kennewick/ench_4.htm (accessed 26 July 2002).

Lewis, D. and Bird Rose, D. (1985) 'Some ethical issues in archaeology: a methodology of consultation in Northern Australia', *Australian Aboriginal Studies*, 1985/1: 37–44.

Lieberman, L. and Jackson, F. (1995) 'Race and three models of human origin', *American Anthropologist*, 97(2): 231–42.

Lipe, W.D. (1974) 'A conservation model for American archaeology', *The Kiva*, 39: 214–45.

—— (1977) 'A conservation model for American archaeology', in M.B. Schiffer (ed.) *Advances in Archaeological Method and Theory, Volume 5*, New York: Academic Press.

—— (1984) 'Value and meaning in cultural resources', in H. Cleere (ed.) *Approaches to the Archaeological Heritage*, Cambridge: Cambridge University Press.

Lippert, D. (1997) 'In front of the mirror: Native Americans and academic archaeology', in N. Swidler, K.E. Dongoske, R. Anyon and A.S. Downer (eds) *Native Americans and Archaeologists: Stepping Stones to Common Ground*, Walnut Creek: AltaMira Press.

Lippmann, L. (1992) *Generations of Resistance*, 2nd edn, Melbourne: Longman Cheshire.

Longacre, W.A. (1970) *Archaeology as Anthropology: A Case Study*, Tucson: University of Arizona Press, Anthropological Papers of the University of Arizona, volume 17.

Lord, K. (2003) 'Stumping for Kennewick Man', *Tri-City Herald*, 1 October. Available online: http://kennewick-man.com/kman/news/story/4053154p-4073040c.html (accessed 2 October 2003).

Lourandos, H. (1970) 'A description of the Aboriginal archaeological sites in Tasmania', in F.D. McCarthy (ed.) *Aboriginal Antiquities in Australia*, Canberra: Australian Institute of Aboriginal Studies.

—— (1977) 'Stone tools, settlement, adaptation: a Tasmanian example', in R.V.S. Wright (ed.) *Stone Tools as Cultural Markers: Change, Evolution and Complexity*, Canberra: Australian Institute of Aboriginal Studies.

Lowenthal, D. (1979) 'Environmental perception: preserving the past', *Progress in Human Geography*, 3(4): 549–59.

—— (1989) 'Nostalgia tells it like it wasn't', in M. Chase and C. Shaw (eds) *The Imagined Past: History and Nostalgia*, Manchester: Manchester University Press.

—— (1990) *The Past is a Foreign Country*, Cambridge: Cambridge University Press.

—— (1995) ' "Trojan forebears", "peerless relics": the rhetoric of heritage claims', in I. Hodder, M. Shanks, A. Alexandri, V. Buchli, J. Carman, J. Last and G. Lucas (eds) *Interpreting Archaeology*, London: Routledge.

Lowenthal, D. and Binney, M. (eds) (1981) *Our Past Before Us, Why do We Save it?* London: Temple Smith.

Lynch, K. (1972) *What Time is this Place?* London: MIT Press.

Lynott, M.J. (1980) 'The dynamics of significance: An example from Central Texas', *American Antiquity*,45(1): 117–20.

Lynott, M. and Wylie, A. (2000) 'Stewardship: the central principle of archaeological ethics', in M. Lynott and A. Wylie (eds) *Ethics in Archaeology*, Washington, DC: Society for American Archaeology.

McBryde, I. (ed.) (1985) *Who Owns the Past?* Melbourne: Oxford University Press.

—— (1986) 'Australia's once and future archaeology', *Archaeology in Oceania*, 21(1) 13–38.

—— (1995) 'Dream the impossible dream? Shared heritage, shared values, or shared understanding of disparate values?', *Historic Environment*, 11(2 and 3): 18–14.

McCall, W. (2002) 'Judge rules tribes can appeal ruling on ancient skeleton', *Seattle Post-Intelligencer*, 22 October. Available online: http://seatlepi.nwsource.com/local/92377_kennewick22ww.shtml (accessed 5 October 2003).

McCarthy, F.D. (1938) 'Aboriginal relics and their preservation', *Mankind*, 2(5): 120–6.

—— (ed.) (1970a) *Aboriginal Antiquities in Australia*, Canberra: AIAS.

—— (1970b) 'Introduction', in F.D. McCarthy (ed.) *Aboriginal Antiquities in Australia*, Canberra: Australian Institute of Aboriginal Studies.

—— (1970c) 'Aboriginal antiquities in New South Wales', in F.D. McCarthy (ed.) *Aboriginal Antiquities in Australia*, Canberra: Australian Institute of Aboriginal Studies.

—— (1970d) 'The Northern Territory and Central Australia', in F.D. McCarthy (ed.) *Aboriginal Antiquities in Australia*, Canberra: Australian Institute of Aboriginal Studies.

—— (1970e) 'Legislation: states without acts', in F.D. McCarthy (ed.) *Aboriginal Antiquities in Australia*, Canberra: Australian Institute of Aboriginal Studies.

Macdonell, D. (1986) *Theories of Discourse: An Introduction*, Oxford: Blackwell.

McGimsey, C.R. (1972) *Public Archaeology*, New York: Seminar Press.

—— (1985) ' "This, too, will pass": Moss-Bennett in perspective', *American Antiquity*, 50(2): 326–31.

—— (2000) 'Standards, ethics, and archaeology: a brief history', in M. Lynott and A. Wylie (eds) *Ethics in American Archaeology*, Washington, DC: Society for American Archaeology.

McGimsey, C.R. and Davis, H.A. (1977) *The Management of Archaeological Resources: The Airlie House Report*, Washington, DC: Special publication of the Society for American Archaeology.

—— (1984) 'United States of America', in H. Cleere (ed.) *Approaches to the Archaeological Heritage*, Cambridge: Cambridge University Press.

McGowan, A. (1992) 'Is Tasmania's cultural heritage legislation effective? Developing criteria for evaluating the effectiveness of cultural heritage legislation', unpublished Graduate Diploma thesis, University of Tasmania.

—— (1996) 'A view from the castle: administering Aboriginal Heritage Legislation in a changing policy environment', in S. Ulm, I. Lilley and A. Ross (eds) *Australian Archaeology '95: Proceedings of the 1995 Australian Archaeological Association Annual Conference*, St Lucia: Tempus Publications, University of Queensland.

McGowan, A., Shreeve, B., Brolsma, H. and Hughes, C. (1993) 'Photogrammetric recording of Pleistocene cave paintings in southwest Tasmania', in M.A. Smith, M. Spriggs and B. Fankhauser (eds) *Sahul in Review*, Canberra: Department of Prehistory, Research School of Pacific Studies, The Australian National University.

McGrath, A. (1987) *Born in the Cattle*, Sydney: Allen and Unwin.

—— (1995a) (ed.) *Contested Ground*, Sydney: Allen and Unwin.

—— (1995b) 'A national story', in A. McGrath (ed.) *Contested Ground*, Sydney: Allen and Unwin.

—— (1995c) 'Tasmania: 1', in A. McGrath (ed.) *Contested Ground*, Sydney: Allen and Unwin.

McGrath, A., Saunders, K. and Huggins, J. (eds) (1995) *Aboriginal Workers*, Sydney: The Australian Society for the Study of Labour History, University of Sydney.

McGregor, R. (1997) *Imagined Destinies: Aboriginal Australians and the Doomed Race Theory, 1880–1939*, Melbourne: Melbourne University Press.

McGuire, R.H. (1989) 'The sanctity of the grave: white concepts and American Indian burials', in R. Layton (ed.) *Conflict in the Archaeology of Living Traditions*, London: Unwin Hyman.

—— (1992) 'Archaeology and the first Americans', *American Antiquity*, 94(4): 816–32.

—— (1998) 'Why have archaeologists thought the real Indians were dead and what can we do about it?' in T. Biolsi and L.J. Zimmerman (eds) *Indians and Anthropologists: Vine Deloria Jr. and the Critique of Anthropology*, Tucson: The University of Arizona Press.

—— (2002) *A Marxist Archaeology*, New York: Percheron Press.

McIntyre, G. (1994) 'Proving native title', in R.H. Bartlett and G.D. Meyers (eds) *Native Title Legislation in Australia*, Nedlands: Centre for Commercial and Resources Law, University of Western Australia.

McKinlay, J.R. (1973) *Archaeology and Legislation*, Wellington: New Zealand Archaeological Association, Monograph 5.

McKinlay, J.R. and Jones, K.L. (eds) (1979) *Archaeological Resource Management in Australia and Oceania*, Wellington: New Zealand Historic Places Trust.

McLeod, D.W. (1987) *How the West Was Lost*, Port Headland: D.W. McLeod.

McManamon, F. (1991) 'The many publics of archaeology', *American Antiquity*, 56(1): 121–30.

—— (1996) 'The Antiquities Act – setting basic preservation policies', *Cultural Resource Management*, 19(7): 18–23.

—— (1999a) 'The Native American Graves Protection and Repatriation Act and First Americans research', in R. Bonnichsen (ed.) *Who Were the First Americans? Proceedings of the 58th Annual Biology Colloquium, Oregon State University*, Covallis: Centre for the Study of the First Americans, Oregon State University.

—— (1999b) 'K-Man undergoes complete physical', reproduced from the *Anthropology Newsletter*. Available online: http://www.washington.edu/burkemuseum/kmanupdate.html (accessed 26 August 2003).

—— (2000a) 'The protection of archaeological resources in the United States: reconciling preservation with contemporary society', in F. McManamon and A. Hatton (eds) *Cultural Resource Management in Contemporary Society*, London: Routledge.

—— (2000b) 'Commemorating an ancient legacy', *Common Ground*, Spring/Summer: 5.

—— (2000c) 'NPS Memorandum to Assistant Secretary, Fish and Wildlife and Parks. Subject: Determination that the Kennewick Human Skeletal Remains are "Native American" for the Purposes of the Native American Graves Protection and Repatriation Act (NAGPRA)'. Available online: http://www.cr.nps.gov/aad/kennewick/c14memo.htm (accessed 26 July 2002).

—— (2000d) 'Results of radiocarbon dating and plans for DNA testing', unpublished compilation from press conference remarks delivered at the Burke Museum, 13 January 2000 and subsequent US Department of Interior News Release, 31 January 2000. Available online: http://www.washington.edu/burkemuseum/kmanupdate.html (accessed 26 August 2003).

McManamon, F. and Hatton, A. (2000) 'Introduction: considering cultural resource management in modern society', in F. McManamon and A. Hatton (eds) *Cultural Resource Management in Contemporary Society*, London: Routledge.

McManamon, F., Roberts, J. and Blades, B. (2000) *Background and Scope for the Cultural Affiliation Reports*. Available online: http://www.cr.nps.gov/aad/kennewick/cultaff_intro.htm (accessed 7 July 2002).

MacNeil/Lehrer Productions (1997) 'The fight for Kennewick Man'. Online NewsHour. Available online: http://pbs.org/newhour/bb/science/jan97/bones_1–3.html (accessed 16 January 2003).

—— (2001) 'Bones of contention'. Online NewsHour. Available online: http://pbs.org/newhour/bb/science/jan-june01/kennewick_6–19.html (accessed 16 January 2003).

McNiven, I. (1994) 'Technological organization and settlement in southwest Tasmania after the glacial maximum', *Antiquity*, 68: 75–82.

McNiven, I., Marshall, B., Allen, J., Stern, N. and Cosgrove, R. (1993) 'The Southern Forests Archaeological Project: an overview', in M.A. Smith, M. Spriggs and B. Fankhauser (eds) *Sahul in Review*, Canberra: Department of Prehistory, Research School of Pacific Studies, The Australian National University.

McNiven, I. and Russel, L. (in press) 'Archaeology and indigenous people', in C. Chippindale (ed.) *Handbook of Archaeology Theories*, Walnut Creek: AltaMira Press.

Maddock, K. (1983) *Your Land is Our Land*, Ringwood: Pelican Books.

Mansell, M. (1985) 'The body snatchers', *Aboriginal Law Bulletin*, 17: 10–11.

—— (1995) 'Letters: *Realpolitik* in archaeology', *Australian*, 4 October.

Marika, W. (1975) 'Statement on sacred sites', in E. Edwards (ed.) *The Preservation of Australia's Aboriginal Heritage*, Canberra: Australian institute of Aboriginal Studies.

Markus, A. (1990) *Governing Savages*, Sydney: Allen and Unwin.

—— (1994) *Australian Race Relations 1788–1993*, Sydney: Allen and Unwin.

Marlow, J. (2002) 'Governmentality, ontological security and ideational stability: preliminary observations on the manner, ritual and logic of a particular art of government', *Journal of Political Ideologies*, 7(2): 241–59.

Marquis-Kyle, P. and Walker, M. (1992) *The Illustrated Burra Charter*, Sydney: Australia ICOMOS.

Marshall, Y. (ed) (2002) 'Community archaeology', *World Archaeology*, 34(2).

Mascia-Lees, F.E., Sharpe, P. and Cohen, C.B. (1990) 'The postmodern turn in anthropology: cautions from a feminist perspective', *Journal of the Steward Anthropological Society*, 17(1–2): 251–82.

Maslen, G. (1995a) 'The death of archaeology', *Campus Review*, 31 August: 7, 31.

—— (1995b) 'Battle of the bones', *The Bulletin*, October: 52–4.

Mason, R. (2000) 'Archaeology and Native American oral traditions', *American Antiquity*, 65(2): 239–66.

Matthews, T. (1990) 'Interest groups', in R. Smith and L. Watson (eds) *Politics in Australia*, Sydney: Allen and Unwin.

May, D. (1994) *Aboriginal Labour and the Cattle Industry*, Cambridge: Cambridge University Press.

May, J. (2001) *Kennewick Man Finds Common Ground in Old Adversaries*. Available online: http://www.indiancountry.com/?2390 (accessed 9 October 2002).

Maykutenner (1995) 'Tasmania 2: "You cannot deny me and mine any longer"', in A. McGrath (ed.) *Contested Ground*, Sydney: Allen and Unwin.

Means, R. with Wolf, M. (1995) *Where White Men Fear to Tread: The Autobiography of Russell Means*, New York: St Martin's Griffin.

Megaw, V.S. (1966) 'Australian archaeology – how far have we progressed?', *Mankind*, 6(7): 306–12.

—— (1980) 'Archaeology down under', *Popular Archaeology*, December: 29–33.

Meighan, C. (1984) 'Archaeology: science or sacrilege?' in E. Green. (ed.) *Ethics and Values in Archaeology*, New York: The Free Press.

—— (1992) 'Some scholar's views on reburial', *American Antiquity*, 57(4): 704–10.

—— (1996) 'Burying American archaeology', in K.D. Vitelli (ed.) *Archaeological Ethics*, Walnut Creek: AltaMira Press.

Meltzer, D. (1989) 'Why don't we know when the first people came to North America?', *American Antiquity*, 54(3): 471–90.

Memo (1968) From Minister for Lands and Works to Chairman, Scenery Preservation Board, re: McCarthy, F.D. submission on protection and preservation of Aboriginal antiquities. Dated 22 November. On PWS File no. 500856, Volume 1.

The Mercury (1982a) 'Ice Age hunters lived in the SW', 27 January. Wilderness Society Newspaper Archives.

—— (1982b) 'Labor blast on dam proposal', 25 January. Wilderness Society Newspaper Archives.

—— (1983) 'Aboriginals seek to rebut claim', 6 June. Wilderness Society Newspaper Archives.

Merriman, N. (1988) 'The heritage industry reconsidered', *Archaeological Review from Cambridge*, 7(2): 146–56.

—— (1991) *Beyond the Glass Case*, Leicester: Leicester University Press.

Merriwether, A.D., Cabana, G.S. and Reed, D.M. (2000) 'Kennewick Man ancient DNA analysis: final report submitted to the Department of the Interior, National Park Service', unpublished report to the National Parks Service, Department of the Interior, Washington, DC. Available online: http://www.cr.nps.gov/aad/kennewick/merriwether_cabana.htm (accessed 10 October 2003).

Meskell, L. (ed.) (1998) *Archaeology Under Fire: Nationalism, Politics and Heritage in the Eastern Mediterranean and Middle East*, London: Routledge.

—— (2002a) 'Negative heritage and past mastering in archeology', *Anthropological Quarterly*, 75(3): 557–74.

—— (2002b) 'The intersections of identity and politics in archaeology', *Annual Review of Anthropology*, 31: 279–301.

Mihesuah, D. (2000) 'American Indians, anthropologists, pothunters, and repatriation: ethical, religious, and political differences', in D. Mihesuah (ed.) *Repatriation Reader: Who Owns American Indian Remains?* Lincoln: University of Nebraska.

Miller, D. (1980) 'Archaeology and development', *Current Anthropology*, 21(6): 709–26.

Miller, D. and Tilley, C. (1984a) 'Ideology, power and prehistory', in D. Miller and C. Tilley (eds) *Ideology, Power and Prehistory*, Cambridge: Cambridge University Press.

—— (eds) (1984b) *Ideology, Power and Prehistory*, Cambridge: Cambridge University Press.

Miller, J. (1986) *Koori: A Will to Win*, Sydney: Angus and Robertson.

Miller, J.J. (1997) 'Bones of contention', *Reason Magazine*, October. Available online: http://reason.com/9710/col.miller.shtml (accessed 22 September 2003).

—— (2002) 'Free at last!', *National Review Online*, 2 September. Available online: http://nationalreview.com/miller/miller090402.asp (accessed 21 February 2003).

Miller, P. and Rose, N. (1993) 'Governing economic life', in M. Game and T. Johnson (eds) *Foucault's New Domains*, London: Routledge.

Minthorn, A. (n.d.) 'Testimony of Armand Minthorn member of the Board of Trustees Confederated Tribes of the Umatilla Indian Reservation before the Senate Committee on Indian Affairs: On NAGPRA oversight hearing'. Available online: http://indian.senate.gov/2000hrgs/nagpra_o725/minthorn.pdf (accessed 16 January 2003).

—— (1996) 'Human remains should be reburied'. Available online: http://www.umatilla.nsn.us/kennman.html (accessed 16 January 2003).

Minute Paper (1968) Re: Lourandos, H. submission on Aboriginal Archaeological Sites. Dated 19 November. On PWS File no 500856, Volume 1.

Mitchell, T. (1991) 'The limits of the state: beyond statist approaches and their critics', *American Political Science Review*, 85(1): 77–96.

Moe, J. (2000) 'America's archaeological heritage: protection through education', in F. McManamon and A. Hatton (eds) *Cultural Resource Management in Contemporary Society*, London: Routledge.

Moore, D. (1975) 'Archaeologists and Aborigines', *Australian Archaeology*, 2: 8–9.

Moore, H. (1990) 'Paul Ricoeur: action, meaning and text', in C. Tilley (ed.) *Reading Material Culture*, Oxford: Blackwell.

Moore, S. (1989) 'Federal Indian burial policy: historical anachronism or contemporary reality?' in R. Layton (ed.) *Conflict in the Archaeology of Living Traditions*, London: Unwin/Human.

Morris, B. (1989) *Domesticating Resistance*, Oxford: Berg.

Morell, V. (1995) 'Who owns the past?', *Science*, 268: 1424–6.

—— (1998) 'Kennewick Man: more bones to pick', *Science*, (279): 25–6.

Moser, S. (1994) 'Building the discipline of Australian archaeology: Fred McCarthy at the Australian Institute of Aboriginal Studies', in M. Sullivan, S. Brockwell and A. Webb (eds) *Archaeology in the North, Proceedings of the 1993 Australian Archaeological Association Conference*, Darwin: North Australian Research Unit, Australian National University.

—— (1995a) 'The "Aboriginalization" of Australian archaeology', in P.J. Ucko (ed.) *Theory in Archaeology: A World Perspective*, London: Routledge.

—— (1995b) 'Archaeology and its disciplinary culture: the professionalisation of Australian prehistoric archaeology', unpublished Ph.D. thesis, University of Sydney.

Mulick, C. (2002) 'Panel looks to ancient bones dispute'. Available online: http://www.kennewick-man.com/news/110902.html (accessed 9 September 2002).

Mulvaney, D.J. (1958) 'The Australian Aborigines 1606–1929: opinion and fieldwork', *Historical Studies*, 8(30 and 31): 131–51, 297–314.

—— (1961) 'The Stone Age of Australia', *Proceedings of the Prehistoric Society*, 27: 56–107.

—— (1963) 'Prehistory', in H. Shiels (ed.) *Australian Aboriginal Studies*, Melbourne: Oxford University Press.

—— (1964) 'Australian archaeology 1929–1964: problems and policies', *The Australian Journal of Science*, 27(2): 39–44.

—— (1968) 'Field research in Australia', in D.J. Mulvaney (ed.) *Australian Archaeology: A Guide to Field and Laboratory Techniques*, Canberra: AIAS.

—— (1970) 'Human factors in the deterioration and destruction of antiquities and their remedy', in F.D. McCarthy (ed.) *Aboriginal Antiquities in Australia*, Canberra: Australian Institute of Aboriginal Studies.

—— (1971a) 'Aboriginal social evolution: a retrospective view', in D.J. Mulvaney and J. Golson (eds) *Aboriginal Man and Environment in Australia*, Canberra: The Australian National University Press.

—— (1971b) 'Prehistory from Antipodean perspectives', *Prehistoric Society*, 27: 228–52.

—— (1977) 'Classification and typology in Australia: the first 340 years', in R.V.S. Wright (ed.) *Stone Tools as Cultural Markers: Change, Evolution and Complexity*, Canberra: Australian Institute of Aboriginal Studies.

—— (1979) 'Blood from stones and bones: Aboriginal Australians and Australian prehistory', *Search*, 10(6): 214–18.

—— (1981a) 'Gum leaves on the Golden Bough: Australia's Paleolithic survivals discovered', in J.D. Evans, B. Cunliffe and C. Renfrew (eds) *Antiquity and Man: Essays in Honour of Glyn Daniel*, London: Thames and Hudson.

—— (1981b) 'What future for out past? Archaeology and society in the eighties', *Australian Archaeology*, 13: 16–27.

—— (1981c) 'The Aboriginal heritage', *The Heritage of Australia: The Illustrated Register of the National Estate*, Melbourne: Macmillan and Australian Heritage Commission.

—— (1983) 'Towards a national consciousness', *Australian Natural History*, 21(3): 88–9.

—— (1985) 'A question of values: museums and cultural property', in I. McBryde (ed.) *Who Owns the Past?* Melbourne: Oxford University Press.

—— (1988) 'Australian anthropology and ANZAAS "strictly scientific and critical"', in R. MacLeod (ed.) *The Commonwealth of Science*, Melbourne: Oxford University Press.

—— (1989) 'Archaeological retrospective 9', *Antiquity*, LX: 96–107.

—— (1990a) 'Afterward: the view from the window', in S. Janson and S. MacIntyre (eds) *Through White Eyes*, Sydney: Allen and Unwin.

—— (1990b) *Prehistory and Heritage*, Canberra: Department of Prehistory, Research School of Pacific Studies, The Australian National University.

—— (1991) 'Past regained, future lost: the Kow Swamp Pleistocene burials', *Antiquity*, 65: 12–21.

—— (1993a) 'From Cambridge in the bush', in M. Spriggs, D.E. Yen, W. Ambrose, R. Jones, A. Thorne and A. Andrews (eds) *A Community of Culture*, Canberra: Department of Prehistory, Research School of Pacific Studies, The Australian National University.

—— (1993b) 'Australian anthropology: foundations and funding', *Aboriginal History*, 17: 105–28.

Mulvaney, K. (1993) 'Which way you look: rock art, a dilemma for contemporary custodians', *Rock Art Research*, 10(2): 107–13.

Murray, P.F., Goede, A. and Bada, J.L. (1980) 'Pleistocene human occupation at Beginners Luck Cave, Florentine Valley, Tasmania,' *Archaeology and Physical Anthropology in Oceania*, 15: 142–52.

Murray, T. (1986) 'Current policies of the Australian Archaeological Association', *Australian Archaeology*, 23: 97–9.

—— (1987) 'Remembrance of things present: appeals to authority in the history and philosophy of archaeology', unpublished Ph.D. thesis, University of Sydney.

—— (1989) 'The history, philosophy and sociology of archaeology: the case of the Ancient Monuments Protection Act 1882', in V. Pinsky and A. Wylie (eds) *Critical Traditions in Contemporary Archaeology*, Cambridge: Cambridge University Press.

—— (1992a) 'Aboriginal (pre)history and Australian archaeology: the discourse of Australian prehistoric archaeology', in B. Attwood and J. Arnold (eds) *Power, Knowledge and Aborigines*, Melbourne: La Trobe University Press.

—— (1992b) 'An archaeological perspective on the history of Aboriginal Australia', *Working Papers in Australian Studies, No. 80*, London: Sir Robert Menzies Centre for Australian Studies, Institute of Commonwealth Studies, University of London.

—— (1992c) 'Tasmania and the constitution of "the dawn of humanity"', *Antiquity*, 66: 730–43.

—— (1993a) 'Communication and the importance of disciplinary communities: who owns the past?', in N. Yoffee and A. Sherratt (eds) *Archaeological Theory: Who Sets the Agenda?* Cambridge: Cambridge University Press.

—— (1993b) 'The childhood of William Lane: contact archaeology and Aboriginality in Tasmania', *Antiquity*, 67: 504–9.

—— (1995) 'Thoughts about the future of archaeology in Australia', *La Trobe University Bulletin*, August–September: 12–13

—— (1996a) 'Creating a post-Mabo archaeology of Australia', in B. Attwood (ed.) *In the Age of Mabo: History, Aborigines and Australia*, Sydney: Allen and Unwin.

—— (1996b) 'Archaeologists, heritage bureaucrats, Aboriginal organisations and the conduct of Tasmanian archaeology', in S. Ulm, I. Lilley and A. Ross (eds) *Australian Archaeology '95: Proceedings of the 1995 Australian Archaeological Association Annual Conference*, St Lucia: Tempus Publications, University of Queensland.

Murray, T. and Allen, J. (1995) 'The forced repatriation of cultural properties to Tasmania', *Antiquity*, 69: 871–4.

Murray, T. and White, J.P. (1981) 'Cambridge in the bush? Archaeology in Australia and New Guinea', *World Archaeology*, 13(2): 255–63.

Murrell, P. (Director Tas NPWS) (1973) Memorandum to Minister for Agriculture, re: protection of Aboriginal relics – proposed amendments to the act. Dated 9 October. On PWS File no. 500856, Volume 1.

—— (1974) Memorandum to Minister for National Parks and Wildlife. Dated 26 July. On PWS File no. 500856, Volume 1.

Murtagh, W. (1997) *Keeping Time: The History and Theory of Preservation in America*, New York: John Wiley and Sons.

Nagel, J. (1997) *American Indian Ethnic Renewal: Red Power and the Resurgence of Identity and Culture*, New York: Oxford University Press.

Nelson, R. and Sheley, J. (1985) 'Bureau of Indian Affairs Influence on Indian Self-Determination', in V. Jr. Deloria (ed.) *American Indian Policy in the Twentieth Century*, Norman: University of Oklahoma Press.

Newman, A. and McLean, F. (1998) 'Heritage builds communities: the application of heritage resources to the problems of social exclusion', *International Journal of Heritage Studies*, 4(3 and 4): 143–53.

Nicholas, G.P. and Andrews, T.D. (eds) (1997) *At a Crossroads: Archaeology and First Peoples in Canada*, Burnaby: Archaeology Press, Simon Fraser University.

Nicholson, B. and Sykes, R. (1994) 'True black: true blue, Aboriginal influence on Australian identity', in L. Dobrez (ed.) *Identifying Australia in Postmodern Times*, Canberra: Bibliotech.

Nordbladh, J. (1990) 'Prehistory as a scout camp: where did the archeology go?', in F. Baker and J. Thomas (eds) *Writing the Past in the Present*, Lampeter: St David's University College.

Norris, C. (1992) 'Old themes for new times', *New Formations*, 18: 1–24.

—— (1995) 'Truth, science, and the growth of knowledge', *New Left Review*, 210: 105–23.

NPWS (National Parks and Wildlife Service) (1989) *Report of New South Wales Ministerial Task Force on Aboriginal Heritage and Culture*, Sydney: NPWS.

NSW, Legislative Assembly (1966), *Debates*, volume 65.

NSW, Legislative Council (1974), *Debates*, volumes 110, 113 and 111.

Officer, J.E. (1984) 'The Indian service and its evolution', in S.L. Cadwalader and V. Jr. Deloria (eds) *The Aggressions of Civilization: Federal Indian Policy since the 1980s*, Philadelphia: Temple University Press.

O'Hagan, M. (1998) 'Bones of contention: the agendas that have brought a 9,300-year old skeleton to life', *Willamette Week*. Available online: http://www.wweek.com/html/cover042298.html (accessed 24 October 2003).

Olivier, L. (2001) 'The archaeology of the contemporary past', in V. Buchli and G. Lucas (eds) *Archaeologies of the Contemporary Past*, London: Routledge.

Olney, J. (1995) 'Judgment in *Sainty (TALC)* vs. *Allen, Murray and La Trobe University*, VG643, 28 July 1995', Melbourne, Federal Court of Australia, Victoria District Registry.

Olsen, B. (1986) 'Norwegian archaeology and the people without (pre)history: or how to create a myth of a uniform past', *Archaeological Review from Cambridge*, 5(1): 25–41.

—— (1989) 'Comments on archaeology into the 1990's', *Norwegian Archaeological Review*, 22(1): 18–21.

O'Malley, P. (2000) 'Uncertain subjects: risks, liberalism and contract', *Economy and Society*, 29(4): 460–84.

O'Meara, K.P. (1999) 'Boneheaded about history', *Insight Magazine*, 15(32). Available online: http://www.n2.net/prey/bigfoot/creatures/kennewick.htm (accessed 25 September 2003).

Organ, M. (1994) 'A conspiracy of silence: the NSW National Parks and Wildlife Service and Aboriginal cultural heritage sites', *Aboriginal Law Bulletin*, 3(67): 4–7.

Outhwaite, W. (1991) *New Philosophies of Social Science: Realism, Hermeneutics and Critical Theory*, London: Macmillan.

Owsley, D. (1999) 'From Jamestown to Kennewick: an analogy based on early Americans', in R. Bonnichsen (ed.) *Who Were the First Americans? Proceedings of the 58th Annual Biology Colloquium, Oregon State University*, Covallis: Centre for the Study of the First Americans, Oregon State University.

Pardoe, C. (1990) 'Sharing the past: Aboriginal influence on archaeological practice, a case study from New South Wales', *Aboriginal History*, 14(1–2): 208–21.

—— (1991) 'Farewell to the Murray Black Australian Aboriginal skeletal collection', *World Archaeological Bulletin*, 5: 119–21.

—— (1992) 'Arches of radii, corridors of power: reflections on current archaeological practice', in B. Attwood and J. Arnold (eds) *Power, Knowledge and Aborigines*, Melbourne: La Trobe University Press.

—— (1994) 'W(h)ither archaeology', *Australian Archaeology*, 38: 11–13.

Parrott, H. (1990) 'Legislating to protect Australia's material cultural heritage – guidelines for cultural resource professionals', *Australian Archaeology*, 31: 75–82.

Patterson, T.C. (1986a) 'Some postwar theoretical trends in U.S. archaeology', *Culture*, 6(1): 43–54.

—— (1986b) 'The last sixty years: toward a social history of Americanist archaeology in the United States', *American Anthropologist*, 88: 7–26.

—— (1989) 'History and the post-processual archaeologies', *Man*, 24: 555–66.

Pavlich, G. (1995) 'Contemplating a postmodern sociology: genealogy, limits and critique', *The Sociological Review*, 43(3): 548–72.

Pearce, F. and Tombs, S. (1998) 'Foucault, governmentality, Marxism', *Social and Legal Studies*, 7(4): 567–75.

Pearson, M. (1984) 'Assessing the significance of historical archaeological resources', in S. Sullivan and S. Bowdler (eds) *Site Surveys and Significance Assessments in Australian Archaeology*, Canberra: Department of Prehistory, Research School of Pacific Studies, The Australian National University.

Pearson, M. and Sullivan, S. (1995) *Looking After Heritage Places*, Melbourne: Melbourne University Press.

Piggott, S. (1981) '"Vast perennial memorials": the first Antiquaries look at megaliths', in J.D. Evans, B. Cunliffe and C. Renfrew (eds) *Antiquity and Man: Essays in Honour of Glyn Daniel*, London: Thames and Hudson.

Pilger, J. (1989) *A Secret Country*, London: Vintage.

Plog, F. (1980) 'The ethics of archaeology and the ethics of contracting', *CRM Archaeology*, 1(1): 10–12.

Porch, N. and Allen, J. (1995) 'Tasmania: archaeological and palaeo-ecological perspectives', *Antiquity*, 69: 714–32.

Powell, J. and Rose, J. (1999) Report on the osteological assessment of the 'Kennewick Man' skeleton (CENWWW.97.Kennewick), unpublished report to the National Parks Service, Department of the Interior, Washington, DC. Available online: http://www.cr.nps.gov/aad/kennewick/powell_rose.htm (accessed 26 July 2002).

Preston, D. (1989) 'Skeletons in our museums' closets: native Americans want their ancestor's bones back', *Harper's Magazine*, February: 66–76.

—— (1997) 'The lost man', *New Yorker*, 73(16): 70–81.

Pretty, G.L. (1970) 'Survey of prehistoric monuments in South Australia', in F.D. McCarthy (ed.) *Aboriginal Antiquities in Australia*, Canberra: Australian Institute of Aboriginal Studies.

Preucel, R.W. (1991) 'Introduction', in R.W. Preucel (ed.) *Processual and Postprocessual Archaeologies: Multiple Ways of Knowing the Past*, Carbondale: Southern Illinois University.

—— (1995) 'The postprocessual condition', *Journal of Archaeological Research*, 3(2): 147.

Price, M.H. (1991) *Disputing the Dead: U.S. Law on Aboriginal Remains and Grave Goods*, Columbia: University of Missouri Press.

Prince, D.R. and Schadla-Hall, R.T. (1987) 'On the public appeal of archaeology', *Antiquity*, 61: 69–70.

Pullar, G. (1994) 'The Qikertarmiut and the Scientist: fifty years of clashing world views', in T. Bray and T. Killion (eds) *Reckoning with the Dead: The Larson Bay Repatriation and the Smithsonian Institution*, Washington, DC: Smithsonian Institution.

Purvis, T. (1996) 'Aboriginal peoples and the idea of the nation', in L. Smith and A. Clarke (eds) *Issues in Archaeological Management*, St Lucia: Tempus Publications, University of Queensland.

Purvis, T. and Hunt, A. (1993) 'Discourse, ideology, discourse, ideology, discourse, ideology ...', *British Journal of Sociology*, 44(3): 473–99.

PWS (Parks and Wildlife Service (no date[a]) State government file 500856 (volume 1) untitled, Hobart: Tasmanian State Government.

—— (no date[b]) State government file 023962, untitled Hobart: Tasmanian State Government.

—— (1992) State government file. 500179 'Acts – Bills Aboriginal Lands Bill', opened 1990, closed 1992, Hobart: Tasmanian State Government.

Pybus, C. (1991) *Community of Thieves*, Melbourne: Heinemann.

Raab, M.L. and Klinger, T.C. (1977) 'A critical appraisal of "significance" in contract archaeology', *American Antiquity*, 42(4): 629–34.

—— (1979) 'A reply to Sharrock and Grayson on archaeological significance', *American Antiquity*, 44(2): 328–9.

Raab, M.L., Klinger, T.C., Schiffer, M.B. and Goodyear, A.C. (1980) 'Clients, contracts and profits: conflicts in public archaeology', *American Anthropologist*, 82: 539–51.

Radford, T. (1998) *Equinox: Homicide in Kennewick. Notes to Accompany Television Production for Channel 4*, first shown October 1998, Manchester: Broadcasting Support Services and Channel 4 Television.

Rains, A., Muskie, E.S., Widnall, W.B., Hoff, P.H., Tucker, R.R., Gray, G. and Henderson, L.G. (eds) (1983 [1966]) *With Heritage so Rich*, Washington, DC: Landmark Reprint Series, Preservation Press.

Raven, S. (1978) 'The doomed Tasmanians', *The Sunday Times Magazine*, London, 21 May: 26, 29–30, 33, 35–6.

Ravesloot, J.C. (1997) 'Changing Native American perceptions of archaeologists', in N. Swidler, K.E. Dongoske, R. Anyon and A.S. Downer (eds) *Native Americans and Archaeologists: Stepping Stones to Common Ground*, Walnut Creek: AltaMira.

Rawls, J.J. (2001) *Chief Red Fox is Dead: A History of Native Americans since 1945*, London: Thomson Learning.

RDF Television Production (1998) *Equinox: Homicide in Kennewick*, first broadcast on Channel 4, UK, October 1998.

Read, D.W. and LeBlanc, S.A. (1978) 'Descriptive statements, covering laws, and theories in archaeology', *Current Anthropology*, 19: 307–35.

Read, P. (1982) *The Stolen Generations, The Removal of Aboriginal Children in NSW 1883 to 1969*, Sydney: NSW Ministry of Aboriginal Affairs.

Read, P. (1995) 'Northern Territory', in A. McGrath (ed.) *Contested Ground*, Sydney: Allen and Unwin.

Redman, C. (1991) 'In defense of the seventies – the adolescence of the New Archaeology', *American Anthropologist*, 93(2): 295–307.

Reekie, G. (1992) 'Women and heritage policy', *Culture and Policy*, 4: 91–6.

Reid, J. (1992) 'Editor's corner: Recent findings on North American prehistory', *American Antiquity*, 57(2): 195–6.

Renfrew, A.C. (ed.) (1973) *The Explanation of Cultural Change: Models in Prehistory*, London: Duckworth.

Renfrew, A.C. (1982) 'Discussion: contrasting paradigms', in A.C. Renfrew and S. Shennan (eds) *Ranking, Resource and Exchange: Aspects of the Archaeology of Early European Society*, Cambridge: Cambridge University Press.

—— (1983) 'Divided we stand: Aspects of archaeology and information', *American Antiquity*, 48(1): 3–16.

—— (1989) 'Comments on archaeology into the 1990s', *Norwegian Archaeological Review*, 22: 33–41.

Renfrew, A.C. and P. Bahn (1991) *Archaeology: Theories, Methods and Practice*, London: Thames and Hudson.

Reynolds, H. (1982) *The Other Side of the Frontier: Aboriginal Resistance to European Invasion of Australia*, Ringwood: Penguin.

—— (1986) 'The breaking of the Great Australian Silence: Aborigines in Australian historiography', in P. Quatermaine (ed.) *Diversity Itself: Essays in Australian Arts and Culture*, Exeter: University of Exeter.

—— (1995) *Fate of a Free People*, Ringwood: Penguin.

Rhoads, J.W. (1992) 'Significant sites and non-site archaeology: a case study from south-east Australia', *World Archaeology*, 24(2): 198–217

Rich, E. (1990) 'Aboriginal historic sites in north east NSW: management study', unpublished report, Sydney: New South Wales National Parks and Wildlife Service.

Richardson, L. (1989) 'The acquisition, storage and handling of Aboriginal skeletal remains in museums: an indigenous perspective', in R. Layton (ed.) *Conflict in the Archaeology of Living Traditions*, London: Unwin Hyman.

Riding In, J. (2000) 'Repatriation: a Pawnee's perspective', in D. Mihesuah (ed.) *Repatriation Reader: Who Owns American Indian Remains?* Lincoln: University of Nabrasca.

Rivera, J.I. (1989) 'The reburial of our ancestors: a moral, ethical and constitutional dilemma for California', *News from Native California*, 3(6): 12–13.

Robbins, R. (1992) 'Self-Determination and subordination: the past, present, and future of American Indian Governance', in M. Jaimes (ed.) *The State of Native America: Genocide, Colonization and Resistance*, Boston: South End Press.

Roberts, F.H.H. (1948) 'A crisis in United States archaeology', *Scientific American*, Winter, December: 12–17.

—— (1952) 'River Basin Surveys: the first five years of the Inter-Agency Archaeological and Paleontological Salvage Program', *Smithsonian Report for 1951*, 1951: 351–83.

—— (1961) 'The River Basin Salvage program: after 15 years', *Smithsonian Report for 1960*, 1960: 523–49.

Robson, K. (1993) 'Governing science and economic growth at a distance: accounting representation and the management of research and development', *Economy and Society*, 22(4): 461–81.

Rose, D. and Rimmer, P. (1979) 'Submission to the Minister for Conservation in response to Alcoa Aluminium Smelter at Portland EES', unpublised document in possession of Denis Rose, Australian Nature Conservation Agency.

Rose, J., Green, T. and Green, V. (1996) 'NAGPRA is forever: osteology and the repatriation of skeletons', *Annual Review of Anthropology*, 25: 81–103.

Rose, N. (1991) *Governing the Soul*, London: Routledge.

—— (1993) 'Government, authority and expertise in advanced liberalism', *Economy and Society*, 22(3): 283–99.

—— (1999) *Powers of Freedom: Reframing Political Thought*, Cambridge: Cambridge University Press.

Rose, N. and Miller, P. (1992) 'Political power beyond the state: problematics of government', *British Journal of Sociology*, 43: 173–205.

Rose, N. and Valverde, M. (1998) 'Governed by law?' *Social and Legal Studies*, 7(4): 541–51.

Rosen, L. (1980) 'The excavation of American Indian burial sites: a problem in law and professional responsibility', *American Anthropologist*, 82(1): 5–27.

Ross, A. (1996) 'Landscape as heritage', in L. Smith and A. Clarke (eds) *Issues in Archaeological Management*, St Lucia: Tempus Publications, University of Queensland.

Rouse, J. (1987) *Knowledge and Power*, Ithaca: Cornell University Press.

—— (1994) 'Power/knowledge', in G. Gutting (ed.) *The Cambridge Companion to Foucault*, Cambridge: Cambridge University Press.

Rowlands, M.J. (1986) 'Modernist fantasies in prehistory?', *Man*, 21: 745–6.

—— (1989) 'A question of complexity', in D. Miller, M. Rowlands and C. Tilley (eds) *Domination and Resistance*, London: Unwin Hyman.

Rowlett, R.M. (1987) 'Comment on Earle and Preucel', *Current Anthropology*, 28(4): 522–3.

Ruppel, T., Neuwirth, J., Leone, M.P. and Fry, G. (2003) 'Hidden in view: African spiritual spaces in North American landscapes', *Antiquity*, 77: 321–35.

Ryan, L. (1972) 'Outcasts in white Tasmania', *Mankind*, 8(4): 249–54.

—— (1981) *The Aboriginal Tasmanians*, St Lucia: University of Queensland Press.

SAA (Society for American Archaeology) (1961) 'Four statements for archaeology', *American Antiquity*, 27(2): 137–8.

—— (1986) *Statement Concerning the Treatment of Human Remains*. Available online: http://www.saa.org/Repatriation_policy.html (accessed 15 September 2001).

—— (1996) 'SAA principles of archaeological ethics', *American Antiquity*, 61(3): 451–2.

—— (2000) *Society for American Archaeology Position Paper: The Secretary of the Interior's September 21, 2000 Determination of Cultural Affiliation for Kennewick Man*. Available online: http://www.saa.org/repatriation/lobby/kennewickc8.html (accessed 15 September 2001).

Salmon, M.H. (1982) *Philosophy and Archaeology*, New York: Academic Press.

Salskov-Iversen, D., Krause Hansen, H. and Bislev, S. (2000) 'Governmentality, globalization, and local practice: transformations of a hegemonic discourse', *Alternatives*, 25: 183–222.

Saunders, A.D. (1983) 'A century of ancient monuments legislation 1882–1982', *The Antiquaries Journal*, 63(1): 11–29.

Sayer, A. (1992) *Method in Social Science: A Realist Approach*, 2nd edn, London: Routledge.

Schaafsma, C.F. (1989) 'Significant until proven otherwise: problems versus representative samples', in H. Cleere (ed.) *Archaeological Heritage Management in the Modern World*, London: Unwin Hyman.

Schiffer, M.B. (1976) *Behavioral Archeology*, New York: Academic Press.

—— (1979) 'Some impacts of cultural resource management on American archaeology', in J.R. McKinlay and K.L. Jones (eds) *Archaeological Resource Management in Australia and Oceania*, Wellington: New Zealand Historic Places Trust.

—— (1988) 'The structure of archaeological theory', *American Antiquity*, 53(3): 461–85.

Schiffer, M.B. and Gumerman, G.J. (eds) (1977) *Conservation Archaeology*, New York: Academic Press.

Schiffer, M.B. and House, J.H. (1977a) 'Cultural resource management and archaeological research: the Cache Project', *Current Anthropology*, 18(1): 43–53.

—— (1977b) 'An approach to assessing scientific significance', in M.B. Schiffer and G.J. Gumerman (eds) (1977) *Conservation Archaeology*, New York: Academic Press.

Schnapp, A. (1996) *The Discovery of the Past: The Origins of Archaeology*, London: British Museum Press.

Schneider, A.L. and Barran. P.A. (2002) 'Plaintiffs statement on judge's decision', Available online: http://www.friendsofpast.org/kennewick-man/press/statement-decision.html (accessed 21 February 2003).

Seldon, R. (2001) 'Bones of contention', *Missoula Independent*, 22 March. Available online: http://missoulanews.com/Archives/ (accessed 5 October 2003).

Senate Report (1966) *Senate Report 1363, Preservation of Historic Properties, S3035*.

—— (1971) *Senate Report 92–340 Amending Act of June 27, 1960 (74 Stat. 220), Relating to the Preservation of Historical and Archaeological Data*.

Shanks, M. (1992) *Experiencing the Past*, London: Routledge.

—— (1995) 'Archaeology and the forms of history', in I. Hodder, M. Shanks, A. Alexandri, V. Buchli, J. Carman, J. Last and G. Lucas (eds) *Interpreting Archaeology*, London: Routledge.

—— (1999) *Art and the Early Greek State: An Interpretive Archaeology*, Cambridge: Cambridge University Press.

Shanks, M. and Hodder, I. (1995) 'Processual, postprocessual and interpretive archaeologies', in I. Hodder, M. Shanks, A. Alexandri, V. Buchli, J. Carman, J. Last and G. Lucas (eds) *Interpreting Archaeology*, London: Routledge.

Shanks, M. and Pearson, M. (2001) *Theatre/Archaeology*, London: Routledge.

Shanks, M. and Tilley, C. (1987a) *Social Theory and Archaeology*, Cambridge: Polity Press.

—— (1987b) *Re-Constructing Archaeology: Theory and Practice*, Cambridge: Cambridge University Press.

—— (1989a) 'Archaeology into the 1990s', *Norwegian Archaeological Review*, 22(1): 1–12.

—— (1989b) 'Questions rather than answers: reply to comments on archaeology into the 1990s', *Norwegian Archaeological Review*, 22: 42–54.

Sharrock, F.W. and Grayson, D.K. (1979) ' "Significance" in contract archaeology', *American Antiquity*, 44(2): 327–8.

Shennan, S.J. (1986) 'Towards a critical archaeology?', *Proceedings of the Prehistoric Society*, 52: 327–38.

Sherratt, A. (1990) 'Gordon Childe: patterns and paradigms in prehistory', *Australian Archaeology* 30: 3–13.

—— (1993) 'The relativity of theory', in N. Yoffee and A. Sherratt (eds) *Archaeological Theory: Who Sets the Agenda?* Cambridge: Cambridge University Press.

Shown Harjo, S. (2002) 'Shame on you, Judge Jelderks for letting scientists pick over ancient one's bones'. Available online: http://www.indiancountry.com/?1031319072 (accessed 9 October 2002).

Sims, P.C. (1971) Letter to Minister for Agriculture re: Aboriginal rock art site – sundown point; Aboriginal antiquities in Australia Conference. Dated 20 September. On PWS File no. 500856, Volume 1.

—— (1972) Letter to Minister for Agriculture re: government policy on aboriginal rock art sites. Dated 26 October. On PWS File no. 500856, Volume 1.

—— (1974) Letter to the Director, National Parks and Wildlife Service re: Archaeological and Aboriginal Relics Bill 1974 – draft. Dated 16 December. On PWS File no. 500856, Volume 1.

—— (1975) 'Legislation and its implementation: Tasmania', in E. Edwards (ed.) *The Preservation of Australia's Aboriginal Heritage*, Canberra: Australian Institute of Aboriginal Studies.

Singleton, T.A. and Orser, C.E. Jr. (2003) 'Descendant communities: linking people in the present to the past', in L.J. Zimmerman, K.D. Vitelli and J. Hollowell-Zimmer (eds) *Ethical Issues in Archaeology*, Walnut Creek: AltaMira Press.

Skeates, R. (2000) *Debating the Archaeological Heritage*, London: Duckworth.

Slayman, A. (1997) 'A battle over bones: lawyers contest the fate of an 8,400-year-old skeleton from Washington State', *Archaeology*, January/February: 16–23.

Smart, B. (1992) *Modern Conditions, Postmodern Controversies*, London: Routledge.

SMH (Sydney Morning Herald) (1967) 'Park Expert Arrives', 11 January. Clipping held on Kingswood 12/1615 (box 1) Correspondence files 1967, State Archives.

—— (1981) 'Find hailed as Tutankhamen of Tasmanian cave archaeology', 17 February. Wilderness Society Newspaper Archives.

Smith, C. (2002) 'Kennewick Man to go to scientists, judge says: Native American coalition had sought 9,300-year-old remains for burial', *Seattle Post-Intelligencer*, 4 October. Available online: http://www.sas.org/E-Bulletin/2002–10–04/features/body.html (accessed 28 November 2003).

Smith, C. and Burke, H. (2003) 'In the spirit of the code', in L.J. Zimmerman, K.D. Vitelli and J. Hollowell-Zimmer (eds) *Ethical Issues in Archaeology*, Walnut Creek: AltaMira Press.

Smith, G.D., Malhi, R.S., Eshleman, J.A. and Kaestle, F.A. (2000) 'Report on DNA analysis of the remains of "Kennewick Man" from Columbia Park, Washington', unpublished report to the National Parks Service, Department of the Interior, Washington, DC. Available online: http://www.cr.nps.gov/aad/kennewick/smith.htm (accessed 10 October 2003).

Smith, L. (1989) 'Aboriginal site planning study: the Cumberland Plain', unpublished report, Sydney: New South Wales National Parks and Wildlife Service.

—— (1991a) 'The Berwick–Pakenham corridor: the archaeological survey of Aboriginal sites', *Occasional Report No. 45*, Melbourne: Department of Conservation and Environment.

—— (1991b) 'Type profiles: open campsites', unpublished report, Canberra: Australian Heritage Commission.

—— (1993a) 'Feminist issues in cultural resource management', in H. du Cros, and L. Smith (eds) *Women in Archaeology: A Feminist Critique*, Canberra: Department of Prehistory, Research School of Pacific Studies, The Australian National University.

—— (1993b) 'Towards a theoretical overview for heritage management', *Archaeological Review from Cambridge*, 12: 55–75.

—— (1994) 'Heritage management as postprocessual archaeology?', *Antiquity*, 68: 300–9.

—— (1995a) 'What is this thing called post-processual archaeology … and what is its relevance to Australian archaeology?', *Australian Archaeology*, 40: 28–32.

—— (1995b) 'Cultural resource management and feminist expression in Australian archaeology', *Norwegian Archaeological Review*, 28(1): 55–63

—— (1995c) 'Gender as "other" in postprocessual archaeology', in J. Balme and W. Beck (eds) *Gendered Archaeology*, Canberra: Department of Prehistory, Research School of Pacific Studies, The Australian National University.

—— (1998) 'Sand in our thongs: feminism, theory and shoe-laces', in M. Casey, D. Donlon, J. Hope, and S. Wellfare (eds) *Redefining Archaeology: Feminist Perspectives*, Canberra: Department of Prehistory, Research School of Pacific Studies, The Australian National University.

—— (1999) 'The last archaeologist? Material culture and contested identities', *Aboriginal Studies*, 1999/2: 25–34.

—— (2000) 'A history of Aboriginal heritage legislation in south-eastern Australia', *Australian Archaeology*, 50: 109–18

—— (2001) 'Archaeology and the governance of material culture: a case study from south-eastern Australia', *Norwegian Archaeological Review*, 34(2): 97–105.

Smith, L. and Campbell, G. (1998) 'Governing material culture', in M. Dean and B. Hindess (eds) *Governing Australia*, Cambridge: Cambridge University Press.

Smith, L. and du Cros, H. (1994) 'Equity and gender in Australian archaeology: a survey of the "Women in Archaeology Conference 1991"', in M.C. Nelson, S.M. Nelson and A. Wylie (eds) *Equity Issues for Women in Archaeology*, Washington, DC: Archaeological Papers of the American Anthropological Association Number 5.

Smith, L., Morgan, A. and van der Meer, A. (2003) 'Community-driven research in cultural heritage management: the Waanyi Women's History Project', *International Journal of Heritage Studies*, 9(1): 65–80.

Smith, L., Rich, E. and Hesp, P. (1990) 'Aboriginal sites on the Kurnell Peninsula: a management study', unpublished report, Sydney: New South Wales National Parks and Wildlife Service.

Smith, L. and van der Meer, A. (2001) 'Landscape and the negotiation of identity – a case study form Riversleigh, north-west Queensland', in M. Cotter, B. Boyd, J. Gardiner (eds) *Heritage Landscapes: Understanding Place and Communities*, Lismore: Southern Cross University Press.

Smith, P. and Warrior, R. (1996) *Like a Hurricane: The Indian Movement from Alcatraz to Wonded Knee*, New York: The New Press.

Smith, R.H. (1974) 'Ethics in field archaeology', *Journal of Field Archaeology*, 1: 375–85.

Snelson, W.J. and Sullivan, M.E. (1982) 'Barbeques at Burrill Lake?', *Australian Archaeology*, 15: 20–6.

Solli, B. (1992) 'Ian Babty and Tim Yates (eds): *Archaeology After Structuralism: Post-Structuralism and the Practice of Archaeology*, Book Review', *Norwegian Archaeological Review*, 25(1): 71–2.

Specht, J. (ed.) (1993) *F.D. McCarthy, Commemorative Papers*, Sydney: Australian Museum.

Sprague, R. (1974) 'American Indians and American archaeology', *American Antiquity*, 39(1): 1–2.

Stannard, B. (1988) 'Bones of contention', *The Bulletin*, 11: 40–1.

Stapp, D.C. and Burney, M.S. (2002) *Tribal Cultural Resource Management*, Walnut Creek: AltaMira Press.

Steel, G. and Powell, J. (1992) 'Peopling of the Americas: paleobiological evidence', *Human Biology*, 64(3): 303–36.

—— (1999) 'Peopling of the Americas: a historical and comparative perspective', in R. Bonnichsen (ed.) *Who Were the First Americans? Proceedings of the 58th Annual Biology Colloquium, Oregon State University*, Covallis: Centre for the Study of the First Americans, Oregon State University.

Stern, N. and Marshall, B. (1993) 'Excavation at Makintosh 90/1: a discussion of stratigraphy, chronology and site formation', *Archaeology in Oceania*, 28: 183–92.

Stiffarm, L. and Lane, P.J. (1992) 'The demography of Native North America: a question of American Indian Survival', in M. Jaimes (ed.) *The State of Native America: Genocide, Colonization and Resistance*, Boston: South End Press.

Stockton, E. (1975) 'Archaeologists and Aborigines', *Australian Archaeology*, 2: 10–12.

Stockton, J. (no date) Comments on the National Parks and Wildlife Bill 1974 pertaining to the protection of aboriginal sites and relics. Paper on PWS File no. 500856, Volume 1 (note authorship attributed to Stockton due to references in paper).

Stone, P. (1986) 'Are the public really interested? Archaeology and the public', in C. Dobinson and R. Gilchrist (eds) *Archaeology, Politics and the Public*, York: York University, Archaeological Publications No.5.

—— (1989) 'Interpretations and uses of the past in modern Britain and Europe, why are people interested in the past? Do the experts know or care? A plea for further study', in R. Layton (ed.) *Who Needs the Past?* London: Unwin Hyman.

Sullivan, K.M. (1986) 'Negotiation, game theory and cultural resource management', *Australian Archaeology*, 22: 36–44.

Sullivan, M.E. (1983) 'Consultants as managers', in M. Smith (ed.) *Archaeology at ANZAAS 1983*, Perth: Western Australian Museum.

Sullivan, S. (1972) 'Aboriginal relics in New South Wales', *Parks and Wildlife*, June: 44–53.

—— (1973) 'Report of a tour of the United States, to study management and protection procedures for prehistoric and historic sites June–September, 1973', unpublished report to the NSW National Parks and Wildlife Service.

—— (1975a) 'Legislation and its implementation: New South Wales', in E. Edwards (ed.) *The Preservation of Australia's Aboriginal Heritage*, Canberra: Australian institute of Aboriginal Studies.

—— (1975b) 'Mootwingee: an example of cultural tourism', in E. Edwards (ed.) *The Preservation of Australia's Aboriginal Heritage*, Canberra: Australian Institute of Aboriginal Studies.

—— (1975c) 'The state, people and archaeologists', *Australian Archaeology*, 2: 23–31.

—— (1983) 'The interim Aboriginal sites committee in NSW, communication between archaeologists and Aborigines', in M. Smith (ed.) *Archaeology at ANZAAS 1983*, Perth: Western Australian Museum.

—— (1984a) 'The "management" in cultural resource management: training for public archaeologists and other cultural resource managers', in G.K. Ward (ed.) *Archaeology at ANZAAS Canberra*, Canberra: Canberra Archaeological Society.

Sullivan, S. (1984b) 'Introduction', in S. Sullivan and S. Bowdler (eds) *Site Surveys and Significance Assessments in Australian Archaeology*, Canberra: Department of Prehistory, Research School of Pacific Studies, The Australian National University.

—— (1985) 'The custodianship of Aboriginal sites in southeastern Australia', in I. McBryde (ed.) *Who Owns the Past?* Melbourne: Oxford University Press.

—— (1992) 'Aboriginal site management in national parks and protected areas', in J. Birckhead, T. DeLacy and L. Smith (eds) *Aboriginal Involvement in Parks and Protected Areas*, Canberra: Aboriginal Studies Press.

—— (1993) 'Cultural values and cultural imperialism', *Historic Environment* 10(2 and 3): 54–62.

Sullivan, S. and Bowdler, S. (eds) (1984) *Site Surveys and Significance Assessments in Australian Archaeology*, Canberra: Department of Prehistory, Research School of Pacific Studies, The Australian National University.

Swain, T. (1993) *A Place for Strangers: Towards a History of Australian Aboriginal Being*, Sydney: Cambridge University Press.

Swidler, N., Dongoske, K.E., Anyon, R. and Downer, A.S. (eds) (1997) *Native Americans and Archaeologists: Stepping Stones to Common Ground*, Walnut Creek: AltaMira Press.

Sykes, R. (1979) 'A re-make: this time with a camera', *Filmnews*, January: 13.

Sykes, R.B. (1989) *Black Majority*, Hawthorn: Hudson.

Tainter, J.A. and Lucus, G.J. (1983) 'Epistemology of the significance concept', *American Antiquity*, 48(4): 707–19.

TALC (Tasmanian Aboriginal Land Council) (1996) 'Will you take next step?', in S. Ulm, I. Lilley and A. Ross (eds) *Australian Archaeology '95: Proceedings of the 1995 Australian Archaeological Association Annual Conference*, St Lucia: Tempus Publications, University of Queensland.

Tatz, C. (1992) 'Aboriginality as civilisation', in G. Whitlock and D. Carter (eds) *Images of Australia*, St Lucia: University of Queensland Press.

Taylor, R.E., Kirner, D.L., Southon, J.R. and Chatters, J.C. (1998) 'Radiocarbon dates of Kennewick Man', *Science* 280: 1171–2.

Terry, J. (1983) 'Damned wilderness and special laws', *Aboriginal Law Bulletin*, 8: 2–3.

Thomas, D. (2000) *Skull Wars: Kennewick Man, Archaeology, and the Battle for Native American Identity*, New York: Basic Books.

Thomas, I. (1993) 'Late Pleistocene environments and Aboriginal settlement patterns in Tasmania', *Australian Archaeology*, 36: 1–11.

Thomas, J. (1990a) 'Archaeology and the notion of ideology', in F. Baker and J. Thomas (eds) *Writing the Past in the Present*, Lampeter: St David's University College.

—— (1990b) 'Same, other, analogue: writing the past', in F. Baker and J. Thomas (eds) *Writing the Past in the Present*, Lampeter: Saint David's University College.

—— (1993a) 'The hermeneutics of megalithic space', in C. Tilley (ed.) *Interpretive Archaeology*, Providence: Berg.

Thomas, J. (1993b) 'Discourse, totalization and "the Neolithic"', in C. Tilley (ed.) *Interpretive Archaeology*, Providence: Berg.

Thomas, J. (1996) *Time, Culture and Identity: An Interpretive Archaeology*, London: Routledge.

Thomas, J. and Tilley, C. (1992) 'TAG and "post-modernism": a reply to John Bintliff', *Antiquity*, 66: 106–10.

—— (1993) 'The axe and the torso: symbolic structures in the Neolithic of Brittany', in C. Tilley (ed.) *Interpretive Archaeology*, Providence: Berg.

Thomas, N. (1981) 'Social theory, ecology and epistemology: theoretical issues in Australian prehistory', *Mankind*, 13(2): 165–77.

Thornton, R. (1998) 'Who owns our past? The repatriation of Native American human remains and cultural objects', in R. Thornton (ed.) *Studying Native America: Problems and Prospects*, Madison: The University of Wisconsin Press.

Thorpe, R. (Secretary, Koorie Cultural heritage Working Group) (no date) Aboriginal Heritage Legislation. AAV file 10–1–24 VAS — Relics Act Review Committee.

Tilley, C. (1989a) 'Interpreting material culture', in I. Hodder (ed.) *The Meaning of Things*, London: Unwin Hyman.

—— (1989b) 'Archaeology as socio-political action in the present', in V. Pinsky and A. Wylie (eds) *Critical Traditions in Contemporary Archaeology*, Cambridge: Cambridge University Press.

—— (1989c) 'Discourse and power: the genre of the Cambridge inaugural lecture', in D. Miller, M. Rowlands and C. Tilley (eds) *Domination and Resistance*, London: Unwin Hyman.

—— (1989d) 'Excavation as theatre', *Antiquity*, 63: 275–80.

—— (ed.) (1990a) *Reading Material Culture*, Oxford: Blackwell.

—— (1990b) 'Claude Levi-Strauss: structuralism and beyond', in C. Tilley (ed.) *Reading Material Culture*, Oxford: Blackwell.

—— (1990c) 'Michel Foucault: towards an archaeology of archaeology', in C. Tilley (ed.) *Reading Material Culture*, Oxford: Blackwell.

—— (1991) *Material Culture and Text: The Art of Ambiguity*, London: Routledge.

—— (1993a) 'Introduction: interpretation and a poetics of the past', in C. Tilley (ed.) *Interpretive Archaeology*, Providence: Berg.

—— (1993b) 'Prospecting archaeology', in C. Tilley (ed.) *Interpretive Archaeology*, Providence: Berg.

—— (1994) *A Phenomenology of Landscape: Places, Paths and Monuments*, Oxford: Berg.

—— (1999) *Metaphor and Material Culture*, Oxford: Blackwell.

Tjamiwa, T. (1992) 'Tjunguringkula Waakaripai: joint management of Uluṟu National Park', in J. Birckhead, T. DeLacy and L. Smith (eds) *Aboriginal Involvement in Parks and Protected Areas*, Canberra: Aboriginal Studies Press.

Trigg, R. (1985) *Understanding Social Science*, Oxford: Blackwell.

Trigger, B.G. (1973) 'The future of archaeology in the past', in C.L. Redman (ed.) *Research and Theory in Current Archaeology*, New York: John Wiley and Son.

—— (1980) 'Archaeology and the image of the American Indian', *American Antiquity*, 45(4): 662–76.

—— (1981) 'Anglo-American archaeology', *World Archaeology*, 13(2): 138–55.

—— (1983) 'American archaeology as Native history: a review essay', *William and Mary Quarterly*, XL: 413–52.

—— (1984a) 'Alternative archaeologies: nationalist, colonialist, imperialist', *Man*, 19: 355–70.

—— (1984b) 'Archaeology at the crossroads: what's new?', *Annual Review of Anthropology*, 13: 275–300.

—— (1985) 'The past as power: anthropology and the North American Indian', in I. McBryde (ed.) *Who Owns the Past?* Melbourne: Oxford University Press.

—— (1986a) 'Prehistoric archaeology and American society', in D.J. Meltzer, D.D. Fowler and J.A. Sabloff (eds) *American Archaeology Past and Future*, Washington, DC: Society for American Archaeology.

—— (1986b) 'Prospects for a world archaeology', *World Archaeology*, 18(1): 1–20.

—— (1989) *A History of Archaeological Thought*, Cambridge: Cambridge University Press.

—— (1991a) 'Constraint and freedom: a new synthesis for archaeological explanation', *American Anthropologist* 93(3): 551–69.

—— (1991b) 'Postprocessual developments in Anglo-American archaeology', *Norwegian Archaeological Review* 24(2): 65–76.

—— (1991c) 'Early Native North American responses to European contact: romantic versus rationalistic interpretations', *Journal of American History*, 77(4): 1195–215.

—— (1995) 'Romanticism, nationalism, and archaeology', in P.L. Kohl and C. Fawcett (eds) *Nationalism, Politics and the Practice of Archaeology*, Cambridge: Cambridge University Press.

Trope, J. and Echo-Hawk, W. (2000 [1992]) 'The Native American Graves Protection and Repatriation Act: background and legislative history', in D. Mihesuah (ed.) *Repatriation Reader: Who Owns American Indian Remains?* Lincoln: University of Nebraska.

Tsosie, R. (1997) 'Indigenous rights and archaeology', in N. Swidler, K.E. Dongoske, R. Anyon and A.S. Downer (eds) *Native Americans and Archaeologists: Stepping Stones to Common Ground*, Walnut Creek: AltaMira Press.

Tunbridge, J.E. and Ashworth, G.J. (1996) *Dissonant Heritage: The Management of the Past as a Resource in Conflict*, Chichester: Wiley.

Turner, E. (1989) 'The souls of my dead brothers', in R. Layton (ed.) *Conflict in the Archaeology of Living Traditions*, London: Unwin Hyman.

TV9 (Channel 9 network) (1995) 'Who Owns the Past?', *Sunday Program*. Broadcast 24 September, distributed by Meditrack, Sydney.

TWS (Tasmanian Wilderness Society) Newsletter (1981) 'Amazing S.W. cave find', March edition, Wilderness Society Newspaper Archives.

Ubelaker, D.H. and Grant, L.G. (1989) 'Human skeletal remains: preservation or reburial?', *Yearbook of Physical Anthropology*, 32: 249–87.

Ucko, P.J. (1983) 'Australian academic archaeology Aboriginal transformation of its aims and practices', *Australian Archaeology*, 16: 11–26.

—— (1986) 'Political uses of archaeology', in C. Dobinson and R. Gilchrist (eds) *Archaeology, Politics and the Public*, York: York University Archaeological Publications No. 5.

—— (1987) *Academic Freedom and Apartheid*, London: Duckworth.

Urry, J. (1990) *The Tourist Gaze*, London: Sage.

Van Dijk, T.A. (1998) *Ideology: A Multidisciplinary Approach*, London: Sage.

Vizenor, G. (1986) 'bone courts: the rights and narrative representation of tribal bones', *American Indian Quarterly*, 10: 319–31.

WAC (World Archaeological Congress) (1990) *World Archaeological Congress First Code of Ethics*. Available online: http://www.wac.uct.ac.za/archive/content/ethics.html (accessed 1 April 2004).

—— (2003) 'Press Release: Kennewick Man', 27 June, Washington, DC.

Wainwright, G.J. (1984) 'The pressure of the past: presidential address', *Proceedings of the Prehistoric Society*, 50: 1–22.

Wallace, A. (no date) Report to the national Parks and Wildlife historical and Scientific Advisory Committee. On PWS File no. 500856, Volume 1.

Walsh, K. (1992) *The Representation of the Past: Museums and Heritage in the Post-Modern World*, London: Routledge.

Ward, G.K. (1983) 'Archaeology and legislation in Australia', in G. Connah (ed.) *Australian Field Archaeology: A Guide to Techniques*, Canberra: AIAS.

—— (1985) 'The Federal Aboriginal *Heritage Act* and archaeology', *Australian Aboriginal Studies*, 1985/2: 47–52.

Watkins, J. (2001a) 'Yours, mine, or ours? Conflicts between archaeologists and ethnic groups', in T. Bray (ed.) *The Future of the Past: Archaeologists, Native Americans, and Repatriation*, New York: Garland Publishing.

—— (2001b) '"The powers that be": power, role, and interaction in the consultation process', unpublished conference paper given at the Session 'Working with Indigenous peoples and other decedent communities', Society for American Archaeology, New Orleans. Available online: http://www.uiowa.edu/~ainsp/saa2001/index.html (accessed 27 October 2003).

—— (2003) 'Archaeological ethics and American Indians', in L.J. Zimmerman, K.D. Vitelli and J. Hollowell-Zimmer (eds) *Ethical Issues in Archaeology*, Walnut Creek: AltaMira Press.

Watkins, J., Goldstein, L., Vitelli, K. and Jenkins, L. (2000) 'Accountability: responsibilities of archaeologists to other interest groups', in M. Lynott and A. Wylie (eds) *Ethics in American Archaeology*, Washington, DC: Society for American Archaeology.

Watson, J. (1995) '"We couldn't tolerate any more": the Palm Island strike of 1957', in A. McGrath, K. Saunders with J. Huggins (eds) *Aboriginal Workers*, Sydney: The Australian Society for the Study of Labour History, University of Sydney.

—— (1973a) 'The future of archaeology in anthropology', in C.L. Redman (ed.) *Research and Theory in Current Archaeology*, New York: John Wiley and Son.

—— (1973b) 'Explanation and models: the prehistorian as philosopher of science and the prehistorian as excavator of the past', in A.C. Renfrew (ed.) *The Explanation of Cultural Change: Models in Prehistory*, London: Duckworth.

Watson, P.J., LeBlanc, S.A. and Redman, C.L. (1971) *Explanation in Archaeology*, New York: Columbia University Press.

Watson, R.A. (1990) 'Ozymandias King of Kings: postprocessual radical archaeology as critique', *American Antiquity*, 55(4): 673–89.

—— (1991) 'What the New Archaeology has accomplished', *Current Anthropology*, 32(2): 275–81.

—— (1992) 'Reply to Wylie', *Current Anthropology*, 33(2): 213–14.

Watson, S. (1992) 'Contested spaces: cross-cultural issues in planning', *Culture and Policy*, 4: 19–33.

Watts, R. (1994) 'Government and modernity: an essay in thinking governmentality', *Arena*, 2: 103–57.

Webb, C. and Allen, J. (1990) 'A functional analysis of Pleistocene bone tools from two sites in southwest Tasmania', *Archaeology in Oceania*, 25: 75–8.

Wendall-Smith, C.P. (1974) Letter to Minister for National Parks and Wildlife, re: exclusion of human remains in legislation. Dated 12 August. On PWS File no. 500856, Volume 1.

Wendorf, F. and Thompson, R. (2002) 'The Committee for the Recovery of Archaeological Remains: three decades of service to the archaeological profession', *American Antiquity*, 67(2): 317–30.

West, A.L. (no date) Archaeological and Aboriginal Relics Preservation Act (Summary of comments supplied to A.L. West by Professor D.J. Mulvaney). AAV file 34–5–3 VAS – Archaeological and Aboriginal Relics Preservation Act 1972.

West, D. (2001) 'The last classic Clinton cover up', *Jewish World Review*, April 27. Available online: http://jewishworldreview.com/0501/west042701.asp (accessed 21 February 2003).

Wetherell, M. (2001a) 'Debates in discourse research', in M. Wetherell, S. Taylor, and S.J. Yates (eds) *Discourse Theory and Practice: A Reader*, London: Sage.

—— (2001b) 'Editor's Introduction', in M. Wetherell, S. Taylor, and S.J. Yates (eds) *Discourse Theory and Practice: A Reader*, London: Sage.

—— (2001c) 'Themes in discourse research: the case of Diana', in M. Wetherell, S. Taylor, and S.J. Yates (eds) *Discourse Theory and Practice: A Reader*, London: Sage.

Wettenhall, G. (1988) 'The Murray Black Collection goes home', *Australian Society*, December/January: 16–19.

White, J.P. (1974) 'Man in Australia: past and present', *Australian Archaeology*, 1: 28–43.

White, R. (1992) 'Inventing Australia', in G. Whitlock and D. Carter (eds) *Images of Australia*, St Lucia: University of Queensland Press.

White Deer, G. (1997) 'Return of the sacred: spirituality and the scientific imperative', in N. Swidler, K.E. Dongoske, R. Anyon and A.S. Downer (eds) *Native Americans and Archaeologists: Stepping Stones to Common Ground*, Walnut Creek: AltaMira Press.

Whitehill, W. (1983 [1966]) '"Promoted to Glory…": the origin of preservation in the United States', in A. Rains, E.S. Muskie, W.B Widnall, P.H. Hoff, R.R. Tucker, G. Gray and L.G. Henderson (eds) *With Heritage so Rich*, Washington, DC: Landmark Reprint Series, Preservation Press.

Whiteley, P. (2002) 'Archaeology and oral tradition', *American Antiquity*, 67(3): 405–15.

Wickham-Jones, C. (1988) 'The road to heri-tat: archaeologists and interpretation', *Archaeological Review from Cambridge*, 7(2): 185–93.

Williams, A. (1975) 'Letter to the editor', *Identity*, October: 29.

Williams, C. with B. Thorpe (1992) *Beyond Industrial Sociology: The Work of Men and Women*, Sydney: Allen and Unwin.

Willmot, E. (1985) 'The dragon principle', in I. McBryde (ed.) *Who Owns the Past?* Melbourne: Oxford University Press.

Wilson, R. (1997) *Bringing Them Home: Report of the National Inquiry into the Separation of Aboriginal and Torres Strait Islander Children from their Families*, Sydney: Human Rights and Equal Opportunities Commission.

Winter, J.C. (1980) 'Indian heritage preservation and archaeologists', *American Antiquity*, 45(1): 121–31.

Woodall, J.N. and Perricone, P.J. (1981) 'The archaeologist as cowboy: the consequence of professional stereotype', *Journal of Field Archaeology*, 8: 506–9.

Woodiwiss, A. (1990) *Social Theory after Postmodernism: Rethinking Production, Law and Class*, London: Pluto.

—— (1993) *Postmodernity USA: The Crisis of Social Modernism in Postwar America*, London: Sage.

Wright, P. (1985) *On Living in an Old Country*, London: Verso.

Wright, R.V.S. (1986) 'Presidential address – changing faces of Australian archaeology: the need to get permission', in G.K. Ward (ed.) *Archaeology at ANZAAS Canberra*, Canberra: Canberra Archaeological Society.

—— (1995) 'Letters: they don't dig it here', *Australian*, 20 September.

Wylie, A. (1992a) 'Rethinking the quincentennial: consequences for past and present', *American Antiquity*, 57(4): 591–4.

—— (1992b) 'On skepticism, philosophy and archaeological science', *Current Anthropology*, 33(2): 209–13.

—— (1993) 'A proliferation of new archaeologies: "Beyond objectivism and relativism"', in N. Yoffee and A. Sherratt (eds) *Archaeological Theory: Who Sets the Agenda?* Cambridge: Cambridge University Press.

—— (2000a) 'Questions of evidence, legitimacy and the (dis)union of science', *American Antiquity*, 65(2): 227–37.

—— (2000b) 'Ethical dilemmas in archaeological practice: looting, repatriation, stewardship, and the (trans)formation of disciplinary identity', in M. Lynott and A. Wylie (eds) *Ethics in American Archaeology*, Washington, DC: Society for American Archaeology.

Xiberras, A. and du Cros, H. (1992) 'Aboriginal involvement in monitoring and protecting cultural sites within the Wurundjeri's tribal boundaries, Melbourne', in J. Birckhead, T. DeLacy and L. Smith (eds) *Aboriginal Involvement in Parks and Protected Areas*, Canberra: Aboriginal Studies Press.

Yates, T. (1988) 'Michael Schiffer and processualism as science with a capital S', *Archaeological Review from Cambridge*, 7(2): 235–8.

Zarmati, L. (1995) 'Popular archaeology, and the archaeologist as hero', in J. Balme and W. Beck (eds) *Gendered Archaeology*, Canberra: Department of Prehistory, Research School of Pacific Studies, The Australian National University.

Zimmerman, L.J. (1987) 'Webb on reburial: a North American perspective', *Antiquity*, 61: 426–30.

—— (1989a) 'Made radical by my own: an archaeologist learns to accept reburial', in R. Layton (ed.) *Conflict in the Archaeology of Living Traditions*, London: Unwin Hyman.

—— (1989b) 'Human bones as symbols of power: Aboriginal American belief systems toward bones and "grave-robbing" archaeologists', in R. Layton (ed.) *Conflict in the Archaeology of Living Traditions*, London: Unwin Hyman.

—— (1996) *Native North America*, London: Macmillan.

—— (1997) 'Remythologizing the relationship between Indians and archaeologists', in N. Swidler, K.E. Dongoske, R. Anyon and A.S. Downer (eds) *Native Americans and Archaeologists: Stepping Stones to Common Ground*, Walnut Creek: AltaMira Press.

—— (1998a) 'Anthropology and responses to the reburial issues', in T. Biolsi and L.J. Zimmerman (eds) *Indians and Anthropologists: Vine Deloria Jr and the Critique of Anthropology*, Tuscon: The University of Arizona Press.

—— (1998b) 'When data become people: archaeological ethics, reburial, and the past as public heritage', *International Journal of Cultural Property*, 7(1): 69–86.

—— (2000a) 'Regaining our nerve: ethics, values, and the transformation of archaeology', in M. Lynott and A. Wylie (eds) *Ethics in American Archaeology*, Washington, DC: Society for American Archaeology.

—— (2000b) 'A New and different archaeology? With a postscript on the impact of the Kennewick dispute', in D. Mihesuah (ed.) *Repatriation Reader: Who Owns American Indian Remains?* Lincoln: University of Nebraska.

—— (2001) 'Usurping Native American voice', in T. Bray (ed.) *The Future of the Past: Archaeologists, Native Americans, and Repatriation*, New York: Garland Publishing.

INDEX